Jazz/Not Jazz

ROTH FAMILY FOUNDATION

Music in America Imprint

Michael P. Roth
and Sukey Garcetti
have endowed this
imprint to honor the
memory of their parents,
Julia and Harry Roth,
whose deep love of music
they wish to share
with others.

Jazz/Not Jazz

The Music and Its Boundaries

EDITED BY

David Ake

Charles Hiroshi Garrett

Daniel Goldmark

UNIVERSITY OF CALIFORNIA PRESS

Berkeley · Los Angeles · London

University of California Press, one of the most
distinguished university presses in the United States,
enriches lives around the world by advancing
scholarship in the humanities, social sciences, and
natural sciences. Its activities are supported by the UC
Press Foundation and by philanthropic contributions
from individuals and institutions. For more information, visit www.ucpress.edu.

University of California Press
Berkeley and Los Angeles, California

University of California Press, Ltd.
London, England

Library of Congress Cataloging-in-Publication Data

Jazz/not jazz : the music and its boundaries / edited by
David Ake, Charles Hiroshi Garrett, Daniel Goldmark.
    p. cm.
  Includes bibliographical references and index.
  ISBN 978-0-520-27103-6 (cloth : alk. paper) —
  ISBN 978-0-520-27104-3 (pbk. : alk. paper) —
  ISBN 978-0-520-95135-8 (ebook)
  1. Jazz—History and criticism. I. Ake, David
Andrew, 1961–   II. Garrett, Charles Hiroshi,
1966–   III. Goldmark, Daniel.
  ML3506.J465 2012
  781.65—dc23
                                      2012003400

Manufactured in the United States of America

21 20 19 18 17 16 15 14 13 12
10 9 8 7 6 5 4 3 2 1

In keeping with a commitment to support environmen-
tally responsible and sustainable printing practices, UC
Press has printed this book on 50-pound Enterprise, a
30% post-consumer-waste, recycled, deinked fiber that
is processed chlorine-free. It is acid-free and meets all
ANSI/NISO (Z 39.48) requirements.

Contents

Illustrations

TABLES

Acknowledgments

The editors extend their deepest appreciation and thanks to the anonymous readers of our drafts; to our indefatigable editor, Mary Francis; and to Eric Schmidt, Kim Hogeland, and everyone at UC Press.

Individually, we offer the following thanks.

From David: To my wife, Kendee Franklin; my son, David Abraham Case Ake; and my colleagues and students in the School of the Arts at the University of Nevada, Reno.

From Charles: To Saleema Waraich and our families, and to my students and colleagues at the University of Michigan, Ann Arbor.

From Daniel: To Cyleste Collins, Milo Goldmark, and Chloe Goldmark; my family; and my students and colleagues at Case Western Reserve University in Cleveland, Ohio.

Introduction

In December 2009 England's *Guardian* newspaper reported on a lawsuit filed that month in Spain. According to the article, a "pistol-carrying Civil Guard police force descended on the Sigüenza Jazz festival . . . to investigate after an angry jazz buff complained that the Larry Ochs Sax and Drumming Core group was on the wrong side of a line dividing jazz from contemporary music. The jazz purist claimed his doctor had warned it was 'psychologically inadvisable' for him to listen to anything that could be mistaken for mere contemporary music."[1] Leaving aside the supposed dangers (or definitions) of "mere contemporary music," this admittedly unusual legal case highlights a reality of which jazz people today are acutely aware: the lines some people draw between "jazz" and "not jazz" can be at once both fiercely guarded and very difficult to discern.

Jazz has never been a monolithic genre, of course, and questions surrounding its definition, ownership, and function hardly emerged with the new millennium. Early critical reception to the music was characterized by clashes between those who heard it as "primitive"—oftentimes corresponding to a broadly racialized, sometimes explicitly racist, conception of composition and performance—and those who celebrated its innovative rhythmic schemes, timbral nuances, and sheer vitality. Commentators at midcentury questioned whether jazz was best understood as a folk expression, a commercial dance style, or an art form deserving of serious treatment alongside highbrow European compositions. Sweet versus hot, trad versus swing (versus bop), electric versus acoustic, avant-garde versus mainstream: these and other debates have been part and parcel of the jazz world for decades and continue to this day. Even such a large-scale and well-meaning attempt as Ken Burns's 2001 documentary, *Jazz,* to crystallize and celebrate the genre's essence only set off a new flurry of arguments and counterarguments.[2] Historians, journalists, and musicians alike expressed dismay at the narrowness of Burns's story, yet no one could seem to agree on exactly what or who should have been left in or out of it. Consider, too, the titles of recent books such as *Jazz in Search of Itself, Is Jazz Dead?,* and *What Is This Thing Called Jazz?*[3]

No doubt, these more recent disputes and quandaries stem in part from broader debates, which began in the 1960s and gained considerable momentum in the 1980s, about the role of public education, government, religion, and the arts. These "culture wars" have typically pitted conservative politicians, religious leaders, and media commentators who champion time-honored works and institutions against left-leaning artists and intellectuals who challenge those same canons—oftentimes deconstructing them in an effort to reveal what they see as the inherent contradictions and inequalities on which they were founded.[4]

But jazz's specific quarrels and dilemmas are also based in and intensified by the rather unique predicament in which the music now finds itself. Call it an identity crisis, if you will, set off in large measure by jazz's meteoric rise from humble, even despised, origins, through global popularity during the swing era, to its current position near the highest reaches of the established cultural hierarchy (and seeming invisibility in most other quarters), a status that has only exacerbated deep-set anxieties over the relevance, health, and future of the art form. And yet despite (or is it because of?) all this apparent confusion, contention, and change, jazz appreciation classes, textbooks, fan magazines, films, and record company advertisements continue to extol many of the same musicians, places, and sounds that they have for decades. It's a paradoxical time for the jazz world in many ways.

Jazz/Not Jazz addresses just this paradox. Accepting that definitions of jazz have been malleable and contested throughout the music's history, these chapters consider some of the musicians who (and concepts, places, and practices that), though deeply connected to established jazz institutions and aesthetics, have rarely, if ever, appeared in conventional jazz narratives. Our goal here is not to map out a supposedly all-inclusive history of jazz, nor even necessarily to salvage the reputations of typically dismissed styles or figures, but rather to explore what these missing people and pieces tell us about the ways in which jazz has been defined and its history told. That is, in focusing our inquiries beyond the veritable hall of jazz greatness we seek to determine what we can learn about jazz as a whole by interrogating its traditionally understood musical and cultural margins (though not necessarily the economic margins: many of the performers and performances discussed in these chapters have been enjoyed by millions of listeners) and to find out what is gained—and what is lost—when particular communities erect their own fences around jazz. As Sherrie Tucker states in her chapter, "We need not only to study those who are missing from the canon but to understand the desires for particular narratives that exclude them."

To be sure, a number of scholars have previously argued for a broader conception of what and who constitutes jazz. Indeed, Scott DeVeaux's formative article, "Constructing the Jazz Tradition: Jazz Historiography," figures prominently as a launching pad for ideas that propel several of these chapters.[5] Yet while other studies have raised important questions about genre, canon, and identity in jazz, this is the first collection to set its sights straight on such a broad range of artists, institutions, and aesthetics. By examining how and why jazz boundaries have been drawn and redrawn, our contributors seek to trouble some of the assumptions on which jazz lore has long rested.

GENRE(S)

The book takes as its basic premise that genre designations play a fundamental role in shaping how we teach, learn, create, access, and assess music. True, people will always play and listen to music, and it might make little difference to some how that music is classified. But there is no denying that a wide array of institutions and businesses—iTunes, radio stations, record stores (those few stalwart ones that remain), Internet websites, grant endowments, magazines, newspapers, libraries, booking agencies, and college curricula, among them—rely on genre classifications to help them organize, present, support, and/or sell music. And because music genres are so prevalent and so powerful, our authors aim to show what is at stake when people construct, maintain, cross, and challenge the boundaries designed to separate one genre from another—in this case, jazz from, well, everything else.

This is no purely academic exercise. Designating oneself (or being designated by others) as "jazz" can hold very real and practical consequences for working musicians. Jazz groups can land gigs at the famed Village Vanguard; klezmer groups cannot (though chapter 1 explains how Don Byron—who is generally understood as a jazz clarinetist—*can* play klezmer music at clubs like the Vanguard). College-level teaching positions exist for jazz saxophonists but not for funk saxophonists. Or consider that musicians can never earn the accolades and financial rewards (currently twenty-five thousand dollars cash, plus increased opportunities for high-paying gigs) that come with the National Endowment for the Arts Jazz Masters Fellowship without first being widely recognized as a jazz artist. Such a statement may seem absurdly obvious in the case of past honorees such as Count Basie, Milt Jackson, and Phil Woods, performers of what has been commonly accepted as "real jazz." But it raises some intriguing questions when considering the work and careers of figures such as bagpiper Rufus Harley, whose distinctive style is addressed in chapter 7, or the *conguero* Ray Barretto, who, as noted in chapter 5, was well aware of the greater professional opportunities afforded to jazz musicians (as opposed to "salsa" musicians) and on whom the NEA *did* eventually bestow the Jazz Master title. On the other side of that same coin, some musicians may find that carrying the jazz label can actually hinder their abilities to perform and market their music more broadly (i.e., in nonjazz venues or on nonjazz radio stations or for nonjazz record labels). It's a line all musicians walk, consciously or not, whenever and wherever they present their work.

Hand in hand with genre boundaries goes the notion of authenticity, the cordoning off of the real (and therefore good, and therefore worthy of praise, study, and sales) from the ersatz. Jazz is far from the only music concerned with this matter. Questions about authentic performance practices fueled some of the most contentious exchanges among practitioners and scholars of European classical music in the 1980s and 1990s.[6] And authenticity, in the form of "real" instruments (read: guitars) and live performances devoid of prerecorded sweetener, is what fans of rock music most often use to separate their music from "mere" pop. But the authenticity question is perhaps most keenly felt in jazz due to its all-too-fluid and uneasy location somewhere between the popular and classical realms.

ESSENTIALS

Recognizing that attempts to enforce strict genre boundaries fail to do justice to the history of a music characterized by continuous change and reinvention, all of our contributors explore the seemingly unavoidable complexities and contradictions inherent in attempting to define jazz once and for all. It should come as no surprise, then, that these authors hold that jazz possesses no essential characteristics. Some jazz performances swing; others feature a different groove or no groove at all. Some jazz highlights improvisation; some of it is meticulously planned in advance (a point of view even that improviser par excellence Charlie Parker maintained).[7] Some jazz adopts an unflinchingly "important" and anticommercial stance; much of it openly courts the marketplace or invites us simply to have a good time. Some jazz musicians possess a strong moral compass and toil to build a more just society; others are self-centered louts.

Nor is jazz ethnically predetermined. Without question, the majority of the most accomplished and influential jazz styles and musicians have emerged from African American communities, and in no way do we wish to diminish or overlook those contributions. Yet one of the consequences of jazz's climb up the ladder of cultural hierarchy has been its increasing acceptance among and adoption by an ever-expanding range of ethnic groups (and also social classes). Perhaps more than any other music genre, jazz reflects, configures, and gives voice to the joys, innovations, and challenges created by increasing commercial globalization, cultural interaction, and individual mobility. It is undeniable that millions of Asian, Latino, Native American, white, and other nonblack musicians, businesspeople, writers, and others create, support, and help to shape how jazz looks, sounds, and is understood.

How to acknowledge and incorporate these participants into the historical and musical narratives represents an important challenge for jazz scholars today. In fact, that issue permeates this entire collection, whether involving the mutual admiration between Louis Armstrong and Guy Lombardo (chapter 2), the sometimes contentious process involved in creating the "jazz" article for *Wikipedia* (chapter 4), the complexities and overlaps produced by Latin jazz (chapter 5), the multiethnic downtown music scene (chapter 8), the avant-garde Asian American jazz scene (chapter 9), or the birth of vocal jazz ensembles (chapter 10).

We also hold that compositions or performances do not contain any eternal meanings or values. One need only look to Nicolas Slonimsky's infamous *Lexicon of Musical Invective* to see that the significance of musical works can change drastically over time.[8] And because they change, it is clear that they are not fixed "within the music." Rather, they are determined and continually redetermined by people—musicians, nightclub owners, record company executives, concert promoters, journalists, scholars, radio station programmers, educators, and listening audiences, among others—who decide which musicians and sounds get heard as good jazz or bad jazz, as jazz or not jazz; indeed, in many ways they determine who and what gets heard at all.

Geography is another significant factor that has helped to define "real" jazz from what some aficionados see as inauthentic practices. While our contributors address jazz practices in famed locales such as New York and New Orleans, we also explore smaller scenes that have developed in the Pacific Northwest, the San Francisco Bay Area, and on college campuses throughout North America. We have consciously chosen to focus the collection on musical activity within the United States because of that country's continued position as global arbiter of jazz tastes, if at this point sometimes only as a perceived establishment against which musicians from other lands might push. Narrowing our geographic scope thus works as a way to focus on other significant jazz debates and other jazz boundaries.[9]

We accept that viewing jazz as an open-ended, multifaceted, ever-changing idea or set of discourses rather than a prescribed and proscribed set of specific musical devices, names, places, or styles opens the door for charges of radical relativism: if anything and anyone can be seen, heard, or described as jazz, then the category becomes meaningless. Theoretically this is a possibility. On the practical level, though, that has not happened, nor is it ever likely to happen. As far as we can tell, the Sex Pistols has never been seen or heard as jazz—neither has Lady Gaga, Snoop Dogg, Bob Marley, Weird Al Yankovic, the Bulgarian Women's Choir, or Gustav Mahler (though Uri Caine's reworkings of some of Mahler's compositions *are* widely understood as jazz). And the inverse is true: John Coltrane will never be heard as a polka musician; Sarah Vaughan will never be heard as a punk rock singer; Steve Coleman will never be heard as a country stylist. Jazz covers immense terrain, sonic and otherwise, but it does not extend everywhere. No doubt, these positions potentially throw into question many of the most deeply held tenets about jazz and the individuals who make and support it. But this book would not exist—would not need to exist—if we felt that jazz (or any other music) was somehow "pure" in any way.

While sharing a fundamental concern with epistemological, ontological, and historiographical matters, the book's contributors are keenly interested in exploring the blurred boundaries and overlaps brought about through exchanges between jazz and various "others," among them popular music, avant-garde experimentalism, and contemporary art music. Above all, though, the authors are explicitly concerned with how music relates to and resonates with living, breathing human beings. Every chapter shows how jazz has provoked, reassured, and inspired (or not) individuals from different backgrounds, whether musical, cultural, or social.

Several contributors also address how and why male instrumentalists continue to dominate conventional jazz narratives while female performers and composers are largely written out of those same narratives, showing how gender still plays a role in shaping current jazz expectations, understandings, and circumstances. Taken together, these chapters survey nearly the entire span of recorded jazz history, while raising fundamental questions regarding musical practices, the meanings people attach to them, and their continued relevance throughout the jazz world today: What characteristics or associations qualify something as jazz? What political, cultural, financial, academic, and aesthetic motivations generate such proclamations and what ends do these positions and debates serve?

We have arranged the book into three sections—Categories, Practices, and Education—that correspond to topics of classification; the expansion and transformation of jazz performance and compositional devices; and the impact of such developments on how and where people teach, learn, talk about, and play jazz. In part 1, Eric Porter opens the collection by confronting the notion of a jazz "essence," showing how musicians' adoption or rejection of this concept can work as a strategy toward shifting musical identities and professional opportunities and suggesting that jazz must be understood through its relationship to other vernacular and popular practices.

Elijah Wald's chapter serves to complicate the entrenched understandings of early jazz styles as either "sweet" or "hot," as well as the musical values and racialized understandings that have come to be attached to those labels. In asking us to take at face value Louis Armstrong's professed admiration for the sounds of the bandleader Guy Lombardo, Wald shows how we can better hear—and thus better appraise, teach, learn, play, and respond to Armstrong's (and also Lombardo's) music. Similar concerns are at the forefront of Charles Hiroshi Garrett's chapter, which considers what's at stake when jazz is approached solely as "serious music" and asks how we might begin to reconcile the music's rich history of humor and crowd-pleasing entertainment with its current status as art. Ken Prouty shows how the rise of the Internet has broadened the field of jazz's public boundary makers (without necessarily changing the fundamental debates about those boundaries). Christopher Washburne points to some of the divergent allegiances and professional strategies of musicians within the inherently multicultural realm of what is widely called (among other names) Latin jazz.

Part 2, "Practices," addresses an array of musical techniques that, while widely utilized by jazz musicians, nonetheless fall outside conventional accounts of the genre. John Howland describes the "jazz with strings" phenomenon of the 1940s and 1950s, a style that has been marginalized within jazz studies even though it represents one of the more commercially successful moments in the music's history. The other chapters in this section examine the ways in which established conceptions of jazz have been challenged and expanded as a result of its intersections with other music cultures. Daniel Goldmark's study of three woodwind players—Roland Kirk, Yusef Lateef, and Rufus Harley, all signed at one point to Atlantic Records' extraordinarily diverse jazz roster—explores how some musicians in the middle to late twentieth century resisted conventionally accepted understandings of jazz timbres, instrumental configurations, and compositional forms.

Tamar Barzel and Loren Kajikawa each recount emerging notions of ethnicity and community in jazz during the closing decades of the twentieth century. Barzel chronicles the birth of New York City's downtown music scene in the 1980s and the effect of its subversive (for some) blurring of musical style on contemporary conceptions of jazz. Kajikawa documents how a prolific group of Asian American musicians on the West Coast drew on the legacy of free jazz and the black nationalist politics of the 1960s and 1970s to produce a distinctively hybrid style at the same time that Wynton Marsalis and other leading African American jazz figures on the East Coast turned away from nationalist ideologies and experimental practices.

Part 3, "Education," centers on how we teach and learn jazz performance and history. Jessica Bissett Perea focuses on vocal jazz ensembles, a subgenre at once immensely popular in certain circles and vilified or ignored altogether in others. Writing from her perspective as a musicologist (and a former vocal jazz performer and ensemble director), Bissett Perea shows the effects of both gender and the institutional structure of most academic music programs on the (non)acceptance of jazz choirs in the wider, and decidedly instrumentalist-oriented, jazz world. David Ake presents a broader analysis of the impact of college-based jazz education on jazz history and historiography, imploring us to rethink our notions of how and where jazz is learned and created in the United States today. To conclude this section, and the collection as a whole, Sherrie Tucker's chapter on the growth of jazz studies in academia serves as both a reflection on the discipline's current state and an impassioned call for scholars to listen more closely—to the music, to the musicians, and to one another—to nurture a field as multifaceted as jazz itself.

Our combined efforts to challenge rigid definitions do not derive from any hope of derailing the significant work carried out by the many individuals and institutions committed to sustaining jazz in the twenty-first century. Rather, by identifying overlooked people, places, and practices, we seek to view in a new light the received wisdom and critical biases that underlie conventional definitions of jazz; to open new lines of musical, historical, and cultural inquiry; and, perhaps most important, to recapture some of the riches lost in the process of elevating, protecting, or otherwise cordoning off jazz. Ultimately, by questioning the common assumptions that fuel jazz debates, we trust that today's scholars and students—and hopefully also fans, music industry professionals, and practicing jazz musicians—can profit by rethinking their own conceptions of this endlessly fascinating, vibrant, and evolving genre.

NOTES

1. Tremlett Giles, "Spanish Fan Calls Police over Saxophone Band Who Were Just Not Jazzy Enough," *Guardian*, December 10, 2009, www.guardian.co.uk/music/2009/dec/09/jazz-festival-larry-ochs-saxophone. As far as we know, that suit is still pending.

2. *Jazz*, directed by Ken Burns (Arlington, VA: PBS, 2001), DVD.

3. Larry Kart, *Jazz in Search of Itself* (New Haven, CT: Yale University Press, 2004); Stuart Nicholson, *Is Jazz Dead? (Or Has It Moved to a New Address)* (New York: Routledge, 2005); Eric Porter, *What Is This Thing Called Jazz?* (Berkeley: University of California Press, 2002). See also Wynton Marsalis, "What Jazz Is . . . and Isn't," *New York Times,* July 31, 1998, 21.

4. See E.D. Hirsch Jr., *Cultural Literacy: What Every American Needs to Know* (Boston: Houghton Mifflin, 1987); Henry Louis Gates Jr., *Loose Canons: Notes on the Culture Wars* (New York: Oxford University Press, 1992); and James Davison Hunter, *Culture Wars: The Struggle to Define America* (New York: Basic Books, 1992).

5. Scott DeVeaux, "Constructing the Jazz Tradition: Jazz Historiography," *Black American Literature Forum* 25, no. 3 (Fall 1991): 525–60. See also Krin

Gabbard, "Introduction: The Jazz Canon and Its Consequences," in *Jazz among the Discourses,* ed. Krin Gabbard (Durham, NC: Duke University Press, 1995), 1–28; Sherrie Tucker, " "Uplift and Downbeats: If Jazz History Included the Prairie View Co-eds," International Association of Jazz Educators, *Jazz Research Proceedings* (January 2001): 26–31; David Ake, "Jazz Historiography and the Problem of Louis Jordan," in *Jazz Cultures* (Berkeley: University of California Press, 2002), 42–61; Porter, *This Thing Called Jazz.*

6. See Richard Taruskin, *Text and Act: Essays on Music and Performance* (New York: Oxford University Press, 1995).

7. *John McLellan:* "What do you feel about a longer piece of music, which is completely scored, which doesn't leave any opening for improvisation—is that still jazz?" *Charlie Parker:* "Well, it depends on how it's written. It could be, yes." Parker, interview by McLellan, Boston, June 13, 1953. Transcript available at "Miles Ahead: Charlie Parker Interviews," Miles Ahead: A Miles Davis Website, www.plosin.com/milesAhead/BirdInterviews.html.

8. Nicolas Slonimsky, *Lexicon of Musical Invective: Critical Assaults on Composers since Beethoven's Time* (1953; repr., New York: Norton, 2000).

9. The past decade has seen the publication of a spate of outstanding books dealing with jazz in parts of Africa, Asia, Australia, South America, and Europe. For recent scholarship on jazz beyond U.S. borders, see E. Taylor Atkins, *Blue Nippon: Authenticating Jazz in Japan* (Durham, NC: Duke University Press, 2001); E. Taylor Atkins, ed., *Jazz Planet* (Jackson: University Press of Mississippi, 2003); Mike Heffley, *Northern Sun, Southern Moon: Europe's Reinvention of Jazz* (New Haven, CT: Yale University Press, 2005); Jeffrey H. Jackson, *Making Jazz French: Music and Modern Life in Interwar Paris* (Durham, NC: Duke University Press, 2003); Michael H. Kater, *Different Drummers: Jazz in the Culture of Nazi Germany* (New York: Oxford University Press, 1992); George McKay, *Circular Breathing: The Cultural Politics of Jazz in Britain* (Durham, NC: Duke University Press, 2005); and Nicholson, *Is Jazz Dead?*

PART ONE

Categories

CHAPTER I

Incorporation and Distinction in Jazz History and Jazz Historiography

ERIC PORTER

Over the past two decades we have seen a flowering of scholarship in what is often termed the "new jazz studies." Jazz historians—but also sociologists, ethnomusicologists, literary scholars, practitioners of American Studies and ethnic studies, and others—have charted the histories of musicians and musical styles and situated them in their broader social contexts. We now have a much better idea of how various social forces have informed the production and consumption of jazz. We have more insights into the ways that musicians, rather than simply being engaged in the pursuit of art or, conversely, expressing in almost-unconscious ways political or cultural imperatives, have instead been positioned by, have responded to, and sometimes have commented on ever-changing social conditions that both inspired and restricted their creativity.

We have seen an array of provocative works that expand our definition of what counts as jazz culture across artistic genres and modes of cultural and intellectual expression. These new studies generally avoid the pitfalls of earlier investigations, which often assumed too homologous a relationship between jazz, American or African American identities and politics, and the aesthetic goals of those working through other modes of creative expression. We now have a much better perspective on critical debates about the music and on the ways jazz and its practitioners have been represented in film, literature, and television. Concomitantly, we know more about the complex ways that jazz has been a vehicle for identity formation and self-actualization for members of disparate cultural communities.

The new jazz studies has generally paid careful attention to racialization and social stratification as fundamental organizing processes of both the political economy of jazz and of its critical representation in the United States. More recently, we have seen work that illuminates the place of women in jazz and the function of jazz as a gendered and sexualized creative, discursive, and institutional practice. Another important growth area is scholarship that considers how such issues of power and identity have played out in places other than the United States.

Recent work has also expanded our definitions of what count as the musical objects of jazz studies. Various scholarly moves bring more, different kinds of music into the story of jazz. For example, as Sherrie Tucker argues, bringing gender into jazz studies expands its referent not simply by being more inclusive of women or by bringing attention to a less studied modality of power. It also enables further investigation into arenas of musical activity—modes of vocal performance, instruments such as flutes often associated with women, sweet bands, novelty bands, music curricula, and so on—marked as "not jazz" because they were feminized.[1] Meanwhile, to cite another trend, serious scholarly work on jazz fusion in the 1960s and 1970s works against the tendency to refuse its inclusion in jazz histories or include it only as an artistic or commercial dead end.[2]

Meanwhile, improvisation studies, a field that overlaps with but is not coterminous with jazz studies, has pushed us to consider musical practices and intercultural exchanges that cross or defy genres. "Improvisation (in theory and practice)," as Daniel Fischlin and Ajay Heble remind us, "challenges all musical orthodoxies, all musical taxonomies, even its own."[3] Such analytical broadening mirrors the long-standing critique of jazz orthodoxy from musicians, many of whom have had a vexed relationship with the term "jazz," because they felt it did not do justice to the breadth of their artistic projects and because of the ways it signified the economic, discursive, and social limitations under which they labored. Indeed, Duke Ellington, who for many is almost synonymous with jazz, issued statements for much of his career suggesting that his musical project exceeded the parameters of the genre. "I am not playing jazz," he said in 1930. "I am trying to play the natural feelings of a people."[4]

Yet as we consider the directions in which jazz studies might go in the future, at a moment when many of the established narratives of jazz history have been complicated, expanded, and in some cases exploded (at least in scholarly circles), I wish to reconsider the generative function of what Scott DeVeaux described in his influential 1991 essay "Constructing the Jazz Tradition: Jazz Historiography" as the widely shared and problematic "article of faith that some central essence named *jazz* remains constant throughout all the dramatic transformations that have resulted in modern-day jazz."[5] While the deployment of this assumption may well have obscured social context and produced a faulty sense of coherence in historiographical practice, I am interested in how the very notion of a jazz tradition and assumptions about its constitutive elements have had complex social and cultural lives intimately related to the creation of music, its political economy, and the discourses that have shaped its meaning.

I begin to explore here how the notion that jazz is a genre with an essence has been both a positively and a negatively productive concept. Contending with the ways that musicians, fans, and critics alike have defined artistic projects by investing in or rejecting elements of jazz's assumed essence, at both musical and symbolic levels, gives us greater insight into the production of this music as a socially situated art and helps us to expand the parameters of jazz history and to rethink its ontology. So does examining the linked process by which musicians and critics have defined jazz projects through the incorporation or acts of distinction from elements and assumed essences of other musical genres.

I start by returning to DeVeaux's essay, considering it, as many of us have done over the past few decades, as a justification for rethinking the parameters of jazz history and for the ways it identifies some of the negatively productive ways in which jazz history is created. Then, drawing primarily on practicing musicians' own musical and textual engagements with jazz history, I identify some of the complicated ways this process is played out in practice, given the complex symbolism of jazz and its musical others. I conclude by suggesting how such acts of incorporation and distinction point to future avenues of scholarly explorations that are less bound to jazz as a framing narrative but that still remain absolutely attentive to the power of jazz as a creative expression and cultural symbol.

In "Constructing the Jazz Tradition," DeVeaux issued a kind of call to arms to jazz historians that helped to energize the emergent field of new jazz studies. While recognizing the status- and capital-producing value of narratives that define jazz as "America's classical music" and the political value in celebrating jazz as an African American achievement, he argued that versions of jazz history that cohered around essentialist understandings of the music's ontological foundations in tradition and progress and that focused on a series of stylistic shifts rather than taking up the messy challenge of analyzing the production of the music in its diverse social and ideological contexts, obscured more than they illuminated. He called, instead, "for an approach that is less invested in the ideology of jazz as aesthetic object and more responsive to issues of historical particularity."[6]

While some musicians, fans, and critics have been interested in understanding these connections between jazz and society since the emergence of this music, DeVeaux's exhortation identified a growing trend in the writing of jazz history during the 1980s and offered inspiration to others (myself included) to think and write in deeper and broader ways about the music as both a creative and a socially situated practice. However, as we contemplate the future of jazz studies—or perhaps a "studies" cast differently or more broadly—I am interested in reexamining the complicated lives of these constructed and obfuscating narratives and their effect on the production and reception of this music.

As a starting point, we need to keep in mind that whatever tyranny may lie in the critical deployments of a jazz tradition, "jazz" as a musical, cultural, and critical practice profoundly emphasizes its own history, and it has done so for many decades. The practice of "encod[ing] the past in symbol form to make a present," as one scholar describes the vernacular practice of history, remains a key component of the performative and reflective aspects of music making.[7] This is something we hear when soloists or composers quote from an existing work or seek to define a style, or a sound, that honors, parodies, or rejects the work of their teachers, colleagues, or prominent predecessors or when the larger ensemble lays down an identifiable or evocative groove.[8]

As listeners, many of us are drawn to particular musicians because of what their engagement with history comes to symbolize on record, through CD marketing campaigns and concert promotion, or when it becomes part of the critical conversation about such artists in jazz magazines and newspapers and in the friendly and not-so-friendly debates among fans about musical worth. The centrality of history to jazz is reaffirmed for us when Wynton Marsalis musically invokes Louis Armstrong, Clifford Brown, or Miles Davis (but only before 1968). But we also hear this centrality of history when clarinetist Don Byron plays the music of pop classical and jazz composer Raymond Scott, R&B icon Junior Walker, or gospel pioneer Thomas Dorsey, or when he collaborates with the spoken word artist Sadiq or the rapper Biz Markie. The historical vision in Byron's work, of course, is different—simultaneously broader in terms of relevant influences and collaborators and more irreverent toward the jazz tradition as some have defined it.

The examples of Byron and Marsalis—two prominent players who for years have been vocal in their explicit and implicit definitions of a jazz tradition—exemplify the ways that the very ontology of jazz as a historically grounded practice is based on choices of how to incorporate or distinguish one's project from particular elements of jazz and its musical others. Marsalis has defined the neoclassical trajectory in his work through invoking antecedents already seen as organic to the jazz tradition or by exploring musical others, like Tin Pan Alley songs, that have long been seamlessly incorporated into the tradition. Byron's more eclectic aesthetic, on the other hand, has celebrated what for some is a less acceptable range of influences. Both visions illustrate how the incorporation of musical others is a long-standing component in the creation of jazz and that musicians make value judgments about where in history one finds musical others worth incorporating.

DeVeaux's essay is similarly valuable for reminding us that the construction of a jazz tradition is relational and negatively productive. Jazz, he shows, is defined in contradistinction to other musical genres. Jazz is jazz because it emphasizes musical characteristics that are deemphasized in other forms or because it lacks those elements seen as central to other forms. But jazz is also defined against itself. "More often than not," he argues, "such definitions [of a jazz tradition revolving around an assumed essence] define through exclusion."[9]

The boundaries of jazz are maintained by calling attention to subgenres or specific musical projects that some might view as jazz but that can also be seen as lacking some essential property (swing, improvisation, the fusion of African and European devices, spontaneity, sounds from black popular music, accessibility) or containing elements, such as commercial appeal, or sounds that some believe reside more comfortably in other musical genres. For example, jazz fusion is perceived to be "not jazz" because it uses elements from rock and funk such as electric instruments and a different rhythmic basis; the avant-garde fails the jazz test for some because it abandons swing and other fundamentals; and the neoclassicists are seen as deficient because they fail to understand that change is fundamental to the art form.[10] One of the striking ironies of definitions of the jazz tradition is that valued components of jazz's ontology (experimentation, black vernacular practices, composition, populism, etc.) become a problem when used in excess, that is, to the extent that they are seen as pushing a particular musical project into territory more properly encompassed by a different genre.

Creating and defining a historically grounded jazz music often involves a multiplicity of incorporative and exclusionary moves that stand in a contradictory but productive relationship with one other. Although the scope of Marsalis's projects over the past thirty years speak is expansive, he has famously, especially during the jazz canon wars of the 1980s and 1990s, defined in interviews and writings and on recordings such as the *Standard Time* series a rather narrow jazz tradition. Marsalis has defined neoclassical jazz—and, in particular, its legitimacy, seriousness of purpose, and moral standing—by casting it in high cultural terms and comparing it with supposedly lesser genres (funk, hip-hop, rock and roll) and deficient jazz subgenres. He has juxtaposed his work with efforts by fusionists like Herbie Hancock to incorporate hip-hop and funk into jazz and also with avant-garde players who strayed too far from their blues roots and wandered too close to modern concert music conventions. Yet Marsalis has done this while integrating a wide variety of vernacular and popular elements (work songs, spirituals, ring shouts, the blues, gospel, New Orleans R&B, Tin Pan Alley, and so on).

Moreover, the legitimacy of neoclassical jazz still depends on its practitioners remaining to some degree populist. Such a populism is crafted, in part, by contrasting the subgenre with a jazz avant-garde whose modernist pretensions make it not populist or popular enough. But, all the while, Marsalis and his colleagues at Lincoln Center incorporate from classical music the ideal that great art exceeds the corrupting influence of the market, as they integrate musical elements and formal qualities of concert music. His *Blood on the Fields* was, of course, composed as an oratorio. Such moves have helped to shepherd the Jazz at Lincoln Center program through a series of prestige-building and capital-improvement projects that brought it at least close to being on par with Lincoln Center's other constitutive organizations: the Metropolitan Opera, the New York City Ballet, and the New York Philharmonic.

Byron, on the other hand, has defined his musical project and, by extension, a more expansive jazz practice through the incorporation of an eclectic range of historical (e.g., Mickey Katz) and contemporary (e.g., hip-hop) influences. Yet this openness is still defined through acts of both incorporation and distinction and by simultaneously rejecting and assimilating different definitions of musical authenticity. Byron created a sense of authenticity on his 1993 album *Don Byron Plays the Music of*

Mickey Katz by reproducing Katz's own orchestrations, suggesting that at least in some cases a kind of authenticating jazz ethos of experimentalism and innovation can be achieved—Byron's recording won him significant critical acclaim in the jazz world—by moving in very visible ways outside of the safety of the jazz tradition and incorporating "other music" in putatively authentic form into one's repertoire.[11]

Some, of course, did not see it this way. Responding in the *New York Times* to explicit comments by critic Stanley Crouch and implicit comments by Marsalis that his music did not fit into the jazz tradition, Byron said, "Me and most of the cats I hang with, we're too left-wing to be around Lincoln Center. . . . They should be presenting the freshest, baddest stuff. I don't even exist in jazz as these people perceive it to be." Byron went on to suggest that a wider vision for jazz, simultaneously historically minded, eclectic, and future-oriented, was prevalent among many musicians of his generation and was defined, at least in part, in productive disagreement with and distinction from the Lincoln Center vision: "One of the fallacies of the Wynton era is that jazz cats don't listen to rap."[12] Such contradictory incorporative and distinctive acts, of course, are often deeply racialized, gendered, classed, and generationalized. They are socially symbolic at the moment of their utterance and when subsequently read by others. As such, they often articulate and challenge power in the jazz world and beyond.

In a 1985 joint interview with pianist Herbie Hancock in *Musician* magazine, Marsalis's erasure of the line between "white" classical music and "black" jazz, with attendant comments rejecting the idea that any race is naturally predisposed to excelling in either genre, coalesced with the idea that African American musicians had a duty to uphold an African American tradition of classical jazz and that they somehow failed their community when they engaged too deeply with popular forms. Marsalis took Prince to task for drawing extensively from a whitened, feminized sphere of youth-oriented rock music (and for what he considered cross-dressing), while he chastised co-interviewee Hancock for incorporating elements from the excessively black, hypermasculine sphere of hip-hop.[13] Yet Marsalis also, as he made clear in multiple interviews and comments, positioned his work against primitivist legacies in jazz criticism, with attendant, narrow conceptions of how (and for whom) black people should act, perform, and think.

Byron labeled *Don Byron Plays the Music of Mickey Katz* a "pro-ethnicity" record, designed in part to recapture what he saw as Katz's challenge to the assimiltationist impulse in U.S. culture after World War II.

By doing so, he not only responded to what he saw as a WASPish cultural dominance still holding sway in the 1990s but also, as David Borgo's analysis of the album suggests, negotiated a widely shared interpretive paradox holding that both ethnic allegiance and cultural boundary crossings sit side by side as generators of jazz (as well as klezmer) authenticity. As an outsider to the cultural tradition that produced klezmer, Byron was compelled to devote significant energy to defining legitimate entry points to and exit points from klezmer and jazz, respectively, while "invigorat[ing] and expanding American Jewish and jazz traditions."[14] Meanwhile, Byron's quirky, nerdy stage persona has provided an alternative to the folksy, respectable, and at times paternal version of jazz (and black) masculinity offered by Marsalis, further defining Byron as authentically experimental while providing a platform for identification by jazz geeks and self-styled intellectuals in his audience.

Recent work on jazz scenes outside of the United States has demonstrated how the Americanness embedded in the practice of jazz has been a touchstone for its authenticity. This scholarship also shows how such gestures are often tied to the power and prestige of the United States and to social transformations in the broader sphere of race relations. Musicians outside of the country have either incorporated or distanced themselves from the putative Americanness or African Americanness of jazz and its subgenres, as they have sought to define a jazz practice relevant to their own creative conception and social experiences.

We see this in E. Taylor Atkins's account of the issue of authenticity in Japanese jazz history over the course of the twentieth century. He shows how in the post–World War II period a strong identification with American jazz was tied up with a sense of Japanese political and cultural failure stemming from the nation's recent defeat at the hands of the United States. Subsequently, a shift by many to disavow American influences and instead create a "Japanese jazz" was linked to a larger critique of U.S. imperialism, a growing sense of Japanese nationalism tied to the nation's economic recovery, and, somewhat ironically, to an identification with black nationalist musical and critical statements from the United States.[15]

Maxine McGregor also explores the phenomenon of identification and disidentification with American jazz in her account of her husband's work with the interracial ensemble, the Brotherhood of Breath. Chris McGregor's group grew out of the South African group, the Blue Notes, which went into exile in Europe in the early 1960s. McGregor's fascinating account gives insight into the complex racial and political terrain in which modern jazz musicians operated under Apartheid during the early

1960s. Among other things, she shows how incorporating elements of U.S.-based modern jazz into South African jazz made the latter politically threatening under Apartheid because of the symbolic interracialism of the American referent.[16]

Her book also documents how expatriate South African musicians' struggles to survive artistically and economically in Europe were made more difficult by the fact that they had diminished authenticity in the eyes of audiences, club owners, and fellow musicians, because they were not American and not African American. Meanwhile, some of these musicians wondered whether they were compromising their African musical roots by incorporating American influences. In one act of distinction, bassist Johnny Dyani left the group and moved to Scandinavia to develop his own musical projects, because he felt that the influence of the American avant-garde put his colleagues and him "in danger of losing their own musical language."[17]

The experiences of members of the Brotherhood of Breath and institutions like Jazz at Lincoln Center remind us that acts of incorporating and marking as distinctive jazz and its others have also been linked to the fundamental challenge for musicians of making a living in the jazz world, which of course is related to broader political-economic factors. Marsalis's neoclassical jazz vision that emphasized the incorporation of black vernacular elements was at least partially engineered to appeal to government and corporate funding entities and to counter the antiblack rhetoric (albeit in ways that reproduced elements of it) and policies of the Reagan-Bush era.[18] And in musicians' statements over the course of jazz history, particularly those of African Americans during the civil rights era, we can see how acts of distancing and incorporation have been explicitly linked to the problem of making a living.

Charles Mingus's musical projects and public commentary during the 1950s and 1960s, particularly his articulation of his vexed relationship with the idea of jazz because of its artistically, socially, and economically limiting aspects, suggests that while we interrogate the idea of a coherent jazz tradition, we also must keep in mind that an investment in creating something called jazz has often gone hand in hand with an equally generative process of troubling the practice of and the very category of jazz. Mingus, in his autobiography, *Beneath the Underdog,* and in other venues, sometimes identified as a jazz musician and sometimes did not. And he positioned his music both inside and outside of the jazz tradition. He characterized it, intermittently and often simultaneously, as serious jazz different from popular music; as experimental music distinct from familiar jazz genres; as genre-defying popular music; as black music steeped in the blues that diverged from that produced by white West Coast musicians; as politicized black music working against white hegemonic culture; and as a universalist expression that defies narrow conceptions of musical blackness.[19]

Such contradictory moves have been assumed by many to be outgrowths of Mingus's mercurial personality and mental instability. They were that, certainly, but they were also responses to the conditions under which Mingus labored. He experienced segregated unions and performance spaces, the financial effects of marketing categories like West Coast jazz and hard bop on his livelihood, and expansions and contractions in the market for experimental jazz and for jazz more generally. His comments about what he was trying to accomplish musically often went hand in hand with analyses of the political economy of jazz. He spoke often and eloquently about jazz and classical music as racialized constructs, linked to the marketing of music and broader class and race relations and determinative of whether and when black musicians could get work. And as he embraced or rejected aspects seen as central to these avenues of musical expression, he was often responding to the personal and professional stakes of distinction and incorporation.[20]

For example, Mingus criticized Dave Brubeck (through his saxophonist Paul Desmond) for not swinging adequately and then apologized for it several months later, after being taken to task by Miles Davis for writing compositions akin to "tired modern paintings." Mingus was, in the first case, distinguishing an African American–centered jazz practice through one of its assumed essences, as he responded to the ways West Coast jazz as a marketing category and marker of critical expectation often benefited white musicians incorporating elements of modern concert music into their work. His apology seems motivated in part by an awareness that such acts of distinction based on racially inflected orthodoxy ran the risk of marginalizing African American experimentalists like himself who were refusing racially coded generic boundaries and similarly seeking to incorporate a wide range of musical referents.[21]

So where do the aforementioned examples leave us when contemplating the future of jazz history and jazz studies? At one level they suggest that we continue to maintain a critical perspective on the problematic jazz historiographical constructs that have constrained creative projects and obscured important stories. But we can also keep in mind the power of these constructs to give meaning to the experience of creating, producing, and listening to jazz. Identifying the complex ways musicians have identified with and distanced themselves from jazz and its subgenres as highly symbolic, multiply coded musical expressions and knowing that such moves are informed by an equally rich set of meanings associated with the genres and elements either incorporated into jazz projects or standing as constitutive others for jazz, provides fodder for expansions and refinements, or perhaps more radical reconceptualizations, of periods and genres.

Such a strategy might enable us, for example, to reimagine the hard bop moment. Historians of hard bop have typically theorized that a fairly wide range of (primarily African American) jazz expressions during the middle and late 1950s and early 1960s developed in relation to currents in black popular music, to the collective artistic and critical desire to reground jazz in an expanding vernacular (as well as its anchoring foundations of the blues and church music), to the demands of a politicizing black public with growing purchasing power, and to the desires of alienated hipsters of various colors for a more "authentic" jazz. Such narratives usually focus on how various jazz modernists—Miles, Mingus, Coltrane, Silver, Blakey, Brown, Roach, and so on—embraced (or at least engaged) popular and contemporary social and political imperatives; these narratives give only obligatory nods to Jimmy Smith, Lee Morgan, and other soul jazz practitioners who, despite unassailable jazz credibility, managed to get more serious play on R&B radio.

Yet one can imagine a history of hard bop more inclusive of artists who worked across genres, paying greater attention to developments in these various genres and to the ways that they were marketed and written about. We might get a better sense of the range of complex meanings that the embrace of the vernacular brought to jazz and to those that jazz brought to other genres. Guthrie Ramsey brings us partway there in his account of the blues-inflected work of Dinah Washington, Cootie Williams, and Louis Jordan during the 1940s and 1950s. Although marketing, critical interpretation, and individual musicians' own artistic goals and politics led to increasing distinction among different styles and genres after World War II, "strong currents of stylistic cross-fertilization continually revitalized each genre." Some musicians moved quite easily across genres, performing and recording with, and thus influencing and being influenced by, a wide range of practitioners. Others engaged in creative collaboration in shared educational, family, or neighborhood spaces.[22]

Dinah Washington's career and critical reception is a particularly interesting case in point. Versed in church music, blues, R&B, and swing, her career took off during the 1950s as she made a concerted effort, with the support of Mercury Records and its new EmArcy imprint, to define herself as a jazz singer. Yet she continued to record R&B hits for the Mercury imprint, and in 1959 she cracked the Billboard pop charts with "What a Diff'rence a Day Makes," recorded with strings and designed to be a somewhat different kind of crossover record.

Nadine Cohodas's survey of Washington's musical activities during the middle and late 1950s illustrates some productive possibilities for reimagining hard bop through a deeper consideration of jazz's musical others. Participants' accounts of Washington's August 1954 recording session in front of a live audience that featured Clifford Brown and Max Roach illustrate that she had significant control of the session. Moreover, it meant a lot to her to be playing with top-flight modern jazz musicians, and it meant a lot to those on the date to be recording with the "Queen of the Blues."[23]

Such reciprocity across genre is generally not evident in written histories of hard bop, in which Washington appears only briefly and only as the steady employer of important rhythm section stalwarts such as pianist Wynton Kelly or drummer Jimmy Cobb or as the leader of recording sessions that featured the likes of Brown and Roach.[24] But one can imagine an alternative account of hard bop that brings more focus to artists like Washington, who crossed genres and provided the catalyst for reconceptualizing jazz through its constitutive others through the give-and-take in the studio, on stage, and in rehearsal and through informal exchanges by members of musical networks. Bringing Washington into the equation would also, of course, temper the androcentrism of histories of hard bop.

Cohodas also shows how Washington's booking agents and record company simultaneously presented her as a blues, R&B, jazz, and, later, crossover artist. Meanwhile, the jazz, popular entertainment, and African American press pondered her musical identities and how they might coalesce. On the one hand, the less than stellar reception Washington received from jazz critics, despite strong record sales and enthusiastic audiences, illustrates the point about the precariousness of the incorporation of musical others into conceptualizations of jazz—that is, how the assumed essences of other forms of music both legitimatize jazz artists and delegitimatize them when they are perceived as being used in excess. Critics were drawn to Washington as "Queen of the Blues" and

"Queen of the Jukebox." She provided something earthy and real, a kind of revitalization of jazz. Yet some viewed her work as somewhat overwrought, lacking nuance, and thus not quite as good as Billie Holiday's, Sarah Vaughan's, or Ella Fitzgerald's.[25] On the other hand, this discourse about Washington also makes clear that understandings among musicians, critics, and fans of a more vernacularly centered jazz were informed by this complex coming to terms with meanings embedded in residual and emergent genres and marketing categories, their similarities, and their divergences.

Through these years Washington performed at jazz festivals and clubs, venues that primarily presented R&B, nightclubs that featured artists across the musical spectrum, and sometimes at concerts that self-consciously juxtaposed artists perceived to be working in different genres. In March 1956 Washington appeared alongside Thelonious Monk, Miles Davis, Terry Gibbs, T-Bone Walker, Little Willie John, and the Clovers at a Detroit concert billed as "Jazz vs. Rock 'n Roll." A January 1957 gig in that city had her appearing alongside Ray Charles, Charlie Ventura, and R&B artist Sil Austin.[26] Although such shows were probably designed to bring in the largest possible audience—rather than instruct them about cross-fertilization among genres—they do point to another potential avenue of exploration for understanding the ways that jazz as roots-oriented music during the late 1950s was constituted in relationship to other popular musical styles.

An awareness of careers like Washington's (or Dakota Staton's or Les McCann's) as well as patterns of musical multiplicity and the productive relationships among musical elements and genres more generally—could also move us beyond simply expanding the parameters of what constitutes a jazz moment or a jazz genre. They might encourage us instead to explore musical phenomena that cannot be contained within a paradigm of jazz studies but whose analysis could still be significantly informed by jazz studies. In other words, rather than placing jazz and invocations of jazz into a larger framework of something like "jazz culture" or expanding the circle of what counts of jazz or who counts as a jazz musician, we might identify and write about various spheres of musical activity that intersect with but are not coterminous with jazz but whose existences are still determined, at least in part, by the idea of jazz and the political economy of the jazz world.

The participants in my recent jazz historiography seminar devoted a significant amount of time talking about how we might continue to push the boundaries of jazz scholarship, even in the new jazz studies moment.

One particularly interesting discussion built off of our reading of the first section ("Rooting Gender in Jazz History") of Nichole Rustin and Sherrie Tucker's *Big Ears: Listening for Gender in Jazz Studies*. We contemplated essays that identified how the gendered exclusions in jazz historical narratives had marginalized or made less than intelligible figures such as Lovie Austin, Lillian Hardin Armstrong, and Hazel Scott, along with all-women's swing bands, women in swing bands, and most jazz singers. These essays also argued eloquently for the inclusion of such figures in more expansive jazz historical narratives.[27]

We were convinced by such inclusionary interventions, but we also found ourselves considering the possibilities of different types of revisionist narratives. Might we, for example, write histories of multigeneric vocal practitioners (say, from Ma Rainey, through Dinah Washington, up to Erykah Badu and other contemporary artists), whose work is informed by jazz and whose reception is conditioned, in part, by the idea of jazz? Or perhaps we should examine the role of talented, female producer-composers (e.g., Lovie Austin, Carla Bley, Miya Masaoka), whose work intersected with but was much broader than jazz, in shaping twentieth-century musical culture?

We might move even further outside established practice by focusing on the various, intricate ways that jazz, as a creative practice and a symbolically rich genre, has helped define, in negative and positively productive ways, other musical genres in the United States and elsewhere. One finds an interesting, albeit brief, account of the productive aspects of a symbolic, American jazz and its genres in Brazilian vocalist Caetano Veloso's memoir. Veloso describes the place of jazz in João Gilberto's early development of the bossa nova and the ways he himself identified with both the bossa nova and jazz while developing an aesthetic and political sensibility in the late 1950s and early 1960s that later inspired him to help launch the tropicalismo movement.

Veloso opens his book by describing his disdain during the late 1950s for Brazil's fascination for what he considered banal forms of American popular culture, and rock and roll in particular. The critique is based on musical quality and on the context of the music's interpretation in Brazil. He hears in "Rock around the Clock" a "stridency and [a] somewhat awkward attempt to be more savagely rhythmic than American music had been up to then; even so it was far less rhythmically intense than Brazilian or Cuban music had always been." In almost Adornian terms, Veloso describes Brazilian consumers of rock and roll as buying into a kind of pseudorebellion, based on style over substance, reflective of middlebrow taste and affluence. The affinity for rock and roll is also symbolic of a stultifying Brazilian cultural nationalism, defined by Rio de Janeiro's assumed metonymic relationship with the rest of the country and by the assumption that Brazil and the United States shared a destiny.[28]

Gilberto and his bossa nova, meanwhile, stand as inspirational models of musical quality. Gilberto is successful, Veloso argues, because, unlike others who synthesize U.S. and Brazilian forms, he maintains a "command of the cool jazz idiom, which was then the cutting edge of musical invention in the United States." And, what distinguishes him from other Brazilian synthesizers of his moment is that he blends cool jazz with what is excellent about Brazilian culture: "that whole world the 'modernizers' had thought it necessary to leave behind as they pursued American styles, which were themselves, ironically, already dated." Such synthesis enables Gilberto to engage in "imagining a different future with the past in a different light."[29]

Veloso, in turn, is inspired by Gilberto to explore the music of U.S. vocalists (Ella Fitzgerald, Billie Holiday, Sarah Vaughan), instrumentalists (Miles Davis, Jimmy Giuffre, Thelonious Monk, the Modern Jazz Quartet), and, especially, the vocal and instrumental project of Chet Baker. Tropicalismo eventually emerged as a product of a series of immersions in and identifications with musical cultures both artistically instructive and socially symbolic—some of which are Brazilian, some of which are from the United States—and as a product of ironic disidentification with (while still incorporating) somewhat less valued musical expressions: "The *tropicalistas* decided that a genuine blend of the ridiculous aspirations of Americanophiles, the naïve good intentions of the nationalists, traditional Brazilian 'backwardness,' the Brazilian avant-garde—absolutely everything in Brazil's cultural life would be our raw material. Genuine creativity could redeem any aspect of it and make it transcendent."[30]

The tropicalismo movement was to be instructive as well as creative: "If we made reference to rock 'n' roll in our songs, the effect was to invite Brazilian rockers and rock fans to join the company of the creators and consumers of quality music." It was also to be political, as the movement's protests against the dictatorship and the subsequent jailing and exile of some of its practitioners indicate. And as it developed, tropicalismo was further nurtured by multigeneric identifications and disidentifications with different musical genres. Ray Charles, on the cusp of jazz, R&B, and pop, provided a particular inspiration through the beauty of this voice and by "fe[eding] our appetite for novelty with a style that was completely different than João's, or from Jimmy Giuffre's, Chet Baker's, or Dave Brubeck's." In addition to that of modern art, literature, and classical music, Veloso notes an eventual openness to work by Bob Dylan, John Lennon, and Mick Jagger, "but every time, I always returned to my passion for João Gilberto to find a base and reestablish a perspective."[31]

In other words, Veloso positions cool jazz as an influence that must be kept at some distance but which also inspires musically. It is a symbol of artistic integrity and a cosmopolitan approach to art. As such, it stands as part of the antidote to a simplistic, stylized identification with America and a dead-end Brazilian nationalism. Yet it is but one element in a complicated process of identifications and disidentifications across genres and national borders. And as the reference to Ray Charles indicates, the public face of an already existing history of jazz-inflected cross-fertilization is also part of the inspirational mix.

The aforementioned examples are by no means a complete list, but I hope they are adequately indicative of historiographical directions in which we might move if we engage productively with the phenomena of incorporation and distinction in jazz history and, importantly, with the way those phenomena have been addressed by musicians. Ultimately, jazz studies—and, by extension, new studies that might exceed it while remaining in dialogue with it—is at its best when scholars remember to take cues from its innovative practioners and their observations on the complex and often contradictory elements of the music and its contexts of interpretation.

NOTES

Elements of this essay were first voiced in presentations sponsored by the Columbia University Jazz Studies Group and the University of Wisconsin–Madison Center for the Humanities. I thank the organizers of these events for the opportunity to share my ideas and acknowledge fellow panelists and audience members for comments that furthered my thinking about these matters. I am grateful to participants in my recent jazz historiography graduate seminar for their sharp insights on the challenges of writing jazz history and for their suggestions for where the field might go in the future.

1. Sherrie Tucker, "Big Ears: Listening for Gender in Jazz Studies," *Current Musicology* 71–73 (Spring 2001–2): 395–96.

2. See, for example, Kevin Fellezs, "Between Rock and a Jazz Place: Intercultural Interchange in Fusion Musicking" (PhD diss., University of California, Santa

Cruz, 2004); and his *Birds of Fire: Jazz, Rock, Funk and the Creation of Fusion* (Durham, NC: Duke University Press, 2011); Steven F. Pond, *Head Hunters: The Making of Jazz's First Platinum Album* (Ann Arbor: University of Michigan Press, 2005).

3. Daniel Fischlin and Ajay Heble, eds., *The Other Side of Nowhere: Jazz, Improvisation, and Communities in Dialogue* (Middletown, CT: Wesleyan University Press, 2004), 31.

4. Duke Ellington, quoted in Florence Zunser, "'Opera Must Die,' Says Galli-Curci! Long Live the Blues!," in *The Duke Ellington Reader,* ed. Mark Tucker (New York: Oxford University Press, 1995), 45 (originally published in *New York Evening Graphic Magazine,* December 27, 1930).

5. Scott DeVeaux, "Constructing the Jazz Tradition: Jazz Historiography," *Black American Literature Forum* 25, no. 3 (Fall 1991): 528.

6. Ibid., 553.

7. Greg Dening, *History's Anthropology: The Death of William Gooch* (Lanham, MD: University Press of America, 1988), 2.

8. Ingrid Monson, *Saying Something: Jazz Improvisation and Interaction* (Chicago: University of Chicago Press, 1996), 97–98.

9. DeVeaux, "Constructing the Jazz Tradition," 528.

10. Ibid.

11. My assessment is complicated a bit by the fact that klezmer in the United States developed in dialogue with jazz, and that of the Mickey Katz era was often influenced by swing and modern jazz. Adding another layer of complexity, Byron's project was not highly regarded by some klezmer aficionados, because Katz's act, dismissed by some as a "novelty," was seen as an inappropriate platform for entering that tradition.

12. Don Byron, quoted in Stephen Sherrill, "Don Byron," *New York Times,* January 16, 1994, www.nytimes.com/1994/01/16/magazine/don-byron.html, p. 9.

13. Robert Walser, *Keeping Time: Readings in Jazz History* (New York: Oxford University Press, 1998), 339–50.

14. David Borgo, "Can Blacks Play Klezmer? Authenticity in American Ethnic Musical Expression," *Sonneck Society for American Music Bulletin* 24, no. 2 (Spring 1998): http://american-music.org/publications/bullarchive/bongo.htm.

15. E. Taylor Atkins, *Blue Nippon: Authenticating Jazz in Japan* (Durham, NC: Duke University Press, 2001).

16. Maxine McGregor, *Chris McGregor and the Brotherhood of Breath* (Flint, MI: Bamberger Books, 1995).

17. Ibid., 116.

18. Eric Porter, *What Is This Thing Called Jazz: African American Musicians as Artists, Critics, and Activists* (Berkeley: University of California Press, 2002), 287–334.

19. Ibid., 101–48.

20. Ibid.

21. Ibid., 118–24.

22. Guthrie P. Ramsey Jr., *Race Music: Black Cultures from Bebop to Hip-Hop* (Berkeley: University of California Press, 2003), 74.

23. Nadine Cohodas, *Queen: The Life and Music of Dinah Washington* (New York: Pantheon Books, 2004), 178–79; see also pages 160–357.

24. We see this treatment of Washington, for example, in David Rosenthal, *Hard Bop: Jazz and Black Music, 1955–1965* (New York: Oxford University Press, 1992) and Kenny Mathieson, *Cookin': Hard Bop and Soul Jazz, 1954–65* (Edinburgh, Scotland: Canongate, 2002).

25. Cohodas, *Queen*, 208, 221–22, 246.

26. Ibid., 224–25, 249.

27. Nichole T. Rustin and Sherrie Tucker, *Big Ears: Listening for Gender in Jazz Studies* (Durham, NC: Duke University Press, 2008), 31–154. The following essays prompted the discussion: Lara Pellegrinelli, "Separated at 'Birth': Singing and the History of Jazz"; Jeffrey Taylor, "With Lovie and Lil: Rediscovering Two Chicago Pianists of the 1920s"; Monica Hairston, "Gender, Jazz, and the Popular Front"; Christina Baade, "'The Battle of the Saxes': Gender, Dance Bands, and British Nationalism in the Second World War"; and Tracy McMullen, "Identity for Sale: Glenn Miller, Wynton Marsalis, and Cultural Replay in Music."

28. Caetano Veloso, *Tropical Truth: A Story of Music and Revolution in Brazil*, ed. Barbara Einzig, trans. Isabel de Sena (New York: Da Capo, 2003), 10, 20, 31.

29. Ibid., 22.

30. Ibid., 28, 20. Later, Veloso says similarly, "To have known rock as something relatively contemptible during the decisive years of our intellectual growth and, on the other hand, to have had bossa nova as the soundtrack of our rebellion signifies for Brazilians of my generation the right to imagine an ambitious intervention in the future of the world, a right that immediately begins to be lived as a duty" (30).

31. Ibid., 30, 40–41.

CHAPTER 2

Louis Armstrong Loves Guy Lombardo

ELIJAH WALD

In the summer of 1949 Louis Armstrong sat down with the English jazz critic and record producer Leonard Feather for one of the "blindfold tests" Feather was then conducting for *Metronome* magazine.[1] The way the blindfold tests worked was that Feather would get together with a prominent jazz performer, play a series of unidentified records, and ask the performer to comment on each and give it a rating from one to five stars.

Armstrong said that he couldn't give any record less than two stars, because he loved all music. As he told Feather, "there's a story about the [church] sisters who were talking about the pastor, and only one sister could appreciate the pastor. She said, 'If he's good, I can look through him and see Jesus. If he's bad, I can look over him and see Jesus.' That's the way I feel about music."[2]

This did not mean that Armstrong loved all music equally. For the first series of records Feather played, he gave three stars to Roy Eldridge's Little Jazz Trumpet Ensemble playing "Fiesta in Brass," four stars to the New Orleans trad men Bunk Johnson and George Lewis playing "Franklin Street Blues," two stars to the Woody Herman Orchestra's "Keeper of the Flame," three stars to Art Hodes and Sidney Bechet playing "Way Down Yonder in New Orleans," and four stars to Benny Goodman's version of "Sometimes I'm Happy," with Bunny Berigan. His comments on the latter were typical: "This has a nice, easy swing . . . like a basketball team, everybody passing the ball just right. . . . This reminds me of when we used to play them good old dance numbers. Real good musicianship here. Sounds like Benny Goodman on clarinet. Four, man!"

Then Feather, who had so far been sticking to trad and swing groups, played a record that sounded rather different: after a hint of understated brass, a choir of mellifluous saxophones came in, murmuring a gentle, waltz-time melody. At the bridge, a lightly flowery piano, redolent of fine hotel lounges, alternated with the whispering reeds. Then a mellow tenor began to sing, "I'll be loving you, always . . . with a love that's true, always." Armstrong's reaction? "Give this son of a gun *eight* stars! Lombardo! These people are keeping music alive—helping to fight them damn beboppers. You know, you got to have somebody to keep that music sounding good. Music doesn't mean a thing unless it *sounds* good. You know, this is the band that inspired me to make 'Among My Souvenirs.' They inspired me to make 'Sweethearts on Parade.' They're my inspirators!"

Armstrong was far from alone in his enthusiasm. Guy Lombardo and the Royal Canadians were by some counts the most popular orchestra of the twentieth century. Pop music chart maker Joel Whitburn names them as the only dance band to sell more than one hundred million records and assigns them twenty-six number one hits between 1927 and 1950.[3] That said, Feather did not play this record for Armstrong simply because of the Royal Canadians' overwhelming popularity. Armstrong was infamous among jazz fans for naming Lombardo's group—which was widely despised as the apotheosis of easy-listening schlock—as his favorite band, a taste he expressed regularly over several decades. Feather probably chose "Always," a particularly syrupy waltz, to highlight the oddity of Armstrong's enthusiasm, and Armstrong would probably have reacted similarly to pretty much any Lombardo selection, just to emphasize his appreciation for the band's unchangingly smooth and melodic style. The fervor of his response was fueled at that moment by his dislike of the young beboppers, but it was also a serious expression of his musical aesthetic.

When jazz historians have bothered to mention Armstrong's admiration for Lombardo, it has almost always been as a bizarre anomaly rather than a measured musical judgment. A *New Yorker* article from 1957, noting that Lombardo had regularly been crowned "King of Corn" by *Down Beat*'s editors and was often misidentified as "Guy Lumbago," suggested that jazz fans "attribute Armstrong's fondness for Lombardo to the same inexplicable quirkiness that occasionally moves a thorough-bred race horse to pal around with a goat."[4]

Since the Royal Canadians sold more records and had a more endur-ing career than any other band of Armstrong's era, the fact that jazz critics and fans considered a taste for this band weird suggests that it was they rather than Armstrong who were quirky, but this interpretation remains common among jazz historians today. Apparently, the idea that Lombardo's syrupy, lilting ballroom style should be discussed seriously alongside the work of the defining hot soloist in jazz has been consid-ered at best odd and at worst insulting to Armstrong's memory. James Lincoln Collier devoted a handful of paragraphs in his Armstrong biog-raphy to Lombardo's influence, but the typical reaction by historians who have bothered to note the connection at all has been to suggest that Armstrong's more Lombardo-flavored records were either lapses of taste or purely commercial choices.[5]

As a result, Armstrong's admiration for Lombardo has almost never been seen as something that need be pursued to understand his work.[6] Looked at from a broader cultural perspective, the casual dismissal of a musical judgment expressed by a major artist over the course of de-cades has a whiff of condescension. Like Robert Johnson, who routinely imitated records by the smoothest urban blues stars of his day but is often recalled as a raw country blues player, Armstrong can apparently be celebrated as a groundbreaking improviser but ignored as a music critic. This choice could perhaps be defended on the grounds that histo-rians and critics have a more distanced and impartial view than that of the artists they study, but even granting that questionable contention, it seems probable that race—and Armstrong's reputation as an impover-ished street urchin who became a grinning, comic entertainer—has also played a part.

What makes this particularly inappropriate in Armstrong's case is that, along with being a broadly knowledgeable musician, he was an extremely prolific writer. He carried a typewriter everywhere he traveled and produced thousands of pages. Many were on matters unrelated to music—unpublished manuscripts include a joke book and a piece on the healthful effects of smoking marijuana—but he also wrote a fair amount about musical matters. And given his stature in twentieth-century music, his opinions should presumably be given some weight. This is especially true of his opinion on Lombardo, since he backed it up with musical choices made at a key point in his career.

Armstrong and Lombardo met and developed an admiration for each other's work in the 1920s, when both were living in Chicago and experiencing their first major successes. They also established a degree of personal affection. Lombardo and his bandmates showed up at Armstrong's gigs, and when Lombardo was playing at venues that did not admit African American patrons, he insisted that Armstrong and his musicians be welcomed as guests.[7] Armstrong would always recall those evenings with pleasure: "I dug that band when they first came from Canada and I used to go out many nights where they were on Cottage Grove in Chicago. People would say, surprised like, 'You sitting in with them?' I'd try to tell them, music is music. Anytime I walk up on that stage with Guy Lombardo, I'm relaxed."[8]

Any jazz fan can understand why the Canadians liked Armstrong's playing—his recordings with the small groups known as the Hot Fives and Hot Sevens established a new standard for jazz improvisation, and with 1929's "I Can't Give You Anything But Love," he pointed the way to swing by blending jazz techniques with Tin Pan Alley melodies. But most find Armstrong's love of Lombardo far more puzzling. Some explain it by noting that Lombardo's band was not as consistently sappy as its reputation suggests. Introducing the Lombardo entry in his landmark jazz discography, Brian Rust wrote, "Although Guy Lombardo has long been associated with the most saccharine form of dance music, a study of his records shows that when required, he and his band could play as 'hot' as any of their contemporaries!"[9] That is an exaggeration—Lombardo's violin playing was notably absent from the band's "hot" discs, and at their best they were no Hot Seven—but records like 1928's *The Cannonball* show that when the mood struck them or the audience demanded it, the Royal Canadians could play quite credible jazz. Still, out of hundreds of Lombardo recordings, Rust includes a mere thirteen in his jazz listing, and none of the discs he selected were commercial successes.

More to the point, it was not Lombardo's hot work that attracted Armstrong's admiration. It was precisely the music jazz critics have consistently loathed, numbers like "Sweethearts on Parade" and "You're Driving Me Crazy." As Armstrong explained many years later, "They inspired us so much with their sense of timing, their beautiful tones. . . . That band plays the tune, they put that melody there, and it's beautiful. You can't find another band that can play a straight lead and make it sound that good."[10] He added that the rest of his band felt the same way: "When we were at the Savoy in Chicago in 1928, every Saturday night we'd catch the Owl Club, with Guy Lombardo, and as long as he played we'd sit right there: Zutty [Singleton], Carroll Dickerson and all the band. We didn't go nowhere until after Lombardo signed off. That went on for months."[11]

This was not simply an example of the broadmindedness Armstrong expressed in his church parable. Lombardo had a sound that he found particularly appealing, and as soon as he got the chance he made it his own. In 1929, on the heels of his Broadway success singing "Ain't Misbehavin'" in the *Hot Chocolates* revue, he finally had the opportunity to lead a full orchestra and, in his own words, "We tried to get our sax section to sound like Lombardo—listen to our records of 'When You're Smiling' and 'Sweethearts on Parade.'"[12]

Indeed, those records show the Lombardo influence so clearly that they have been reviled by many of Armstrong's fans. George Simon, though more receptive to "sweet" dance orchestras than most jazz critics were, wrote that of all the black players who dabbled in Lombardo's sound, "no musicians did so to more absurd effect than Armstrong's saxists. What an incongruous sound it was, that virile trumpet backed by those simpering saxophones!"[13] This is not quite fair, or perhaps the disjuncture is just less startling to modern ears. Certainly, when Armstrong comes in over the Lombardoesque reeds and violin, the effect is less jarring than Ray Charles's appearance over the strings and choir of "I Can't Stop Loving You"—a somewhat similar exercise and similarly reviled by many fans when it first appeared.

In fact, while "When You're Smiling" is far from Armstrong's hottest record, he sounds very comfortable with the arrangement—his claim that he found Lombardo's style relaxing is borne out by both the instrumental and vocal sides of the disc. Compared to the older New Orleans trumpeters, Armstrong always had a particularly clear, smooth tone. It was certainly more vibrant and exciting than the Lombardo sound, but when one compares Armstrong's playing with King Oliver's, it is not hard to understand how an affection for more sedate stylists contributed to his innovations. Furthermore, Armstrong's insistence on playing lilting, romantic melodies rather than sticking to the blues-inflected repertoire of his mentors was one of the key factors in his transformative effect on jazz.

Armstrong loved both heat and sweetness, and he always kept one foot in either camp, a practice not rare among the black jazz musicians of his day. The pressures on white and black musicians were very different, and a frequent complaint from that generation of black players is that they were stereotyped as hot bands, although they could play as smoothly and gently as the white bands. Lombardo always took pride in the number of black orchestras that imitated his style, and Simon's comment on the incongruity of Armstrong in that setting highlights the fact that other black bands created more fully integrated variations on the Lombardo approach.

A perfect example is the second strain of Duke Ellington's "Black and Tan Fantasy," which finds a Lombardoesque saxophone chorus so seamlessly blended into the overall feel of the piece that few commentators have noted the influence.[14] Once it is pointed out, though, it is unmistakable: Ellington's 1927 OKeh recording, in particular, is so permeated with Lombardo's approach that I have played it for rooms of quite astute music listeners back to back with the opening section of Lombardo's "Too Many Tears" and challenged them to guess which is Ellington and which Lombardo. Admittedly, there is some cheating involved in this particular juxtaposition, since on "Tears" Lombardo included a growling trumpet along with the usual cooing saxophones—but that is precisely my point: Lombardo copied Ellington on occasion, and vice versa.

This is not to suggest that Lombardo was in any way as great or exciting a musician as Ellington. But they were both playing for broad, overlapping audiences, and in the late 1920s and early 1930s pretty much any popular dance orchestra in the United States was trying to get some of the Lombardo sound. Jimmie Lunceford's "Cherry" is such an obvious steal from Lombardo's "Little Coquette" that it is surprising no one sued. And if the recording industry had allowed it, we would have far more examples of black orchestras playing his kind of sweet dance music.

Rex Stewart, who replaced Armstrong in the Fletcher Henderson Orchestra, recalled that Henderson was explicitly prevented from preserving this treasured side of his repertoire: "The record executives categorized Smack's [Henderson's] band as a stomp band. They didn't accept the fact that a Negro band could play sweet, though as a matter of fact, we used to get tremendous applause at Roseland and other places for playing waltzes beautifully. . . . Smack was very disappointed at not being permitted to record his famous *Rose* medley [a selection of waltzes with 'rose' in their titles]."[15] Though celebrated for creating the hard-swinging arrangements that would make Benny Goodman a sensation, Henderson had more than thirty waltzes in his band book, and Armstrong recalled that the first selection he played with the orchestra was "By the Waters of Minnetonka."

It's easy to dismiss such facts by saying, "Yes, of course the black orchestras played some sweet arrangements, because everybody who wanted to make decent money had to play for white folks." That was certainly true—*Variety* dubbed Henderson "the Ivy League prom king"—but it's not that simple.[16] On the one hand, Stewart is quite clear that Henderson loved the "rose" medley, and Ethel Waters famously complained that Henderson was so refined that he couldn't get a blues feel until she forced him to practice along with some James P. Johnson piano rolls.[17] On the other, one of the odd little facts of pop history is that in 1930 Lombardo and his Royal Canadians set an attendance record at Harlem's Savoy Ballroom.

The Savoy was Harlem's most popular dance hall, famed as a venue for battles of the hottest bands and for the most exciting dancers in the United States. But history can be tricky. What attracted writers to document the Savoy was the heat and swing that distinguished it from more sedate, white ballrooms, so they had no interest in visits by the less flamboyant dance bands or in the public those bands attracted. Lombardo was clearly a change from the typical Savoy fare, but what drew the average customer to the Savoy was the same thing that draws most customers to dance halls anywhere: the opportunity to spend a romantic evening with a member of the opposite sex. And for that purpose, Lombardo's band was unsurpassed. As George Simon wrote, "It hits superb tempos, and though it doesn't produce a rhythmically inspiring beat, it produces a succession of steady, unobtrusive beats that make it a pleasure to take your girl out on the floor and move around to the best of your ability. If you can dance at all, you can dance to Lombardo's music."[18] Or as Panama Francis, who was the Savoy's house drummer for many years, explained, "Guy Lombardo had a helluva beat! [Francis hummed a bit of 'Blue Room,' clapping in time.] It didn't swing, but it had rhythm. I love Guy Lombardo—he had a great band."[19]

This raises a broader issue: The evolution of American pop music has to a great extent been driven by the work of black innovators, but its history has been written overwhelmingly by white critics and scholars. This is by no means a blanket indictment of American pop music historians, but it has led to some misunderstandings, and the popularity of Lombardo at the Savoy highlights a curious double standard: hundreds of books have documented the racially integrating effects of popular music, but their examples are always white youth dancing to Louis Armstrong or Little Richard, not black youth swaying to the gentle strains of Lombardo and Lawrence Welk (whose recording of "Calcutta" made it to number ten on *Billboard*'s R&B chart in 1961). It seems fair to suggest that this is at least in part because the critics and historians have themselves tended to be white kids who enjoyed Armstrong and Little Richard, and who detested Lombardo and Welk.

There are other reasons, of course. When a minority group adopts the music of the dominant culture, that does not change that culture—or at least not as drastically as when the dominant group adopts a minority style. Though one could build an interesting argument to the contrary, it is probably true that Elvis Presley singing rhythm and blues had a more transformative effect on American culture than Marian Anderson singing opera. But that does not justify treating the tastes of the white fans who love African-rooted music seriously, while ignoring or dismissing the tastes of black fans who have loved European-derived styles.

Such dismissals, whether explicit or subtle, have become only more common since the ragtime and jazz eras. In 2005 a CD set called *Lost Sounds* was issued by the Archeophone record label to accompany a book of the same title, surveying recordings of African American performers before 1920. The CD's compilers divided the recordings into four groups: "Vocal Harmonies," "Minstrel & Vaudeville Traditions," "Dance Rhythms," and "Aspirational Motives." The aspirational section included the composers Will Marion Cook and Harry T. Burleigh, the poet Paul Laurence Dunbar, and various classical singers and musicians.[20]

Classical music—especially opera and choral works—was a staple of the black entertainment world. Even minstrel shows often included operatic excerpts, and when Bessie Smith made her Chicago debut in 1924, it was on a vaudeville bill that also included a black "prima donna."[21] Such performances were the primary focus of the first African American–owned record label, Broome Special Phonograph Records, and the two important black-owned labels of the 1920s were both named after opera singers, Black Patti for Sissieretta Jones and Black Swan for Elizabeth Taylor Greenfield. This is a huge subject, which has received almost no attention in the past fifty years and desperately needs to be explored. As an example of quite how huge, the first full-length book on African American classical music was published in the 1880s and had chapters on artists like Justin Holland, who translated the works of Sor and Carcassi into English and was the author of the most respected American classical guitar instruction books of the period.[22]

Given the widespread and long-lasting role of classical music in the African American community, both as a professional performance style and as an amateur avocation, why should it be categorized as "aspirational"? Over the course of the twentieth century, thousands of white singers and musicians have attempted to play like Charlie Parker or sing like Aretha Franklin, but I have never seen these attempts labeled "aspirational," nor is that term typically used for the many eastern European Jews from poor families who tried to better their economic condition by mastering central European concert styles. So why was it aspirational for black Americans to write poetry (in Dunbar's case, much of it in southern black dialect) or to compose and perform music that drew on the European tradition?

Classical music has always been considered something of an elite taste, but for that very reason it was the common musical language of the educated middle class, black and white, throughout the nineteenth and most of the twentieth century. Reading the works of, say, James Weldon Johnson, one finds classical music treated as the unifying style of all educated musicians—the hero of his *Autobiography of an Ex-colored Man* aspires to blend classical styles with African-inspired rhythms but takes his basic classical repertoire for granted as what any piano teacher would provide to students. Anyone who took music lessons learned classical music—that was what music lessons meant. For the son or daughter of a black working-class family to take such lessons can be deemed aspirational—but no more so than for the child of a working-class white family to do so, or for the same child to study English literature or chemistry. Indeed, in the latter case arguably less so, since musicians were not generally accorded the same societal stature as college professors.

In this context, on average, the black bandleaders who were most popular in the 1920s and 1930s were just as middle class and well educated as the white bandleaders. Guy Lombardo never attended college, but *Metronome* noted that the Jimmie Lunceford Orchestra was made up almost entirely of college graduates.[23] Other black collegians in the band business included Fletcher Henderson, Don Redman, Teddy Wilson, Cab Calloway, and Erskine Hawkins, and would have included Ellington—who was awarded a scholarship to study art at Brooklyn's Pratt Institute—had he not already been making enough money from music that he decided to let the opportunity pass.

Likewise, most of the musicians in the black dance orchestras had some classical training. To work in an orchestra, they needed to be able to read and often to play a range of music that included light classical pieces as well as pop tunes and jazz. And the long tradition of classical playing—both professional and amateur—in black communities meant that there were plenty of opportunities to get that training.

There are good reasons why black classical artists have received far less attention than their peers who turned to ragtime and jazz—they did not change the world, and those peers did—but it is impossible to understand the evolution of the popular genres without having some sense of the broad classical foundation that underlay the later black concert styles. James Reese Europe, whose orchestras presented the first evening of African American music at Carnegie Hall in 1912 and over the next decade helped bridge the transition from ragtime to jazz, started out as a classical violinist. In 1894, at the age of fourteen, he entered a classical composition contest in Washington, DC, and came in second, the winner being his younger sister, Mary.

Though given short shrift by history, Mary Europe was an active and respected figure in Washington for more than forty years, working as a teacher, pianist, organist, and choral director, and many black people saw her and her associates as providing a desperately needed antidote to the stereotypical "coon songs" and dance rhythms that made her brother famous. Today, it is common to dismiss such views as archaic and to applaud jazz as the true "black classical music," but we lose touch with reality if we ignore the reasons why many black people chose to distance themselves from popular and dance styles, or forget that many of the pioneering jazz players and composers were influenced by their relatives, peers, and mentors who sought a place for black musicians and composers in the classical world. It was not accidental that Duke Ellington, the most celebrated composer in jazz, came out of Washington, a town with a black classical scene that included a symphony orchestra, chamber music groups, the Original Colored America Opera Troupe, the Washington and Columbia conservatories, and the editors of the *Negro Journal of Music* and the *Negro Musician*.

Pianists were particularly likely to have classical training, since unlike guitars, trumpets, and violins, pianos tended to be available only to people who had a stable home and enough money to buy or rent one. The piano was widely considered a parlor instrument, favored by proper young ladies—musicians as varied as Jelly Roll Morton and Fred Wesley (the musical director of James Brown's band in the early 1970s) recalled being wary of the piano in their youth because it was considered a girl's instrument. It was also the standard middle-class training instrument, with piano lessons typically serving as an introduction to classical music and thus what was unself-consciously termed "music appreciation." As a result, virtually all the early jazz piano virtuosos were also knowledgeable classical players. On his Library of Congress recordings, Morton demonstrates this aspect of his training by playing an excerpt of the "Miserere" from Verdi's *Il Trovatore,* and he took great pride in his repertoire of opera music. When he came to Chicago, Lil Hardin—Louis Armstrong's second wife and the piano player for King Oliver's band and later Armstrong's Hot Five—says that she had a contest with him, and he outplayed her on jazz and ragtime, but she won because she was better on Chopin. James P. Johnson and Fats Waller also prided themselves on their Chopin, and both composed classical pieces. Johnson had started out as a classical player, taught by his mother and a skilled Italian music master in his native New Jersey, and he recalled that he honed his technique by studying the top concert pianists of his youth: de Pachmann, Rachmaninoff, and Hofmann.[24]

The fact that many black jazz musicians had classical training has of course been acknowledged by jazz historians over the years, but it has rarely if ever been explored in any detail, nor has there been more than the most cursory focus on the black classical music scene and its relationship to popular styles. Though few writers have phrased their views so explicitly, many seem to regard the black musicians who devoted their lives to classical styles as little better than race traitors, or at best misguided figures seduced by the gilt and velvet of the European concert hall. As a result, the fact that Miles Davis studied at Juilliard is often singled out as an anomaly, followed by the observation that he shortly quit because he was learning more on Fifty-Second Street. Even historians who acknowledge that any literate musician had to have a bit of classical education seem to assume that anyone who ended up in the jazz field was there as a matter of taste and preference. But it's not that simple. For a lot of black musicians jazz was a choice, but for at least a few the jazz orchestras were like the all-black baseball leagues—wonderful places to play, as far as they went, but also the only option they had.

Rex Stewart said of Art Tatum that "his secret ambition was to be known as a classical composer" and that "Tatum also wanted, very definitely, to be featured as a soloist accompanied by the Boston or New York symphony orchestras, which he considered among the world's best."[25] Or take Buster Bailey, who grew up in Memphis and played with

Armstrong, W.C. Handy, King Oliver, and Fletcher Henderson. In the 1950s, talking about the advances in integration, he said, "If it had been like this when I came up I would have been able to play with some symphony orchestra. I would have had more of an incentive to study because there would have been more of a prospect of my making a living the way I wanted to. Sure, we played concerts and overtures and numbers like that in the theaters, but when I started you couldn't even think, if you were a Negro, of making symphony orchestras. . . . I guess you could say the only regret I have is that I didn't have a chance to make it in symphony music."[26]

In recent years, I have heard similar complaints from Cuban dance musicians. In the Cuban system, classical training is required for anyone who wants to be a professional musician, so one might assume that dance-oriented players just grind away at their class work, waiting for the chance to get out and perform the hot music they love. But when I interviewed David Calzado of Charanga Habanera, one of the most popular and funky bands of the 1990s, he expressed regrets about not being able to make a living as a classical violinist: "I always dreamed of being a concert artist, but here in Cuba the market for classical music is very limited. People don't go to symphonic concerts. So I realized that to take that career path would be very difficult, very demanding—I like complicated things, but I thought it would be impossible. So I decided to lean toward popular music. But I have always had an itch to be able to play Mozart in a beautiful hall with a good symphony orchestra behind me."[27]

Neither Bailey nor Calzado sounds as if his regret is simply a matter of cultural aspiration, in the sense of wishing that they could have been more respectable or upper class. Calzado has played lots of nice rooms—he worked in Monte Carlo for several summers—and I assume that by the 1950s Bailey had as well. Of course, one cannot dismiss the weight of societal expectations, but it seems reasonable to think that both of them genuinely liked classical music. And why should it be any odder for a black or Latino musician to love Mozart than for a white musician to love jazz or R&B? Even granting for a moment that musical taste may simply be an unconscious marker of cultural aspiration, why should we not grant the same respect to black working-class listeners who love the music of the academy that we accord to white middle-class listeners who love the music of the bars and dancehalls? Nostalgie de la boue is surely no nobler than upward mobility, nor is there any evidence that it produces better music.

We will never know how many black musicians in the first half of the twentieth century would have preferred to play symphonies or Lombardo-styled waltzes but were forced to choose between playing hot or finding another profession. My guess is that most would have been happiest if they had not had to make such choices; musicians tend to pride themselves on their breadth of taste and skill, and given a society that encouraged versatility, I suspect that most would prefer to play a wide variety of music, rather than spending their lives locked into a particular style or genre.

Which brings us back to Louis Armstrong. He was by no means from a middle-class background, nor did he get any formal music lessons in his childhood. He learned to read music competently only after becoming a professional player, when he got a job with Fate Marable's band on the riverboats, and was still shaky about sight-reading when he joined Henderson's orchestra. But that does not mean that his tastes were limited to what he heard in the streets, bars, and parks of New Orleans (a pretty wide range of music, as it happens: Lonnie Johnson's street band played opera tunes, and concerts in the parks included everything from classical orchestras to Mexican and Italian bands). One of his most prized possessions was a wind-up Victrola, and though he recalled that most of the records he owned were by the Original Dixieland Jazz Band, he added, "I had Caruso records, and Henry Burr, Galli-Curci, Tettrazini—they were all my favorites. Then there was the Irish tenor, McCormack—beautiful phrasing."[28]

For a trumpet player of that time, the affection for opera is not coincidental, nor was it unique to New Orleans. In the rage for brass band music that extended a couple of decades on either side of the turn of the twentieth century, transcriptions of opera were common, and brass virtuosos regularly showed their stuff by playing operatic arias. Few jazz players were ever asked about such influences, but Dan Morgenstern reports that when he asked the trombonist Vic Dickenson about his early models, "he pulled out an ancient disc of 'Celeste Aida' performed by Arthur Pryor, who'd been John Philip Sousa's star trombonist before starting his own concert band."[29]

Armstrong was thoroughly familiar with the work of the mainstream bandmasters. When he got his most prestigious job in New Orleans, with the Tuxedo Brass Band, he described it not as a jazz gig but as a brass band gig: "I felt just as proud as though I had been hired by John Philip Sousa or Arthur Pryor. It was a great thrill when they passed out the brass band music on stiff cards that could be read as you walked along."[30]

Success as a jazz artist by no means blunted Armstrong's enthusiasm to explore classical styles. In 1926, after making his reputation with King Oliver's band and then as the featured trumpet soloist for the Henderson Orchestra, he returned to Chicago and his first regular gig as a bandleader. His group worked at the Dreamland Ballroom, advertised with a banner hailing him as "The World's Greatest Trumpet Player." Nonetheless, he recalled being thrilled when a more formal orchestra offered him an opportunity to work outside the dance milieu: "I had become so popular at the Dreamland, Erskine Tate from the Vendome Theater came to hire me to join his Symphony Orchestra. I like to have fainted. Erskine Tate had a 20 piece orch. . . . [I'd been trying] to get the experience of playing classic and symphony music, etc. Well, here's your chance, I said."[31] Armstrong's period with Tate overlaps his first recordings with the Hot Five, but what he played at the Vendome would have surprised anyone who typed him by those records: "We played the scores for the silent movies, and a big overture when the curtain would rise at the end of the film," he recalled. "I got a solo on stage, and my big thing was *Cavalleria Rusticana*."[32]

Armstrong never recorded any of this light classical repertoire, but it would be wrong simply to dismiss the Tate gig as an anomaly or to suggest that all Armstrong got out of playing such music was some personal satisfaction and an improvement in his reading skills. In 1928 he would set the jazz world on fire with his introduction to "West End Blues," a virtuoso, unaccompanied trumpet cadenza. Brilliant as this solo is, and startling as it was in the context of a small jazz group, it takes on a quite different flavor when placed in relationship to the work of earlier trumpet virtuosos.

For example, if one listens to the "West End Blues" cadenza alongside Herbert L. Clarke's unaccompanied cadenza to "Caprice Brilliante (The Debutante)," recorded with Sousa's Band in 1908, there are clear similarities between the two performances. Clarke was the most famous cornet virtuoso in the United States, and it is easy to see how his performance would have inspired Armstrong's. Nor is this mere idle supposition: in 1954 Armstrong was still excited about Clarke's playing, telling Leonard Feather, "I've heard trumpet solos from 1908 up to the present day—Herbert Clarke and all those boys that really used to blow them horns and it sounds like it was recorded yesterday." At the end of his life, Armstrong's record collection still contained ten of Clarke's 78s, including "Caprice Brilliante."[33]

This is not to say that Armstrong's famous solo was derivative in any but the broadest sense. Not only is his choice of notes unique, but he had a rhythmic drive Clarke lacked and his tone and execution are stronger. And Armstrong had composed his solo and was to some extent improvising, while Clarke was playing from written notation.[34] Nonetheless, it improves our understanding of Armstrong's cadenza if we place it in this broader tradition and look at it as a virtuoso trumpet display that has been categorized as jazz because of the band performance that follows and because Armstrong's work has always been filed in that category.

If we want to understand music history, we must always remember that, while genre labels are useful, they often blind us to connections between artists and styles that have been separated for commercial, social, or pedagogic reasons.[35] Armstrong was certainly a jazz musician, as Clarke was a classical musician and Lombardo played a smooth dance style that even in its time was considered by many critics to be the antithesis of jazz. But it is equally true that Armstrong and Clarke were both cornet virtuosos and that Armstrong's and Lombardo's orchestras were both popular dance bands, playing an overlapping repertoire and exchanging techniques. And, at least in the case of Armstrong and Lombardo, a lot of the same people—both white and black—were listening and dancing to both of them.

It is hard to tease loose any reliable statistics on this listenership and harder still to sort out the extent to which black (or white) listeners were in thrall to racially slanted decisions by recording company and radio programmers rather than following their own tastes. Still, it seems fair to say that the black listenership for bands like Lombardo's has never received its due from popular music historians. As an African American correspondent wrote me after hearing a discussion of this subject on a Los Angeles radio program, "on the West Coast, before 1965 . . . most other black people I knew were as comfortable with Lawrence Welk, Liberace, and Mitch Miller as they were with Bobby Bland, Ray Charles, or even Mighty Sparrow, or Perez Prado. The variety was well out of proportion with what I have seen as hindsight or recreation of the late 1950s and 1960s black American."[36]

I am not suggesting that historians need necessarily celebrate the music of Herbert L. Clarke or Guy Lombardo. But we cannot understand an artist like Louis Armstrong without making an effort to explore the breadth of his taste and education, nor do we do either ourselves or his memory any favors if we dismiss his opinions as ridiculous. When we seek to understand jazz—or classical music, or rock, or any other style—while dismissing massively influential figures as irrelevant mediocrities, we may be listening to a lot of great music, but we are not dealing with the reality of what the players of that time were doing, of the societies they were working in, or of how their music evolved.

NOTES

This chapter originally appeared as "Louis Armstrong Loves Guy Lombardo! Acknowledging the Smoother Roots of Jazz," *Jazz Research Journal* 1, no. 1 (2007): 129–45.

1. "Lombardo Grooves Louis!," *Metronome,* September 1949, reprinted in *Louis Armstrong, in His Own Words,* ed. Thomas Brothers (New York: Oxford University Press, 1999), 165–66. Feather later moved the blindfold tests to *Down Beat,* where as of 2011 they remain a regular feature.

2. Gary Giddins, *Satchmo: The Genius of Louis Armstrong* (New York: Da Capo, 1992), v. This quotation is apparently drawn from the second installment of the 1949 *Metronome* blindfold test, though Giddins credits it to *Down Beat.*

3. Joel Whitburn, *Pop Memories, 1890–1954* (Menomonee Falls, WI: Record Research, 1986), 276. Whitburn's pre-1940s chart listings are largely conjectural, and he does not give a source for his sales figures, so neither number should be taken as definitive, but they are indicative of Lombardo's popularity in this period.

4. E. J. Khan, "Powder Your Face with Sunshine," pt. 1, *New Yorker,* January 5, 1957, 42.

5. George T. Simon, *The Big Bands* (New York: Schirmer Books, 1981), 323; James Lincoln Collier, *The Making of Jazz* (Boston: Houghton Mifflin, 1978), 56.

6. There have been a few exceptions to this rule. James Lincoln Collier devotes a bit more than a page in his *Louis Armstrong: An American Genius* (New York: Oxford University Press, 1983) to the relationship with Lombardo, and Dan Morgenstern, though he has written little if anything on this subject, was immediately responsive to my question about it and eager to provide examples of Lombardo's influence (Morgenstern, conversation with the author, Institute of Jazz Studies, Rutgers University, Newark, NJ, ca. 2008).

7. Dave Peyton's column in *Chicago Defender,* September 22, 1928, cited in Collier, *Louis Armstrong,* 219.

8. Richard Meryman, *Louis Armstrong: A Self-Portrait* (New York: Eakins, 1971), 58.

9. Brian Rust, *Jazz Records, 1897–1942* (Chigwell, Essex: Storyville, 1969), 1028.

10. Meryman, *Louis Armstrong,* 58.

11. Max Jones and John Chilton, *Louis: The Louis Armstrong Story, 1900–1971* (New York: Da Capo, 1988), 130.

12. Leonard Feather, *Esquire,* March 1954, quoted in Collier, *Louis Armstrong,* 243.

13. Simon, *Big Bands,* 323.

14. I am indebted to Dan Morgenstern for pointing out this example (Morgenstern, conversation).

15. Rex Stewart, *Jazz Masters of the Thirties* (New York: Macmillan, 1972), 26.

16. Joshua Berrett, *Louis Armstrong and Paul Whiteman: Two Kings of Jazz* (New Haven, CT: Yale University Press, 2004), 50.

17. For example, the black Kansas City bandleader Clarence Johnson, who performed primarily for white ballroom patrons, also named Lombardo as his hero and model. See Sherrie Tucker, "Nobody's Sweethearts: Gender, Race, Jazz, and the Darlings of Rhythm," *American Music* 16, no. 3 (Autumn 1998): 263.

18. George Simon, "Guy's Group Treats Its Dancers with Respect and Intelligence: Danceable, If Not Too Musical," *Metronome,* February 1942, reprinted in Simon, *Big Bands,* 321.

19. "Robert Crease Discussion," Savoy: World's Finest Ball Room, accessed November 15, 2011, www.savoyballroom.com/background/discussion.htm.

20. Tim Brooks and David Giovannoni, liner notes to *Lost Sounds: Blacks and the Birth of the Recording Industry, 1891–1922,* Archeophone Record 1005, 2005, compact disc.

21. Advertisement, *Chicago Defender,* May 10, 1924, sec. 1, p. 6.

22. James M. Trotter, *Music and Some Highly Musical People* (Boston, 1881; repr., Chicago: Afro-Am Press, 1969).

23. *Metronome,* August 1938, reprinted in George T. Simon, *Simon Says: The Sights and Sounds of the Swing Era, 1935–1955* (New York: Galahad Books, 1971), 110.

24. Gunther Schuller, *Early Jazz: Its Roots and Musical Development* (New York: Oxford University Press, 1968), 215.

25. Stewart, *Jazz Masters,* 189.

26. Buster Bailey, quoted in Nat Shapiro and Nat Hentoff, eds., *Hear Me Talkin' to Ya: The Story of Jazz as Told by the Men Who Made It* (New York: Dover, 1955), 331–32.

27. David Calzado, quoted in Elijah Wald, *Global Minstrels: Voices of World Music* (New York: Routledge, 2006), 95.

28. Meryman, *Louis Armstrong,* 24.

29. Dan Morgenstern, liner notes to *Louis Armstrong: Portrait of the Artist as a Young Man,* Columbia Legacy 57176, 1994, 40, compact disc.

30. Louis Armstrong, *Satchmo: My Life in New Orleans* (New York: Da Capo, 1986), 219.

31. Armstrong, "Goffin Notebooks" (unpublished), cited in Giddins, *Satchmo,* 59–60.

32. Jones and Chilton, *Louis,* 212. *Cavalleria Rusticana* is a one-act Italian opera by Pietro Mascagni that premiered in 1890.

33. Terry Teachout, *Pops: A Life of Louis Armstrong* (New York: Houghton Mifflin Harcourt, 2009).

34. Lewis Porter was the first to note that Armstrong had recorded a substantial section of the "West End" cadenza almost four years earlier in a break

on Margaret Johnson's 1924 recording, "Changeable Daddy of Mine" (Morgenstern, liner notes to *Louis Armstrong*, 10).

35. For his Juilliard audition, Miles Davis played Herbert Clarke's "Youth Dauntless." John Szwed, *So What: The Life of Miles Davis* (New York: Simon and Schuster, 2002), 32.

36. Terry Williams, brother of the novelist M. Dion Thompson, e-mail message to author, January 29, 2004.

CHAPTER 3

The Humor of Jazz

CHARLES HIROSHI GARRETT

I am serious about my music, but I like to have fun, too.
—Dizzy Gillespie

When the cornetist Bix Beiderbecke was asked in 1929 to define jazz, he replied, "Jazz is musical humor." The celebrated composer and pianist Duke Ellington offered similar guidance to budding players: "you have to have a good sense of humor before you're a really great jazz musician. Horace Silver, the hard bop and soul jazz pioneer, embraced this musical aesthetic as well, explaining that "I try to keep it on the light hearted side with some fun and laughter in it. It's uplifting and it's entertaining. . . . A lot of my music has a sense of humor. . . . [My compositions] have humorous titles. They have humorous lyrics to them." Such commentary by renowned jazz figures suggests that humor has played an integral role in the history of the music. Following these lines, jazz critic Gary Giddins has argued, "A ripe sense of humor is indigenous in jazz. It's a music quick to enlist whatever barbs can best deflate pomposity and artificiality." Indeed, jazz would seem to be an ideal wellspring for musical humor, because the music delights in reinvention, improvisation, unexpected turns of phrase, and rhythmic play.[1]

But not all jazz performers and observers share such views, if we are to judge from the scant attention given to humor within contemporary jazz discourse. On the contrary, as jazz has declined in commercial popularity while rising in cultural stature, it is the seriousness of jazz artists, practices, and traditions that is typically championed. When the jazz pianist and educator Billy Taylor famously characterized jazz as "America's classical music," he made this very point in his opening paragraph: "Though it is often fun to play, jazz is *very serious* music."[2] I am not attempting here to undercut notions about the value or significance of jazz, but I am convinced that the relative lack of acknowledgment for its humor-laden heritage suggests how current understandings of jazz as a genre have been shaped by its shifting stance toward humor, comedy, and popular entertainment.

By viewing jazz through the lens of humor, I seek to outline the key ways in which this relationship has transformed over the past century and to explore how these developments have shaped musical practice and audience expectations. Rather than present a blow-by-blow account of recorded humor in jazz history, I am more interested in how jazz humor intersects with musical aesthetics, genre definition, and jazz criticism. Asking what humor can tell us about jazz not only helps identify its various permutations as an artistic strategy but also raises broader questions concerning the relationship of humor and beauty as well as the distinctions often drawn between humorous and serious music. It is clear that the diminishing role of humor in jazz practice has changed the nature of the performance, function, and reception of jazz. Correspondingly, the widespread dismissal of jazz humor has shaped perceptions about whether certain figures, practices, and modes of performance should be considered essential to a jazz tradition. In addition to engaging with such notions about the jazz canon, this alternative perspective suggests that jazz has contained, and still holds, greater possibilities for creative musical expression than are commonly acknowledged.

As the comments that open this essay demonstrate, it is not as if jazz artists and critics have failed to notice the existence of humor in jazz. Increasingly, however, and especially since the advent of bebop, it has become a challenge to acknowledge the presence of humor in jazz while simultaneously paying respect to the significance and unquestionable artistry of this musical tradition. Instead, a hierarchy that places serious art above everyday humor often emerges in the critical literature about jazz humorists. Dorothy Donegan, an immensely talented and downright outrageous pianist who performed for more than five decades, is one of many artists to receive such a mixed reception. Her piano chops and imagination were highly regarded. The critic Whitney Balliett compared her "rich, flying left hand" and her "roller-coaster lines and ten-pound chords" to the playing of Art Tatum, one of her mentors.[3]

But Balliett also felt that Donegan's melodramatic style and her vaudeville performance gestures obscured her jazz artistry. "She has been showing off so long," he observed, "she probably doesn't remember what you are really supposed to do when you sit down at a keyboard." Few critics were sure what to make of her performances of tunes such as the classic number "St. Louis Blues," in which she sometimes shifted tempo midway to unleash a flashy boogie-woogie passage, or her stage act, which incorporated salty jokes, stylistic parodies of other jazz pianists, and humorous asides. Donegan was quick to profess her penchant for humor and entertainment: "I like audiences, I like people, and I like having fun with them." But such explanations were not enough to satisfy writers such as Robert Doerschuk, who compared her ostentatious persona to "circus acts or plate spinners" rather than "anything that passes for serious jazz." Although the critic Leonard Feather appreciated her distinctive style, he also commented that "Donegan's problem is that she has never appeared to take herself seriously."[4]

Presenting oneself in a serious manner, these comments imply, has become an expected part of modern jazz performance. Since similar expectations were not firmly in place during earlier stages of jazz history, we can understand such responses as part of a larger historical arc. At the same time, gaining a better understanding of performers like Donegan may require us to reverse the terms of Feather's critique. Rather than wondering whether Donegan took herself seriously enough, her music asks whether the critical assumptions and aesthetic criteria typically employed in jazz scholarship are equipped for examining her brand of jazz.

Many scholars across the sciences and the humanities have taken humor seriously, seeking to answer central questions about human belief and behavior as well as to discover what humor reveals about human psychology, social interaction, creative expression, playfulness, and pleasure. Such research is quite rare in the field of musicology, however, and is confined mainly to a handful of studies centered on canonical figures, including Mozart, Haydn, and Beethoven, whose credentials as serious artists are already firmly established. If mentioned at all in general treatments of jazz, musical humor is usually dismissed as frivolous and inconsequential, unworthy of sustained consideration.

Scholarly reticence when it comes to humor can be explained in part because musical scholarship has historically championed aesthetic coherence and unity—music that makes sense—whereas musical humorists often poke fun at aesthetic conventions and embrace irreverence. Furthermore, musical humor generally seeks to be accessible and relevant, offering immediate rewards rather than requiring deep contemplation, serving as a timely intervention rather than bidding for transcendence. Musical humor also presents an unusual analytical challenge, as Leonard Bernstein bemoaned, "The main trouble is that the minute you explain why something is funny, it isn't so funny any more."[5] As a result, it proves a formidable task to analyze musical humor without either draining its comic life or failing to do justice to its creative spark.

Aesthetic coherence, formal unity, and idealized transcendence play similarly important roles in the contemporary reception of jazz, as Gabriel Solis, David Ake, Ingrid Monson, and other scholars have discussed.[6] In the early years, however, jazz artists frequently produced accessible, humor-filled entertainment. "Accustomed to a place on the outside looking in," writes Gary Giddins, "jazz took pleasure in skewering anything that made the mainstream feel safe and smug." But as jazz critics on both sides of the Atlantic worked to promote the music as a significant art form, jazz discourse gradually developed a reputation for its solemn bent. By 1962 Leonard Feather, one of the music's leading advocates, would admit that "jazz criticism . . . often takes itself so seriously that the reader may be disconcerted, even turned off by its pretentiousness." Jazz musicians also had changed gears by this time, and the rise of bebop-based aesthetics in midcentury declared jazz to be a modernist art built on authenticity, virtuosity, complexity, and steadfast commitment. To understand and examine these artistic strategies has prompted similar analytical dedication to technical mastery and the critical treatment of jazz as high art. Jazz studies has developed into a "serious intellectual endeavor," according to Gabriel Solis, accompanied by a "corresponding discomfort with humor and playfulness."[7]

The rapid spread of jazz education has raised the cultural profile of jazz, just as its presence in the academy has garnered the music further accolades and critical scrutiny. That jazz has earned such cultural standing is both a cause for celebration and a remarkable and unexpected achievement in light of the music's humble origins. In persuasive work that recognizes this accomplishment, Ingrid Monson has written about the musical and cultural significance of the bebop movement within the context of the fight for civil rights. "The trappings of art," she explains, "brought dignity and prestige to African-American musicians struggling to overturn the legacy of minstrelsy and its demands for smiling buffoonery."[8] Accordingly, jazz scholars have treated jazz musicians and their artistic endeavors with due admiration. My interest in jazz humor is not an effort to undercut such triumphs but rather to explain how humor lends useful perspectives for better understanding various aspects and eras of jazz history. This is a particularly suitable approach for jazz because humor has been an integral part of African American expressive culture not only as an enjoyable aspect of everyday life but also as a means of survival, liberation, and protest.[9] The humor of jazz assumes a variety of shapes—as a mask for social critique, a display of comic artistry, a mode of communication, a fount of pleasure, and sometimes all of these at once.

Philosophers have long debated the nature, purpose, and meaning of humor, and although no single theory has been universally accepted, three general theories of humor are broadly recognized today. The first centers on the notion of superiority, or what the English philosopher Thomas Hobbes described as "our sudden glory when we realize that in some way we are superior to someone else."[10] *We* wouldn't be the ones to slip on that banana peel, for example, or to take a pie in the face.

The second theory, now commonly associated with Sigmund Freud, characterizes humor as a method for releasing internal tension that can bring pleasure and relief to a joke teller and an audience. For Freud, humor is not necessarily frivolous or light; rather, it can mask and release our aggressions surrounding topics we may be unwilling to discuss in polite company. Letting off steam in this manner, whether by engaging with taboo subjects or ridiculing authority figures, enables humor to create feelings of liberation.

The third theory, advanced by Immanuel Kant and later Arthur Schopenhauer, ties humor to the concept of incongruity: humor occurs when a sense of anticipation is created, and then confounded by something unexpected. Not every incongruous event will make audiences laugh—some may cause shock and confusion or require further contemplation—but this theory proposes that incongruity is fundamental to the nature of humor.

Most studies of musical humor rely on the third approach, viewing humor in terms of incongruity. In his book *Sweet Anticipation* music theorist David Huron describes in close detail how musical incongruities can be generated by foiling a listener's expectations.[11] Musical surprises can be fashioned using many techniques that break rules and upend conventions, including intentionally "wrong" notes, unexpected sounds or noises, and sudden changes in timbre, tempo, style, harmony, dynamics, and more. In addition, Huron argues that understanding a musical joke often requires a listener to have some knowledge about genre conventions as well as the ability to quickly relate new musical information to what has already been heard. Without sufficient preparation and attention, a musical punch line will fall on deaf ears.

Huron's approach to humor, which examines the nuts and bolts of musical rhetoric, can be applied directly to how jazz musicians play with expectations. These moments can occur when Thelonious Monk makes listeners wait for . . . just that extra sliver of time or when Sarah Vaughan startles us by beginning a new phrase in her deepest register, an octave or two lower than we expected. Although not all musical incongruities are intended to be humorous, there is no question that arguably incongruous moments permeate jazz—whether Charlie Parker quoting a passage by Stravinsky or Louis Armstrong quoting "Pop Goes the Weasel." In fact, the humor of jazz may be more difficult to isolate for that very reason—because we have come to expect the unexpected in the form of improvised solos, freely interpolated quotations of musical material, and personalized renditions of even the most time-honored tunes.

Huron's analysis of musical humor concentrates on the ways in which musicians create anticipation and introduce incongruities, and he bases this section of his larger study on how the classical humorist P.D.Q. Bach (Peter Schickele) is able to amuse his audiences and make them laugh. Because Huron focuses on how humor works in instrumental music, his observations are particularly useful for understanding the techniques by which jazz instrumentalists produce humor, but I wish to extend his work in several directions.

First, the humor of jazz exists beyond any musical incongruities intrinsic to an individual work. For example, when jazz musicians allude to or directly quote other musical compositions, they may choose an ironic or openly comedic bent to take advantage of any humorous extramusical associations. Imagine a lick from a cartoon theme like "Meet the Flintstones" popping up in the middle of a rendition of a jazz standard. Second, jazz humor extends beyond instrumental capabilities, since singers have been responsible for producing much humor in jazz performances and recordings. Their imaginative vocals, lyrical play, and comedic stagecraft have opened up wide vistas for creating jazz humor.

Third, jazz humor is not limited to a written score or to the sounds of an individual performance. We can locate elements of jazz humor in song titles, comic lyrics, and visual imagery or watch it take shape between live musicians in their facial expressions, performance gestures, and stage banter. Because mediation may confine or unleash comedic possibilities, jazz humor takes varying forms in the studio, on stage, in print media, and on film. Fourth, jazz musicians use humor not only to evoke laughter but also to establish group rapport and a sense of intimacy with their audiences. As the jazz bassist and composer Steve Swallow describes, "humor used as a tactic is very effective. For one thing it sets the musicians themselves at ease. It's relaxing to play funny music, and it puts the audience in a similar place."[12]

Finally, jazz humor moves beyond the comic production of musical incongruity to encompass a variety of artistic strategies, including wit, comedy, slapstick, irony, parody, and satire. It is also possible to manufacture musical humor in the form of accidental gaffes—mistimed entrances, misplaced notes, and other unintentional mistakes—although I will place my attention here on the ways in which jazz artists make intentional efforts to produce humor.

By choosing to focus on the creation of humor I do not meant to suggest that audience response is insignificant, for humor is an "eminently social phenomenon" and one that relies on the ability of joke tellers and audiences to reach some degree of common ground. The cultural historian Lawrence Levine adopted this stance for his work on African American humor from French philosopher Henri Bergson, whose work frames humor as a process to be understood as an interactive exchange, as participants seek common ground, rather than an activity artificially split into separate acts of production and reception.[13]

I believe that we can learn from both perspectives. In other words, the search for social signification, the give-and-take between musicians and their audiences, has much to tell about the power and the various mechanisms of humor. At the same time, it is important to recognize not only that humor can be created intentionally by musical artists but also that specific audiences, or audience members, can be more or less receptive and prepared to accept such meanings. I am sure that future reception studies and ethnographic projects centered on jazz would do well to investigate the social function of musical humor.

What we do know is that individual responses to musical humor remain difficult to predict or pin down, because they are shaped by so many factors, including musical background, cultural beliefs, aesthetic preferences, mood, and attention span. As a result, any given attempt at musical humor may cause one listener to break out laughing while leaving another unmoved. Sarah Vaughan's 1954 recording of Gershwin's "They Can't Take That Away from Me" presents such an example. Vaughan begins this performance by offering a fairly straight rendition of the tune, but she changes her approach when reaching the third chorus, taking a phrase ("the way you sing off-key") and humorously exaggerating its lyrical commentary on musical practice by singing the word "key" three times on playfully nasal, blaringly off-key notes.

Different reactions to this moment are to be expected. Some listeners may laugh or smile; some may feel that her over-the-top-delivery panders to the audience; some will miss the joke entirely if they are unfamiliar with the musical concepts of key and pitch. Because of its referential nature, jazz humor yields extra rewards for experienced audiences, listeners who carefully process musical information and who have a reserve of knowledge about jazz on which to draw. Just as familiarity with other versions of Gershwin's tune helps listeners to appreciate other aspects of Vaughan's performance, familiarity with other jazz artists enables us to contextualize her decision to turn to humor at this moment.

Vaughan's repeatedly off-key delivery signals her witty engagement with jazz, placing her in a lineage of vocal humorists ranging from Louis Armstrong to Bobby McFerrin. Although this performance represents only one instance in her lengthy career—not all of her recordings contain such audible levity—I believe Vaughan's comic sensibility has been greatly underrated, especially when it comes to manufacturing vocal humor with her remarkable range, timbral manipulation, and sense of timing. Jazz scholars have a tendency to analyze such moments by applauding Vaughan's artistry, her creative approach to interpreting text, her quick and clever mind—all valid and necessary approaches—but forget to mention how she could be downright funny. Vaughan's knowing wit raises questions for all scholars interested in humor. Are we to conceive of musical humor as a craft, as a distraction from serious musical performance, or as a sign of commercial aspirations? Is it possible to construct aesthetic criteria to gauge the success or failure of musical humor?

In this rendition of Gershwin's tune, Vaughan clearly chose her notes carefully to spotlight this moment, rather than to detract or distract from her overall performance. Consequently, whether individual audience members understand this as a highlight or a blemish depends more on personal taste and aesthetic preference. Although it is difficult to determine the degree to which Vaughan's humor was appreciated, we can recognize that Vaughan intended to reach and entertain audiences through this lighthearted gesture, one that stands out further because she so seldom turns to humor elsewhere in this studio recording. Adjustments of pitch, harmony, rhythm, and timbre will always differentiate a straight version from a more humorous take. Listening for such bright moments, where humor takes musical life, helps us to identify the range of aesthetic choices available to jazz artists, just as recognizing the relative absence of incongruity or outright humor in a given recording offers us different indications about an artist's intentions.

In comparison to a figure like Vaughan, who inserted occasional moments of humor into her recordings and performances, jazz artists such as Slim Gaillard mined humor for everything it was worth. During the late 1930s and early 1940s, Gaillard teamed with Slam Stewart to form Slim & Slam, a partnership that entertained audiences with comic spoofs, irreverent parodies, ethnic humor, and songs that verged on nonsense, often reveling in what Gary Giddins calls a "barely restrained lunacy."[14]

Throughout his career Gaillard had the knack for writing song titles that could tease a smile—such as "Banana Skins Are Falling" or "Serenade to a Poodle"—and staged subversive performances that mixed hard-swinging jazz, humorous chatter, and Vout, an imaginative comic language invented by Gaillard. His sense of humor comes across on his glee-filled studio releases, but recordings of his live performances best capture his relentless and effective efforts to get crowds laughing. *The Legendary McVouty,* a compilation of sides recorded during World War II to buoy the troops, contains a number of uproarious tracks, including "Avocado Seed Soup Symphony, Part I" (of a two-part concoction). During the course of this live recording the audience's response sometimes obscures the musicians' performance. Gales of laughter ring out, as the crowd reacts to the madcap exchange of Vout-inflected scat singing along with occasionally recognizable phrases (e.g., "Jingle Bells" and "Avocado Soup") that emerge from the chaotic mix. The frequency of noise and laughter throughout the recording, responding to comic musical gestures but also arising during seemingly sober musical passages, reminds us that Gaillard complemented his musical rhetoric and vocal play with exaggerated stage gestures.

Slapstick, comic entertainment, parody, and satire all were integral to Gaillard's brand of artistic creativity. Whereas critical responses to performers like Vaughan sometimes underplay or bypass elements of humor in favor of exploring less comedic aspects of a musician's artistry, for an artist like Gaillard it becomes impossible to ignore how music engages with humor without having to altogether dismiss him. It is unclear how best to read Gaillard's work in terms of classical theories of humor. One might argue that some audience members laughed because they feel superior to Gaillard's antics. I am more inclined to understand the situation from the perspectives of humor relief theory and the concept of incongruity: that Gaillard's frenzied display, especially during the dark passage of wartime, could present light entertainment, poke fun at the concept of making serious music or serious jazz, and offer audiences all kinds of unexpected turns. Either way, artists like Gaillard force us to either embrace humor wholeheartedly—to examine the intersections between music, play, pleasure, and subversion—or to tailor our notions about what constitutes true jazz.

The degree of difference between Vaughan's wit and Gaillard's comic antics indicates that jazz humor has contributed to a broad range of artistic strategies. But both of these performers gained prominence before the rise of bebop and bop-based aesthetics in the later 1940s. As a result, they were accustomed to encountering jazz as a popular form of musical entertainment at a time when humor was a regular part of jazz practice. Even the first group to record jazz packed their recordings with comic punch. In 1917 the Original Dixieland Jass Band (ODJB) produced "Livery Stable Blues," a hit recording that integrated musical incongruities into a parody of rural life, complete with imitation barnyard sounds. At that moment in jazz history, the contrast between the slapstick comedy of this primitivist novelty and, say, a classical symphony or a parlor song, was inordinately clear to amused record buyers, and the ODJB emphasized their knack for clowning around in their promotional materials.

Changing responses to the ODJB, however, indicate how jazz humor can serve as a barometer of social attitudes, expectations, and values. Their slapstick delighted many record buyers, among them the young Louis Armstrong, but the ODJB's "Livery Stable Blues" does not elicit the same level of enthusiasm today, even though the sounds remain unchanged. This results in part from heightened familiarity: polyphonic ensemble jazz by the ODJB and the groups they influenced no longer seems as fresh, and certain jokes may reach a particular audience at a specific moment while others fall out of fashion. More significantly, listener's expectations about what jazz should be have changed dramatically; rather than seeking out the latest comic novelty, we are more apt to understand such raucous and unruly sounds as products of an earlier, unrefined age of jazz.

The existence of such dated humor has much to tell us about jazz history, for contemporary critical responses to the ODJB also have been shaped by the group's vexed relationship to black musical culture. Reactions today are either mixed or strongly unfavorable not only because the all-white group delivered comic exaggerations of black musical practice but also because their leader, cornetist Nick LaRocca, claimed that jazz was invented by white men and had no relationship to African American creativity. Consequently, the ODJB has been excoriated for at once appropriating and demeaning the musical traditions on which they drew—garnering financial profits as Jazz Age minstrels. Heard from this perspective, the animal sounds of "Livery Stable Blues" suggest that the ODJB was simultaneously mimicking and debasing jazz, drawing on its comic exuberance while establishing their distance from the music's true creators. Consequently, the ODJB reminds us that jazz humor is not necessarily innocent or timeless. As Freud claimed, it can be full of aggression and reveal much deeper meanings. Jokes are commonly made at the expense of someone or something, and humor can obtain very different meanings in different historical and social contexts.

Integrating humor into jazz performance remained common practice into the 1940s. This was an era, as Leonard Feather later noted, when "the line between jazz as art and jazz as entertainment was scarcely drawn at all," and "we tended to take ourselves and our music a little less seriously." Although such lines have hardened over recent decades, many top jazz artists of the prewar period pitched themselves as popular entertainers and complemented their live performances with stage pizzazz, vaudeville tricks, and comic patter. Cab Calloway, one of the most successful bandleaders to follow this artistic path, made no secret of his intentions: "Some artists make you think, others make you dream, and still others, like me, want to entertain." Reflecting on his career, Calloway explained that he was looking for "a way of communicating joy to people," recognizing that "it's rough out there, but drop that heavy load for a while. Laugh and enjoy yourself."[15]

By treating humor as a social phenomenon, in the sense recommended by Bergson, we can understand Calloway as reaching out to audiences during the Depression era and helping them to let go of their cares. In addition to creating a sense of intimacy through shared experience, Calloway's humor also enabled his audiences to engage with dangerous topics while keeping them at arm's length, negotiating with and letting off steam in the Freudian sense. Taking advantage of his dramatic delivery and theatrical flair, Calloway recorded the song "Minnie the Moocher" and a series of equally irreverent spin-offs that cataloged the illicit behavior of Minnie and her friend Smokey Joe, including their misadventures with cocaine, opium, and marijuana. Alternating verses that mixed humor and intrigue with Calloway's amusing scat choruses, songs like "You Gotta Ho-De-Ho (To Get Along with Me)" (1932) encouraged listeners to join in a communal call and response—shouting "Ho-De-Ho" or "kick the gong" (a slang phrase for smoking opium)—and thus lend approval to Calloway's act and participate in the fun. In addition to building an active audience, his musical humor can be seen as an attempt to distinguish between insiders and outsiders, establishing an in-crowd of listeners who were keen to enlist in Calloway's creative bedlam. Reflecting Freud's notion of humor as a release of tension, Calloway's humor can be interpreted as a type of risqué playfulness or as a strategy for upending societal norms.

But that is not how Calloway typically has been read. He is usually treated as a figure peripheral to the jazz canon, dismissed as more caricature than musician. To a certain extent, this has to do with critical bias against any musical figures who blend humor, jazz, and popular entertainment.[16] Calloway has been criticized because of his band's lighthearted repertory, because he perpetuated certain stage techniques long associated with blackface minstrelsy, and because he was an African American performer who catered largely to white audiences at venues such as the Cotton Club. Decked out in spectacular garb and flashing an enormous grin, he went so far to entertain these audiences that his early career has been depicted as something of a tragedy in which he was allowed only to play a demeaning, subservient role, as if his aim to please defeated any opportunity for producing real art. At the same time, of course, Calloway can be defended for being able to establish his career, doing his best under especially challenging circumstances, and using humor as a strategy to entertain audiences, connect with them, and earn a living.

Regardless of whether we wish to condemn Calloway's choices or recuperate his reputation, it is clear that the study of musical humor always requires understanding the nature of the relationship formed between individual artists and their audiences. Are the relationships of power equal? To what degree must a musician balance the need to indulge an audience and the desire to satisfy individual aesthetic goals? How do musical humorists position themselves to reach out to their listeners? How might we describe the ideal relationship between jazz artists and their audiences? Each of these questions ends up pointing back to the debate over jazz as entertainment versus jazz as art. As a result, answering them depends fundamentally on whether we believe musical humor is a valid artistic strategy, whether humor and art can coexist. If we conceive of art as a purely serious endeavor, if there is no room in jazz for humor, then both our definition of jazz and our method of critical inquiry will be equally curtailed.

Although answers to these questions remain subject to debate, many jazz scholars have attempted to understand certain brands of jazz humor by framing them as critical acts, demonstrating how jazz can be very humorous and extremely serious at once. One rationale for this particular line of inquiry has been outlined by the critic Martin Williams, who writes, "I think that many native American arts and artists have functioned best with a mask, a valid artistic persona, of light-heartedness. And whoever receives that light-heartedness as mere lightness or superficiality will probably not understand our artists, nor appreciate the size and depth of the comments on the human condition which the best of them have made."[17]

Attempting to look behind the jazz performer's mask has resonated with scholars interested in figures such as Louis Armstrong and Fats Waller, who combined brilliant musical artistry, humor, and crowd-pleasing entertainment. For example, Robert O'Meally has tried to reconcile Armstrong's artistic achievements with his down-home stage persona, which featured exaggerated mugging, grinning, and humorous banter. Echoing Williams, his work seeks to discover what lies behind Armstrong's smiling face and reveals that jazz is a "rippling, subversive comic art," one well suited for Armstrong to poke fun, issue critiques, and experiment freely behind the mask of humor. Likewise, Paul S. Machlin has persuasively shown how the larger-than-life persona adopted by Fats Waller enabled him to experiment with comic antics and linguistic play in the process of producing biting satire and subversive parody.[18]

O'Meally and Machlin are among a growing number of contemporary scholars to examine how certain modes of jazz humor operate as political or social critique, as if to sugarcoat or to partially conceal a more serious message in the sense that Freud suggested. Such work, often drawing heavily on Henry Louis Gates's theory of Signifyin(g), positions individual jazz musicians within the long tradition of tricksters seeking to operate within and upend dominant culture, often by using an array of rhetorical strategies to dislodge fixed meanings. Indeed, in the process of developing his theory, Gates himself cites the influence of Freud's *Jokes and Their Relation to the Unconscious* and *The Interpretation of Dreams,* and he explains how the types of references, substitutions, and playful shifts characteristic of Signifiyin(g) "tend to be humorous."[19]

Integrating Gates's perspective has encouraged scholars to seek out the connections between jazz and African American humor, because, as Ingrid Monson explains, "irony and parody are more central and *expected* means of aesthetic expression in the African-American tradition." Extending this argument, Monson has suggested that musical irony can be produced easily when African American jazz musicians insert musical quotations taken from outside the jazz tradition or when jazz composers make humorous references to earlier jazz genres. Research by Monson, Josh Kun, and others has explored how jazz artists Charles Mingus and Rahsaan Roland Kirk wielded satire to address contemporary issues—most famously in the recordings by Mingus that lampooned Orville Faubus, the segregationist governor of Arkansas.[20] This work has been vital for acknowledging the political dimensions of jazz humor. Not only do such efforts suit the scholarly impulse—to dig deeper, to unearth what is brewing beneath the surface—but they have lent greater respectability to the study of irony, satire, and parody in jazz, demonstrating how strategies of humor can be quite serious after all.

To date, most studies of jazz humor have centered on a handful of canonic figures, such as Armstrong, Mingus, Gillespie, and Waller, jazz musicians whose relationship to humor is undeniable. Future considerations of humor might extend to other major figures for whom the relationship between jazz and politics is less clear or to humor-laden artists who have been pushed for that very reason to the margins of the jazz canon. Because scholars are so well trained to find a valuable core beneath the surface of pleasure, these inquiries may require adjusting our typical balance that tilts toward considering depth over surface. This is not to say that humor should be equated with a lack of substance but rather that jazz humor is not always clearly underpinned by social activism or political action.

For that reason inquiries into jazz humor also need to account for elements of play, delight, pleasure, persuasion, and joy. What can humor tell us about carving out individual artistic space or building group solidarity, surviving in the world or temporarily escaping from it, engaging in witty exchanges with a close circle of confidants or filling a large hall with peals of laughter?

One productive means for approaching these sorts of questions may be found in the writings of Mikhail Bakhtin, whose work on the Renaissance and the nature of humor and laughter has made a remarkable and wide-ranging impact on scholarship across the humanities over the last quarter century.[21] Bakhtin's conception of the "carnivalesque"—in particular, the power of humor and chaos to enact liberation or to subvert dominant culture—has inspired a great deal of research on humor, parody, and satire. Bakhtin claims that what we might deem as the lightest or most flimsy types of comic expression often can reveal something very significant about the human condition—that playful pandemonium and comic bedlam can function as much more than a mass of bewildering chaos.

His work has been especially influential when it comes to understanding the power of folk culture and popular culture, and particularly influential in literary and cultural studies, but jazz scholar David Ake has shown convincingly how the concept of the carnivalesque can apply as well to today's jazz, at least as practiced by slide trumpet player Steven Bernstein and his band Sex Mob.[22] Ake explains how the band's carnivalesque aesthetic—their raucous language and imagery; visceral, clownish sounds; earthy, growling timbres; loose, improvisatory feel; and surprising, gleeful covers of pop/dance tunes such as "Macarena"—works in direct opposition to the type of serious, orderly, distinguished style of jazz that characterizes much of the contemporary scene.

It remains to be seen how broadly the carnivalesque can be applied to current jazz practice—it certainly holds great potential for earlier moments in jazz history—but Bakhtin gives another productive resource for conceptualizing the ways in which jazz humor creates different possibilities, offers alternate forms of communication and collectivity, and helps us to negotiate new musical relationships with the world around us.

We have already seen how the humor of jazz often hinges on racial, cultural, and political dynamics, but a useful analytical framework may integrate additional perspectives. For instance, we might examine how jazz humor is calibrated differently along lines of gender. Prominent jazz vocalists such as Sarah Vaughan and Ella Fitzgerald incorporated humor into their recordings and live performances, but fewer female jazz instrumentalists have embraced humor to the same degree, perhaps because they have had to struggle so hard just to be taken seriously as female performers in a field dominated by men.

The pianist Dorothy Donegan accepted this challenge by welcoming musical humor into her act, a penchant that began early in her career. At the age of nineteen she appeared as part of a splashy number in the Hollywood film, *Sensations of 1945*. Seated at a white grand piano, wearing a formal white dress, Donegan solemnly plays the opening phrases of Franz Liszt's *Second Hungarian Rhapsody* (1847). Slowly, however, Liszt's piece dissolves, and Donegan transforms the original melody, harmony, and tempo into an up-tempo boogie-woogie number. She speeds forward, now smiling and kicking her foot to the beat, while improvising freely and demonstrating her remarkable facility. Midway through the number, the platform supporting Donegan and her piano begins to rotate slowly, revealing a second piano, helmed by jazz pianist Gene Rodgers. As the dueling pianists attempt to outmaneuver each other, conductor Cab Calloway appears to animatedly conduct them to a grand finish.

This was by no means the first or only time that American popular culture exploited the comic potential of poking fun at classical music. The same Liszt rhapsody was at the center of numerous cartoons, including two released the following year—one starring Bugs Bunny (*Rhapsody Rabbit*), the other Tom and Jerry (*The Cat Concerto*).[23] In comparison to these cartoons, which presented exaggerated, distorted, yet recognizable versions of the original rhapsody, Donegan's transformation is much more thorough, as the rhapsody is quickly overtaken by the high-flying momentum of boogie-woogie. Donegan was not the first jazz artist to display such an impish attitude. Pianists Hadda Brooks and Hazel Scott had gained fame earlier in the decade through their own attempts to boogie the classics. For that matter, Donegan's approach was just one of various methods of "jazzing" the classics that had been employed for decades within jazz circles. During the war years, however, humorous attempts to overturn the European classical tradition with a vernacular African American approach packed extra punch, this time delivered by a young, stylish artist.

Whether one considers this performance entertaining, funny, virtuosic, or appalling, the intentional humor of Donegan's performance revolves around one transformative moment, the incongruous musical pivot when the piece shifts from Liszt's rhapsody to Donegan's boogie-woogie. All listeners can recognize that the dour, slow, minor opening shifts into something new—here, a spirited, up-tempo, major number. But audiences familiar with Liszt will realize something is especially out of order when she starts to boogie, and they may also react when Donegan later inserts brief quotations from the original composition. Ironically, even though the humor of the performance may upset classical purists, the ideal listener for such a musical joke is someone who is familiar with both classical music and boogie-woogie.

For that matter, Donegan, who was classically trained, sought to be a concert pianist to the extent that she set aside her jazz career during her twenties to pursue classical music full-time. After finding few opportunities available for a female African American classical pianist in that era, Donegan returned to the jazz world and later recorded many boogie-woogie renditions of classical pieces, from Beethoven's Menuet in G to Grieg's Piano Concerto. Playing the trickster with Liszt thus represents for Donegan both an early professional highlight and a sign of later career roadblocks. It is terribly difficult to resist the infectiousness and humor in her performance, even as we realize what this signaled about the range of her musical opportunities in midcentury America.

Like all forms of humor, the impact of Donegan's performance depends on the composition of her audience. For example, her target audience in this case could refer to contemporary jazz enthusiasts who seek out this specific performance clip, to the cast and crew on the film set, or to filmgoers who watched *Sensations of 1945,* a musical comedy starring Eleanor Powell and Dennis O'Keefe, produced by a major studio (United Artists), and marketed as a mainstream film for white audiences. In 1963 LeRoi Jones (Amiri Baraka) criticized the phenomenon of concert boogie-woogie played for white middle-class music lovers as an embarrassment, a burlesque, a form of modern-day minstrelsy.[24] His harsh assessment of this practice, given nearly two decades after the film's release, reflects a gradual shift in published views about what constituted an appropriate stance for African American performers.

Weighing such criticism against the few available options for female jazz instrumentalists, how might we analyze Donegan's humorous brand of entertainment in its original context? Does her appearance reflect a small victory for jazz women, or a dated artifact best ignored? Can we discover here an example of trickster politics, subservience, comic artistry, or everything at once? These are the sorts of questions that demonstrate how exploring humor can expand our understanding of individual jazz figures, a chosen era in jazz history, and the changing nature of the genre itself.

As jazz has slowly transformed into an art music that now occupies prestigious conservatories, college classrooms, and concert halls, audience expectations have changed accordingly. Jazz no longer functions primarily as a popular music for dancing, socializing, and lighthearted entertainment, and jazz performances attract respectful audiences who remain quiet and often save their applause for the end of completed numbers. Although moments of humor still emerge in live performance, typically prompted by off-the-cuff stage banter, neither today's jazz musicians nor their audiences anticipate a night's worth of humor-filled entertainment. Instead, contemporary jazz is quite serious and professional, if we are to trust the brochures that market jazz concerts and festivals, the imagery on CD jackets and liner notes, and the visual materials used in jazz textbooks and educational websites.

When Horace Silver was learning his craft in the late 1940s, *Down Beat* occasionally featured cover images of jazz musicians adopting comic poses—for instance, using the bell of a trombone as a hat or a pair of drumsticks as chopsticks. In contrast, today's jazz magazines typically present their musicians as professional artists, so devoted to their craft that they sometimes have little inclination to break a smile. Not all musicians are delighted by these developments. Recalling the ties between earlier jazz and show business, the jazz pianist Cooper-Moore (Gene Y. Ashton) frets, "a lot of [today's] music doesn't have any humor. Monk was a funny cat. Dizzy and Monk and Satchmo, these were funny cats. And I don't see it. I know guys. They are funny, but when they get on stage, they've got no humor. Like you can't laugh and talk to people."[25]

Acknowledging the same historical swing, Horace Silver chose to title his latest studio album *Jazz . . . Has . . . a Sense of Humor* (1999). This sentiment was nothing new for Silver, a musician who cites as influences not only jazz performers such as Lester Young but also popular standup comedians. He has always attempted to reach audiences by releasing accessible tunes and giving them memorably humorous titles such as "The Skunky Funky Blues," "Filthy McNasty," "Hard Bop Grandpop," and "I Love Annie's Fanny." Next to staid album titles released by other contemporary jazz artists, Silver's claim may seem either overly optimistic or nostalgically out of step; however, coming from an artist who began releasing earthy, audience-friendly music in 1952, Silver's reminder urges fellow musicians and listeners to retain a broader aesthetic view, to remain open to all sorts of musical possibilities.

The seriousness of jazz has reached a point that some artists have begun to explore specific ways of injecting humor back into jazz practice. "I have been trying to develop a humorous voice, because it's hard to get serious when playing 'Stella by Starlight,'" explains the jazz pianist Dave Frank. "It's time to just make it funny or just take it out someplace for a joke, because it's been done a million times."[26] Where humor primarily resides in today's jazz world, however, it increasingly reflects the turn to an ironic sensibility in American culture, an aesthetic strategy that typically presents intriguing juxtapositions without offering a clear stance toward them. One can find this sensibility in the droll creations of jazz postmodernists who play with traditional perceptions of jazz. Sometimes this strategy applies to song titles or cover songs. How else are we to understand a group like The Bad Plus, which releases jazz versions of heavy metal classics such as "Iron Man" and gives their own tracks titles such as "Rhinoceros Is My Profession"?

One might also point to the open-minded approach to repertory taken by vocalist Cassandra Wilson, who has recorded songs by the Monkees and Glen Campbell, and clarinetist Don Byron, who has covered the music of Mickey Katz, Puccini, Raymond Scott, and the Four Tops. Considering the performance aesthetic employed by The Bad Plus, a sly but knowing hipness that draws on aspects of modern jazz and rock, these strategies do not indicate the rebirth of jazz slapstick in the twenty-first century; instead, the irony created by these juxtapositions enables these artists to mix traditional and unconventional practices while establishing territory for themselves within today's music world.

Whether taking shape as irony, satire, wit, parody, slapstick, or comedy, musical humor should not be seen as an amusing tangent to conventional narratives of jazz history but rather as an indication of the richness and complexity of jazz, enlivening what Scott DeVeaux has described as its "chaotic diversity of style and expression."[27] Using humor as an analytical lens not only can help to enlighten various aspects of jazz—from aesthetics to reception, from political engagement to social function—but also can work to challenge our musical expectations and scholarly assumptions. If we look for serious artistry in jazz, we will certainly find it, but in the process will we end up discounting alternative modes of expression or bypassing other forms of communication?

At the conclusion of his liner notes to *Jazz ... Has ... a Sense of Humor,* Horace Silver writes, "This album is dedicated to the memory of Thomas 'Fats' Waller. His talents brought a smile to many sad faces throughout the world. We pray that this recording will not only provide you with some good toe-tapping music, but also provide you with a laugh or two. In that laughter may you find the strength to overcome your present problems."[28] How laughter transforms into strength is perhaps a question typically outside the province of musicology. But how music can inspire a smile or a laugh, how musicians forge different modes of communication with audiences, how jazz humor can entertain, please, surprise, and educate: the search for answers to all these questions can enrich our understanding of jazz.

NOTES

1. "'Jazz Is Musical Humor,' Says Davenport Composer and Cornetist of Whiteman's Band," *Davenport Sunday Democrat*, February 10, 1929; "Ellington Speaks Out on Jazz," *Los Angeles Sentinel*, February 3, 1955, 10A; Fred Jung, "My Conversation with Horace Silver," *All About Jazz*, September 1999, www.allaboutjazz.com/iviews/hsilver.htm; Gary Giddins, *Visions of Jazz: The First Century* (New York: Oxford University Press, 1998), 143.

2. Italics in the original. William "Billy" Taylor, "Jazz: America's Classical Music," *The Black Perspective in Music* 14, no. 1 (Winter 1986): 21, reprinted in Robert Walser, ed., *Keeping Time: Readings in Jazz History* (New York: Oxford University Press, 1999).

3. Whitney Balliett, *Collected Works: A Journal of Jazz, 1954–2001* (New York: St. Martin's Press, 2002), 526.

4. Wilma Dobie, "Dorothy Donegan Did It Her Way: Fans Loved but Critics Belittled," 1999, *JazzHouse.org*, www.jazzhouse.org/gone/lastpost2.php3 ?edit=920665948; Robert Doerschuk, *88: The Giants of Jazz Piano* (San Francisco: Backbeat Books, 2001), 56; Leonard Feather, "Jazz," *Los Angeles Times*, December 19, 1982, U84.

5. Leonard Bernstein, "Humor in Music," *Young People's Concerts*, accessed November 5, 2011, www.leonardbernstein.com/ypc_script_humor_in_music.htm.

6. Gabriel Solis offers detailed commentary on the relationship of jazz, humor, and historiography in his book *Monk's Music: Thelonious Monk and Jazz History in the Making* (Berkeley: University of California Press, 2007), 49–56. See also David Ake, *Jazz Cultures* (Berkeley: University of California Press, 2002), and Ingrid Monson, "Doubleness and Jazz Improvisation," *Critical Inquiry* 20, no. 2 (Winter 1994): 283–313.

7. Giddins, *Visions of Jazz*, 143; Leonard Feather, *Laughter from the Hip: The Lighter Side of Jazz*, with Jack Tracy (New York, Horizon, 1963), iii; Solis, *Monk's Music*, 54.

8. Ingrid Monson, "Monk Meets SNCC," *Black Music Research Journal* 19, no. 2 (Autumn 1999): 187.

9. Lawrence W. Levine, *Black Culture and Black Consciousness: Afro-American Folk Thought from Slavery to Freedom* (New York: Oxford University Press, 1977), 300–359.

10. Thomas Hobbes, quoted in *The Philosophy of Laughter and Humor*, ed. John Morreall (Albany: State University of New York Press, 1987), 19.

11. David Huron, *Sweet Anticipation: Music and the Psychology of Expectation* (Cambridge, MA: MIT Press, 2006).

12. John Corbett, "Feeding Quarters to the Nonstop Mental Jukebox: Carla Bley and Steve Swallow in Conversation," *Down Beat* 68, no. 5 (May 2001): 38.

13. Levine, *Black Culture*, 358; Henri Bergson, *Laughter: An Essay on the Meaning of the Comic*, trans. Cloudesley Brereton and Fred Rothwell (New York: Macmillan, 1911).

14. Gary Giddins, *Rhythm-a-ning: Jazz Tradition and Innovation in the '80s* (New York: Oxford University Press, 1985), 162.

15. Leonard Feather, "Gaillard at Donte's," *Los Angeles Times*, April 18, 1978, E1, E11; Cab Calloway and Bryant Rollins, *Of Minnie the Moocher and Me* (New York: Crowell, 1976), 5.

16. For more on this phenomenon, see David Ake's discussion of jazz historiography and Louis Jordan in *Jazz Cultures*, 42–60.

17. Martin Williams, *The Jazz Tradition*, rev. ed. (New York: Oxford University Press, 1983), 253n3.

18. Robert O'Meally, "Checking Our Balances Ellison on Armstrong's Humor," *boundary 2* 30, no. 2 (2003): 123, 136; see Paul S. Machlin's introduction to *Thomas Wright "Fats" Waller: Performances in Transcription, 1927–1943*, ed. Paul S. Machlin (Middleton, WI: A-R Editions, 2000).

19. Henry Louis Gates, *The Signifying Monkey: A Theory of Afro-American Literary Criticism* (New York: Oxford University Press, 1988), 49, 58.

20. Monson, "Doubleness and Jazz Improvisation," 303n47; Josh Kun, *Audiotopia: Music, Race, and America* (Berkeley: University of California Press, 2005), 113–42.

21. Mikhail Bakhtin, *Rabelais and His World*, trans. Hélène Iswolsky (Bloomington: Indiana University Press, 1984).

22. David Ake, "Sex Mob and the Carnivalesque in Postwar Jazz," in *Jazz Matters: Sound, Place, and Time since Bebop* (Berkeley: University of California Press, 2010), 54–73.

23. Daniel Goldmark, *Tunes for 'Toons: Music and the Hollywood Cartoon* (Berkeley: University of California Press, 2005), 44–76.

24. LeRoi Jones (Amiri Baraka), *Blues People: The Negro Experience in White America and the Music That Developed from It* (New York: Morrow, 1963), 218.

25. Cooper-Moore, quoted in Michael J. Kramer, "They All Laughed When I Sat Down at the Piano . . . ," *Jazziz* 17, no. 9 (September 2000): 76.

26. Dave Frank, quoted in Stephen Flinn, "Tradin' Fours: Laughing at Standards," *Down Beat* 63, no. 6 (June 1996): 38.

27. Scott DeVeaux, "Constructing the Jazz Tradition: Jazz Historiography," *Black American Literature Forum* 25 (Fall 1991): 525.

28. Liner notes for Horace Silver, *Jazz . . . Has . . . a Sense of Humor*, GRP 293, 1999, compact disc.

CHAPTER 4

Creating Boundaries in the Virtual Jazz Community

KEN PROUTY

The boundaries of jazz have long been discussed and debated in the pages of magazines, newspapers, and journals, and in films and other media, as critics, scholars, and musicians have expressed opinions on what qualifies as "real jazz." Largely absent from this discussion has been the voice of the music's fans, of the average jazz listener. While letters to the editors of *Down Beat* and other periodicals have occasionally captured fans' opinions on important issues in jazz, those letter writers represent only a small sliver of the jazz audience and their messages were mediated through publishers and editors. With the advent of interactive Internet platforms, however, this dynamic has begun to change, as fans have found new ways of expressing and disseminating their views.[1]

Through sites such as All about Jazz, *Wikipedia*, YouTube, and Twitter, as well as blogs and other digital outlets, fans can now engage more directly in the ongoing discourse that seeks to define jazz—to erect, challenge, and defend the music's boundaries—in an arena not subject to traditional gate keeping by commercial media. As with their critical and scholarly counterparts, virtual jazz communities are a function of a knowledge economy of jazz; yet these new communities reflect a particular expression and type of knowledge, one negotiated in chat rooms, on message boards, and in the comments sections of web pages.[2]

Virtual communities differ, of course, from traditional communities in that their interactions exist only in the realm of cyberspace. That is, members of the group do not typically encounter one another face-to-face, but rather connect through a network of computers and web servers. At the same time, however, they are also not simply "imagined communities," a term popularized by Benedict Anderson in his book of the same name. Anderson defines mass-mediated communities as "imagined because the members of even the smallest nation will never know most of their fellow-members, meet them, or even hear of them, yet in the minds of each lives the image of their communion."[3] Virtual communities function somewhat outside of the realm of "print capitalism," a term used by Anderson to refer to the one-way mass production and dissemination of information. For while members of the virtual community rarely meet one another in person, they do interact regularly and in a manner that differs profoundly from Anderson's model. This interactive nature of digital communication helps foster its own senses of belonging and membership, its own "sense of community."

The notion of a sense of community, advanced in the 1980s by social psychologists David McMillan and David Chavis, rests on a number of specific criteria that define a subjective sense of involvement. As McMillan and Chavis argue, "Membership [in the community] is a feeling that one has invested oneself to become a member and therefore has a right to belong." What is notable here is the emphasis on individual agency and perspective. A "feeling that one has invested oneself" implies that community membership is largely a process of self-selection and self-identification. Following this idea, anyone can, given the proper "feeling" and level of "investment," acquire this sense of community membership. Another critical concept in McMillan and Chavis's argument, most germane to this discussion, is that communities must have boundaries: "There are people who belong and people who do not."[4] They note, too, that the seriousness with which communities regard boundaries is reflected in the "pain of rejection and isolation" they can create and that the concept is, in their own words, "troublesome."[5]

The interactions within "real world" jazz communities often follow these types of practices and patterns in the establishment of genre boundaries and, by extension, of membership in these communities, particularly among musicians, where the "pain of rejection and isolation" can play out publicly. The same is often true of virtual communities devoted to jazz, despite the frequently invoked rhetoric that virtual communities are "unbounded."[6]

Indeed, the establishment of boundaries in virtual environments is often a core activity among community members, many of whom engage directly in policing them, sometimes quite forcefully. For example, perceived "intrusions" into the community, in the form of discussions of artists or topics not deemed to be jazz related, are often flagged for review by administrators of Internet forums.[7] And when the intellectual and emotional heart of an online community is not so clearly defined, the nature of boundary creation moves well beyond simple administrative action, into the very discourse of the community itself. This is, in fact, oftentimes the case with virtual jazz communities, where discussions of what is or is not jazz abound. In the constantly growing expanse of the World Wide Web, such debates take on many forms and can be seen in many contexts.

ENTERING THE VIRTUAL JAZZ WORLD: *WIKIPEDIA* AND JAZZ

There is a staggering amount of material about jazz on the Internet. A simple Google search for the term "jazz," which as of July 17, 2011, registered more than 186 million hits, illustrates the vastness of the topic. Even so, these results can very quickly point to some crucial sites of community formation, where the boundaries of jazz and of jazz community are negotiated.

One of the first jazz-related sites to appear in a Google search is the "Jazz" article on *Wikipedia,* the open-source reference site that has revolutionized the construction of and engagement with knowledge since it first went online in January 2001.[8] By its own definition, *Wikipedia* is a "community-built" reference, and there is a "possibility for error" in article content. Communities often display a multiplicity of viewpoints in the accumulation of knowledge, and *Wikipedia* lays these differences bare, as the editing of articles is generally transparent. That is, the history of edits and discussions on the site is archived, so that users can see who wrote what and when.[9] As with most other Internet-based communities, *Wikipedia* also provides the possibility of anonymity to these users and editors. In this way, *Wikipedia* editors construct a quasi-public knowledge for a particular topic, one that is publicly accessible, yet affords its participants more privacy (and, it is argued, freedom to speak openly) not available in most physical media.[10]

The most readily observable boundary in the creation of a *Wikipedia* article involves what its founders refer to as "consensus." Beyond a simple agreement about what should be included in an article, consensus is a key process in the generation and presentation of knowledge in the *Wikipedia* universe. As *Wikipedia*'s own article on consensus states,

"Editors typically reach a consensus as a natural outcome of wiki-editing. Someone makes a change to a page, then everyone who reads the page has an opportunity to leave it as it is, or change it. When two or more editors cannot reach an agreement by editing, consensus is sought on article talk pages."[11]

Consensus about *Wikipedia*'s jazz article, therefore, involves the establishment of a boundary, which tries to contain only the body of knowledge and work deemed to be "jazz." But just as in the "real world" of jazz discourse, the process of reaching consensus online is often contentious. Perspectives are presented and challenged, credentials and expertise are called into question, and the resulting article is a reflection of where the community *feels* the boundary should be drawn. The article itself might be seen as a moving manifestation of that boundary: while debates might rage over whether or not John McLaughlin is in fact a jazz artist, the public text of the article has to reflect one side or the other; the community consensus (i.e., the text of the article itself) cannot portray him as both "jazz" and "not jazz." Either he belongs or he does not.

Since its first appearance in November 2001, the *Wikipedia* jazz article has been the site of many types of controversies and debates, as reflected both in the article's edit logs and the discussion pages. One of the fiercest debates on the discussion pages took place over two weeks in July 2008, concerning the wording of the lede (opening) of the essay that sought to define jazz in relation to African and European forms. One user, identified as "Editor437," wrote in a post from July 10, 2008, "I doubt any serious work on Jazz would deny that Jazz originated, at least primarily, in African-American communities in the South and that 19th and 20th century American popular music was based upon (with, of course, further developments) European music."[12] Another user, by the screen name of "Verklempt," responded the same day: "There are many jazz scholars who argue that the music arose in a variety of locales, and some of these scholars are covered in the source cited. . . . Since most of these elements have other origins in addition to Africa (which is also addressed in the cited source), it's misleading to attribute them to Africa alone."[13]

The debate that ensued was similar to an earlier squabble involving a user referred to as "deeceevoice," an editor who had invested significant time, beginning in 2004, to working on the jazz entry, and this person's experiences speak to the contested nature of jazz's historiography in the virtual world. One of deeceevoice's earliest discussions involves the characterization of jazz in terms of race; a post from July 8,

2004 states, "I'll probably catch a lot of flack *[sic]* for this, but as an African-American, it galls me when people try to act like black folks aren't the originators of jazz. I've edited this article extensively to reflect that fact."[14]

Deeceevoice's subsequent work on the article (and that of others at the time) did not go unnoticed; by September 2004 the article was nominated to be "featured" on the *Wikipedia* site, an envied status among Wikipedians, as featured status represents a public expression by the *Wikipedia* community that an article reflects what is best about the site. These are the articles that *Wikipedia* wants the public to see. But there is seldom a "final product" in the *Wikipedia* universe. On September 1, 2007, after devoting much time and attention to an article, deeceevoice noted in the discussion page that it was now a "whitewash," with the contributions on jazz's early history and African American identity deemphasized.[15]

On the other side of this debate, in a post to the article's discussion page from October 25, 2007, Verklempt wrote, "I still object to the 'African American communities' phrase [in the article lede]. The history is quite clear that early jazz was performed on riverboats, at resorts on Lake Ponchartrain, and in the Storyville brothel district. It is inaccurate to describe these locales as 'African American communities.'"[16] Throughout the fall of 2007 and into 2008, the discussion intensified about not only the procedures and practices of editing *Wikipedia* sites but also the nature of jazz itself.[17] With Verklempt leading one side of the debate, and deeceevoice the other, the cultural identity of jazz was argued and counterargued. The central question came down to whether jazz should be classified as a historically African American idiom or whether discussion of the music should be more "race neutral."[18]

In seeking to define jazz's cultural and historical boundaries, the tension in community-consensus knowledge formation came to the fore. Two prolific members of the community, neither of whom backed down from their positions, engaged in a fierce, sometimes bitter discourse, all of which was archived by *Wikipedia*. What happens to consensus and community when two vastly different perspectives on the nature of the music cannot be reconciled? Where is the boundary to be drawn? As of July 2011, the lede of the jazz article reads as follows: "Jazz is a musical style that originated at the beginning of the 20th century in African American communities in the Southern United States: it was born from a confluence of African and European music traditions. From its early development until the present, jazz has incorporated music from 19th and 20th century American popular music. Its West African pedigree is evident in its use of blue notes, improvisation, polyrhythms, syncopation, and the swung note."[19]

It would seem, for the moment, that the perspectives of deeceevoice and like-minded editors have won the day and that the discursive boundaries of the *Wikipedia* jazz community reflect the belief that jazz has a fundamentally African American character. Though Verklempt was not ultimately successful in placing such perspectives outside the boundary of the article, all the arguments remain behind the scenes in *Wikipedia*'s discussion pages, spotlighting the contentious nature of discourse in the online world. This is a remarkable shift from the world of traditional publishing, where works such as jazz history textbooks or the *New Grove* dictionary are not accompanied by a list of edits and corrections. The printed results of the communities' discourses from authors, editors, and publishers rarely see the light of day.

DEFINING THE BOUNDARIES BETWEEN JAZZ AND NOT JAZZ IN THE VIRTUAL COMMUNITY

One of the most visible and frequently visited gathering points for virtual jazz communities today is the message board at the website All about Jazz. Established in 1995 by Michael Ricci, All about Jazz filled the (virtual) hole left by the demise of Jazz Central Station by offering reviews, original feature articles, profiles of member musicians, and a wealth of information on seemingly every conceivable aspect of jazz.[20] All about Jazz seemed from the outset to be better suited to the transition to what has become known as "Web 2.0," a reference to the shift from corporate-centered web ventures to a more user-centered virtual experience.[21]

The All about Jazz message board features many of the same boundary-defining debates and discourses as *Wikipedia,* a point underscored by a recent post to the forum. A user identified as "NoScrub" introduced himself to the community as a "3rd year student currently doing a dissertation on Jazz," involving "a critical investigation into the problem of defining jazz as genre." NoScrub asked of the forum's membership, "What is jazz?" Many users responded by noting the difficulty of the very act of defining jazz; despite this, a number attempted to do just that. One user, identified as "ksjazzguitar," opined that jazz exhibits " 5 basic qualities," which include "Swing," "complex harmonies," "complex rhythms/ syncopation," "improvisation," and "blues inflection/vocabulary," though it is worth nothing that this writer also qualified the response by writing that jazz "didn't need to have all 5, but should have at least 4." A short time later, another user called "Vaughan" responded that this definition "doesn't work for me because it discards the free/avant garde jazz I hold so dear." Another user, "Lee Gato," supported ksjazzguitar's contribution as "pretty good," but added to this list "personal style" and a clear influence from an extensive list of jazz musicians. Yet another user, "Hutch Fan," attempted to put these debates in perspective, noting that "Bird said 'No, bop isn't jazz.' He considered bop to be something entirely new. Dizzy said 'Yes, bop is jazz.' He saw bop as an extension of the existing jazz tradition. If two of the *founders* of bebop don't agree, I don't expect that we will either!"[22]

These virtual participants acknowledge that erecting boundaries around jazz as a genre is a difficult, if not impossible, proposition. But without such boundaries, can the community really exist? Or more to the point, are not such efforts to create boundaries an essential act of community, as McMillan and Chavis might argue? Despite Hutch Fan's well-intentioned perspectives on the inherent disagreement in defining jazz, and the seeming desire to leave them aside, debates such as these continue as a central facet of community formation.

These sorts of discussions are found frequently in other sites of virtual jazz communities, in some cases, even those whose identities extend beyond jazz itself. A 2011 thread on the Sax on the Web discussion board raised many of the same points; the original poster, a user called "Coooljazzz," opened the discussion: "I've always found it interesting to see how many different definitions of 'jazz' there are among the population here at SOTW. My personal view is that jazz is a huge umbrella term encompassing many different styles of music, but a surprisingly large number of people seem to have a much narrower definition of jazz."[23]

The exchange that followed, as in the case of the previously mentioned thread at All about Jazz, featured a number of users debating what is or is not jazz. The original poster later contributed the following: "I don't expect anyone to change their minds about their own definition of jazz, especially those of us who have formed our opinions over multiple decades of exposure and experience (old folks like us)."[24] One wonders if the intent is not to change anyone's mind, then what is the purpose of all this debate? Perhaps, in this sense, it is not the actual boundaries themselves that define the community as much as it is the act of trying to create them.

As one might expect, those subgenres that are seen to be more closely allied to popular forms are often the subject of intense scrutiny among members of virtual jazz communities. Smooth jazz is a particularly frequent target, with claims that it is "not jazz" or merely a "radio format" often tossed about in discussions. A relatively early example of this type of debate appeared on Jazzcorner.com's "Speakeasy" forum that originated in May 2003. Originally intended as a discussion of Branford Marsalis's opinions on smooth jazz, users eventually (and perhaps inevitably) moved on to their own assessments and opinions.[25] In a post on May 21, a user called "stonemonkts" added the oft-cited opinion that the problem with smooth jazz is not the music per se, but only that it is included in discussions of jazz at all, a sentiment echoed in several subsequent posts.[26]

Some users defended smooth jazz and its connection to the larger jazz world, while others expressed a sense of antipathy toward the whole discussion. Within the span of one day, three major discursive stances had been invoked: (1) there is a clear boundary for jazz that *excludes* smooth jazz, (2) there is a clear boundary for jazz that *includes* smooth jazz, (3) discussions of boundaries such as these are ultimately pointless.

In each case, members defined their own view of jazz community in different ways. For some, jazz is strictly bounded, a genre whose stylistic identity does not include the likes of certain (sub)genres: this might be regarded as a conservative stance on the surface, but some members in this group also included avant-garde forms (which illustrates the idea that even within relatively narrowly defined boundaries, jazz's identity is often contested). For a second set of members, jazz is still stylistically bounded, but the boundaries encompass a broader range of approaches, including, in this case, smooth jazz and other noncanonical forms. For the last set of members, the notion of boundedness is antithetical to jazz itself: the very act of establishing boundaries flies in the face of what jazz stands for. In all these perspectives, however, it is the act of establishing boundaries itself that serves as a catalyst for community discourse, perhaps even more than any particular aesthetic perspective on the music.

As noted, members of virtual jazz communities are often quick to condemn what they see as intrusions into their virtual space, particularly those that involve forms or genres of music whose pedigrees as clearly defined jazz styles are questionable. In a thread on the All about Jazz forum from January 2004, a number of users debated whether or not fusion is more appropriately classified as rock. The discussion kicked off with a post by a user named "coypu" praising Sean Malone's new release, *Emergent*. Though the original post made no claims to the classification of this work as jazz/not jazz, responses went almost immediately into this area. The very next post, coming several hours later from a user called "jazzypaul," addresses what he sees as coypu's overemphasis (referencing copyu's discussion of death metal in prior posts to the board) on nonjazz idioms: "Instead of going on and on (and on and on and on) about all of these death metal players, tell us how you went out and bought a Cannonball CD, and that it blew your mind. Fusion is not jazz, and death metal, even when it improvises, is still not jazz. You're on a jazz chat. Talk about jazz, JUST ONCE!!!"[27]

What began as a post about an individual recording quickly developed into a referendum on Malone's music, jazz fusion, nonjazz genres, and, ultimately, the boundaries of music and community. I wish to underscore jazzypaul's pointed advice to coypu: "You're on a *jazz* chat" and should "talk about *jazz*." I emphasize the word jazz here to draw attention to what jazzypaul seems to believe is a violation of the boundaries that define the community by discussing a nonjazz style. He asserts that Sean Malone's recording is *not jazz* and that by extension such discussions should not be part of this community's discourse. In defining the music as *not jazz*, the writer is simultaneously attempting to maintain the virtual jazz community's boundaries. A site called "All about Jazz" is not, in this view, the place to discuss what this person considers death metal.

Of course, such a determination depends by necessity on one's definition of jazz. Some members of the virtual community have grown tired of the constant attempts to define the music. A user identified as "johndunlapjazz," argues on July 23, 2008, "I think the movement to narrowly define Jazz is just as contrived as the movement to widley *[sic]* define it. The people who say Jazz is just the Trad stuff are making an artistic statement *[sic]* The people who say Jazz is everything in the Jazz section including fusion and whatnot are making a statment *[sic]* too. That's it. No one has the moral authority. Our Links to EITHER version of the past are usually somewhat tenuous."[28]

Another user, "Bill McCloskey," writing in a post on July 24, 2008, is not ready to throw in the towel just yet, making a counterargument with a palpable sense of exasperation: "What a great idea! Everything is jazz. Rolling Stones? jazz. George Jones? He sang sort of jazzy. Jazz. The Greatful *[sic]* Dead are one of my favorite jazz groups. Bach is one of my favorite jazz composers. Have you heard the new Britney Spears jazz

CD? Amazing. Now that we have that settled, there is no real need for this forum. Let's add some new forums: country jazz. rock jazz. Wagner's Ring Cycle jazz. Philip Glass jazz. Jazz is meaningless. It is whatever you want it to be. It is the most popular music there is because it is all music. There is no jazz. Everything is jazz. Is Emenem [sic] good jazz or bad jazz. Is fity [sic] cent good jazz or bad jazz? How about Mozart? Good jazz or bad jazz?"[29]

One might surmise that on a website called "All about Jazz" users would find some common ground on which to discuss the music. But this last set of debates seems to indicate that this is not the case; it is not simply about what jazz is or is not, but whether it needs a definition in the first place. Is the virtual community therefore defined simply by those who participate in it, those who (in McMillan and Chavis's words) "self-identify?" I would suggest that this might not be far from the mark, as community is ultimately a construct of the individual in negotiation with other stakeholders, and the boundaries that define the community are constructed through such interactions.

Occasionally, virtual jazz communities enthusiastically take up the discussion of other forms that are more clearly identified as not being jazz. One prolific thread appeared in response to an article by pianist Kenny Drew Jr. titled "What the F**k Happened to Black Popular Music?," which appeared on the main All about Jazz site on April 6, 2006. Though claiming to critique black popular music in general, Drew's essay is, in fact, a scathing critique of the contemporary rap scene.[30] After the article's appearance on the main site, a thread was started to discuss the article on the All about Jazz forum, and many users were willing and able to participate in debates over nonjazz forms.[31]

Nevertheless, not all users of the site shared this sentiment. Newly registered user "Jeffery Newton, Esq." wrote on April 13, commenting on what he perceived as the out-of-place nature of this debate in this forum: "I just joined this forum, and this thread caught my eye. This *is* a Jazz forum, is it not???"[32] Here the user suggests that a boundary has been crossed, that a discussion of hip-hop has invaded a jazz community forum, and that such a discussion is out of place. This is a fair point: why *is* this topic so actively and forcefully argued on a jazz message board? Why should a self-identified community of jazz fans care about hip-hop, even if, ironically, the subject generated more extensive discussion than many other threads? In this context, talking about the state of black popular music might be read as an exercise in which *this* jazz community can define and redefine itself in relation to other forms.

The establishment of boundaries for jazz discourse provides a crucial framework, a set of assumptions within which the community can operate, what McMillan and Chavis refer to as the "common symbol system."[33] This type of system also helps to foster a sense of membership in the community, as with the oft-repeated slogan "jazz is spoken here" (even when it is not).[34]

INSIDE OR OUTSIDE: JAZZ ARTISTS AND THE VIRTUAL COMMUNITY

Discussions of musical style and practice are always important to the establishment of the community's boundaries. But communities are composed first and foremost of *people,* and the single most basic function of a boundary in the formation of a community is to determine *which* people are included in its membership and which are not. The Bad Plus provides an excellent example of the dynamics of these debates. Widely lauded (or derided) for their fusions of mainstream acoustic jazz with contemporary popular forms, the group has been the subject of an enormous amount of writing in the jazz press, much of which eventually comes around to the topic of whether or not they play jazz. The group itself recognizes—and perhaps even fuels—this debate, as evidenced in a comment by drummer Dave King in an interview for the *Minnesota Post*'s website: "We like being hard to classify. All of our heroes were hard to classify."[35]

Discussions of the group in virtual communities have reflected similar ambiguities. In a thread on the All about Jazz forum, from late 2004, a user called "Andy D" posted a message to the community soliciting opinions on whether The Bad Plus is "Jazz or what?" Responses stretched for nearly a year, but no real consensus was reached, though the general tone of the debate seemed to favor their identification as jazz artists, albeit ones who stretched the genre's boundaries by their incorporation of pop song forms. On the *Wikipedia* site for the band, the article lede clearly identifies them as a "jazz trio," with absolutely no discussion about whether this is an accurate assessment. It seems that in these virtual communities, at least, members are generally willing to include The Bad Plus within the boundaries of jazz.[36]

While virtual communities have tended to be relatively accommodating of an acoustic trio such as The Bad Plus, the determination of a jazz-based identity for artists whose music draws on electric and digital forms is often more hotly contested. In a discussion of the *Wikipedia*

"Talk: Jazz" article from September 24, 2006, a user identified as A.M.L. took issue with the inclusion of audio samples of the Mahavishnu Orchestra's "Birds of Fire" and Courtney Pine's "The Jazzstep" in the "Jazz" article: "If 'Birds of Fire' is jazz (or at least has something in common with it), then I am Charlie Parker. And how 'The Jazzstep' can be called *modern jazz*, while it is just a simple tune played over a synthesized background?" (italics in the original). Another user called Mutze responded just minutes later, arguing, "Well, if you are Charlie Parker and/or haven't read the article, you indeed wouldn't know that the development of Jazz didn't completely halt after the exploration of Bebop. The Mahavishnu Orchestra's Fusion is just as much Jazz as the first Dixie bands and Ornette Coleman's free experiments."[37]

A.M.L. responded again a few hours later, reiterating that "Birds of Fire" was "[not] ever fusion, it's straight rock." Even in this brief exchange, we can observe members of the community disputing where the boundary should be drawn: should Mahavishnu and Courtney Pine be in or out? They cannot be both in a single *Wikipedia* entry. As with The Bad Plus, the consensus of the community, and thus the boundary of jazz itself as expressed in the article, seems to be that they *are* jazz, as both audio clips still appear in the article as of early 2011.

Virtual jazz communities have not been as accommodating toward other artists, however. Above all, the saxophonist Kenny G is often cast as a perversion or watering down of jazz.[38] In these cases, the discourse of the community often not only reflects an assessment of the artist's style and approach but also moves into the area of ostracizing the individual in question. For many members of virtual jazz communities, Kenny G is not simply "not jazz"; the very suggestion that he *might* be jazz is an affront to the sensibilities of the community, and criticisms of him from members are often much more personal and visceral than with other artists. Numerous posts and threads at the All about Jazz forum assert with absolute certainty Kenny G's status as not jazz, and very few users seem to want to take up his defense.

In a comment thread from June 2000 on the dustup between Kenny G and Pat Metheny, a user identified as "drew" notes that "What Mr. Metheny argues is not that Kenny G is not jazz—which ought to be apparant [sic] to us all," a viewpoint that seemed to be validated in the community by numerous posts echoing the same idea. In a more recent post a user identified as "Bill Williams" notes in a thread from December 12, 2008, "We all know Kenny G is NOT jazz and that's why we're all here on this forum."[39] This, I think, is a telling comment. Not only is

Kenny G squarely identified as "not jazz," but also the ability of the virtual community to express and affirm this idea is something that brings the community together. The certitude of this boundary, and the lack of challenges to it, seems to be recognized by the community's members. To underscore this point further, the comment by Bill Williams was made in response to another user's complaint that he had dismissed free jazz. Thus, even though two users may not agree on the merits of the avant-garde, they can *at least* agree that Kenny G is not jazz, and this act of exclusion, of emphatically deciding that "Kenny's out," marks a boundary that the community as a whole can agree on, one of the very few points of broad agreement in some areas.[40]

Along with assessing artists who might be regarded as jazz or not jazz, members of virtual jazz communities also engage in discussions of those from the "real world" whose attempts to define and defend jazz instigate their own virtual debates. Defining the boundaries of jazz is a frequent topic of critical and scholarly discourses and also a topic of discussion among artists themselves. Some artists have rejected the term "jazz" outright: Ellington, Mingus, and Max Roach all famously eschewed the term. And yet members of the virtual jazz community are unlikely to regard these artists as not being jazz, and most are likely to jump to defend jazz from attack, reflecting "real world" attitudes among members of jazz communities.

More often, what incites members of virtual communities are statements by artists that seem to limit jazz discourse rather than broaden it. Wynton Marsalis's perspectives on jazz often provide grist for this particular mill. Marsalis, whose own views on the boundaries of jazz have come under frequent criticism (as well as some praise) from critics, scholars, and other artists, is a regular topic in the virtual world, with numerous discussions devoted to the merits (or lack thereof) of his music. But what often draws the attention of virtual jazz communities are his comments about the nature of the music itself.

In a thread on the message board at his official website, which began in October 2008, members debated recent comments by Quincy Jones, who criticized Marsalis for his stance on hip-hop. Some users immediately rose to defend Marsalis, as might be expected on his official site. This in itself is a nod to the boundaries of community: at the official website for Wynton Marsalis, the tone of debate tends to skew in his favor, and excessive criticism of him might be regarded as a violation of the boundary. A user called "wvtrumpet" makes clear that "Wynton has made his stance firm on what is and is not jazz. Hip Hop is NOT JAZZ, nor is RAP!!!"[41] Very few posts challenged this idea, again underscoring the idea that in this particular virtual jazz community, one allied with Marsalis himself, the artist's ideas serve to define the discourse.

On other sites, this is not necessarily the case. In a thread at All about Jazz that began in October 2004, a user identified as "tpt1" starts off a conversation titled "I Like What Wynton Said," an entry almost guaranteed to touch off debate. Regarding comments Marsalis made in an interview with Frank Matzner for All about Jazz's main site, tpt1 states, "You know what? I think he absolutely makes sense. I am not wed to the term 'jazz' and I would have no problem saying that 'jazz' is strictly music that has a 'swing' rhythm, walking bass line, ding-ding-a-ding on the ride cymbal, etc.—and all instruments must be acoustic. . . . I am not a 'jazz purist'—far from it—my tastes are way to diverse for that term, but Wynton makes sense here, and I agree."[42]

As if on cue, another user called "monk" responds, "Total bullshit, sorry," and states that such claims amount to "musical fascism."[43] The thread continued for several days, with the merits of Marsalis's statements, and of the artist himself, hashed out among members. Nowhere do these members of the community question whether or not Wynton Marsalis's music is jazz (though some do question whether it is good jazz). The point, rather, is to show how "real world" discussions about jazz's boundaries find their way into the virtual community, with members taking up the debates between jazz's major public stakeholders among themselves.[44] The final entry to the thread, on October 22 from the user "annieds," points to a broadening of the original topic away from Marsalis specifically and concludes on a philosophical note: "Jazz and not-Jazz depends on what you like."[45]

This final comment might provide us with a productive way of assessing the dynamics of virtual jazz communities. Despite the efforts of community members to define themselves through the boundaries they set around the music, such boundaries will always remain fluid, continually determined and redetermined by groups and individuals whose distinct interests, histories, and knowledge are themselves constantly evolving. In this regard, the web generation is no different from those formed through print media, in a jazz club, or around a stereo in someone's apartment. What virtual communities do offer is the opportunity for a wider group of jazz people to engage in this ongoing and long-standing conversation, across vast geographic and demographic spaces. For scholars of jazz, the virtual jazz world also affords us a window through which we can observe—and participate directly in—these conversations as they take place, more rapidly and more broadly than before. It's an ever-shifting work in progress, much like the music itself.

NOTES

This piece is derived in part from the fourth chapter of my book *Knowing Jazz: Community, Pedagogy and Canon in the Information Age* (Jackson, MS: University Press of Mississippi, 2012). I am grateful to Craig Gill and the University Press of Mississippi for permission to reuse this material.

1. Among the first major jazz websites to appear with the rise of the World Wide Web in the 1990s was Jazz Central Station (JCS). Featuring current jazz news, artist profiles, audio and video clips, and feature articles—as well as sales offerings—JCS aimed to be a "one stop shop" for jazz enthusiasts. Most relevant to the purpose of this chapter, the JCS Café became a critical early example of online community activity, providing users with the opportunity and space to exchange ideas about jazz, emerging into what might rightly be termed the first significant virtual jazz community. See Jason Ellis, "Booking Passage through Jazz Central Station," jellis.org, May 4, 1998, http://jellis.org/work/jcs-study/jcs -paper.html.

2. As I argue in my book *Knowing Jazz,* jazz communities are a function of *knowledge* about jazz, which itself is a product of mediation. Members of jazz communities construct their knowledge of the music, with rare exceptions, through media such as texts, records, films, and so forth.

3. Benedict Anderson, *Imagined Communities* (London: Verso, 1983), 6.

4. There are four other components to this aspect of their theory: emotional safety, a sense of belonging and identification, personal investment, and a common symbol system.

5. David McMillan and David Chavis, "Sense of Community: A Definition and Theory," *Journal of Community Psychology* 14, no. 1 (1986): 6–23, quotes from page 9.

6. See, for example, Lelia Efimova and Stephanie Hendrik, "In Search for a Virtual Settlement: An Exploration of Weblog Community Boundaries," blog. mathemagenic.com, November 18, 2004, http://blog.mathemagenic.com/2004/ 11/18/in-search-for-a-virtual-settlement-an-exploration-of-weblog-community -boundaries-draft/.

7. One example can be seen in a thread on All about Jazz from early 2010, in which Lady Gaga came up as a topic of conversation. Several users objected to the discussion, as she was clearly and unambiguously not a jazz artist (unlike, say, a contested figure such as Kenny G), an assertion which itself did not generate debate. In other cases, users have introduced posts by acknowledging that the topic might be outside the recognized boundaries of the community, with a disclaimer like "This may be off topic, but . ..." In these cases, users seem to recognize the boundary they might be violating.

8. In my July 17, 2011, search, *Wikipedia*'s "Jazz" article was the second result, behind only the official website of the Utah Jazz basketball team. The order of search results on Google is determined by a mechanism called Page-

Rank, a "link analysis algorithm" that determines, in essence, the relative popularity of a site as measured through the number and frequency of other sites linking to it. See "PageRank," *Wikipedia*, last modified November 12, 2011, http://en.wikipedia.org/wiki/PageRank.

9. This is not always the case, as *Wikipedia*'s administration has at times been accused of "scrubbing" its edit logs; cofounder Jimbo Wales was accused of doing just that in the controversy over the *Wikipedia* article for John Seigenthaler. See "Seigenthaler and Wikipedia: A Case Study on the Veracity of the Wiki Concept," Journalism.org, October 1, 2005, www.journalism.org/node/1672.

10. The topic of web anonymity has generated a great deal of debate and discussion, with some arguing that it is an essential tool in stimulating open discourse, and others argue that the shielding of user's "real" identities endangers the trust that develops between users in the virtual community. Jason Ellis's aforementioned study of Jazz Central Station's community, for example, noted one incident in which an anonymous user solicited information on listening habits by identifying herself as a student: it was later found that the user was working for a rival company and was engaged in market research. For a discussion of web anonymity, see John Markoff, "Taking the Mystery out of Web Anonymity," *New York Times*, July 3, 2010, www.nytimes.com/2010/07/04/weekinreview /04markoff.html.

11. *Wikipedia* editors, "Consensus," *Wikipedia*, last modified November 12, 2011, http://en.wikipedia.org/wiki/Wikipedia:Consensus.

12. Editor437, "Talk: Jazz," *Wikipedia*, July 10, 2008, http://en.wikipedia .org/wiki/Talk%3AJazz.

13. Verklempt, "Talk: Jazz," *Wikipedia*, July 10, 2008, http://en.wikipedia .org/wiki/Talk%3AJazz.

14. deeceevoice, "Talk: Jazz," *Wikipedia*, July 8, 2004, http://en.wikipedia .org/wiki/Talk%3AJazz/Archive1.

15. deeceevoice, "Talk: Jazz," *Wikipedia*, September 1, 2007, http://en.wiki pedia.org/wiki/Talk%3AJazz/Archive_3.

16. Verklempt, "Talk: Jazz," *Wikipedia*, October 25, 2007, http://en.wikipe dia.org/wiki/Talk%3AJazz/Archive_3.

17. The intensity of these debates can be gauged in part by word count. The previously referenced debate on changes to the article between Verklempt and deeceevoice (as well as a few other users) logged around six thousand words, about the length of a typical scholarly journal article. The length of the entire "Jazz" entry, including links and references, was just over five thousand words at the end of October 2007, when this discussion wrapped up, meaning that the discussion of changes to the article was 20 percent longer than the article itself. Most of this debate took place in the first few days of September 2007, though it was kept alive into the following month.

18. At the end of 2007 deeceevoice's editing activity on this article dropped off sharply, and posts to the user profile http://en.wikipedia.org/wiki/User: Deeceevoice express a great deal of dissatisfaction with the entire *Wikipedia* enterprise.

19. *Wikipedia* editors, "Jazz," *Wikipedia*, last modified November 11, 2011, http://en.wikipedia.org/wiki/Jazz.

20. Owned by record label N2K, Jazz Central Station went off-line in 1999, a casualty of the bursting of the "dot-com bubble." See John Szwed, "Keyword: Jazz," *Jazziz*, September 1999, 64.

21. The term "Web 2.0" was coined by Darcy Dinucci in the article "Fragmented Future," *Print* 53, no. 42 (1999): 32.

22. NoScrub, "What Is Jazz? Dissertation," All about Jazz, May 23, 2011, http://forums.allaboutjazz.com/showthread.php?t=49077; ksjazzguitar, "What Is Jazz?"; Vaughan, "What Is Jazz?"; Lee Gato, "What Is Jazz?"; Hutch Fan, "What Is Jazz?," May 24, 2011.

23. Coooljazzz, "Bernstein on Jazz (What IS Jazz?)," *Sax on the Web*, May 6, 2011, http://forum.saxontheweb.net/showthread.php?159223-Bernstein-on-Jazz-(what-IS-jazz-).

24. Ibid.

25. In this article, which consists of an interview in *Jazziz*, Marsalis gives a tepid defense of smooth jazz and its public face, Kenny G. See Larry Blumenthal, "Family Man," *Jazziz*, June 2003, 40–45.

26. stonemonkts, "Branford on Jazz vs Smooth Jazz," *Jazzcorner.com*, May 21, 2003, www.jazzcorner.com/speakeasy/speakeasy/showthread.php?t=1075.

27. copyu and jazzypaul, "I Just Got Sean Malones New Album *Emergent*," All about Jazz, January 15, 2003, http://forums.allaboutjazz.com/showthread.php?t=156. The mention of death metal players is most likely in reference to a previous thread initiated by copyu that discussed the "glory of Death-Jazz" and looked at bands that fused jazz and death metal. The Cannonball CD alludes, presumably, to alto saxophonist and hard bop stalwart Julian "Cannonball" Adderley. This massive and meandering thread, featuring a spirited debate between copyu and other users (including jazzypaul), lasted until February 2003 and had 548 individual posts when it ended; it can be accessed at http://forums.allaboutjazz.com/showthread.php?t=118.

28. johndunlapjazz, "What Do You Call Jazz? And What Rock?," All about Jazz, July 23, 2008, http://forums.allaboutjazz.com/showthread.php?t=34656.

29. Bill McCloskey, "What Do You Call Jazz?," July 24, 2008.

30. Kenny Drew Jr., "What the F**k Happened to Black Popular Music?," All about Jazz, April 6, 2006, www.allaboutjazz.com/php/article.php?id=21243. The article is accompanied by a photo of a menacing, shirtless 50 Cent.

31. The thread, which was initiated by a user called "jazz man" the same day that the article appeared, was the site of a spirited debate that stretched into August and had, by the time debate wrapped up, more than one thousand posts. With the exception of the monthly "What are you listening to?" threads, to date it is the single longest discussion in the "General Music Discussion" section of the forum, the most active area of the message board. A post in December 2007 commented that the thread was "legendary." This thread encapsulates many different aspects of the experience of the online jazz community, which I discuss in much greater depth in my book *Knowing Jazz*. It can be accessed at http://forums.allaboutjazz.com/showthread.php?t=14077.

32. Jeffery Newton, Esq., "What the F**k Happened to Black Popular Music Article," All about Jazz, April 13, 2006, http://forums.allaboutjazz.com/showthread.php?t=14077&page=22.

33. McMillan and Chavis, "Sense of Community," 10. The "common symbol system" includes categories such as language, dress, ritual, and so forth. In a sense, the bashing of rap might be seen as something of a ritual in establishing jazz community on this message board, a replication of an act that is frequently observed among "real world" jazz communities.

34. The common phrase "jazz is spoken here" was also the title of a 2000 documentary on pianist Ellis Marsalis.

35. Dave King, quoted in Pamela Espeland, "Back in Town: The Bad Plus Still Defy Easy Definition," *minnesotapost.com*, December 24, 2008, www.minnpost.com/pamelaespeland/2008/12/24/5518/back_in_town_the_bad_plus_still_defy_easy_definition. The band has also cited, in other venues, relatively canonical artists such as Thelonious Monk as primary influences. While Monk's style may have been eclectic, few would argue that his music is hard to classify as jazz, at least with respect to mainstream perspectives.

36. Andy D, "The Bad Plus—Jazz or What?," All about Jazz, November 25, 2004, http://forums.allaboutjazz.com/showthread.php?t=7095; *Wikipedia* editors, "The Bad Plus," *Wikipedia*, last modified October 20, 2011, http://en.wikipedia.org/wiki/The_Bad_Plus.

37. A.M.L., "Talk: Jazz," *Wikipedia*, September 24, 2006, http://en.wikipedia.org/wiki/Talk:Jazz/Archive_2; Mutze, "Talk," September 24, 2006.

38. It is worth noting the lede to *Wikipedia*'s "Kenny G" article refers to him specifically as a "smooth jazz" artist, and not simply as a "jazz" artist (as in the case with The Bad Plus).

39. drew, "Do You Agree with Pat Metheny's Comments about Kenny G? Why? Or Why Not?" All about Jazz, June 27, 2000, www.allaboutjazz.com/threads/patmetheny.htm (this discussion actually predates the All about Jazz message board itself); Bill Williams, "Terrible Albums by Great Players," All about Jazz, December 12, 2008, http://forums.allaboutjazz.com/showthread.php?t=36959&page=2. This individual's profile currently lists him as a "banned user."

40. Even in Internet forums not devoted to jazz, Kenny G's nonjazz nature is asserted. At YouTube, rarely are Kenny G videos or audio tracks posted without at least one user comment that his music is not jazz. There are also at least two Facebook pages dedicated to the proposition that "Kenny G is not jazz."

41. wvtrumpet, "Quincy Jones Calls Wynton Out," *wyntonmarsalis.org*, October 16, 2008, www.wyntonmarsalis.org/forum/read.php?2,9498.

42. Frank Matzner, "Wynton Marsalis Speaks Out," All about Jazz, February 27, 2004, www.allaboutjazz.com/php/article.php?id=1209; tpt1, "I Like What Wynton Said," All about Jazz, October 14, 2004, http://forums.allaboutjazz.com/showthread.php?t=6456.

43. monk, "What Wynton Said."

44. In another example of "real world" discourses becoming a site for community identity, there was a great deal of discussion in the virtual community regarding Keith Jarrett's caustic comments at the 2007 Umbria Jazz Festival, in which the pianist berated his audience and the host city, after he observed fans taking photos and recording the event. Users were split on the merits of his actions (though most thought he went too far), but there was a real consensus

that Jarrett's actions had cast the "jazz community" in a negative light. Many users stated emphatically that they did not want his actions to reflect on them and did not want him standing as a representative of the community to which they belonged.

45. annieds, "I Like What Wynton Said," All about Jazz, October 22, 2004, http://forums.allaboutjazz.com/showthread.php?t=6456&page=3.

CHAPTER 5

Latin Jazz, Afro-Latin Jazz, Afro-Cuban Jazz, Cubop, Caribbean Jazz, Jazz Latin, or Just . . . Jazz

The Politics of Locating an Intercultural Music

CHRISTOPHER WASHBURNE

Jazz music is global and transcultural in its stylistic scope. It has been so since its inception. No more is this apparent than in the form of jazz that embodies a nexus of intercultural exchange, where African American musical practices are blended with Latin American and Caribbean forms. Today, we see an unprecedented interest in this music both institutionally and within popular realms, spawning a number of published histories, documentaries, compilations, recordings, and festivals. In short, we are experiencing a thriving moment in the music's history, while only beginning to grasp and theorize the forces at play in this open and inclusive reinvention of jazz. Taken in total, all of these developments impel musicians, scholars, and spokespersons alike to position, define, and prescribe generic boundaries. Just the variety of names chosen for the music—Latin jazz, Afro-Latin jazz, Afro-Cuban jazz, Cubop, Caribbean jazz, jazz Latin, and jazz, to name a few—suggest how nationalistic, ethnic, geographic, and racial agendas inform discursive exercises of generic prescription.

In a similar vein, such agendas are key to understanding why, in spite of growing interest and popularity, this music, along with the musicians who make it, are persistently marginalized and separated economically, politically, ethnically, and racially by the media, educational institutions, jazz producers and promoters, consumers, and musicians. The music is frequently segregated into allotted programming and promotional slots that neatly compartmentalize and pigeonhole—reserved exclusively for the exotic, the novel, the lightweight, the not real jazz music for cats who can't play changes—and is often billed with cliché terms such as "hot," "fiery," or "*caliente*" (fig. 5.1). Though an in-depth discussion concerning the multiple reasons for this type of continued marginalization is beyond the scope of this essay, economic concerns and the intense competitive environment of the jazz business are certainly key factors. Especially as the popularity of Caribbean and Latin-inflected jazz styles grows, thus raising the economic stakes, strong resistance continues to fester among various groups within the jazz community who have benefited in the past from a more exclusive delineation of what jazz is.

What comes to mind are these questions: Is this chapter just another one of those examples in which Latin American– and Caribbean-inflected jazz is segregated from the mainstream, black-versus-white, U.S.-centric "real jazz" world? Should this music remain a separate category? Why is the music of Chico O'Farrill, Tito Puente, and Machito rarely treated simultaneously with, or with equal weight as, the music of Duke Ellington or Louis Armstrong? Should it be this way?

This continuing, but uneasy marginalization, in turn, heightens the stakes involved in the discourse concerning genre. The ramifications of nominal choices alone are significant in terms of the economic and cultural capital that each can potentially yield. Furthermore, the burden of signification that each label carries, embodying complex subjectivities, yields productive analysis for scholarly inquiry, serving as a lens into the fundamental political girding of intercultural production. What becomes apparent is that self-conceived notions held by musicians of how to label this music are not static or terminal in nature but rather mobile, fluid, and changeable; always strategic; and at times even seemingly fickle.

In this chapter I explore the pendular, self-positioning discourse that makers of this music engage to navigate through and strategically position themselves within this, at times, adversarial milieu. I demonstrate that genres are not only performed but carefully imagined, constructed, and maintained in ways that reveal "the ideologies and power arrangements that underlie local impositions of generic order."[1] The politics of nation, class, economics, ethnicity, and race underpin a fluid dance of genre imaginings, as well as the complex relational dynamics of center and periphery, that is, mainstream and margins.

Specifically, I examine two case studies of musicians, Arturo O'Farrill and Ray Barretto, positioned in divergent and revealing ways. Reflecting

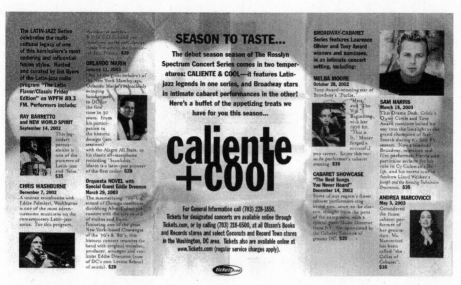

FIGURE 5.1. Program from Spectrum Theater in Arlington, Virginia (2002).

my own position and research energies, this chapter focuses primarily on New York City, although this is only as the first step in examining the global implications of this generic discursive dance. I acknowledge that New York–centrism is problematic when studying jazz as a global phenomenon, but since much of jazz business and performance is centered there, it can aptly serve as a productive microcosm for examining the wider global field.

Before we look at the individual cases, however, I first want to explain how I am conceiving the forces at play. The music and musicians associated with jazz and Caribbean and Latin American mixings operate on a stylistic continuum of sorts. The sphere, consisting of Caribbean and Latin American traditional, folk, dance, and popular forms, as well as their associated performance practices, exists on one end of the spectrum and that of jazz forms and performance practices inhabits the other (see fig. 5.2). These generic entities are obviously far from mutually exclusive, both having a closely shared history. Neither is bounded, nor has an essentially pure or authentic past. In fact, there has been a continual intercultural dialogue among practitioners of these styles since the inception of the music traditions we now locate under the auspices of jazz (roughly over the past hundred years).

J. Lorand Matory has written about the misleading notions of Africa's unidirectional influence on diasporic styles, often conjured up solely

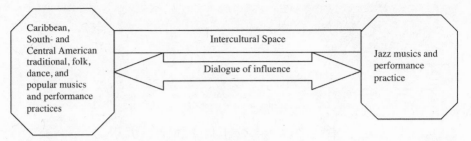

FIGURE 5.2. The "Latin Jazz" continuum.

to serve as root source material.[2] He critiques the limitation of such an outdated notion and instead points to the fundamentally dialogic nature of the relationship between Africa, on the one hand, and the Americas and Caribbean on the other, stating that these places have been, and still remain, in a state of constant exchange, rooted in real contacts by people and their artifacts operating within a living reciprocal relationship. The same can be said about the relationship of the types of music located on this continuum, yet often with notions of Africa serving as the fundamental point of departure for intercultural exploration and stylistic mixing. I am presently focusing on the music situated in the fluid intercultural space between the two ends of the continuum, at times leaning more heavily toward one side or the other but embodying enough stylistic diversity to be simultaneously excluded from both domains. Yet they remain indebted and imbedded in the two ends, in this dialectical middle ground, a multicultural one at that. Obviously, both spheres at each end of this imagined continuum have at their core interculturality a prominent productive and generative force.

On the surface level, one might ask, "What isn't intercultural music?" The pervasive and rather vague character of the term often reduces some of its explicatory power when considering its most basic meaning. What seems to be called for, though, is a theoretical specification of the very notion of interculturality. The truly intercultural artifact is not explicated by any simple reference to cross generic or cross stylistic origins (which would take us straight back to the stale insights of traditional historicist source studies) but by that which retains at its core a certain level of fluidity and ambivalence in the way it is positioned in relation to these various cultural inputs. What is actually happening in this in-between shared space of real, lived experience is a dynamic field of forces at play, where cultural difference and commonality is negotiated, battled, allied, and explored. In short, my use of the term "interculturality" must be seen in light of this dialectic movement between the two ends of the continuum.

At times, musicians delve into this interstitial space simply in search of fodder for innovation and change while exploring sonic alchemy; others enter simply seeking their cultural roots. As the musicians fulfill particular agendas, new affiliations and alliances are forged in this hybrid space. These agendas frequently are instigated by institutional urges of naming, labeling, and classifying, all of which are rather artificially static activities that tend to be relatively reductive in nature. But the naked fact of the functional necessity remains: due to economic and political pressures, we are repeatedly forced to specify generalities that essentialize our music. Such classifying choices make a real difference in the lives of musicians by determining how their music is produced, marketed, and programmed. Efficient labeling can mean the difference of making a living or not. Yet in reality musicians rarely inhabit one place along this continuum but freely and fluidly migrate, changing positions even within one composition or from one song to the next. Thus, it is just as important to identify the counterpresence of resistance to generic sedimentation and acknowledge that most music thrives on the ability to remain operative and evasive within the fluidity of indeterminacy.

ARTURO O'FARRILL AND WYNTON MARSALIS

Beginning in the mid-1990s the growing appeal of Latin American and Caribbean music prompted Wynton Marsalis, artistic director of the Jazz at Lincoln Center program, to schedule a number of themed concerts, including The Latin Tinge: Jazz Music and the Influence of Latin Rhythms, featuring Tito Puente, the Fort Apache Band, and Arturo Sandoval, in March 1995; Afro-Cuban Jazz: Chico O'Farrill's Afro-Cuban Jazz Orchestra, in November 1995; Con Alma: The Latin Tinge in Big Band Jazz, in September 1998; and The Spirit of Tito Puente, in November 2001, for the Jazz at Lincoln Center Annual Gala Concert.

At the last event, both the Lincoln Center Jazz Orchestra (LCJO) and the Tito Puente Orchestra shared the stage, alternating numbers and also performing together. Puente had died in 2000, so his band was led by his longtime musical director Jose Madera and was made up of seasoned veterans who had performed with Puente over the years, including saxophonists Mario Rivera, Bobby Porcelli, and Mitch Frohman; trumpeters Ray Vega and John Walsh; percussionist Johnny Rodriguez; pianist

Sonny Bravo; bassist Ruben Rodriguez; and trombonists Lewis Kahn, Reynaldo Jorge, and yours truly. The LCJO was directed by Wynton Marsalis and was composed of mostly younger accomplished musicians, none of whom had extensive experience playing Caribbean or Latin American rhythms. During rehearsals Marsalis became concerned about his band's lack of experience performing the music of Puente, so he hired Arturo O'Farrill, son of the influential Cuban composer and arranger Chico O'Farrill, as an assistant conductor and coach for his LCJO musicians.

As work progressed with O'Farrill, Marsalis gained confidence in his band and during the final rehearsal, and to the surprise of the Puente musicians, decided to perform one of Puente's most famous originals, "Picadillo," solely with his own band, instead of having Puente's band join in. During the concert, the Puente veterans sat idly on stage watching as Marsalis's band struggled to execute the sharp rhythmic breaks that made Puente famous among dancers. Immediately following this lackluster performance, the Puente band launched into a particularly inspired performance of the Latin standard "Mambo Inn," leaving LCJO "in the dust," as the Puente musicians later proclaimed (fig. 5.3).

During his life, Tito Puente complained of an imbalance between the knowledge Latino musicians are expected to have of jazz styles and how little "American" jazz players think they need to know to play Latin music styles.[3] Arranger and percussionist José Madera commented, "It is a well-known fact that a good jazz band cannot really play Latin music, but a good Latin big band, such as Machito or Puente or Tito Rodriguez could play jazz fairly well."[4] This disparity was clearly demonstrated that evening at Lincoln Center. Arturo O'Farrill recalls, "There was a benefit performance pairing Wynton's orchestra with Tito Puente's, [and] Wynton had me lead a rehearsal of the Latin numbers. I wanted them to play a Cuban phrase, but they just could not articulate it authentically. They would 'jazz' it up. They could not 'Afro-Cubanize' it. Wynton had this faraway look in his eye. I think that's when he realized that it takes a specialized group of musicians. It's a different approach—artistically, mentally and emotionally."[5]

Shortly after this concert, Wynton Marsalis and the powers that drive Lincoln Center conceded LCJO's lack of expertise in Caribbean- and Latin American–inflected jazz and launched a second band in July 2002 that was solely dedicated to that body of music. Arturo O'Farrill was chosen to lead the new band, which was modeled on the group led by Marsalis. The programming at Lincoln Center has been a powerful marketer for redisseminating the "jazz" word, especially through its effective

FIGURE 5.3. The Tito Puente Orchestra (*right*) and the Lincoln Center Jazz Orchestra (*left*) with Wynton Marsalis (*upper far left*) and dancers performing at Avery Fisher Hall in November 2001 for the Jazz at Lincoln Center Annual Gala Concert. Photo © 2001 by Jack Vartoogian/Front Row Photos.

educational branch, for which Marsalis and LCJO tour the country presenting numerous programs. Similar educational programs were planned for O'Farrill's band. With unprecedented institutional support, O'Farrill was thrust from the shadow of his father to what was potentially an extremely powerful position. Virtually overnight, this arena of jazz became historicized, worthy of preservation quasi on par with the repertoire played by Marsalis's LCJO.

Then came the problem of what to call this new band to differentiate it from Marsalis's group. The very choice of O'Farrill's leadership reflected the hegemonic position of Cuba in the development of the music throughout the twentieth century (O'Farrill is half Cuban and half Mexican). Cuba's influence was rooted in numerous historical factors, ranging from its rich music heritage, a long economic relationship with the United States, its geographic proximity, large Cuban immigration, and the sheer number of exceptionally gifted and skilled performers coming from the island.

Furthermore, Cuban musicians were some of the first important progenitors of pan-African explorations in jazz, prompting a number of intercultural collaborations that sought to sonically explore the common musical heritages of African-derived traditions. As Jason Stanyek writes, it was Cuban percussionist Chano Pozo's and trumpeter Dizzy Gillespie's music ventures and "their ability to juxtapose different histories without sacrificing identities . . . as well as their reflexive use of notions of cultural difference as a basis of collaboration" that created the fulcrum of pan-Africanism and a dialogic space of interculturality in jazz.[6] Other Cuban musicians associated with these early intercultural explorations are Frank "Machito" Grillo, Mario Bauzá, and Chico O'Farrill.

Choosing the same instrumentation as the big band of Dizzy Gillespie in the mid-1940s (that is, a jazz big band, plus a three-piece Cuban percussion section) and hiring New York–based musicians seasoned in Afro-Cuban jazz styles, O'Farrill's band was a fairly traditional Afro-Cuban jazz band, for all intents and purposes. But, concerned with not promulgating a Cuban centricity from such a powerful position, O'Farrill, in collusion with Marsalis, shied away from the more commonly used "Latin jazz" or "Afro-Cuban" labels and instead chose the name "Lincoln Center's Afro-Latin Jazz Orchestra" (LCALJO). According to O'Farrill, "Wynton wanted 'Latin jazz' or 'Afro-Cuban' in the name of the band, but I did not think that these reflected the diversity of the music. So I chose a name that I had never heard used before in a band's name. As a Cuban I find the Cuban centrism offensive. It is a small view of the world. It does not reflect the global nature of the music. I have found great big band traditions in Haïti, the Dominican Republic, and Mexico."[7]

The choice was particularly strategic, because it referenced not only pan-Africanism with "Afro" but also pan-Latinismo with "Latin." The concept of pan-Latinismo was first associated with the ferment for unity and ethnic revitalization that began in the 1960s among Latino communities in the United States.[8] Predicated on notions that the African diaspora and Latino cultures share essential commonalities, both pan-Africanism and pan-Latinismo are intercultural concepts and frequent tropes that have been played out repeatedly as a way to negotiate cultural space. Both are part of a larger phenomenon of strategic panethnic movements that have been fueled largely by political and economic pressures, promoting common unity for empowering a minority or marginalized group with mass mobilization toward a common goal. As such, both pan-Africanism and pan-Latinismo exist in constant tension with specific national, ethnic, class, and racial identification and distinction.

But combining these two lineages conjures an even larger, more powerful coalition—that of a "circum-Atlantic" world. As Joseph Roach writes, "The concept of the circum-Atlantic world (as opposed to a transatlantic one) insists on the centrality of the diasporic and genocidal histories of Africa and the Americas, North and South, in the creation of the culture of modernity. In this sense, a New World was not discovered in the Caribbean, but was truly invented there." This model of intercultural encounter offers an alternative historical narrative of American culture by emphasizing the truly astonishing multiplicity of cultural encounters in circum-Atlantic America and the adaptive creativity produced by the interaction of many peoples. Such a model calls for "a performance genealogy in which the borderlands, the perimeters of reciprocity, become the center."[9]

Considering that Roach was writing about expressive culture in New Orleans, his discursive centering move comes uncomfortably close to challenging the origins of jazz as solely an expression of African American culture, or at least calls for a redefinition of African American culture. Ironically, his centering strategy echoes those employed by Marsalis, who posits jazz as an essential and significant part of "American culture," a strategic discourse that helped launch the Jazz at Lincoln Center program in the first place.

Regardless of this possible ideological conflict with his boss, O'Farrill did not tread lightly in this regard, which may have contributed to his eventual demise. O'Farrill stated, "The music [Latin jazz] was created here [the United States], but it has the unfortunate stigma of being perceived as foreign. Latinos speak a different language, which makes it seem foreign to some people. It's not. It's as American as apple pie. Let's stop pretending it's a subset, a subgenre." But then a moment later in the same interview, a pendular discursive dance is revealed as O'Farrill backs away from following through with a logic that could have led to his own obsolescence at Lincoln Center. "Afro-Latin, Afro-Caribbean music is different enough from standard big band repertory that it deserves to be understood as a separate specialty and discipline."[10] This position, of course, strategically affirms the necessity for his LCALJO by emphasizing and maintaining a basic distinction between the music played by Marsalis's LCJO and that of O'Farrill's LCALJO. Thus, a specialized space on the continuum is reserved exclusively for "Afro-Latin jazz specialists," all the while maintaining the exclusive rights of Marsalis's band to "jazz proper."

Acts of genre labeling are unavoidable necessities and serve the utilitarian requirements of the economic strictures imposed by current music business practices involved in promotion, production, sales, and booking. However, I view this exercise of labeling as an act of discursive violence, because what it often cloaks and ignores, though simultaneously reflects, is a murkier layer located beneath the institutionalized game of naming, which involves the slippery complex of intercultural exchange. This exchange operates as a disruptive force, spawning new levels of heterogeneity and complexity, where commonalities are forged and collaborative space is created, but where differences and diversities are deemphasized or ignored, and cultural specificity is erased. Thus, with all acts of naming, a discrepancy becomes apparent between actual lived experience and its idealized projection.

In the case of the LCALJO, the concern for a delimited yet inclusive discourse had little specific relation with the diversity in cultural affiliations of the actual band members: seven Puerto Ricans, two Dominicans, and one Costa Rican, along with six Anglo-Americans and one African American, all of whom resided permanently in the New York City area.[11] O'Farrill was the only member with Cuban ancestry. No doubt some of these musicians self-identified, to some extent, with the less specific Afro-Latin cultural affiliation, but certainly not all. So on a basic level, the Afro-Latin designation represented only a portion of the individual membership of the group (fig. 5.4).

Moreover, most of the music they performed was firmly rooted in what is commonly referred to as Afro-Cuban traditions, and on the few

FIGURE 5.4. Publicity photo of the Lincoln Center Afro-Latin Jazz Orchestra. *Left to right:* Pablo Calogero, baritone; Papo Vasquez, trombone; Erica von Kleist, alto; Andy Gonzalez, bass; Milton Cardona, congas; Michael Philip Mossman, trumpet; Jim Seeley, trumpet; Ray Vega, trumpet; Bobby Porcelli, alto; Luis Bonilla, trombone; Arturo O'Farrill, piano; Joe Gonzalez, percussion; Doug Purviance, bass trombone; Felix Rivera, drums; John Walsh, trumpet; Bobby Franceschini, tenor; Reynaldo Jorge, trombone; Mario Rivera, tenor. Photograph by John Abbott, 2003. Courtesy of Jazz at Lincoln Center.

occasions when non-Cuban-based music was programmed, they (quite revealingly) hired freelance ringers who specialized in those forms to compensate for their lack of expertise. Regardless, the discourse concerning LCALJO remained strategically open throughout the group's tenure at Lincoln Center, from 2002 to 2007. Reflecting how these debates intersected with hiring practices, O'Farrill stated,

> When Wynton came to the first rehearsal of the band he asked me, "Where are all the black people?" I wish I could hire all Latinos with dark skins, but that does not reflect who has made this music throughout history. You would often have Latin rhythm sections with Italian and Jewish horn sections. I base my hiring on artistic decisions. If there is a group of great Polish musicians who could play this music, I would have a bunch of Polish guys in the band. . . . Then maybe we would be playing Afro-polkas![12]

The notion of required specialization and expertise served O'Farrill well by maintaining a privileged space for LCALJO within the Jazz at Lincoln Center program; however, the broader implications of the band's name bore little resemblance to the actual music played.

RAY BARRETTO

Conguero and bandleader Ray Barretto provides a contrasting example. Barretto led a hugely successful salsa band throughout the 1960s and 1970s, but for the last twenty-five years of his life, he dedicated most of his performance energies to jazz-inflected septets and sextets (he died in 2006). Consciously hiring musicians known as gifted jazz soloists but not considered specialists in Caribbean- and Latin American–inflected jazz, he favored a traditional jazz quintet instrumentation (trumpet, saxophone, piano, bass, and drums), plus congas. Stylistically, his music inhabited a space on the continuum comparable to that of O'Farrill's, favoring Afro-Cuban rhythms and styles. But he positioned himself in a markedly different way.

While Barretto was performing in France at the Jazz à Vienne festival with his sextet in 2003, during a softer ballad, one drunken fan started shouting out requests for Barretto's most famous salsa tunes from the 1970s. After attempting to ignore the disruption, the fan's persistence caused Barretto to stop the band and exclaim, "Do you see a singer on stage? Do you see timbales and bongos? This is a jazz band, and this is a jazz festival, and that is what we play. . . . Jazz? This music is for listening, not dancing. So shut up and listen, and you just might learn something." The fan became increasingly irate and just continued to call out salsa tunes, then several other audience members joined in, shouting out similar requests. Enraged, Barretto stood up (he was tall with a muscular build and huge swollen hands, not an unassuming character) and shouted, "Fuck you. And fuck all of France." He then sat back down behind the congas and counted off the next tune, a straight-ahead swing tune with no pronounced Latin rhythms. The audience quickly simmered down by the end of that selection. They played the rest of the concert without any other disruptions (fig. 5.5).[13]

Barretto's omission of any reference to the Latin or Caribbean influences heard in his music, while defending his musical choices to the French salsa fan, was the manifestation of a conscious self-positioning strategy that he employed on many occasions. For instance, when he negotiated for his annual weekly engagement at the Blue Note jazz

FIGURE 5.5. Ray Barretto
playing congas with bassist
Jairo Moreno. Photo © 2011 by
Enid Farber.

club in New York City, he pleaded to share the bill with straight-ahead
jazz musicians, such as Horace Silver or Johnny Griffin, and to not be
paired with other musicians performing Caribbean- or Latin American–
inflected jazz, such as Eddie Palmieri, Dave Valentine, or Poncho San-
chez (he was rarely successful in this venture and mostly appeared on
Latin jazz–themed weeks). In other words, he did not want to be rele-
gated to a separate marginalized space, or what he referred to as the
"Latin jazz *Barrio*."[14] He wanted his music to be taken as a part of the
jazz sphere.

This perspective is not surprising considering Barretto's background.
Of Puerto Rican heritage, raised in New York City, he musically matured
playing next to jazz musicians such as Philly Jo Jones, Art Taylor, Lou
Donaldson, Red Garland, and Kenny Burrell. As a Nuyorican musician
in the 1950s playing congas, an instrument that had not solidly become
part of the jazz scene, he was inevitably seen as a liability. In spite of this,
however, he developed a playing style that adapted itself to swing feels in

an unprecedented way. In the liner notes of the 1958 release of *Manteca,* on which Barretto performs as a featured soloist, critic Ira Gitler attests to his accomplishments and adaptability: "A conga and the title [Manteca] might lead you to believe that this is an Afro-Cuban jazz album. This is not the case. Due to Barretto's rhythmic conception, the standards do not assume a Latin flavor, in spite of the instrument. Barretto, although of Latin descent, does not think, musically, like a Latin."[15]

From this quote we can surmise the type of racism the young Barretto faced and the hard work required to overcome such prejudice. In spite of his difficulties and his financially rewarding salsa career, he steadfastly believed that his alignment with jazz yielded greater prestige and cultural capital. One revealing example occurred while I was performing with his salsa band in California in 2003. I voiced a complaint with Barretto when the band did not receive individual hotel rooms, a common courtesy and something he could have easily lobbied for and obtained as the headliner in a large salsa festival. His response was "What do you think this is? This is a salsa gig, not a jazz gig! In salsa they do not treat musicians like they do in jazz. This is why I stopped playing salsa and prefer to play with my jazz band."[16]

Regardless of the cause of this disparity in the treatment of musicians, for Barretto, there was a sharp social divide and disjunction in the practices and expectations between the different spheres of the continuum. And although he did not disparage generic labels, such as "Latin jazz," he was bothered by their misuse, especially by musicians who dabbled in mixtures and did not respect and maintain what Barretto referred to as the "true essence of both musical traditions." Though he did not provide specific names of guilty musicians, he insisted, "I have no interest in being associated with those cats."[17] As such, he preferred to erase any doubt where his music should be located: firmly within the jazz tradition.

On the one hand, this clear distinction was at the expense of erasing his own rich cultural roots (at least discursively); on the other hand, it strategically centered Caribbean- and Latin American–inflected jazz as inseparable from the jazz tradition. And by extension, it served to acknowledge the significant contribution Caribbean and Latin American musicians have made to a music tradition held as something authentically "American."

Even though Caribbean- and Latin American–inflected jazz styles have been performed since the birth of jazz, it was not until after Machito audaciously named his band "The Afro-Cubans" in 1940, and Dizzy

Gillespie coined the label "Cubop" for his collaborative work with Chano Pozo in 1947, that musicians began to actively engage with the ideologies that underlie impositions of generic order associated with this body of music. During the postwar years, significant stylistic shifts reflected changes in the social landscape, particularly concerning issues of race, and an emboldened younger generation of innovative musicians were asserting difference and striving for artist independence from their predecessors. Labeling became an important signifying tool in this discourse. Machito and Gillespie's influential positions guaranteed a significant presence of Caribbean and Latin American jazz exploration for future generations; however, their insistence on alternative generic labels located their pan-African explorations as something related to, but not a part of, jazz, ensuring a sense of otherness and alterity for generations.

The labels "Cubop" and "Afro-Cuban jazz" predominated until the early 1960s, when the less specific label "Latin jazz" came into fashion. This change was prompted both by the United States' embargo against Cuba, beginning in 1960, which prevented continued exchange with Cuban musicians, and by a number of musicians who began exploring and incorporating musical traditions from many other places throughout the Caribbean and Latin America. The broader term "Latin jazz" aptly captured the growing diversity in musical styles as well as the diminished role of Cuban musicians working abroad. Since the 1960s various other labels that reference specific national, racial, or generic traditions have been used, such as Afro-Colombian jazz, Brazilian jazz, mambo jazz, and Afro–Puerto Rican jazz, but none have been as widely used as the term "Latin jazz."

Regardless, the body of music to which these labels refer has been systematically marginalized ever since the labeling began, evidenced by a "Latin jazz" Grammy category, distinct radio programming formats, and separate programming slots for festivals, clubs, and concert series.[18] O'Farrill's and Barretto's discursive engagements with generic order are the result of the historical legacy of labeling introduced by Machito and Gillespie and the resultant marginalization of that body of music.

This institutionalized differentiation has exposed the music at its very core, and on a foundational level, to the dynamic tensions of center and periphery, mainstream and margins. In this case, I am conceiving of the center as a location of empowerment, authority, and privileges (imagined or real), in terms of economics, nationalism, or cultural capital, while the periphery is a marginal location of a somewhat disempowered difference and alterity. There is a reciprocal relationship between both (one needing the other for its existence), sustained by a dialogic flow of energy and influence. This relationship is not static and can easily be flipped. Like polarized magnets, center and margins never exist in the same space but constantly remain polar opposites and at times can change positions. According to Henry Louis Gates Jr.,

> The threat to the margin comes not from assimilation or dissolution—from any attempt to denude it of its defiant alterity—but, on the contrary, from the center's attempts to preserve that [and contain] alterity, which results in the homogenization of the other as, simply, Other. The margin's resistance to such homogenization, in turn, takes the form of breeding new margins within margins, circles within circles; an ever-renewed process of differentiation, even fragmentation. . . . For the very logocentricity of the center has, at least in certain spheres, conferred special authority on the marginal voice.[19]

Gates's perspective succinctly captures how musicians navigate their position along the continuum (and in stark contrast to the violence of generic labeling), fluidly moving from center to periphery or choosing to remain at the margins, using a discourse of alterity to claim power or create space for innovation.

For musicians, a centered position is not always the most conducive for creativity and many would agree with the observations of Mikhail Bakhtin that "the most intense and productive life of culture takes place on the boundaries."[20] Moreover, musicians often adopt multiple musical identifications or subject positions, which are in sharp contrast to the "apparent 'unities' of collective experience" and thus may inhabit several contrasting positions within an imagined relational framework of the mainstream and marginal.[21]

Within this fluid framework of center and periphery, both O'Farrill and Barretto, each in their own way, attempted to attain a privileged position through divergent inscriptions of the logic of empowerment. In both instances, quite obviously, the act of positioning led to strategic advantages, even at the cost of erasure and cultural denial. In Barretto's case, the center to which he aspired is the jazz mainstream, wanting his Caribbean- and Latin American–inflected jazz to be undifferentiated rather than set apart. O'Farrill, on the other hand, deliberately exploited a marginal position, invoking powerful tropes of alterity (pan-Africanism and pan-Latinismo) to add credence and accentuate the advantages his position could potentially yield. O'Farrill and Barretto shared similar goals, not only seeking better performance opportunities and recognition but also advocating against the continued marginalization of Caribbean- and Latin American–inflected jazz. Each chose to pursue these goals from a differing vantage within a center/periphery framework. In the end, one could argue that Barretto's strategy had a greater impact; however, in fairness to O'Farrill, who is a generation younger, it may still be too early to tell.

Barretto's untiring advocacy from stages across the world (the incident in France being one example) and his performance with a number of renowned jazz musicians culminated in one of the most prestigious jazz honors, a National Endowment of the Arts Jazz Masters Fellowship in 2006. This was quite a remarkable accomplishment, especially when considering that since the program's inception in 1982, only 3 of the 114 Jazz Masters Fellowship recipients have been musicians who primarily played Caribbean- and Latin American–inflected jazz (Paquito D'Rivera in 2005, Barretto in 2006, and Candido Camero in 2008). The fact that all of these awards have been granted within the last few years is significant, representing not only the growing popularity of Caribbean- and Latin American–inflected jazz, but possibly a relational shift between center and periphery and the long overdue recognition of the Caribbean and Latin American contribution to jazz.

Throughout his association with the Lincoln Center, O'Farrill continued to advocate for recognition, both in terms of Afro-Latin jazz's relationship to jazz, and within the interinstitutional dynamics of the Jazz at Lincoln Center program. O'Farrill once stated, "Latin jazz is a misnomer. It doesn't exist. It's part of the same tree as jazz. Jazz and Latin are intertwined in ways that nobody has yet to even understand. In the music drawn from Latin roots we can find keys to both jazz's past and its future. . . . [It is as] worthy of attention as any genre. In fact, in some ways it's more so because it is a music that harkens closer to Africa than anything else in the current jazz pantheon."[22]

Words such as these challenge jazz's status quo and represent O'Farrill's growing frustration working from his marginal position. According to several musicians in the LCALJO, who wished to remain anonymous because they still perform regularly with O'Farrill, he grew increasingly frustrated with his relationship with Lincoln Center, feeling that the LCALJO was not enjoying the same touring schedule and opportunities nor receiving compensation commensurate with Marsalis's LCJO. O'Farrill believed that, once again, this disparity was just one more example of the continued marginalization of Caribbean and Latin American inflected jazz, lamenting, "Ultimately, as in the larger American culture, the Latin group became nothing more than a stepchild" [at Lincoln Center].[23] When he lobbied for greater opportunity and compensation, he was duly fired and the LCALJO was discontinued. Caribbean- and Latin American–inflected jazz performances are still programmed at Lincoln Center, but freelance musicians are now hired for each performance and Paquito D'Rivera is often employed to serve as musical director. O'Farrill continues to lead the Afro Latin Jazz Orchestra under the auspices of his own nonprofit organization, the Afro Latin Jazz Alliance, and they perform a few times a year at New York's Symphony Space.

Fabian Holt observes, "At a basic level genre is a type of category that refers to a particular kind of music within a distinctive cultural web of production, circulation, and signification. That is to say, genre is not only 'in the music,' but also in the minds and bodies of particular groups of people who share certain conventions."[24] The cases of both Arturo O'Farrill and Ray Barretto demonstrate how, in a "distinctive cultural web of production," musicians actively resist, collude, and navigate within the dynamics involved in the framework of center and periphery and how musical genre serves as a communicative field of action, a highly contested arena where ethnic, national, geographic, economic, social, and racial affiliations are forged, and identifications are created and erased. Ultimately, the marginalization of this music presents both advantages and disadvantages to the musicians who make it. Studying how musicians chose to position themselves along the continuum and the discursive strategies involved in acts of self-positioning provides an opportunity to witness the multiplicity and complexities involved in the processes of intercultural production.

NOTES

Special thanks to Ingrid Monson, Kay Shelemay, Richard Wolf, Virginia Danielson, and Katherine Hagedorn for their comments on earlier drafts of this chapter.

    1. Charles Briggs and Richard Bauman, "Genre, Intertextuality, and Social Power," in *Linguistic Anthropology: A Reader,* ed. Alessandro Duranti (1995; repr., Chichester, UK: Wiley Blackwell, 2009), 238.

    2. J. Lorand Matory, "Afro-Atlantic Culture: On the Live Dialogue between Africa and the Americas," in *Africana,* ed. Kwane Appiah and Henry Louis Gates (New York: Basic Civitas, 1999), 36–44.

    3. Tito Puente, interview with the author, 1998, New York.

    4. José Madera, telephone interview with the author, 2001.

    5. Larry Blumenthal, "Cultural Conversation: Arturo O'Farrill, the Son Also Rises—and Embraces His Musical Roots," *Wall Street Journal,* April 29, 2008, D7.

6. Jason Stanyek, "Transmissions of an Interculture: Pan-African Jazz and Intercultural Improvisation," in *The Other Side of Nowhere: Jazz, Improvisation and Communities in Dialogue,* ed. Daniel Fischlin and Ajay Heble (Wesleyan, CT: Wesleyan University Press, 2004), 89.

7. Arturo O'Farrill, interview with the author, December 9, 2005, New York.

8. See Felix M. Padilla, *Latino Ethnic Consciousness: The Case of Mexican Americans and Puerto Ricans in Chicago* (Notre Dame, IN: University of Notre Dame Press, 1985).

9. Joseph Roach, *Cities of the Dead: Circum-Atlantic Performance* (New York: Columbia University Press, 1996), 4, 189.

10. Arturo O'Farrill, quoted in Bill Meredith, "The Latin Tinge: Latin Jazz Is Pounding, Pulsing, Grooving—and Underappreciated," *Jazz Times,* November 2007, 70.

11. The personnel did fluctuate throughout the band's tenure at Lincoln Center; however, the racial and ethnic balance remained fairly stable.

12. Arturo O'Farrill, interview.

13. Vince Cherico (Barretto's drummer), interview with the author, November 4, 2003, New York.

14. Ray Barretto, interview with the author, September 2005, New York.

15. Ira Gitler, liner notes to *Manteca,* Prestige 7139, 1958, compact disc.

16. Ray Barretto, personal communication with author, May 23, 2003.

17. Ibid.

18. Some might argue that a Latin jazz Grammy and separate radio and concert programming are triumphs that represent wider recognition. Indeed, three of Barretto's recordings received nominations in the "Best Latin Jazz Recording" category, and he won a Grammy for the "Best Tropical Latin Performance" in 1989 for the song "Ritmo en el Corazon" with Celia Cruz. O'Farrill also won a Grammy for "Best Latin Jazz Recording" in 2008. Most likely neither musician would have won or received nominations without these specialized categories.

19. Henry Louis Gates Jr., "African American Criticism," in *Redrawing the Boundaries,* ed. Stephen Greenblatt and Giles Gunn (New York: Modern Language Association of America, 1992), 315.

20. Mikhail Bakhtin, *Speech Genres and Other Late Essays,* ed. Caryl Emerson and Michael Holquist (Austin: University of Texas Press, 1986), 2.

21. Georgina Born and David Hesmondhalgh, introduction to *Western Music and Its Others: Difference, Representation, and Appropriation in Music,* ed. Georgina Born and David Hesmondhalgh (Berkeley: University of California Press, 2000), 33.

22. Blumenthal, "Cultural Conversation," D7.

23. Ibid.

24. Fabian Holt, *Genre in Popular Music* (Chicago: University of Chicago Press, 2007), 2.

PART TWO

Practices

CHAPTER 6

Jazz with Strings

Between Jazz and the Great American Songbook

JOHN HOWLAND

In the 1940s and early 1950s there were several important trends in popular music that merged standard big band instrumentation with lush, urbane, string-based backgrounds. These trends, first evident in the early 1940s when a number of prominent bandleaders expanded their ensembles, developed into a highly successful commercial canon of both jazz-with-strings recordings and lush, Nelson Riddle–inspired "American Songbook" vocal recordings. Such mixtures of jazz and popular music idioms with orchestral textures borrowed from film music, musical theater, and certain popular symphonic literature.

As these emulations might suggest, this broad jazz-with-strings repertory is closely related to midcentury trends in American "middlebrowism," a connection especially prominent in this music's overriding glorified entertainment aesthetic and its often presumed dilutions of "higher" musical traditions. While the expression first emerged in the early 1930s, "middlebrow" first gained its negative connotations in the 1940s, when the term was adopted by white cultural critics as a means to describe the pervasive hybridization of mass and highbrow cultures, or rather the watering down or vulgarization of high-culture standards and symbols in popular culture.[1] This demonizing of both commercialism and stylistic hybridity is a direct outgrowth of class politics at midcentury, and these cultural debates are openly reflected in the negative critical reception of much of the jazz-with-strings repertory. Through considerations of select artists, arrangements, contemporary cultural discourses, and criticism, this essay articulates the larger aesthetic issues and cultural conditions that shaped the hybrid, middlebrow ideals of these postwar jazz-with-strings subgenres.

SYMPHONIC JAZZ. ROOTS

The idiomatic symphonic jazz sound, which was widely disseminated across American popular culture of the 1920s and 1930s, provided a musical aesthetic that shaped nearly all postwar big-band-plus-strings trends. Along with the prevalent class hierarchy discourses of the day, the interwar era's growing white interest in black culture initially emerged from 1920s' white artistic celebrations of the American vernacular, and these trends marked an early recognition of the nation's inherent cultural "mongrelization," as historian Ann Douglas has termed it.[2] Symphonic jazz was a central musical nexus for these intersecting cultural discourses. The mongrel cultural aesthetic of this idiom is absolutely key to appreciating the rich cultural threads that define certain postwar jazz trends, for the creators, practitioners, and proponents of the symphonic jazz sound sought not so much to position their music as high culture but rather to mold the musics of Tin Pan Alley, jazz, and the jazz-derived entertainments of Broadway, Harlem, and Hollywood into elegant, glamorous, witty, and refined popular culture. In the interwar era, however, such musico-cultural elevation could be achieved only by bridging the social chasm that separated the privileged highbrow culture of the concert hall and the lowbrow stigma of commercial entertainment, Tin Pan Alley, and black jazz. According to the social politics of the era, this glorification of popular music had to occur under a sophisticated stylistic veneer that emulated the symphonic tradition.

The foremost exponent of the idiom across the 1920s and 1930s was the bandleader Paul Whiteman, whose symphonic jazz paralleled the era's broadly inclusive journalistic uses of the term "jazz"—as both an adjective and a verb—to imply a mildly irreverent interbreeding of high and low (and white and black) cultures. By contrast, the symphonic characterization of this idiom specifically referenced the music's heightened theatricality and heterogeneous stylistic significations: its comparatively complex episodic, multithematic formal structures and especially its emphasis on orchestrational and stylistic variety.

The heart of the artful entertainment aesthetic that shaped the symphonic jazz idiom is found in the music's indiscriminate but purposefully playful juxtapositions of both elevated and vernacular, and black and white, musical idioms. This ideal closely parallels what the cultural critic H.L. Mencken once described as the American penchant for creating novel and colorful new slang locutions through juxtaposition, modification, and playful contextual manipulation.[3] These attributes are also key to this music idiom's often gilded and heterogeneous formal sensibility. The jazzy orchestral sound of this expanded ensemble ultimately came to dominate many American interwar entertainment traditions, and these attributes also provided exemplary targets in the later midcentury critical war against culturally homogenizing middlebrow commercialism.

While important roots for symphonic jazz can be found in the 1910s, it was in the early 1920s that this idiom first emerged. Prior to Paul Whiteman's now-famous 1924 Aeolian Hall concert that premiered *the* cornerstone concert work of symphonic jazz—George Gershwin's *Rhapsody in Blue*—the term "symphonic jazz" was associated with a highly influential style of dance-orchestra arranging popularized by Whiteman's band. The symphonic aspect of this music is more a matter of relative structural, orchestrational, and textural complexity than it is of actual high-culture posturing, and the description of this idiom as symphonic in the early 1920s did not necessarily reflect the Whiteman band's instrumental makeup, whose nine to twelve members fell within the standard hotel- and theater-orchestra instrumentation used in this period (there was typically some configuration of the rhythm section, doubling reeds, brass, and one or two violins). Only in 1924 did the Whiteman outfit expand to the twenty-three-piece concert orchestra—an early big band instrumentation with doubling reeds and an additional full string section—that debuted the *Rhapsody in Blue*.

Despite the multitude of popular manifestations of the symphonic jazz sound well into the 1940s, the early 1930s marked a turning point in its critical reception in jazz historiography. This shift occurred just as jazz-styled concert music had been largely dropped from the topical and aesthetic interests of contemporary art music circles. This lack of highbrow respect or interest—in tandem with the idiom's growing commercial associations (particularly its connections to the more jazzy scores of Hollywood and Broadway) and the tensions between earlier critical claims that the idiom was elevating or legitimating "authentic" jazz (a concept that was ideally captured in the 1920's aphorism about symphonic jazz "making a lady of jazz")—only helped to make white symphonic jazz an easy critical target during the rise of a new post-1930 jazz criticism tradition that defined the music through the rich legacy of African American performers, an emphasis on improvisation, and black musical sounds and aesthetics.

While the term "middlebrow" was not in full public circulation until the mid-1940s, the highbrow reception of such middle-culture activities as "high culture diluted for mass sales and consumption" was definitely present, and for many music critics, symphonic jazz was a primary manifestation of such activities.[4] For better or worse, in pandering to an anti-intellectual American tradition, many of the proponents of symphonic jazz readily promoted their activities as a cultural middle ground and an entertaining art. In general, however, most of the critics of interwar middlebrowism would likely agree with critic Dwight Macdonald's midcentury assessment that "there is something damnably American about Midcult" (his term for middlebrow culture).[5] Indeed, the great achievement of the Whiteman symphonic jazz formula was its ability to bridge urban entertainment styles and the aesthetic tastes of the populations that lived outside of America's cities.

THE JAZZ "CORE" AND GLORIFIED POP

In contrasting symphonic jazz with both the swing era and certain postwar jazz trends, it is useful to bear in mind Scott DeVeaux's distinction between the "core and boundaries" of the jazz tradition. By the "core" tradition DeVeaux means "the essence of the idiom as we have defined it," that is to say, the tradition that has been canonized in post-1930 jazz scholarship. John Szwed has aptly noted that the "boundaries" of this tradition, which he characterizes as "jazz," or jazz-in-quotes, represent a large family of "jazzy," syncopated popular musics that extend from Tin Pan Alley to stage and film musicals, Hollywood film underscoring, 1950s mood music, and the stylizations of various modern pop subgenres, among other trends.[6] That is, the boundaries of the jazz tradition actually include a wealth of sounds and approaches that musicians, critics, and aficionados have resisted calling jazz, despite the fact that much of this music overlaps with core jazz practice in performance, style, arranging conventions, and even in the participation of musicians from the accepted core tradition. Meanwhile, less ideologically invested contemporaries among the general public, promoters, and the press often have had no qualms to explicitly characterize much of this music as jazz.

In retrospect, we can see now that one area the accepted narrative of "authentic" jazz has marginalized is the extensive dialogue, interchanges, and musical overlaps among the worlds of the core jazz tradition and its boundary relations to American popular culture in the early twentieth century. While there is significant value in our narrower, present-day definitions of jazz, in a rich and highly diverse cultural melting pot such as the 1920s and early 1930s in New York, what we now take to be the core jazz tradition by no means existed in an isolated cultural domain. In many ways, it did not exist at all. Even at the height of the swing era in the late 1930s and early 1940s, many of the same professional and stylistic divisions between the hot-jazz/sweet-jazz/commercial dance-band idioms continued to be blurred, because jazz (used here in a broadly inclusive manner) was the very definition of commercial popular music. Jazz was an integrated part of a larger interwar American pop culture centrally defined by an entertainment aesthetic and a myriad of cross-cultural, democratizing trends.

The popular 1920s term "glorified" is appropriate for describing the relation of the symphonic jazz sound to the "hotter" jazz and other popular traditions this music sought to elevate or glamorize. In 1928 the radio conductor B.A. Rolfe characterized the stylistic intent of his Lucky Strike Dance Orchestra's Whiteman-modeled music as "Glorifying American Jazz."[7] Likewise, in his review of Whiteman's 1928 Carnegie Hall concert, the critic Abel Green noted, "*Whiteman is always box-office,* always was and will continue so to be. . . . For all the concert hooey and high-hat aura of . . . Carnegie, [Whiteman] is *too much the showman* to concern himself about such things, so long as he is creating discussion. . . . After all, Whiteman . . . is attuned to the jazz tempo. If this tempo is *symphonized* and *glorified* to approach [the style of a] symphony, it is still basically jazz, and it is manifestly in error to judge Whiteman by any other standards."[8]

In this passage, Green seems to capture succinctly the nature of Whiteman's music, which, Green calls simply "jazz." Most important, Green cautions his *Variety* readers not to be misled by the "glorified" trappings of "the concert hooey and high-hat aura of . . . Carnegie" Hall. Like other critics of the day, Green uses the popular adjective "glorify" to characterize an entertainment act of superficial cultural elevation, an attempt to make something seem better (i.e., more sophisticated, elegant, glamorous, or higher). In my use of this term to describe symphonic jazz, "glorified" is also employed in part as a paraphrase of the time-worn slogan of the Ziegfeld Follies, the influential Broadway revue series that, since 1922, had used "glorifying the American Girl" as both its official theme and literal rubric.

In her book *Ziegfeld Girl: Image and Icon in Culture and Cinema,* the scholar Linda Mizejewski explores both the contextual cultural discourses that surrounded the over-the-top Ziegfeldesque entertainment traditions of female pageantry and grand tableau productions and also this tradition's powerful iconographic reflection of contemporary consumerist desires. The Ziegfeld Girl represented a key embodiment of period concepts of glamour, which, as Mizejewski explains, "is a fairly modern concept involving [the] public visibility of a desirable object, its management or control, and its resulting value as class marker or commodity."[9] In light of Ziegfeld's renowned aesthetic taste and the extravagant costs of his shows, his revues—and their influential entertainment aesthetic model—represented the epitome of contemporary style and fashion.

Similarly, in terms of their close relations to certain production-number arranging traditions in popular music, musical theater (including Ziegfeld's productions), the lavish prologue stage shows of the deluxe movie palaces, and film music of the late 1920s and 1930s, the luxuriant, lush sounds of both symphonic jazz and later jazz-with-strings idioms tap into common period musical codes for glamour and elevated cultural refinement. The self-conscious, overt juxtapositions of culturally high and low musical signifiers in this music (in instrumentation, form, and performance presentation) are central to its aesthetic. Specifically, the elevated gestures of these idioms—their heightened theatricality, their use of strings and other typically symphonic instruments, their complex formal structures—are meant to impart a sense of sophistication, elegance, and artfulness to what some saw as the mundane traditions of popular song. This hybrid instrumental and formal aesthetic has a very long history in American popular music, extending well back into the nineteenth century, through the swing era and into the legacy of postwar American jazz and popular music.

SYMPHONIC SWING

An abbreviated post-1920s outline of strings in jazz orchestration reads something like this: At the onset of the Depression, many of the large, Whiteman-style, symphonic jazz dance bands were forced to downsize

or eliminate string sections. Radio, theater, and film orchestras nevertheless continued to present music in the Whiteman mold. Then came the
1935 boom in the big band business following the rise of Benny Goodman's orchestra. This period saw a near-exclusive adoption of the
brass/reeds/rhythm band model for dance orchestras. Yet by the spring
of 1942 the pendulum had swung back, as *Metronome* magazine remarked on the "mounting number of bands that are adding strings."[10]

A key model for the early 1940s big-band-plus-strings vogue lies in
the arranging conventions of interwar radio orchestras. A fine example
of the growing popularity of elaborate radio production numbers can be
heard in Adolph Deutsch's arrangement of Gershwin's "Clap Yo' Hands"
for Whiteman's orchestra in a 1934 broadcast of the Kraft Music Hall
program. Table 6.1 shows an outline of the extravagant arranging routine for this number. The arrangement unfolds over four different key
areas. It displays a wealth of varied scoring textures that rapidly change
at every four to eight bars. The arrangement includes 1920s Broadway
orchestral textures; pre–swing-era, big band sax soli; Dixieland-jazz
textures; various hot-style solos; a vocal solo by Johnny Mercer; pseudo-
spiritual choral passages; and even vocal contributions from the
band.

Many other bandleaders of the big-band-plus-strings outfits of the
early 1940s had extensive work experience in 1920s symphonic jazz
radio, theater, and dance orchestras. Tommy and Jimmy Dorsey (who
had been members of Whiteman's orchestra in the late 1920s) briefly
recorded grandiose, Whiteman-style arrangements as the studio-based
Dorsey Brothers Concert Orchestra. On at least one recording, the young
conductor Eugene Ormandy directed the ensemble. Despite this self-
conscious classical connection, though, the orchestra was packed with
future swing-era musicians such as Glenn Miller, Phil Napoleon, Chauncey
Morehouse, Hal Kemp, and Skinny Ennis, among others.[11]

A similar trajectory can be seen in the early career of Artie Shaw,
who is often said to have gained overnight success in 1936, but this sudden fame came not with his famous big band but rather with a hybrid
ensemble that consisted of his clarinet, a string quartet, and a rhythm
section. This transition to bandleader was facilitated by his participation in a 1936 New York concert held in Broadway's Imperial Theater.
In his 1952 autobiography, Shaw notes, "up to this time American
dance music had always been a sort of bastard child of 'real' music [i.e.,
classical music]—good enough to be danced to but hardly to be taken

TABLE 6.1. Formal outline to Adolph Deutsch's 1934 radio arrangement of "Clap Yo' Hands" for the Paul Whiteman Orchestra (composed by George and Ira Gershwin)

Section	Measures	Key	Texture
Introduction, part A	4	A♭ major	Broadway show music. Trumpets and trombones exchange with reed background.
Introduction, part B	4 + 4 + 4		Gershwinesque. Tutti.
Chorus 1 (A^1)	8		Sax soli. Pre–swing era, big band texture with sustained string backing. Brass exchange into next phrase.
Chorus 1 (A^2)	8		Varied repeat of (A^1).
Chorus 1 (B)	8		Bix-like trumpet solo (paraphrase improvisation based on written). Sustained strings and reeds background.
Chorus 1 (A^3)	6 (truncated)		Slight variation on texture of (A^1).
Interlude/extension 1	4		Tutti.
Vamp/verse 1 (*not* from original song verse)	8	C minor	"Moaning" trombone solo (Teagarden) with pizzicato strings and reeds background.
Verse 2 (*not* from original song verse)	8		Vocal solo (Mercer) with shouted band/choir responses and a solo vocal response (Teagarden). Repeats background to verse 1.
Chorus 2 (A^1)	8	E♭ major	Solo vocal (Mercer) with Gershwinesque tutti backing and a jazz-styled trumpet section into next phrase.
Chorus 2 (A^2)	8		Varied repeat.
Chorus 2 (B)	8		Quasi-oriental scoring effect with oboe lead backing vocal ("On the sand of time").
Chorus 2 (A^3)	(6 truncated)		Vocal continued. Prominent string backing, often in unison with vocal. Sustained reeds.
Interlude/extension 2	8		Repeated choral "Hallelujah!" passage with light tutti backing and pedal strings.
Interlude/verse 3	4	C major	Vocal solo and chorus (including band) exchanges. Loosely related to original song verse materials. Background largely based on rhythm section with guitarist on prominent banjo part.

TABLE 6.1 *(continued)*

Section	Measures	Key	Texture
Chorus 3 (A^1 varied)	8		Varied repeat.
Chorus 3 (B)	8		Dixie-style big band texture with "hot" clarinet solo (paraphrase improvisation on written solo). Strings out.
Chorus 3 (A^3)	8		Out-chorus big band texture (trombone lead).
A^3 extension (varied repeat)	4		Trombones and saxes continue riff texture (with string backing on beats 2 and 4).
Coda	4		Rising choral "Hallelujah!" ending with tutti backing on beats 2 and 4.

seriously as anything to listen to." He further suggests that in this concert, there was the "rather revolutionary concept" that "'swing' music, as an American idiom, was something to be listened to for itself." With this high-minded intent, Shaw introduced his *Interlude in B-flat,* which was written for clarinet, string quartet, rhythm section, and a "little big band" of tenor saxophone, trumpet, and trombone.[12] At this premiere performance, however, Shaw performed the number without the added little big band. Shaw's *Interlude* is scored with a self-conscious, chamber-style quintet texture that initially features the string quartet alone, followed by a suitably rhapsodic clarinet cadenza over the held strings. At measure 13 of the manuscript score though, modern swing bursts forth in a hybrid chamber jazz scoring for solo clarinet, a lightly swinging rhythm section, little big band interjections (by trumpet, tenor saxophone, and trombone), and sustained strings.

Shaw was one of a growing number of musicians concerned about the social and class stigma of performing in commercial dance bands. The string quartet obviously was added to impart an air of sophistication that tapped into the highbrow aura of classical music. While Shaw's account of the genesis of the *Interlude* emphasizes this work's inspiration in the "clarinet-and-string literature" of Mozart and Brahms, the form of this arrangement comes directly out of a three-strain Whiteman-esque popular concert work tradition of the 1920s and 1930s.[13] Nevertheless, Shaw's *Interlude* is an early example of the idea later embodied in the *Charlie Parker with Strings* sessions.

According to Shaw, there was not a sustaining audience for this unusual ensemble, and he was soon encouraged to organize a conventional big band in its stead. In December 1938, however, Shaw's Whitemanesque aspirations were apparently rekindled when he was invited to be the featured soloist in a bluesy concert number at Whiteman's 1938 Carnegie Hall concert. By the spring of 1940 Shaw had disbanded his standard big band, and he and his newly enlarged studio orchestra, with a full woodwind section and strings, were recording in Hollywood. Several months later, a version of that orchestra was shown in the 1940 film *Second Chorus*. Shaw's cameo role in this 1941 film features rehearsals of his Concerto for Clarinet, as well as a dance production number in which Fred Astaire's character guest conducts a bestringed Shaw orchestra in a bluesy, symphonic jazz concert number.[14]

This Hollywood studio outfit had distinct ties to the late 1920s Whiteman band in that it included such former Whiteman musicians as Charlie Margulis on trumpet, Bill Rank on trombone, and Mischa Russell on violin, as well as arrangements by the sometime Whiteman arranger William Grant Still. Within several months, Shaw reduced this outfit to a standard big band plus strings, though of course the saxophone players were expected to double on other woodwind instruments, in the influential fashion of the Whiteman orchestra. (There were also occasional studio additions of other orchestral woodwinds and French horns.) This latter ensemble was billed as Shaw's Symphonic Swing band. As the critic Paul Grein aptly argues, in Nelson Riddle's later choice to mix "strings with swing orchestra" in his influential work for Frank Sinatra, the arranger "developed an idea that the band leader Artie Shaw had experimented with a decade-and-a-half earlier." Grein also rightly notes that "Riddle's swing-with-strings fusion was more elegant than Shaw's," but the success and sophisticated arrangement of Shaw's Symphonic Swing ensemble notably inspired other top-tier 1940s bandleaders to follow suit with string-section expansions.[15]

Despite the occasional concert-style work recorded by these 1940s outfits, the bulk of their repertory was based on popular song arrangements. According to Shaw, "a string section provides a broader musical palette, just as a wider spectrum of color enables a painter to do more complex things." He likewise broadened his band's instrumental palette through the hiring of the ex–Count Basie trumpeter and singer Oran "Hot Lips" Page, who acted as "kind of a spark plug" to this ensemble.[16]

Shaw's interracial, hot-and-sweet jazz mixed with string section formed the aesthetic heart of the symphonic swing band sound, and this ensemble model is a key forebear to the Sinatra-Riddle sound that emerged in the mid-1950s. Despite the growing popularity of his outfit, Shaw broke up the band after the December 1941 attack of Pearl Harbor and joined the navy.

Example 6.1 presents an excerpt from the bridge to the first chorus from the September 2, 1941, recording of "Blues in the Night," a number that features the trumpet work and singing of Hot Lips Page.[17] From the first notes of Page's opening trumpet solo, it is clear that Shaw's ensemble intended to infuse this big-band-plus-strings texture with a distinctly "hotter" style than Whiteman had featured in the late 1930s. (Though the Whiteman orchestra of this later period included a number of star swing soloists, including trombonist Jack Teagarden, as well as the author of "Blues in the Night," the singer/composer Johnny Mercer.)

In this bridge passage, the string section is employed as an added third texture to contrast the brass and reed sections. Here, the strings seemingly replace the saxes in what might have been a typical texture with reeds backing a vocal alongside blues-based responsorial interjections by the trombones. That said, this textural substitution is not direct in either melodic and harmonic content or phrasing. The use of the strings here clearly displays various idiomatic commercial string textures, as can be seen, for instance, in the prominent use of swooning glissandi between key harmonies in the progression. Likewise, note that Shaw purposefully sets the three-note harmony voicings in the violin section with prominent octave-spread outer voices set in dissonant diminished and augmented fifth relations with an internal voice. The strings are set homophonically as a section; thus the octave-based countermelody of the violins is quite prominent, and even more so since it equally favors both chromatic movement and dissonant intervallic leaps in its melodic contour. The quasi-modernist effect of this dissonant, nonlinear string arrangement is likely meant to distance the string texture here from the saccharine commercial style of string writing found in contemporary radio orchestras, yet it is also different in style from the typical saxophone voicing that one might expect to underscore this number in Shaw's earlier big band. The string scoring conventions seen here, then, are key components in Shaw's efforts to create a concert-style band for listening rather than dancing, and they

EXAMPLE 6.1. Artie Shaw, "Blues in the Night," measures 34–42
(Harold Arlen and Johnny Mercer; arranged by Sy Oliver).

resonate with similar string textures in the concert-style numbers of this outfit.

Following the success of the similarly expanded Shaw and Harry James bands, a number of major swing orchestras added strings in the early 1940s. For instance, the 1944 big band of the famous black pianist and bandleader Earl Hines featured for several months an all-female string section and a harp.[18] During this period, Hines notably told *Metronome* of his long-standing desire to "do something like . . . Whiteman [but] along jazz lines."[19] Like the Whiteman band in the 1920s, these swing-era hybrid ensembles were employed as multidimensional musical units. While these outfits featured hot-style big band arrangements, they equally emphasized sweet-style ballads and occasional concert-style numbers, thereby intentionally building an ensemble and band book suitable for dance dates as well as theater, hotel, or radio work. These groups also usually included a coterie of singers and often featured a small group within the group that performed hot jazz. These all-in-one types of symphonic swing bands of the early 1940s—especially Tommy Dorsey's outfit—form the foundations of the later Sinatra-Riddle sound, and indeed this lineage is fairly direct, as many of the Capitol Records studio musicians on Sinatra's mid-1950s recordings were alumni of the early 1940s Dorsey orchestra.

The full potential of these symphonic swing orchestras was chiefly realized in the critically overlooked big band venue of movie theater prologue revue shows. These jobs were highly prized among both white and black bands, with or without strings. Most of these revues featured bands set amid extravagant stage settings, with performances of current hits; ballads and up-tempo pieces, hot-style numbers; event-specific extended production or medley arrangements; instrumental soloist features; and backgrounds for novelty numbers, comedians, acrobats, and dancers. In vocal-heavy, sweet-style big bands such as Tommy Dorsey's, singers were also featured in what critic Will Friedwald has aptly termed "movie-style production numbers—three-ring circuses that involved several spotlighted singers, a vocal group, and any number of instrumental soloists."[20]

In early 1942 Dorsey annexed Shaw's violin section en masse.[21] At that time, Dorsey's main arrangers were the ex–Jimmy Lunceford arranger Sy Oliver, an up-tempo specialist, and Axel Stordahl, who specialized in scoring romantic ballads for the young Frank Sinatra. Oliver's arranging in the 1930s defined the sound of Lunceford's 1930s orchestra. When he left this celebrated band for the greater monetary rewards and broader audience of the Dorsey ensemble, his arranging, trumpet work, and distinctive vocals infused this first-tier white orchestra with a greatly valued quality of hot Harlem-style jazz. This interracial collaboration was obviously not without precedents, since Benny Goodman's breakthrough swing band was built on the arrangements of Fletcher Henderson and other black arrangers, and Goodman had hired various black musicians for small ensemble work. Likewise, Artie Shaw's Symphonic Swing orchestra included Hot Lips Page as a central instrumental voice. This interracial jazz texture of sweet-style white swing and black instrumental voices is yet another important model that points to the later Sinatra-Riddle sound, with musicians such as Count Basie's one-time star trumpeter, Harry "Sweets" Edison, performing the comparable role to Page and Oliver in most mid-1950s Sinatra-Riddle recordings.

This connection is not coincidental. Both Sinatra and Riddle looked back to Oliver's work for the Dorsey band-plus-strings configuration as the foundation for their 1950s collaborations. According to Riddle, at the beginning of their association, he and Sinatra had numerous discussions about their "mutual admiration for Tommy Dorsey." He once noted that "in planning [the landmark 1956 Sinatra-Riddle album] *Songs for Swingin' Lovers,* Frank commented on 'sustained strings' as part of the background to be used. Perhaps unconsciously my ear recalled some of the fine arrangements Sy Oliver had done for Tommy, using sustained strings but also employing rhythmic fills by brass and saxes to generate excitement. The strings . . . add to the pace and tension of such writing. . . . It was a further embroidery to add the bass trombone . . . plus the . . . fills of Harry 'Sweets' Edison on Harmon-muted trumpet."[22]

This description provides the basic outline of the characteristic uptempo idiom that Riddle employed for Sinatra's Capitol recordings. The opening of Oliver's celebrated 1944 arrangement of "On the Sunny Side of the Street" for the Dorsey Orchestra demonstrates the basic band-plus-strings texture that Riddle admired in Oliver's writing.[23] This recording was Oliver's biggest hit with this ensemble. Despite the string section, the disc underscores Oliver's assertion that Dorsey "wanted a Swing band," and that the bandleader had "changed personnel until he got the guys that *could* do it." Oliver was one of these personnel additions, and his hiring highlights the point that

Dorsey specifically wanted to infuse his orchestra with key elements of the trademark Lunceford sound. As Oliver noted, "when I moved from the Lunceford band to Tommy Dorsey, I didn't change my writing approach."[24]

While this statement clearly holds some truth, it also neglects to note the expansion of his style to include his use of strings. This added texture, when combined with the basic musical identities of both Dorsey and Oliver, created a somewhat gentler version of the two-beat rocking, rhythmic swing of the Lunceford band. Many of the Oliver swing and popular-song arrangements for Dorsey are built on a soft, two-beat rhythmic feel borrowed directly from Oliver's Lunceford work. This swing sensibility is immediately felt in the "Sunny Side" arrangement. Likewise, Oliver's trademark Lunceford-era interests in novelty effects and extreme textural and dynamic juxtapositions and contrasts is evident in the eight-bar introduction's layering of sforzando, two-chord brass and reed punctuations (brass on the first note, the reed color dominating the second), set against a mezzo forte baritone sax tonic pedal-point ostinato, occasional arpeggiated obbligato piano interjections, and an even softer foundational layer of strings that harmonically cushion the whole episode. At the entry of the instrumental statement of the first chorus, the strings segue to a harmonic background of saxophones and guitar-dominated rhythm section, which underscores the muted trumpet section melodic statement.

While the string section clearly adds a pleasant contrapuntal line against the primary melodic materials of the introduction, the strings are not given a distinctive melodic line themselves. Rather, they take on the "sustained" quality that Riddle appreciated. Throughout the chart, the string part generally moves by stepwise rising motion, primarily following the harmonic rhythm by adding half-note shifts or sustaining across chords on common tones between chords. The rising contrapuntal line of the string part, to paraphrase Riddle, adds to the "pace and tension" of the episode "without getting in the way." The part infuses the introduction with a sense of dramatic shape, melodically and harmonically. The harmony is fundamentally built on an elaborated I-IV-V-I progression. Dramatic tension rises through the dissonances created between the tonic pedal and the primary melodic notes of the violin section. Melodically, the four notes of the string part form a rising arc. The first note of measures 1–2 is the third of the tonic, which in turn moves up a half step in measures 3–4. The new note becomes the root of the subdominant chord but forms an eleventh with the baritone sax dominant. The arc then peaks as the violin line moves up to a flat-9 tone for the dominant chord, which forms the dissonance of a flat-13 (or augmented fifth) tone above the tonic pedal in measures 5–6. In measures 7–8, the strings subtly reduce dynamics and the line moves a half step downward to a resolution on the fifth note of the tonic chord. This introduction and its segue to the first chorus show Oliver's imaginative craft in designing a rich musical fabric built from a series of simple elements. The introduction, for instance, derives maximum dramatic effect from a very spacious and aurally transparent setting of a few discrete elements. Such a sensibility is of central importance to Riddle's later postwar, jazz-pop swing style.

LUSH POP IN THE 1940S: FROM SINATRA AND STORDAHL TO MOOD MUSIC

An important early outgrowth of the 1940s big-band-plus-strings vogue was the rise of melodramatic, quasi-symphonic ballad orchestrations for popular vocalists such as Frank Sinatra, who began his solo career in September 1942. Sinatra's post-Dorsey "crooner" period is defined by the arrangements of the ex-Dorsey arranger Axel Stordahl.

In comparing the 1940s Columbia recording and persona of Sinatra with the 1950s Capitol Records rebirth of the singer, the *New York Times* critic John Rockwell has noted,

> The musical style captured in this Columbia Sinatra set will strike most non-nostalgists and non-Sinatra cultists as bland and sticky-sweet. . . . Everything is insistent ingenue vulnerability, pretty at the expense of almost every other emotional or musical virtue.
>
> The arrangements [of the Columbia era], mostly by Mr. Sinatra's standby during this decade, Axel Stordahl, have dated badly, however much we may try to be sympathetic to the conventions of yesteryear. Twinkling harps, swooning strings and above all those terrible mewling [vocal] choruses all subvert even the strongest performances.[25]

Rockwell's comments reveal a typical post-1960 critical assessment of the differences between the Stordahl and Riddle arrangements for Columbia and Capitol, respectively. The idiom of the earlier period is heard to be dated, while the latter continues to be held up as a timeless cornerstone in American popular culture—indeed, the latter idiom is now held to be "traditional pop." Rockwell's remarks reflect a stylistic predilection rather than a characterization of arranging skills, of course, as close attention reveals Stordahl to be one of the most adroit vocal arrangers of the 1940s, a figure who crafted very finely tuned backgrounds for the era's defining pop music voice.

Despite this Columbia/Capitol division, an ideal example of this sound can be found in Sinatra's first recordings for the latter company in 1953. The lack of commercial sales for these Capitol sides ultimately led to the singer's celebrated partnership with Riddle, who had also worked for Dorsey. Example 6.2 shows the lush, melodramatic opening of the 1953 Columbia-style arrangement of "I'm Walking behind You."[26] This chart, too, abounds in the sort of "twinkling harps" and "swooning strings" that Rockwell abhorred. The ensemble also features such overtly symphonic instruments as French horns, flutes, oboes, and harp (though at times Shaw's band included several of these instruments). The melodramatic arrangement further employs string glissandi as part of the swooning, romantic effects that likely were meant to underscore the sorts of vocal portimento effects that Sinatra employed to send bobby soxers into amorous delirium. More important, Stordahl clearly places great emphasis on constructing richly harmonized, strong section countermelodies that compliment the non-doubled vocal part. Despite the classical aura his string writing might impart, this association has more to do with the cultural- and class-based aura of the instrument family rather than the writing itself. If reduced to simply a piano part (which seems to be how Stordahl approached arranging), one can readily hear a great similarity to the quasi-orchestral piano style of the era's cocktail piano traditions. In fact, the entire arrangement can be transcribed note for note to be comfortably played by a single pianist.

Despite the somewhat densely harmonized and frequently moving string parts, Stordahl leaves plenty of room for Sinatra's voice. Accompanimental motion regularly slows when the vocal part moves, and it provides ornamental fills where Sinatra's part pauses. Harmonically, the arrangement is rather straightforward when compared to the riches of the big band arranging tradition. Dissonance is used sparingly for dramatic effect, such as the Db 9/#5 harmony that Stordahl introduces for a "pained" effect in response to the lines "Though you may forget me." The aforementioned semiclassical textures are readily heard in the introduction's rubato call-and-response between the sweeping strings, a texture complemented with two clarinets, an oboe, and harp glissandi, on the one hand, and the horn answers, on the other hand—all of which

EXAMPLE 6.2. Frank Sinatra, "I'm Walking behind You," measures 1–14 (Billy Reid; arranged by Axel Stordahl).

EXAMPLE 6.2 (continued)

is performed sans rhythm section, which enters subtly under the vocal chorus.

Another major figure in the continued commercial expansion of the 1940s big-band-plus-strings vogue was the ex-Dorsey arranger, Paul Weston. By 1944 Weston was the musical director for the newly formed Capitol Records. Along with Stordahl, Weston's arrangements for Capitol singers such as Jo Stafford and Peggy Lee epitomize the pop vocal arranging conventions of the day. However, it was Weston's instrumental albums that created the highly successful new genre of "mood music." This latter development has important ties to earlier trends, such as the sweet-style dance orchestras of the swing era, the rise of the Muzak corporation in the mid-1930s, and the 1930s light music repertories of certain radio orchestras.

The Weston mood music model notably favored prewar hit songs from the 1920s through the early 1940s—that is, the repertory that we now call "standards." Weston later described his arranging and big band performance formulas for these recordings as "underplayed," "underarranged," and "on-the-melody." This approach can be heard in Weston's 1946 version of "You Go to My Head,"[27] a recording that employed the sort of subdued big band textures that were held to have fallen out of taste with postwar audiences. Here tempo is greatly reduced, blaring brass textures are entirely absent, and there is an emphasis on lush, Glenn Milleresque five-part, close-position sax voicings. These settings further include a restrained, pianoless rhythm section. Weston's charts also typically involve lush introductions, featuring strings, harp, and reed textures. The arrangements as a whole leave only a small amount of room for ornamental improvisation from soloists. In direct contrast to the design-intensive "sophistication" of the symphonic jazz tradition, Weston's arranging routines are regularly reduced to one- or two-choruses with no modulation and at most only a few additional measures for either an introduction, single interlude, or tag coda.

MAKING A LADY OF MODERN JAZZ

In a postwar environment that saw both the decline of the dance-band industry and an increase in concert-setting performances of jazz, various bandleaders and arrangers began to experiment with new harmonic and formal devices and further symphonic-leaning ensemble augmentations. In contrast to the overtly commercial intent of Weston's "underarranged" mood music formula, several arrangers notably began to explore comparatively complex textures that stylistically emulated the music of prewar modernist composers such as Igor Stravinsky and Paul Hindemith. By the late 1940s this new, self-consciously complex big band music was called "progressive jazz," but its roots lay several years earlier. In 1946 the producer Norman Granz began to commission recordings for his landmark album, *The Jazz Scene* (which was released in 1949).[28]

Two of the artists to use strings in this project were the arrangers Neal Hefti and George Handy, both of whom were later associated with progressive jazz. Significantly, saxophonist Charlie Parker's first performance with strings occurred in the 1946 recording of Hefti's composition "Repetition." Handy's contribution to *The Jazz Scene,* his composition "The Bloos," ably illustrates several early intersections between progressive jazz and the burgeoning big-band-plus-strings vogue. As seen in table 6.2, this work is built from three strains, one of which is a simple blues chorus that is repeated twice for an improvised tenor sax solo. Like "Clap Yo' Hands," Handy's arrangement for "The Bloos" restlessly shifts scoring textures at every four- to eight-bar phrase.[29] Beyond his use of dissonant harmonic extensions, Handy's progressive textures are built from melodramatic, widely varying tempi and performance gestures, a hyperactive palate of dynamic shadings, and smatterings of ritards and rubato cadenzas.

While progressive jazz originally received front-page press coverage, and its leading proponents, such as Stan Kenton's orchestra and its arranger Pete Rugolo, routinely won *Down Beat* readers' polls, many critics remained wary of the idiom. This concern was expressed by the jazz scholar Marshall Stearns, who suggested in 1956 that progressive jazz "reversed Paul Whiteman's formula by adapting jazz to academic [modernist] music," thereby resulting in a negative "diffusion of [real] jazz." This concern for the mutual watering down of both modern jazz and modern classical music reflects larger period concerns about middlebrowism. *Down Beat*'s record reviewer saw similar middlebrow modernist pretensions in the "[Warner Brothers] big movie brass effects" of "The Bloos," though he read these elements as indications of "a brilliant . . . satire."[30]

These critical suspicions of middlebrow intent were most prominently leveled at the high-profile career of Stan Kenton, the bandleader who most popularized the term "progressive jazz." In 1949 Kenton unveiled his Innovations in Modern Music Orchestra. The Innovations Orchestra was a standard big band augmented by a sixteen-piece string section, an expanded woodwinds section, French horns, and harp. A 1950 concert program notes that with this group, Kenton had "grown into manhood—and with manhood comes . . . musical maturity."[31] This mature repertory ranged from atonal concert-style works with occasional bebop episodes, to more traditional big band arrangements with room for improvisation. The orchestra also featured elaborate vocal arrangements by Pete Rugolo written for June Christy. The February 1950 recording of "Lonesome Road" offers an ideal representation of the hybrid art/entertainment aesthetic of these production arrangements

TABLE 6.2. Formal outline for George Handy's arrangement of "Bloos" (composed by George Handy)

Section	Measures	Key	Texture
Strain 1 (A^1)	8	C major/minor	Oboe lead with strings and celeste background (rhythm out). "Progressive" two-measure reed and brass answer to phrase.
Strain 1 (A^2)	8		Varied repeat.
Strain 1 (B)	8		Brass-heavy, melodramatic extension of the previous answer to A phrase. Single violin and oboe emerge out of held chord and bridge into next phrase.
Strain 1 (A^3)	8+2		Variation on A phrase with added solo violin and oboe. Includes two-measure extension pickup.
Strain 1 (C^1)	8+8	G major	Brass-heavy concert jazz antecedent phrase (without rhythm section) and a symphonic-style consequent phrase led by woodwinds (oboe, bassoon, contra bassoon).
Strain 1 (C^2)	8+8		Varied repeat (with new French horn soli).
Interlude, part 1	8	—	Variation on motives from phrase C over high violin pedal. Call-response between concert-jazz and symphonic textures. Gives way to sustained *Tristan* prelude type string texture.
Violin cadenza	3	—	Overt "classical" effect. Violin cadenza over held "symphonic" chord in reeds and strings.
Interlude, part 2	6	—	"Progressive" jazzy chord stabs in response to cadenza. Dovetailed into jazz trombone solo (over strings and celeste).
Strain 2	20 (6+6+2 ext.+6)	[unstable]	Jazz trombone solo over shifting harmonic progression. Melodramatically backed by oboe and strings (ref. both pop and symphony orchestra traditions) with alternately subdued and bombastic big band. Closing four-measure trombone cadenza.

TABLE 6.2 *(continued)*

Section	Measures	Key	Texture
C³ phrase variation	4 + 4	G major	Repeat of opening Strain 1 (C) phrase, with improvised jazz sax solo ending backed by rhythm section and pizzicato strings.
Blues chorus 1	12	D	Improvised sax solo with rhythm section only.
Blues chorus 2	12		Continued.
Interlude	4		Screeching big band interjections followed by odd "symphonic" oboe cadenza.
Strain 1 (A¹)	8	C major/minor	See previous.
Strain 1 (A²)	8		See previous.
Coda	3		Varied repeat of phrase A² material with ominous ensemble swell.

(see table 6.3).³² The arrangement's introduction displays a bombastic, dissonant, "progressive" texture with Christy's vocalise on top and a slow, rubato tempo (see ex. 6.3). Chorus 1 develops this melodramatic pop-modernist texture through phrase turnaround and scoring shifts at each phrase. Big band jazz fully enters at the double-time interlude.

The progressive textures of "Lonesome Road" are largely scoring effects superimposed on top of a standard vocal arrangement routine, though Rugolo's design-intensive approach clearly recalls the production arrangements of symphonic jazz dance bands and radio orchestras. This sort of connection was not lost on Kenton's detractors. One reviewer noted that he had "the terrifying thought that maybe . . . [Kenton] was the Paul Whiteman of the day."³³ This reception was ultimately the undoing of Kenton's position in the modern jazz canon.

PARKER, GRANZ, AND JAZZ SOLOISTS WITH STRINGS

Unlike Kenton's progressive jazz, which has mostly faded into obscurity, the recordings of *Charlie Parker with Strings* from this same period sell remarkably well to this day. But despite the commercial success and their influence on generations of jazz-soloist-with-strings recordings and events, they have had a problematic critical reception in jazz historiography. Notwithstanding their intention to showcase the "modern" improvisational voice of Parker, the "with strings" backing charts are

TABLE 6.3. Formal outline for Pete Rugolo's arrangement of "Lonesome Road" for Stan Kenton (composed by Gene Austin and Nathaniel Shilkret)

Section	Measures	Key	Texture
Introduction	12	B♭ major	Slow, bombastic, quasi-atonal concert texture (tutti) with semipop vocalise. Variations on chorus (A) themes, including "progressive" response motive. Rhythm section out.
Chorus 1 (A^1)	6 + 2		Sultry vocals with reed-led (oboe, tenor, bassoon) background with low brass and strings. "Progressive" motive (two measures). Light rhythm (brushes).
Chorus 1 (A^2)	8		Vocal with background of muted strings and brassy, flag-waving jazz ensemble segue to next phrase (two measures).
Chorus 1 (B)	8		Melodramatic "symphonic" texture with rubato tempo, tremolo strings, and brass-heavy stabs. Rhythm out.
Chorus 1 (A^3)	6 (truncated)		Lush, sultry strings. Similar to phrase A^1 with strings varying the previous reed part. Light rhythm (brushes).
Interlude	16		Big band jazz enters in double time (with rhythm). Vocal out. Vamplike, with motivic interplay and gradual building of forces. Very light string use.
Chorus 2 (A^1)	8	B♭ major	Big band texture in tempo, with vocal and string interjections.
Chorus 2 (A^2)	8		Vocal and background of reeds and French horns with brassy segue (two measures).
Chorus 2 (B)	8		Vocal and lush, jazz-styled pop strings (akin to sax writing).
Chorus 2 (A^3)	6 + 2		Recalls Chorus 2 (A^1) (six measures) and "Progressive" motive (two measures).
Chorus 3 (A^1)	8		Recalls Chorus 1 (A^1).
Coda	5		Variation on introduction.

fairly conventional, radio-orchestra–style arrangements with only rare touches of Rugolo-leaning progressive textural coloring.

The 1949 recording of "Just Friends" notably became the best-selling record of Parker's career.[34] Jimmy Carroll arranged this chart for Parker's alto along with five strings, harp, oboe, and rhythm section. As seen

EXAMPLE 6.3. Stan Kenton, "Lonesome Road," measures 5–14 (Gene Austin and Nathaniel Shilkret; arranged by Pete Rugolo).

continued

EXAMPLE 6.3 (*continued*)

in example 6.4, the arrangement begins with a four-bar, Stordahl-style mock-concert texture of a cello solo backed by swelling tremolo strings and sweeping harp arpeggios. At the fifth bar, Parker enters in double time with cadenzalike flourishes over a sustained, shimmering tremolo string backing. Parker then seamlessly glides into his embellished statement of the chorus melody. In the manner of many of the glorified arranging models discussed earlier, the backgrounds of the initial chorus are varied with each eight-bar phrase. Table 6.4 charts out the remainder of the arrangement. Carroll's work on "Just Friends" has been singled out by jazz critics as the highlight of these Parker recordings because, unlike many of the other "with strings" charts, it gave Parker ample space for full improvisation across another chorus and a half, plus the coda.

In interviews of this period, Parker regularly expressed his keen interest in the music of various prewar modernist composers (e.g., Stravinsky and Hindemith). With these statements in mind, many critics have been deeply puzzled by the overtly commercial sound of the "with

EXAMPLE 6.4. Charlie Parker, "Just Friends," measures 1–11 (John Klenner and Sam Lewis; arranged by Jimmy Carroll).

continued

EXAMPLE 6.4 (continued)

strings" arrangements. Some critics have suggested that Parker was contractually coerced into making these recordings. In response, Parker noted that "my friends said 'Oh, Bird is getting commercial.' That wasn't it at all. I was looking for new ways of saying things musically. . . . I asked for strings as far back as 1941." This claim is backed by Parker's producer, Norman Granz. In 2001 Granz further remarked that "I'm most criticized for . . . *Bird with Strings,* like this [project] was a crime against humanity. . . . Charlie . . . virtually put a gun to my head, insisting he wanted . . . strings. . . . [Likewise] . . . Lester Young . . . Ben Webster . . . [and] Johnny Hodges [all] wanted strings."[35] The negative reception of these recordings in jazz critic circles may have been

TABLE 6.4. Formal outline for Jimmy Carroll's arrangement of "Just Friends" for Charlie Parker (composed by John Klenner and Sam Lewis)

Section	Measures	Key	Texture
Introduction, part 1	4	A♭ major	Mock concert texture: cello solo and strings, harp.
Introduction, part 2	4 + 2		Jazz texture: Parker solo and rhythm, strings, harp.
Chorus 1 (A^1)	8		Parker solo (ornamented melody) and strings, harp, rhythm.
Chorus 1 (B^1)	8		Same (with occasional pizzicato strings).
Chorus 1 (A^2)	8		Strings soli and harp, rhythm (Parker out).
Chorus 1 (B^2)	8		Parker solo (ornamented melody) and strings, harp, rhythm.
Interlude	4	A♭ major	Oboe solo and tremolo strings, rhythm (Parker out).
Chorus 2	30 + 4 mm. extension	B♭ major	Parker solo and rhythm, strings (arco and pizzicato), harp.
Chorus 3 (A^1 + B^1)	16		Piano solo and rhythm, strings, harp.
Chorus 3 (A^2 + B^2)	30 (truncated)		Repeated texture from chorus 2 (A^2 + B^2).
Coda	8		Parker, strings, harp, rhythm.

sparked by Granz's liner notes for the original LP release of these recordings, in which he wrote,

> Unfortunately . . . the [mass] public has been slow in its acceptance of [Parker's music]. . . .
>
> All of the music in this album shows a new Parker to most listeners. He plays the melody very closely and it's good that he does, for the tunes are truly beautiful. . . . Some of the harsh effects achieved heretofore by Parker's [bebop] ensemble are nowhere noticeable here, [with] the strings softening and prettying Parker; and Parker, for the first time, plays with truly great [legitimate] musicians, which meant he had to be, as it were, on his best musical behavior.[36]

These gendered, classist comments about "softening and prettying" Parker with a backing string ensemble of "great musicians" resonate loudly with a long history of commentary around various jazz-with-strings endeavors. Most important, in the 1920s, it was a popularly held notion that Gershwin "made a lady of jazz" and that Whiteman was the musician who had brought dignity and highbrow respect to this supposedly lowbrow music.

In the opinion of mid-1930s jazz critics such as Winthrop Sargeant, however, the symphonic jazz idiom was seen as a commercial vulgarization of "true" jazz. To Sargeant and his critical peers, the former music was characterized by its "fusion of the pretentious and commonplace," its "slick and striking," "gilded, exotic, orchestral effects."[37] These damning claims against Whiteman's jazz aptly foreshadow Granz's "criminal" characterizations of the 1950s and 1960s jazz-with-strings vogue, which was critically received through similar class-hierarchy culture filters that strictly read the music in terms of the never-to-be-combined cultural roles of modern jazz, middlebrow musical kitsch, commercial entertainment, and "legitimate" concert music.

To paraphrase the Whiteman camp, it sounds like Granz was worried that he might be accused of "making a lady" of modern jazz—a metaphorical notion that post-1930 jazz critics would likely have equated with a sort of musical emasculation and as a clear cultural opposite to highbrow, "legitimate" music. This class-oriented and gendered reading stands in direct contrast to the hypermasculine, modernist arranging strategies of Kenton and his progressive jazz peers, musicians who self-consciously sought to avoid associations with the new, culturally devalued (read "overtly commercial") sounds of mood music and the *Your Hit Parade*-style radio orchestras of the day. While this self-described "musically mature" *progressive* (instead of "regressive"?), often bombastic sound ideal sought to evoke the highbrow cultural aura of then-current notions of modernist concert music, Kenton's clear ties to popular music ("Lonesome Road"), jazz, and huckster-style showmanship (which is readily apparent in various Kenton poses on his publicity literature and several albums covers), clearly repositioned these trends squarely back in the territory of midcentury middlebrow culture.

CONCLUSION

This chapter's focus has been concerned with the often critically disparaged gray area that lies between the "core and boundaries" of the canonic jazz tradition ("the essence of the idiom as we have defined it") on the one hand, and the emerging idiomatic sound of the celebrated midcentury vocal recordings that we now identify as the "Great American Songbook" repertory on the other. The music trends I have outlined ultimately led to a highly successful *commercial* jazz canon that includes both jazz-soloist-with-strings recordings and the vocal American Song-book repertory and its big-band-plus-strings arranging conventions.

While the post-1950 golden age of the latter tradition is, of course, a topic for another essay, we must recognize that jazz emerged as a *marketing* category distinct from popular music only *after* jazz was no longer a popular music for the dancing and youth markets of the swing era. Indeed, while the core jazz tradition was certainly a concern for many musicians, critics, and aficionado fans through much of the 1930s and 1940s, major music business sources reveal that this idiom was commonly viewed by the broader public and industry alike as an intertwined facet of larger, overarching popular music genre conceptions of the day.

One observes, for example, that over *Down Beat*'s first several years of operation (in the mid-1930s), the title banner of the magazine proudly proclaimed that its coverage extended to "Ballroom, Cafe, Radio, Studio, Symphony and Theater." *Jazz* was not even mentioned (though, of course, jazz was a subject in the magazine's pages). Moreover, it was not until 1953 that for the first time the genre categories of the magazine's annual readers' polls refer to jazz among their "best of" categories. That same year the magazine inaugurated its critics' poll, which initially focused *only* on the core jazz tradition, thus underscoring this later period's role as a key historiographic moment in the critical elevation of jazz from its popular culture roots.[38]

Similarly, it was not until 1953 that *Billboard* finally introduced a "Jazz" recording sales column. On April 23, 1955, however, the magazine featured a front-page pronouncement that "Jazz Disks, Paced by LP, Hit Cool 55% Jump in Hot Year," accompanied by several companion articles on jazz, including an editorial titled "The Jazz Renaissance." For *Billboard*, this mid-1950s "Jazz Renaissance" boom marks the very moment that jazz became a marketing category distinct from popular music.[39] This moment arrives in near parallel with the initial flowering of the aforementioned, midcentury vocal Songbook tradition. Most notably, since the late 1980s, Sinatra's—and also Ella Fitzgerald's—recordings from this period have come to embody the quintessential big-band-plus-strings sound of what the National Academy of Recording Arts and Sciences has characterized as "traditional pop," regardless of their performance and stylistic proximity to the core jazz tradition.

While the Parker-with-strings recordings have long been appreciated among both the record-buying general public and lay jazz fans, that model has routinely been situated as a commercial, bastard stepchild of jazz proper (i.e., the core of this tradition) by many aficionados, critics, and jazz historians. Even so, through sheer sales numbers and their back-catalog staying power in the marketplace, the Parker-with-strings recordings represent an anomaly—a commercial success—in the history of postwar jazz. Despite the occasional critical appreciation afforded some other "with strings" efforts—like those by trumpeter Clifford Brown (e.g., his 1955 album, *Clifford Brown with Strings*) or saxophonist Stan Getz (beginning with the 1960 album, *Cool Velvet*)—the most prominent popular commercial success in this tradition after Parker is likely found in the many "with strings" contributions of pianist Oscar Peterson, which in some cases sound conspicuously close to being updates on the Weston mood music formula for easy listening ballads.

Such connections can be heard and seen, for example, in a release such as the 1957 Peterson album, *Soft Sands,* which features gentle piano-plus-orchestra arrangements of ballads, as well as a typical period "vinyl vixen" album cover, the latter of which reflects a widespread, midcentury mood music marketing practice that featured gauzy cover images of alluring women in seductive and romantic poses (in this case, the album cover involves a close-up head shot of a young blond beauty lying in the sand with a sultry red flower in her hair), a marketing trend that began at Capitol Records in the early 1950s with the jazz-with-strings-inflected mood music albums of Jackie Gleason.[40] While these sorts of images appeared on album covers for many music genres, they were absolutely central to the fashionable jazz-inflected mood music and "Music for [fill in the activity; e.g., 'a Rainy Day']" easy listening albums of the 1950s and 1960s. Indeed, there are a host of big-name jazz artists—for example, pianist George Shearing (his 1956 *Black Satin* and *Velvet Carpet* albums) or saxophonist Sonny Stitt (*The Sensual Sound of Sonny Stitt* from 1961)—who released such overtly commercial jazz albums in this vein (vinyl vixen covers and all).

One goal of this essay has been to articulate a greater—and more nuanced—historical context for the emergence of the jazz-soloist-with-strings traditions. But while these improvising-soloist-with-strings albums seem to form a mass-market, popular canon of jazz recordings, they are decidedly *not* deemed to be part of the accepted canon of jazz that is taught in classrooms or that has been the traditional concern of jazz historiography. Even if some might argue that the Parker-with-strings releases could be considered as part of the jazz canon (unlike the big-band-plus-strings efforts of Kenton or Weston, for example), they have been viewed this way solely because of Parker's indisputable canonic role in jazz history and the considerable strengths of his inspired solos in these recordings. In fact, the backing textures (the "with strings" part) of these releases have been routinely characterized by critics as extraneous, dispensable, irrelevant, or embarrassing facets of these recordings—not something worthy of the jazz canon or of serious critical consideration, even despite the recurrent historical popularity of similar backing textures among jazz artists (including, among others, Wynton Marsalis). Such a mixed-message critical stance—wherein a critic praises Parker's performance while simultaneously disdaining the schmaltzy character of the arrangements—can be seen in the comments of prominent writers such as Gary Giddins, for example, who wrote that Parker's string arrangements "were painfully banal in several instances; [but] they seemed to enervate his playing with their pseudo-serious melodrama."[41]

As both Riddle's early career history and his comments confirm, there are important and undeniable (and even obvious) connections between the core jazz tradition and the emerging Great American Songbook tradition, and the broad midcentury jazz and jazz-pop practices that blossomed in the fertile popular musical culture that lay between these two bounding (and now-venerated) traditions. In fact, the cultural idea of the cherished canon of popular song standards represented in this latter territory seems to have arisen in the 1940s and 1950s through the mood music and vocalist-plus-orchestra branches of the jazz-with-strings legacy. In terms of sales and marketing presence, the jazz-with-strings tradition has ironically come to function as one the most prominent representatives of the jazz legacy in popular culture.

Beyond 1930, jazz historiography has been based largely on the cornerstone premise that jazz is an art form. After World War II, this debate was historically framed in terms of midcentury cultural politics that recognized only a rigid division between the cultural spheres of art and entertainment. As such, the jazz canon came to be built with questionable boundaries based on similarly rigid cultural binaries such as art/commerce and pure/contaminated—that is, ideas wholly based on the devaluation of, and subjective assessments of, commercial and entertainment intent. In turn, this hard-won consensus of jazz as art continues to carry an essentialist policing mechanism that does not often acknowledge the many gray, pluralistic middle areas that exist in American culture; our identity politics of race, gender, commerce, and class; and our social sites of racial interchange. What the narrative of a core jazz tradition has ignored is the extensive dialogue, interchanges, and musical overlaps among a large family of American popular musics that grew out of these midcentury jazz-with-strings trends.

NOTES

1. In the period following World War I and leading up to the rise of "middlebrow" as a disparaging critical term ·in the mid-1940s, there was an ever-increasing public trend toward cultural democratization (or "homogenization," as the American cultural critic Dwight Macdonald later termed it). Such trends prompted Frankfurt School cultural critics such as Theodor Adorno, as well as later American critics Clement Greenburg and Dwight Macdonald, into both their collective defense of highbrow cultural authority against the onslaught of mass culture and their persistent attacks on the predisposition of American culture toward middlebrow, or *entertaining*, art. From 1933 to 1941, the Frankfurt School theorists were living in exile on the Columbia University campus in New York. By the mid-1940s traces of their negative views on the American popular "culture industry" (Adorno's famous term) had entered public discourse by way of the mass-circulation newspaper and magazine essays of Greenberg, Macdonald, Russell Lynes, and other American cultural critics. See Dwight Macdonald, "Masscult and Midcult," pt. 1, *Partisan Review* 27 (Spring 1960): 203–33; and Theodor Adorno, *Dialectic of Enlightenment*, with Max Horkheimer, trans. Edmund Jephcott (Stanford, CA: Stanford University Press, 2002).

Over the past decade plus, there has been growing cross-disciplinary research interest in class hierarchy discourses and in middlebrow culture. See especially John Howland, *Between the Muses and the Masses: Symphonic Jazz, "Glorified" Entertainment, and the Rise of the American Musical Middlebrow, 1920–1944* (PhD diss., Stanford University, 2002), and *Ellington Uptown: Duke Ellington, James P. Johnson and the Birth of Concert Jazz* (Ann Arbor: University of Michigan Press, 2009); Lawrence Levine, *Highbrow/Lowbrow: The Emergence of Cultural Hierarchy* (Cambridge: Harvard University Press, 1988); and Joan Shelley Rubin, *The Making of Middlebrow Culture* (Chapel Hill: University of North Carolina Press, 1992). Each of these texts includes citations of important primary midcentury literature. On middlebrow culture in general, also see the bibliography page of the Middlebrow Research Network's website, University of Strathclyde, accessed January 5, 2009, www.middlebrow-network .com/Bibliography.aspx.

2. Ann Douglas, *Terrible Honesty: Mongrel Manhattan in the 1920s* (New York: Farrar, Strauss, and Giroux, 1995).

3. H.L. Mencken, *The American Language: An Inquiry into the Development of English in the United States*, 3rd ed., rev. (New York: Knopf, 1923), 30.

4. Joseph Horowitz, *Understanding Toscanini* (New York: Knopf, 1987), 7.

5. Dwight Macdonald, "Masscult and Midcult," pt. 2, *Partisan Review* 27 (Fall 1960): 628.

6. Scott DeVeaux, from the abstract to his conference paper titled "Core and Boundaries," Leeds International Jazz Conference, Leeds, UK, March 11, 2005;

John Szwed, *Jazz 101: A Complete Guide to Learning and Loving Jazz* (New York: Hyperion, 2000), 6–10.

7. See Rolfe's "Radio's Favorite Conductor" advertisement in *Variety,* October 23, 1928, 64.

8. Italics added. Abel Green, "Paul Whiteman's Concert," *Variety,* October 10, 1928, 53.

9. Linda Mizejewski, *Ziegfeld Girl: Image and Icon in Culture and Cinema* (Durham, NC: Duke University Press, 1999), 11.

10. Otto Cesana, "Cesana Analyzes Use of Strings in Dance Bands," *Metronome,* April 1942, 39.

11. An ideal example of this ensemble can be heard in their nine-minute arrangement of "Was It a Dream" from 1928. The Dorsey Brothers Concert Orchestra, "Was It a Dream," pts. 1 and 2, Okeh 41083, 78 rpm.

12. Artie Shaw, *The Trouble with Cinderella: An Outline of Identity* (Santa Barbara, CA: Fithian, 1992), 291. A transcription recording of the works premiere performance can be found on *Aircheck #1: The 1930s,* vol. 1, Aircheck Records (Vancouver, Canada) [no number], n.d., LP. The manuscript score exists in the Artie Shaw Collection, School of Music, College of Fine Arts, University of Arizona, Tucson. Scott DeVeaux provides additional context for this work in his rich essay, "The Emergence of the Jazz Concert, 1935–1945," *American Music,* Spring 1989, 6–29, esp. 12–14.

13. Shaw, *Trouble with Cinderella,* 293–94. On the Whiteman concert work tradition, see Howland, *Muses and the Masses* and *Ellington Uptown.*

14. "Blues," on *Aircheck #1; Second Chorus,* directed by Henry Potter (1940; Los Angeles: Paramount, 2004), DVD.

15. Paul Grein, *Capitol Records: Fiftieth Anniversary, 1942–1992* (Hollywood: Capitol Records, 1992), 58.

16. Artie Shaw, "Good Enough Ain't Good Enough: Artie Shaw Looks Back, Reflects, and Sums Up," liner notes to *Self-Portrait,* Bluebird RCA 63808, 2001, compact disc box set, 61.

17. Artie Shaw and His Orchestra, "Blues in the Night," Victor 27609, 1941, 78 rpm; reissued on Shaw, *Self Portrait.*

18. A photograph of the orchestra can be seen in Stanley Dance, *The World of Earl Hines* (New York: Charles Scribner's Sons, 1977), 96–97.

19. Earl Hines, quoted in Barry Ulanov, "The Fatha!," *Metronome,* February 1945, 19.

20. Will Friedwald, *Sinatra! The Song Is You: A Singer's Art* (New York: Da Capo, 1997), 79.

21. See Peter J. Levinson, *Tommy Dorsey: Livin' in a Great Big Way* (New York: Da Capo, 2005), 152.

22. Nelson Riddle, *Arranged by Riddle* (n.p.: Nelson Riddle, 1985), 169.

23. Tommy Dorsey, "On the Sunny Side of the Street," 1944; reissued on Tommy Dorsey, *The Sentimental Gentleman of Swing: Centennial Edition,* Bluebird 711672, 2005, compact disc box set.

24. Sy Oliver, quoted in Les Tomkins, *The Sy Oliver Story,* pt. 1, accessed February 13, 2009, www.jazzprofessional.com/interviews/SyOliver_1.htm.

25. John Rockwell, "6-LP Set, 'The Voice,' Samples Sinatra Years on Columbia," *New York Times,* November 23, 1986, H25, H27.

26. Frank Sinatra, "I'm Walking behind You," Capitol, 1953; reissued on Frank Sinatra, *The Complete Capitol Singles Collection,* Capitol 38089, 1996, compact disc box set. The score is held in the Capitol Records Manuscript Collection, School of Music, Brigham Young University, Salt Lake City, Utah.

27. Paul Weston, quoted in Joseph Lanza, *Elevator Music: A Surreal History of Muzak, Easy-Listening, and Other Moodsong* (London: Quartet Books, 1994), 72; Paul Weston, "You Go to My Head," *Music for Memories,* Capitol BD-37, 1946, 78 rpm; reissued on Paul Weston and His Orchestra, *Music for Dreaming/Music for Memories/Songs without Words,* Vocalion (Austria) CDUS 3023, 2002, compact disc. The "You Go to My Head" orchestration was generously made available to me by Tim Weston, Paul Weston's son.

28. *The Jazz Scene,* prod. Norman Granz, Clef Records 10413, 1950, 78 rpm vinylite box set; reissued as Verve 314521661-1, 1994, compact disc box set.

29. For an excellent extended study of Handy's "Bloos," see Benjamin Bierman, "George Handy Composes *The Bloos,*" *Jazz Perspectives* 3 (August 2009): 87–122.

30. Marshall Stearns, *The Story of Jazz* (New York: Oxford University Press, 1956), 224; Michael Levin, "Calls 'Jazz Scene' Most Remarkable Album Ever," *Down Beat,* January 1950, 14.

31. Stan Kenton and His Orchestra, concert program to *Innovations in Modern Music for 1950,* in the author's possession, 3.

32. Stan Kenton and His Orchestra, "Lonesome Road," *Innovations in Modern Music,* Capitol P-189, 1950, ten-inch LP; reissued on Stan Kenton, *The Innovations Orchestra,* Capitol 59965, 1997, compact disc.

33. "The Jazz Beat," May 28, 1949, n.p., from the "Kenton, Stan" clippings file of the Institute of Jazz Studies, Dana Library, Rutgers University, Newark.

34. Charlie Parker, "Just Friends," *Charlie Parker with Strings,* Mercury/Clef MGC-501, 1949, ten-inch LP; reissued on Charlie Parker, *Charlie Parker with Strings: The Master Takes,* Verve 314523448, 1995, compact disc. Source for sales ranking is Joe Goldberg, liner notes to *Charlie Parker with Strings: The Master Takes,* n.p.

35. Charlie Parker, quoted in Nat Hentoff, "Counterpoint," *Down Beat,* January 20, 1953; reprinted in *The Charlie Parker Companion: Six Decades of Commentary,* ed. Carl Woideck (New York: Schirmer Books, 1998), 80; Norman Granz, interview by Elliot Meadow, London, February 27, 1987, transcript provided by Tad Hershorn, Institute of Jazz Studies, Dana Library, Rutgers University, Newark.

36. Norman Granz, liner notes to *Charlie Parker with Strings,* 1949.

37. Winthrop Sargeant, *Jazz: Hot and Hybrid* (New York: Dutton, 1938), 232.

38. See the "Down Beat Critics Poll Archive" and the "Down Beat Readers Poll Archive," *Down Beat,* accessed January 14, 2011, www.downbeat.com/default.asp?sect=cpollindex.

39. See the various related jazz articles: I.S. Horowitz, "Jazz Disks Paced by LP, Hit Cool 55% Jump in Hot Year," 1, 13; "Concert and Nitery Fields Get Shot in Arm from Jazz Boom," 13; "The Jazz Renaissance," 13; Bill Simon,

"Categories of Jazz Disks," 14, 22, 24; June Bundy, "Resurgence of Jazz Deejay: Part and All-Jazz Program Get Good Reception Coast to Coast," 14, 22; Gary Kramer, "Taste in Jazz Albums: Modern School Head Best-Sellers' Class," 18; "Jazz Best Sellers," 18, 20, 24; and Orrin Keepnews and Bill Grauer, "Jazz Packaging: Re-issue Albums Have Solid Sales Potential," 20, 22; all in "Buying—Selling—Programming Jazz Records, Tunes and Talent: The *Billboard* 1955 Review and Preview Section," *Billboard*, April 23, 1955.

40. The term "vinyl vixen" is borrowed from Benjamin Darling, *Vixens of Vinyl: The Alluring Ladies of Vintage Album Covers* (San Francisco: Chronicle Books, 2001).

41. Gary Giddins, liner notes to *Bird with Strings: Live at the Apollo, Carnegie Hall, and Birdland*, Columbia Records, 1977, LP; reissued as TriStar Music 80913, 1994, compact disc.

CHAPTER 7

"Slightly Left of Center"

Atlantic Records and the Problems of Genre

DANIEL GOLDMARK

It's 1966, and a neatly dressed African American man walks onstage as the first mystery guest of the evening on *I've Got a Secret,* a CBS game show hosted by Steve Allen. This man, Allen says, is "a professional musician who is truly unique in the world of jazz music." The mystery guest whispers to Allen the secret that sets him apart from all other jazz musicians, which is shown on the screen for the studio and home audience: "I play jazz on the bagpipes." After narrowing down the guest's idiosyncrasy to an instrument, one of the four celebrity guests, trying to guess what he plays, asks several times if he plays a "novelty" instrument—this after one of the panelists dismissively states, "No, *no* jazz musician plays the bassoon." The panel is stumped, not surprisingly, and Allen finally reintroduces "Mr. X" as Rufus Harley, "a great musician who, believe it or not, plays jazz, both cool and hot, on, of all instruments, the bagpipes!" After a few questions, Harley is invited to play; large plaid cloths hang on the stage wall behind where Harley's trio awaits. In contrast to the rough attempt at Scotch surroundings, Harley and his band are clad in suits and ties, and all sport close-cut hair styles. They go through three choruses of "Feeling Good," the lead track from his latest album, *Scotch & Soul* (1966), on Atlantic Records.[1]

Of all the record companies in the United States, how did Atlantic Records—widely known as an R&B label—come to be the ideal home for an artist with Rufus Harley's unique attributes? Atlantic began releasing jazz recordings as soon as the label was formed in 1947, including sides by Pee Wee Russell, Erroll Garner, Mary Lou Williams, and Don Byas, among others. But the label's diverse R&B-heavy roster of performers kept it from developing a distinctive jazz identity in its early years. When Nesuhi Ertegun joined Atlantic in 1955, his arrival corresponded with the crystallization of several trends in the industry, particularly the move to twelve-inch long-playing records and the advent of true stereo. Within a few years, renowned artists on Ertegun's Atlantic roster—including Charles Mingus, John Coltrane, the Modern Jazz Quartet, and Ornette Coleman—gave the label jazz visibility and focus that had not existed previously. If we look at the entirety of Atlantic's output from the late 1950s to the mid-1970s, however, we find an array of artists—all marketed as jazz—that nonetheless fall outside of the typical representations of jazz during that era: Ray Charles, Chris Connor, Hubert Laws, Les McCann, Shorty Rogers, Dorothy Ashby, Herbie Mann, and Joe Zawinul, to name just a few. Among this diverse group, Rufus Harley does not seem at all out of place.

I want to consider the concept of genre as it applies to jazz labels by examining the especially eclectic evolution of Atlantic Records' jazz output during the tenures of both Nesuhi Ertegun and Joel Dorn, who took over stewardship of the jazz catalog at Atlantic in 1967. While the former signed names long since concretized in the jazz canon, Dorn's tastes went in a decidedly different direction, in terms of both whom he signed and how he produced albums. Harley represents a fine example of Dorn's predilection to more unusual sounds, one that clearly had a large role in the direction of Atlantic's output; looking back on his career in 2006, he (under)stated, "I've always been drawn to the stuff that's been slightly left of center."[2] This tendency became especially evident in the late 1960s and early 1970s, when Ertegun left much of the A&R (artists and repertoire) work to the younger and more plugged-in Dorn. By the time of Dorn's departure, Atlantic's jazz catalog was a microcosm of the diffuse, category-repelling state of jazz in the mid-1970s.

ATLANTIC JAZZ IN BRIEF

It's revealing that Atlantic's story, which has been told numerous times by journalists and in the trade press, has received little attention by scholars.[3] Founded in New York in 1947 by record producer Herb Abramson and R&B and jazz fan Ahmet Ertegun, the label began as a way for the two men to explore their mutual love for jazz, gospel, and race records. The lack of scholarly attention to Atlantic may come from the label's inability to settle in one genre. Additionally, just as the jazz artists on the label were eclectic, so too were their other performers, from R&B singers Ruth Brown and Joe Turner to cabaret acts Bobby Short and Mabel Mercer.

The story of Atlantic's jazz division is a lesser-known tale, one that begins with Nesuhi Ertegun (1917–1989), Ahmet's elder brother, whose interest in jazz went back to 1932. As he recalled, "I had purchased Ted Lewis records in Switzerland when I was 12 years old, but I felt the full impact of jazz when I saw Coleman Hawkins introduced from the [London] Palladium stage. We used to listen to Lew Stone's band broadcast every Tuesday evening on the BBC. . . . When the Duke came to London in '33 with what most persons consider his 'finest band,' I was very impressed with work [sic] of Hodges and Bigard." While a student at the Sorbonne in Paris, Nesuhi also had the opportunity to see Django Reinhardt, Eddie South, Dicky Wells, and Coleman Hawkins play. Nesuhi and his younger brother, Ahmet, finally had the opportunity to collect jazz and blues records in earnest when their father, a Turkish diplomat, was posted to Washington, DC. Nesuhi remembered, "I prowled around Virginia and North Carolina accumulating records. We picked up Bessie [Smith], [Louis Armstrong's] Hot 5s, Ma Raineys, etc."[4]

Before joining Atlantic, Nesuhi had founded his own label, Crescent Records, in 1944 (largely to record music by the recently out-of-retirement Kid Ory); with his wife, Marili Morden, he also ran another label, Jazz Man, through the late 1940s. Just as he seemed on the verge of becoming permanently entrenched in Hollywood, his brother Ahmet, afraid that Nesuhi was going to join Imperial, a rival label, lured him to Atlantic. As Nesuhi remembered it, he came in to Atlantic "as the LP man, so-called in those days." He focused on the "album projects," while his brother and Jerry Wexler produced pop and R&B singles and records.[5] Atlantic was especially keen on the vocals-driven race records that would come to be known as R&B and doo-wop, released by the Clovers, Ruth Brown, The Chords, Joe Turner, and many others. Granted, Atlantic was still a small, independent label in the early 1950s—nothing compared to the era's juggernauts such as Columbia and RCA-Victor.[6] Part of Atlantic's reputation in the business derived from its interest in and support of black artists, as well as its willingness to take chances on music, both of which would play into its relationship to jazz.

Atlantic had recorded and released jazz albums before Nesuhi joined the company, including those by Tiny Grimes, Erroll Garner, Johnny Hodges, and Dizzy Gillespie.[7] When he was asked, just prior to joining

Atlantic, to name his favorite jazz artists, Nesuhi's response shared a similar aesthetic: "[Jimmie] Noone, Louis [Armstrong], [Kid] Ory, [Jelly Roll] Morton, and Darnell Howard. Among the more recent jazzmen, [Django] Reinhardt, Turk Murphy, Bob Helm, and . . . Charlie Parker!" He then went on to praise Parker and criticize Lennie Tristano, saying that "attempts by men like Tristano to get away from the roots of jazz is an abortive thing. I'm very suspicious of THEIR contributions to jazz."[8]

The image we get of Nesuhi at that moment is of someone steeped in older jazz—even verging on the description of one of the "moldy figs" so excoriated during the defense of bebop in the 1940s.[9] Sure enough, within his first year at Atlantic, Nesuhi recorded albums by Paul Barbarin and Wilbur DeParis, both of whom played New Orleans–style jazz. He also made numerous records with key West Coast artists he had come to know while living in Los Angeles. By 1956, however, his attitude toward contemporary jazz seemed to be shifting; he told *Down Beat,* "Jazz has never before been so thoroughly adventurous." In the same article, he rattled off a list of the many artists he had worked with since his arrival at the label: "During the last 15 months, I made record dates on the west coast with Jimmy Giuffre, Jack Montrose, Shorty Rogers, Jess Stacy, and Betty Bennett; in Chicago with Bill Russo; in New York with the Modern Jazz Quartet, Lennie Tristano, Lee Konitz, Charlie Mingus, Milt Jackson, Wilbur de Paris, Tony Fruscella, Teddy Charles, and Chris Connor."[10] Note that Nesuhi mentions Tristano as an artist he had recorded, just a few years after bashing him in print. Clearly his tastes had changed.

The year 1956 saw a continued shift for Atlantic jazz. First came the signing of the Modern Jazz Quartet, which would stay with the label until its initial breakup in 1974. Other important artists signed that year included Mingus, Connor, and Giuffre, as well as another performer, already on Atlantic, that worked with Nesuhi on several jazz-oriented recordings: Ray Charles. After Charles left the label in 1959, Nesuhi signed two of Charles's sax players, David "Fathead" Newman and Hank Crawford, to record deals.

Mingus's experimentalism brought the label to one plateau of innovation, while the 1959 signing of both John Coltrane and Ornette Coleman pushed Atlantic to the tip of the cutting edge. Coltrane's work at Atlantic included *My Favorite Things* and *Giant Steps;* the core of Coleman's most important recorded work took place during this time, including *The Shape of Jazz to Come* and *Free Jazz.* Over the next six years, many new artists (Mose Allison, Mel Tormé, Eddie Harris, Charles

Lloyd, and Herbie Mann) signed with Atlantic, and numerous others (Art Farmer, Nat Adderley, Max Roach, Thelonious Monk, and Art Blakey) recorded for the label. By the end of his active period as a producer, we can see that Nesuhi succeeded in turning Atlantic into a home for modern and adventurous jazz.

It was around this time that Joel Dorn (1942–2007) entered the picture. A disc jockey for WHAT-FM in Philadelphia, Dorn had been an acolyte to the Erteguns and Atlantic since he first heard Ray Charles's music as a teenager. Nesuhi fostered Dorn's interest in music by inviting him to recording sessions and eventually gave Dorn a bigger opportunity in 1964: Dorn was given a total budget of $1,500 to find and record an artist who had never recorded as a leader. Dorn's choice? Hubert Laws, *a jazz flutist*. This unusual choice reveals much about Dorn's preferences as an A&R man and producer. Rather than trying to find the next sax prodigy, he opted for someone who offered a different sound and approach. Dorn wrote that his experience as a DJ, fielding phone calls from listeners, "showed me what it was that moved them, good or bad, and how certain songs by certain artists affected certain kinds of people." Thus, when a club owner told Dorn about Mongo Santamaria's flute player, Dorn was intrigued: "I'd never heard anybody play like that in my life. He had symphony chops and a jazz head."[11]

Laws's premiere album, *The Laws of Jazz,* sold well, although not enough for Dorn to land the full-time job he wanted with Atlantic. Nesuhi Ertegun did agree, however, to distribute a jazz series produced by Dorn (and funded by a friend of Dorn's) under the Atlantic name; Ertegun dubbed it the "3000 series."[12] Dorn put out eight albums in this series: two by Rufus Harley, two by Duke Pearson, and one each by Valerie Capers, Sonny Stitt, Joe Zawinul, and Roland Kirk (his first for Atlantic Records). According to Dorn, it was Harley's album that put him over the top with Ertegun. Dorn recalled,

> The word was kind of out among local musicians that I had produced a few records for Atlantic, or I had produced a few records independently, and that I was looking to become a record producer full time. So [Rufus] brought by an acetate of a cut he had done by himself called "The Bagpipe Blues." I've always been drawn to the stuff that's been slightly left of center, and I really liked it. . . . And all of sudden, of all the things I'd done with established people like Stitt, Duke Pearson, and a few others, that record started to sell, and that was basically the reason I got my job at Atlantic. I had been pitching Nesuhi for years; I had apprenticed to him as a producer while I was on the air, and he agreed to distribute the label that I had gotten financing for. But the bagpipe record took off! Now, when I say, took off, it sold five, six thou-

sand copies. But for a jazz album by an unknown artist, and one who played the bagpipes? That was a big deal. And it especially sold in Detroit. . . . It was a big record in my life.[13]

By the spring of 1967, after the Harley album "took off," Ertegun offered Dorn, now twenty-five, a full-time position at Atlantic Records in New York, essentially to take Ertegun's place as the main producer of the jazz division. Dorn recalled Ertegun saying at that meeting, "My time in the studio is pretty much over. I'll still make albums from time to time, especially with friends like John Lewis, but I'm not in the clubs anymore, and I'm not on the scene, and most of the artists I've worked with are no longer with the label. This is your time."[14] This observation is an important point to consider when we think about how Dorn's tenure began: most of the transformative jazz figures that recorded for Ertegun's Atlantic—Coltrane, Coleman, and Mingus—had moved on to other labels by the mid-1960s. Ertegun may have been a hard act to follow, but Atlantic was ready for new direction.

And yet it was indeed Dorn's time. His full-time position followed within a year; he was made "executive assistant to Nesuhi Ertegun," a job that included "assisting Ertegun in album promotion, artist negotiations, signings and a&r work."[15] He got to work quickly, as *Billboard* reported, "Dorn is cutting a number of unknown performers because 'the real joy in recording is finding something new.' Among his acts are the new Jimmy Owens (trumpet), Kenny Barron (piano) quintet, Hank Crawford, Rufus Harley, Nat Adderley, Freddie Hubbard, Junior Mance, Roland Kirk, Yusef Lateef, Earl Coleman, Billy Taylor, Jack McDuff, and Fathead Newman."[16] The writer here lumps together all the artists that Dorn recorded, as opposed to just the newer names, and rightly so— Dorn's reputation as a producer would be built not just on his discoveries, but on the albums he created with known quantities (such as Adderley or Taylor) as well. From 1967 until Dorn left the label in 1974, he also produced performers that worked in a variety of styles, instruments, and genres, including Jimmy Scott, Gary Burton, Les McCann, Keith Jarrett, Herbie Mann, and Roberta Flack.

In addition to their adventurous signings, Ertegun and Dorn each had their own distinctive approach to production. In many interviews Dorn revealed his admiration for Ertegun's production style: "He was more of a capturer. He put money on talent and captured what they did. He wasn't one of those guys who said, 'Let's do a Broadway album, and I'll give you a big drum sound.'"[17] At the same time, Dorn seemed more than happy to embrace the young up-and-comer label with which Erte-gun had tagged him. Dorn commented in 1967, "To promote jazz, you have to be emotionally involved with the music. . . . We're trying to come up with new frameworks for our artists. Labeling music as jazz is bad. My generation and the generation behind me has [sic] open ears. They don't want to know from labels. People just aren't getting locked into musical categories any more."[18] Considering that the counterculture in America was on the verge of new heights in the late 1960s, Dorn's com-ment about his "generation" seems aptly rebellious, even if not every-one seemed thrilled with Atlantic's shift in direction. Eliot Tiegel wrote in *Billboard* in 1966 that "Atlantic, which has always had a stylish jazz catalog, has of late been experimenting with unusual releases, e.g., 'Bag-pipe Blues' by Rufus Harley, and 'The Fantastic Jazz Harp of Dorothy Ashby.' "[19] We couldn't ask for a more backhanded critique of Dorn's early work at the label.

Dorn also embraced a more conceptual approach to making albums, something that (as the earlier quotation indicates) Ertegun largely avoided. Take, for instance, three albums from 1969: Yusef Lateef's musi-cal envisioning of his hometown in *Yusef Lateef's Detroit Latitude 42°30' Longitude 83°;* Roland Kirk's enormous suite "Expansions" with twenty-eight musicians, including sixteen string players, on *Left & Right;* and Shirley Scott's "horns meet organ" summit released as *Shirley Scott & The Soul Saxes,* featuring Hank Crawford, Fathead Newman, and King Curtis on saxes and flutes (and Chuck Rainey, Eric Gale, and Bernard Purdie in the rhythm section).[20] Whether it was small group or large ensembles, Dorn had no trouble working with and encouraging experimentation from his artists.

After Dorn left Atlantic in 1974, the label's jazz output dropped pre-cipitously. Ertegun became more involved in running WEA Interna-tional, and his jazz days were largely over (although, as Bob Porter re-minds us, Ertegun did bring Mingus back to Atlantic for his final years of recording before his death in 1979).[21] Dorn continued producing, including the first (and many subsequent) albums of Bette Midler and Leon Redbone, among many other artists. It seems especially apt that Dorn's last project before his death in 2007 was compiling and produc-ing a five-disc retrospective of Atlantic's jazz output, titled *Hommage à Nesuhi.* Interestingly, and not surprisingly, one artist *not* included in this extended paean to his mentor is Rufus Harley; in spite of the fact that he was an Atlantic jazz artist, Harley was entirely Dorn's discovery. I wish to turn here to Harley, because of his improbable (if short-lived) mainstream acceptance, because of the role he played in launching Dorn's career, and because his story has not been chronicled in any significant form elsewhere.[22]

"NOBODY WANTED TO PLAY WITH ME"

Rufus Harley was born in 1936 near Raleigh, North Carolina; he and his family moved to Philadelphia within a few years (not unlike the path taken by Percy Heath and John Coltrane). He earned enough money from selling newspapers to buy a C-melody saxophone and eventually played in his high school band. By age sixteen he had left school to work but continued his pursuit of music, which included playing jazz gigs (now on tenor saxophone and flute) nights and weekends; his professional debut came in the early 1960s with local big band drummer Mickey Collins.[23]

Harley told the story of his discovery of the bagpipes as follows: the state burial of John F. Kennedy had the nation at a standstill on November 25, 1963, with millions watching their televisions or listening on their radios. Somewhere in Germantown, a suburb of Philadelphia, Harley, a civil servant ("a maintenance man for the Philadelphia Housing Authority," or as Harley put it, "cleaning up the dumpsters and sweeping the streets), watched the proceedings on television.[24] Nine pipers of the Black Watch Royal Highlanders Regiment played four songs during the procession of the funeral cortege from the White House to St. Matthew's Cathedral. At this point of the funeral Harley had an epiphany, an understanding that the unique sound he had been trying in vain to produce on the saxophone could be realized on the bagpipes. He searched for bagpipes in Philadelphia before finding a set in a New York City pawn shop for $120. Having a sympathetic teacher in guitarist Dennis Sandole (a swing band regular in the 1940s, who had mentored John Coltrane in the late 1940s), Harley adapted to the bagpipes' distinctive breathing and fingering techniques (an unusual approach compared to a saxophone) within about six months.

To make the bagpipes work with traditional jazz instruments, Harley tuned his pipes' drones to F and B-flat. With the drones playing, Harley could thus play only in one key. Another restriction came with the chanter, the only fingered pipe on the instrument, which can typically play only nine notes, further limiting his ability to sit in with a group of players, regardless of whether they were sympathetic to his sound. In addition, intonation presents a challenge on the bagpipes, especially if, as in Harley's case, one is trying to play with equally tempered instruments. Because the player's mouth has no direct contact with the chanter, there is no way to force notes high or low, whether by lipping, overblowing, or any other technique. The air being pushed out from the bag determines the pitch, though a very skilled player can bend pitches slightly by how they control the bag.

Despite these limitations, Harley was able to develop a convincing enough approach to playing jazz on the bagpipes to get Dorn's attention. His first two albums for Dorn on Atlantic were *Bagpipe Blues* (1965) and *Scotch & Soul* (1966). The albums contain a mixture of contemporary songs then popular with other jazz musicians ("Feeling Good"), original tunes ("Bagpipe Blues"), and a few standards ("A Nightingale Sang in Berkeley Square"). After some touring, Harley made two more albums—*A Tribute to Courage* (1967) and *King/Queens* (1970)—at which point his contract with Atlantic lapsed.

Harley's albums garnered a great deal of media attention; *A Tribute to Courage* actually reached number 32 on *Billboard*'s R&B album chart, reflecting Harley's appeal as a crossover artist. His appearance on *I've Got a Secret* was not an isolated incident; during the span of his time with Atlantic, he also showed up on *What's My Line?* and *To Tell the Truth*, as well as talk or variety shows including *The Mike Douglas Show*, *The David Frost Show*, *The Skitch Henderson Show*, and *The Tonight Show*.[25] He also toured fairly extensively, including performances at the International Jazz Festival and Berlin Jazz Days in West Berlin, both in 1966, as well as several high-profile concerts, including the Newport Jazz Festival in 1968.

Critical coverage of Harley's albums and gigs appeared in magazines such as *Newsweek, Down Beat, Billboard,* and *Melody Maker,* in addition to reportage of shows in local newspapers. Not surprisingly, critics seemed torn on how to deal with Harley's music: gimmickry or innovation? Or, better yet, jazz or not jazz? Atlantic didn't promote Harley as a gimmick—as Dorn points out, for a largely unknown *jazz* artist, his first album sold well. So well, in fact, that his second album was pictured in an advertisement among those by Herbie Mann, Eddie Harris, Hubert Laws, Duke Pearson, and Mose Allison, all under the header "Jazz Best Sellers are on Atlantic."[26] Despite the attempts to place Harley securely among Atlantic's jazz stable, he was never seen as something other than an anomaly. His media appearances always focused on his unique instrument and never touched on his *ability* with the bagpipe (let alone his skills on the saxophone or flute). The announcement in the *New York Times* of Harley's appearance at Newport in 1968, for instance, amounted to a few words of the last sentence of an eleven-paragraph summary of the festival to come: "and Rufus Harley, who plays jazz on bagpipes."[27] Even the liner notes to his first album, *Bagpipe Blues* (written by jazz critic Dave Bittan), refer to the bagpipes as "the odd instrument."[28]

One of the more critical takes on *Bagpipe Blues* and Harley in general appeared in *Saturday Review,* where critic Stanley Dance wrote, "Rufus Harley: *Bagpipe Blues.* A superficial acquaintance with Indian music seems to have accounted for a great deal of recent 'droning' on the part of jazz saxophonists. Now, logically, we have jazz on the bagpipes, an instrument members of the avant-garde have been approximating for some time. No doubt it makes a good gimmick by the decade's standards (the liner shows Harley resplendent in full Highland gear—kilt, sporran, and tartan), but it is a mercy that the pipes are heard on only three of the seven numbers." Dance not only derides the wave of interest in Eastern music in the 1960s but basically describes the bagpipe as the natural point of devolution for avant-garde jazz. *Newsweek's* Hubert Saal, after comparing Harley to a tamed circus animal, described the sounds he heard as "screeching," "barbarous" (quoting Samuel Pepys), and "provocative," while the reviewer in *Melody Maker* seemed unimpressed with Harley's musicianship: "He manages to play jazz on them. Not the greatest jazz you ever heard, but unmistakably jazz." While largely dismissive, these critiques also remind us that reviewers—and, presumably, listeners—heard Harley as jazz, even as his music hit the R&B charts.[29]

Not all the critics were distracted by Harley's chosen instrument; many took what he was doing quite seriously. In 1968 James D. Dilts compared Harley's solo on soprano sax at a Left Bank Jazz Society concert as having "lapsed into an Easter motif and ended with Shepp-like shriek." His next solo, on tenor, drew praise as well. Once the bagpipes came out, however, the playing was first described as "more sound than substance." After a few more tunes, the show ended with "Windy," which "turned out to be the perfect combination of material and instrument and brought the crowd, which had been enthusiastic but not demonstratively so throughout the afternoon, to its feet." This tune seems to have fared especially well with critics; concerning his appearance at the Newport, Whitney Balliett wrote that, in Harley's version of "Windy," "he somehow supplied all the notes that have been missing from the instrument since it was invented." Likewise, a reviewer for *Ebony* stated, "And his versions of *Wendy [sic]* and *Sunny* can start any audience swinging as soon as everyone overcomes the initial reaction to the novelty of the sound and lets the music take over."[30]

The closest Harley ever came to being accepted into the folds of mainstream jazz occurred several years later. Along with Dizzy Gillespie and Charles Mingus, Harley joined Sonny Rollins in a Carnegie Hall concert on May 3, 1974. The *New York Times* review described Harley as one "who is rarely heard here" and who "gave some virtuoso demonstrations of the potentials of the bagpipes."[31] Rollins subsequently invited Harley to join his group for a tour of Europe that summer, including playing bagpipes and soprano saxophone. The group's tour included a performance at the Montreux Jazz Festival on July 6, 1974; their performance was released as *The Cutting Edge,* with Harley playing on one song, "Swing Low, Sweet Chariot." For a brief moment it seemed as if Harley might reach a wider audience, but his time with Rollins did not translate into any lasting change. And while Rollins welcomed Harley into his ensemble, the leader didn't see the pipes as crossing over from novelty to standard: "I didn't really get a sense that the bagpipe would be something which could find a place in the normal jazz group."[32]

Rollins's comment, as with all the reviews, makes it clear that listeners would likely never move beyond the novelty of his instrument; this fixation on instrument (or mode of production) plays a key role when drawing the lines between jazz and not jazz. Even Dorn acknowledged Harley's image when he described *Bagpipe Blues* as being "well on its way to becoming the off-the-wall jazz record of the year." The message is clear: it's not about the music but rather the instrument.[33] According to Dorn, most critics stereotyped Harley in this way: "I was recording guys at that time like Rahsaan and Yusef and people like that. Any time back then when you did something that was slightly different, the regular jazz community looked at it as if it was gimmicky, or vaudeville-like. People looked at it as an oddity or a one-off. Real people liked it. But the critical community just looked at him like it was odd."[34] Dorn certainly didn't help the projection of Harley as a gimmick when he suggested that Harley wear a traditional Highland piper's outfit—kilt, sporran, and so on—on the cover of *Bagpipe Blues,* especially at a time when so many jazz musicians had embraced the look and feel of more Afrocentric attire. By the time of his last two Atlantic albums, Harley sported a more au courant wardrobe; he can be seen wearing a dashiki on several of his television appearances in 1967 and 1968, as well as on the covers of his last two Atlantic albums.

THE MULTI-INSTRUMENTALISTS

Dorn's mention of Lateef and Kirk provides a useful way to contextualize Harley: as one of a trio of Atlantic artists Dorn produced, all of whom were sax players who moved on to atypical winds: Yusef Lateef to oboe, English horn, numerous flutes, and bassoon (contrary to the panelist's opinion on *I've Got a Secret*); Roland Kirk to an array of instruments (many of his own manufacture); and Harley to bagpipes and flute. Doubling for sax players is nothing new, of course, but these were particularly unusual instruments for jazz: flute, oboe, bassoon, bass clarinet—essentially all the parts of a traditional orchestral woodwind section. As Kirk recalled, there was some resistance to multi-instrumentalists at the time: "Back in the early '60s there were just two or three of us going on the bandstand with more than one horn. Some people would laugh and ask, 'What do you need *this* for? Why can't you learn one instrument?' Eric Dolphy and Yusef Lateef and myself—we were the ones bearing that load back then."[35] Lateef recalls in his memoir that he learned a great deal from Dolphy while they were both playing for Mingus—and then immediately goes on to discuss his admiration of Kirk, who joined Mingus as well during that time.[36] It was as if one instrument should have been enough.

Before signing to Atlantic, Kirk had an extensive career as a sideman and leader (mostly on Mercury). Blind from age two, he evinced a talent for wind instruments early on and had begun experimenting as a teenager with many of the atypical winds he played later as a professional musician. A review in *Down Beat* recounted an (apparently typical) early studio session: "During one of Kirk's wilder passages, [Argo A&R man Jack] Tracy slapped his thigh, laughed, and said, 'I can just hear the critics! They're going to say, "My God, first Ornette Coleman and now this!"'" Kirk's response is telling: "'I'm afraid of what the critics are going to say. I know what they'll say. They'll say I play out of tune.' 'That's a drag,' said a musician sitting nearby. 'If Ornette Coleman plays out of tune, they say it's freedom.'" Even this early in his career (at the age of twenty-four), Kirk had become used to defending and justifying what he was doing as a musician.[37]

Kirk was an easy target, written off as a musical circus act not just for playing three horns simultaneously, or for the many other instruments hanging from his neck during performances, but also for his ability to play without having to stop for a breath. Having strong political beliefs and being blind did not help make him seem any more ordinary. In his examination of blind African American musicians, Terry Rowden positions Kirk next to nineteenth-century virtuoso Blind Tom Bethune for how "the relationship between blindness and 'freakishness'" characterized the reception of their music. What set Kirk apart, Rowden argues, was that critics and musicians alike argued "that his music was neither exceptional nor even 'real' jazz," pointing to his "antimusical antics, political diatribes, and qualitatively inconsistent performances and recordings."[38] Over time, however, more critics and fans alike began to take him seriously, both as a skilled player and as an inventive performer and composer.[39]

Like Kirk, Yusef Lateef came to Atlantic after recording numerous albums as a leader for Savoy, Prestige, Riverside, and Impulse! He was already well-known as a multi-instrumentalist, although, like Harley, he moved beyond the saxophone later in life. Lateef had already had his big break as a tenor player with Dizzy Gillespie's band in 1948. When he returned to his hometown of Detroit for personal reasons, he began exploring more contemporary jazz sounds with other locals (including Paul Chambers, Donald Byrd, and Kenny Burrell), while also pursuing a music degree at Wayne State University. It was Burrell who suggested the flute to Lateef as a way to expand his timbral palette; he added oboe a few years later. He also picked up several non-Western instruments including the *shinai* and *rabat*. In his autobiography Lateef does not give much attention to his time at Atlantic, although he does mention that he was "given a lot of latitude to record whatever I wanted to with Joel Dorn as my producer."[40]

Perhaps the biggest difference among these three performers is that Kirk and Lateef were well-known before coming to Atlantic. Both became known first as sax players; their reputations as compelling musicians no doubt helped them in their transition to the wider world of instrumentation. Harley had not recorded prior to his picking up the bagpipes. This may offer one reason why he was taken much less seriously than Kirk or Lateef—he never had (or took) the opportunity to make a name for himself as a "legitimate" sax player before expanding his range to include the pipes. What ultimately brings these men together, however, is that they were not hemmed in by Dorn but rather encouraged to explore new ideas and new sounds.

If we look at the many albums Kirk and Lateef made into the 1970s, there exists an increasing reliance on complex and involved production. Harley's final album fits this description as well, not only for his covering of rock tunes ("Eight Miles High"), but also for the use of electrified bagpipes. Harley, Kirk, and Lateef were not the only ones bucking reputations for gimmickry, however; Dorn gained his own renown for constructing artificiality in the studio. He acknowledged this in 2001, stating "Half of the music I made, people thought was a gimmick. They thought Rahsaan was a gimmick. They thought that I ruined Yusef. They thought that the things we did with Les were gimmicks. They hated it when I put 'Fathead' with strings, all that stuff."[41] Gimmick or not, Dorn's approach to production moved Atlantic jazz to a whole new location on the spectrum of jazz taste, far from where Ertegun had left it less than a decade earlier. Atlantic had boasted an identity as a serious, notable jazz label, demonstrated by the artists they signed, the albums they released, and the styles of jazz those releases promoted. Where was the label now?

GENRE AND JAZZ

While Rufus Harley was far from alone at Atlantic as a man of many winds, it was Atlantic's growing profile as an adventuresome jazz label that allowed Dorn to experiment with such unconventional artists. Taken together—Harley and his multi-instrumentalist associates, Dorn's explorational bent, Atlantic's nontraditional stance—this nexus ultimately leads us to question the role of genre in defining jazz.

Genre is a complex and contentious issue, and applying it to jazz is no exception, as we know from many practitioners. Some artists wish to be associated with a particular genre, because they feel it represents their interests or influences as a musician; others bristle at the idea of being pigeonholed or stereotyped into a pat category; some make music that intentionally defies the idea of genre. From a different perspective, record companies market albums and artists according to perceived desires in the consumer, and the entire industrial complex surrounding mass-produced music depends on the conceptual order and stability provided by genres and other organizational categories. Consumers likewise often use the (sometimes arbitrary and ambiguous) associations they make with labels like "swing," "West Coast," or "hard bop" to guide them in deciding what they do and do not prefer, and likewise in what they should or should not purchase.

Taken from the perspective of the historian, genre labels typically provide blunt, ham-fisted explanations of a complex time in history, usually one that coexists with a dozen or so other genres and thus does little to explain what the music is about or why it was important. Yet historians must reckon with genre regularly as one of many guiding forces in the ebb and flow of popular trends in any form of music, jazz or otherwise.

Strangely enough, the topic of genre in jazz has received very little direct discussion by scholars. The *New Grove Dictionary of Jazz* (original and second edition) offers no entry on the subject, and most books on genre and popular music avoid jazz altogether. Fabian Holt's book on genre is an exception, laying out many of the uses and the related pitfalls of genre with all forms of popular music. But Holt also explains that far more substantive work on genre has appeared in areas outside music, particularly in film studies (including work by Steve Neale, Rick Altman, and Thomas Schatz, among many others), where it has shaped the discipline for several decades.[42] Unlike film, music uses more forms of production (labels, venues, an endless variety of ensembles), and involves far more nonspecific representation (i.e., not typically visualized) than film (or literature, for that matter), making it much more difficult to apply generic categories usefully to popular music.

Although I do not aim to put forward a unifying theory on jazz genres, the history of Atlantic and Dorn prompts two observations. First, record labels often become genres unto themselves if they specialize in a particular style, genre, or even approach. In the jazz world, labels such as Blue Note, ECM, and Impulse! have an established sound and even "look" to them: Blue Note represents the home of hard or post bop; ECM evokes modern, experimental jazz; Impulse! is inextricably tied up with Coltrane and the avant-garde; and Atlantic translates into R&B and eclecticism. Outside of jazz, labels such as SubPop, Chess, Motown, or Sire immediately evoke particular genres for which they are known (alternative, blues, soul, punk/new wave), even if those labels release music in other areas as well. A label's mission could even translate into a genre: Rhino Records was one of the first major reissue labels, which led many former pop figures to fear the day their music was anthologized by the label, meaning they had officially become a has-been.

Jazz records were not always confined to jazz labels—far from it. Like practically all recorded music, the earliest jazz records appeared as outliers, niche releases, or one-offs on long-established labels, such as Brunswick, Vocalion, and Victor. Labels capitalizing on new music pop up almost immediately, while larger organizations dedicate new imprints or numerical series to specific genres or styles. We eventually find that while some companies endeavored to have a broad roster of artists, others became known—intentionally or otherwise—for a particular kind of music.

Second, historians and critics alike have long fixated on instruments as the defining characteristic for jazz musicians (frequently taking precedence over style, period, nationality, etc.). Witness *Down Beat*'s longstanding critics' and readers' polls, which ask for the best in any number of categories—all based on mode of production (i.e., type of instrument, as well as a few categories for ensembles and vocalists, which also point to where the music comes from). While not one of the choices for the earliest years of the polls (the readers' began in 1936, the critics' in 1953), the magazine added a "Miscellaneous Instrument" category in 1950 and 1959 (to the readers' and critics' polls, respectively).[43]

Likewise, *The Oxford Companion to Jazz* from 2000 features dozens of short essays on important figures and trends in jazz history. Two-thirds of the way through the 852-page tome is a series of brief explorations, each by a different writer, on the development and reception of key instruments in jazz history: the clarinet, saxophone, trumpet, trombone, electric guitar and vibraphone, and bass (the piano receives four separate chapters). Sandwiched between the chapter on the bass and the "Batteries not Included" chapter on the electric guitar and vibraphone, we find Christopher Washburne's valorous "Miscellaneous Instruments in Jazz." He immediately acknowledges that certain players "have defied orthodoxy by developing their voices on instruments that have not attained a prominent role in jazz."[44] Each instrument is explored mainly through the names and provenances of those known for playing them. Harley's distinction as a "miscellaneous" instrumentalist seems as least somewhat confirmed by his appearance—in 1975!—on the ballot of fifteen names for *Ebony*'s Black Music Poll under "Miscellaneous Instrument," sharing the ballot with the likes of Ornette Coleman, Alice Coltrane, Sun Ra . . . and Roland Kirk and Yusef Lateef.[45]

David Ake's discussion of Louis Jordan's longtime omission from most histories of jazz as emblematic of larger issues in the construction of genre boundaries reminds us that historians have deep investments in the fabrication of such boundaries and that bemoaning his exclusion from jazz history accomplishes far less than questioning the aesthetic or cultural values that his exclusion benefits.[46] Applying that idea here, we might begin to question exactly why musicians who play one instrument (à la a person specializing in a single trade, whether as a doctor, a carpenter, or a musician) are taken more seriously than those who play more than one instrument regularly (perhaps giving the impression they are merely "dabbling" and not serious). We might also use this point of view to better understand how instrumentation plays into the larger story being told of the history of jazz, and Atlantic's place in it: the label is considered pivotal to jazz history in the late 1950s, tied to Coleman, Mingus, and Coltrane, before it disappears once more. Does equating jazz with certain instruments strengthen the traditional narratives? Do nontraditional instruments equal nonseriousness or nonimportance?

Perhaps Atlantic's challenge is that it has been too difficult to categorize, and happily so. Does its general profile from the mid-1950s to the 1970s fit the description of "beyond category"? Not really—unless "category" refers to the semistandardized story told regarding jazz in the 1960s, in which Blue Note dominated hard bop and postbop, and Impulse! was "made" by Coltrane, who reigned supreme until Miles Davis "created" fusion in the late 1960s. Dorn himself apparently subscribed to this narrative, stating, "Blue Note owned and operated the postbop small groups; Atlantic's universe was much more eclectic."[47]

In the early 1960s, Atlantic could claim an extraordinarily diverse roster, which extended even beyond the artists that made numerous records for the label. The year 1966 offers a perfect example. Alongside recordings by Atlantic regulars Herbie Mann, Hank Crawford, and Joe Zawinul, both Dorothy Ashby and Joe Harriott recorded two sessions. Ashby was a bop harpist who made a dozen or so albums from the 1950s to the 1980s on as many labels. She provided Atlantic with breadth in terms of the definition of what made a viable jazz instrument. The Jamaican-born Harriott became known on the soprano sax while playing in England, largely for his exploration of improvisatory techniques that drew (often unfavorable) comparisons to Ornette Coleman. His two albums released by Atlantic feature his collaboration with violinist John Mayer and a trio of musicians (sitar, tabla, tambura) from India: *Indo-Jazz Suite* (1966) and *Indo-Jazz Fusions* (1967) saw Harriott pushing the idea of expanding the vocabulary of jazz (and Western music in general) into new directions around the time that prominent popular musicians were getting interested in Indian music as well.

Where Atlantic jazz stood, stylistically, at the end of Dorn's tenure is debatable. In his 1974 history of Atlantic Records, Charlie Gillett declares, "But since ABC signed Coleman and Coltrane to its Impulse jazz label in 1962, Atlantic seemed to lose interest in nurturing experimental but expensive jazzmen and more or less abandoned the frontiers of modern jazz. Instead, much of Atlantic's current 'jazz' catalogue sounds like hip muzak, played well and fashionably to back up conversations at parties. Nesuhi explains that he doesn't like most avant garde jazz, 'And I think it is important to record music you like. I do like Eddie Harris, Les McCann, Herbie Mann, and we record them.'"[48]

It's no surprise that he names Harris and McCann in one breath: the first collaboration between the two men, *Swiss Movement,* recorded live at the Montreux Jazz Festival in 1969 (and coproduced by Ertegun and Dorn), spawned a huge hit, "Compared to What," and the album itself hit number 1 and 2 on *Billboard*'s jazz album and R&B album charts, respectively.[49] What would be one of the most successful recordings (according to the charts, at least) tied to Atlantic jazz ultimately was a synthesis of styles: not just between the two artists but also between the two producers.

By 1968 Dorn was quoted as saying, "Jazz has become so broad that it is getting difficult to pigeonhole, and jazz stations no longer say that a certain album belongs in a jazz category while another doesn't. This has become evident in the abundance of plays on the jazz stations of pop disks and the overlap of the same albums in the pop and jazz charts."[50] After only a few years at Atlantic, Dorn could see how genre lines were becoming less distinct, or fading away altogether. His own career would follow this trajectory, as he went on to work with more pop- or rock-oriented performers.

There are many other factors to consider when trying to get a clear image of Atlantic through the 1960s and onward. Much of their jazz output does not fit neatly into any of the old categories. New trends like bossa nova and other forms of Latin jazz make inroads, but so does soul, gospel, and rock, all of which are adopted, adapted, and recorded by Atlantic artists, and often end up on the same record! Herbie Mann, for instance, traveled to Tennessee to record an album (*Memphis Underground,* 1969) that firmly straddles the line between jazz and soul and integrates two of the label's best-loved sounds: Mann's flute and the Memphis rhythm section. Atlantic was not the only eclectic jazz label during this period—all the other major labels had their own category-defying artists. But Atlantic's willingness to take chances on unproven or unusual artists gave it an exceptionally diverse and eclectic roster and a perfect example of how difficult it is to categorize music under a label, a genre, or in any way whatsoever.

For their part, Kirk, Lateef, and Harley each made their own important contributions to jazz. All three men took seriously the idea of expanding the music they played beyond the traditional notions of "jazz." The limitations of Harley's bagpipes compelled him and his listeners to hear the standards he played very differently. Kirk's penchant for playing several instruments simultaneously—including sirens, whistles, and screams—expanded the notion of what sounds might be acceptable in a club or concert setting. And Lateef's repudiation of the word "jazz" continues to inform all his music, from his use of atypical instruments to his move away from standards and toward "world music." Taken together, these three represent trends at Atlantic and in the jazz world in general in the 1970s: the hybridization of jazz, rock, pop, and world music through the embracing of sounds and forms new to jazz.

Two years before his death in 1989, Nesuhi Ertegun gave an interview for *Jazz Times,* in which he reminisced about his days as a producer and discussed the ongoing transition to compact discs, including a multivolume collection of hits from the Atlantic jazz catalog that he was spearheading. Near the article's end, he opined, "The current reissue boom will be over by the end of 1988, simply because everything by then that is worth reissuing will have *been* reissued. There is a limited amount of material."[51] Ertegun did not live to see the massive reissue craze that began around the time he made this statement, nor did he see Rhino Records make available hundreds of out-of-print Atlantic albums as well as previously unreleased material by Atlantic artists found in archives and personal collections. As disparate as their stable of jazz artists were, it would no doubt make Ertegun and Dorn happy to know that Atlantic jazz still has an identity more than a half century after its inception.

NOTES

1. "I've Got a Secret," YouTube video, 8:29, originally televised by CBS on October 17, 1966, posted by "rrgomes," February 21, 2010, www.youtube .com/watch?v=PnvAu3CoGb4.

2. Joel Dorn, telephone interview with the author, November 2005.

3. Besides the coffee table book *"What'd I Say": The Atlantic Story; 50 Years of Music* (New York: Welcome Rain Publishers, 2001), with Ahmet Ertegun listed as the primary author, there are several biographies and memoirs by those

involved in Atlantic's creation, including Dorothy Wade and Justine Picardie, *Music Man: Ahmet Ertegun, Atlantic Records, and the Triumph of Rock 'n' Roll* (New York: Norton, 1990), and Jerry Wexler and David Ritz, *Rhythm and the Blues: A Life in American Music* (New York: Knopf, 1993). There is also Charlie Gillett's *Making Tracks: Atlantic Records and the Growth of a Multi-Billion-Dollar Industry* (New York: Dutton, 1974), which covers precisely the period on which I focus here. Gillett, though, largely covers Atlantic's rock and pop output.

4. Floyd Levin, "Crusader for Jazz," *Second Line* 3, no. 11–12 (Nov–Dec 1952): 1.

5. Max Jones, "That's Jazz—That's Nesuhi," *Melody Maker,* July 24, 1976, 36.

6. Atlantic remained one of the last major independent labels until 1967, when it was bought by Warner Bros.

7. Some of these albums were recorded by Blue Star and leased by Atlantic for release.

8. Levin, "Crusader for Jazz," 17.

9. For a meticulous analysis of this war of the critics, see Bernard Gendron, *Between Montmartre and the Mudd Club: Popular Music and the Avant-Garde* (Chicago: University of Chicago Press, 2002), esp. ch. 6, "Moldy Figs and Modernists," 121–41.

10. Nesuhi Ertegun, "Unpredictable . . . Is the Word Atlantic Records Exec Uses to Describe Recording of Jazz," *Down Beat,* May 16, 1956, 13.

11. Joel Dorn, "Makin' the Connection," liner notes for *Hommage à Nesuhi: Atlantic Jazz, a 60th Anniversary Collection,* Rhino Handmade RHM2 7760, 2008, 15, five compact discs.

12. Ibid., 16.

13. Dorn, interview.

14. Dorn, "Makin' the Connection," 19.

15. "Executive Turntable," *Billboard,* May 18, 1968, 6.

16. Eliot Tiegel, "Jazz Beat," *Billboard* November 18, 1967, 14.

17. John Kruth, "The Second Coming of Hip," *Wax Poetics* 34 (2009): 103.

18. Tiegel, "Jazz Beat," 14.

19. Tiegel, "The Jazz Beat," *Billboard,* January 22, 1966, 20.

20. Granted, Dorn had his limits: "I hate that far-out, make-believe jazz/out/downtown shit. It's unlistenable. . . . When Mingus or Ornette went out, they usually left enough bread crumbs for you to find your way out of the woods. When Yusef or Rahsaan went out, it was cool, you could still hear it." Kruth, "Second Coming of Hip," 109.

21. Bob Porter, "Atlantic History," liner notes for *Hommage à Nesuhi: Atlantic Jazz, a 60th Anniversary Collection,* Rhino Handmade RHM2 7760, 2008, 67, five compact discs.

22. Harley's four Atlantic albums were collected into a two–compact disc anthology in 2006, *Courage: The Complete Atlantic Recordings,* for which I wrote the liner notes. Rhino Handmade RHM2 7725. A volume consisting of an extended interview and several reproduced photos was published the following year: Charles A. Powell, *The Jazzish Bagpiper in Conversation* (Stuart, FL: W.I.T. Books, 2007).

23. Title quote from Bob Houston, "Jazz Bagpipes Are No Laughing Matter," *Melody Maker,* November 19, 1966, 8; Peter Relic, "It's Piping Hot," *Mojo* 81 (August 2000): 18.

24. Dave Bittan, liner notes for Rufus Harley, *Bagpipe Blues*, Atlantic 3001, 1966, LP; Rufus Harley, telephone interview with the author, December 2005.

25. According to an interview in 1981, Harley appeared on *To Tell the Truth* a second time, in 1981, where "the panel had the tough job of guessing his occupation—midwife." Harley was discussing the fact that he helped to deliver his (at the time) nine children. Clover A. Linton, "Rufus Harley: Jazz and Vegetables Are His Bag," *Vegetarian Times,* May 1982, 63.

26. Advertisement, *Billboard,* September 3, 1966, 41. Another example of the company still trying to situate Harley as mainstream was the inclusion on his version of "Eight Miles High" from *King/Queens* on a sampler album (*Atlantic Sales Meeting Atlantic Jazz Series Winter 1970 Special Promotional Record*, Atlantic SD JSM 1) distributed to record retailers in 1970, along with tracks from other Atlantic releases by Bobby Short, Les McCann, Freddie Hubbard, and Yusef Lateef.

27. John S. Wilson, "Jazz in Newport Attracts 7,500," *New York Times,* July 5, 1968, 21.

28. Bittan, liner notes for Rufus Harley.

29. Stanley Dance, "Recordings Reports: Jazz LPs," *Saturday Review* 49 (January 15, 1966): 50; Hubert Saal, "Skirling the Blues," *Newsweek,* January 30, 1967, 97–98; Houston, "Jazz Bagpipes," 8.

30. James D. Dilts, "Rufus Harley: Left Bank Jazz Society, Baltimore, Md.," *Down Beat,* May 2, 1968, 35; Whitney Balliett, *Collected Works: A Journal of Jazz, 1954–2001* (New York: St. Martin's Press, 2002), 295; "Rufus Harley's Black Bag," *Ebony,* July 1969, 101.

31. John S. Wilson, "Jazz Greats Join Rollins's Session," *New York Times,* May 5, 1974, L74.

32. Sonny Rollins, telephone interview with the author, June 22, 2006.

33. Dorn, "Makin' the Connection," 16. Harley is not the only jazz musician to take on the bagpipes, but he was the only one to take them on as his primary instrument. Albert Ayler and Sonny Rollins, among others, experimented and even recorded on the pipes. One of Harley's favorite anecdotes was how John Coltrane called him in the middle of the night, asking for a lesson on the bagpipes. At one point, Harley suggested that the two men could collaborate on an album, leading Coltrane to respond, "What am I going to play?" Harley, interview.

34. Dorn, interview.

35. Todd Barkan, "Rahsaan Speaks His Peace," *Down Beat* 41, no. 14 (1974): 14. My curiosity in this theme grew when, early in my research on Harley, I ran across a record review from a local Southern California newspaper. After an opening paragraph about jazz "in recent years," the reviewers write, "Rufus Harley, Roland Kirk, and Yusef Lateef are some of the most creative members of the new composer-player breed." The irony is that the review was *not* exclusively about Atlantic artists but rather about players of atypical winds.

Harvey Waterman and Joe Roberts, "Record Rack," *Evening Star-News, Culver City; Venice Evening Vanguard,* October 1, 1968, 12. Joel Dorn Papers, 1967–82, Archives Center, National Museum of American History, Smithsonian Institution, Washington, DC.

36. Yusef Lateef, *The Gentle Giant: The Autobiography of Yusef Lateef,* with Herb Boyd (Irvington, NJ: Morton Books, 2006), 86–87. One could certainly add Eric Dolphy to this list, not only because of his work as a sideman and leader on the bass clarinet and flute, but also because of the nexus that he seemed to share with Kirk and Lateef: having all played for Charles Mingus in the early 1960s. It's interesting to imagine one possible outcome for Dolphy's career had he not died so young, at age thirty-six in 1964—he might have ended up lured to Atlantic by either Ertegun or Dorn.

37. "The Man Who Plays Three Horns," *Down Beat,* August 4, 1960, 13. Dorn mentioned that when he was still a young DJ, listeners liked Kirk's music, but "if I would talk to other people about Rahsaan, they would kind of sneer that there was this guy who played three horns at once. It was just considered a gimmick." Stanley Crouch, liner notes for *Does Your House Have Lions: The Rahsaan Roland Kirk Anthology* Rhino R2 71406, 1993, 27, compact disc.

38. Terry Rowden, *The Songs of Blind Folk: African American Musicians and the Cultures of Blindness* (Ann Arbor: University of Michigan Press, 2009), 91.

39. See also Josh Kun's discussion of Kirk's engagement with sound and black politics, "Basquiat's Ear, Rahsaan's Eye," in *Audiotopia: Music, Race, and America* (Berkeley: University of California Press, 2005), 113–42.

40. Lateef, *Gentle Giant,* 50–53, 65, 75, 101.

41. Fred Jung, "A Fireside Chat with Joel Dorn," *Jazz Weekly,* March 12, 2001, www.jazzweekly.com/interviews/dorn.htm.

42. Barry Kernfeld, ed., *The New Grove Dictionary of Jazz* (New York: St. Martin's Press, 1994); Fabian Holt, *Genre in Popular Music* (Chicago: University of Chicago Press, 2007), 2.

43. Compilation of readers' and editors' polls, *Down Beat,* accessed August 6, 2011, www.downbeat.com/default.asp?sect=stories&subsect=story_detail &sid=756.

44. Christopher Washburne, "Miscellaneous Instruments in Jazz," in *The Oxford Companion to Jazz,* ed. Bill Kirchner (New York: Oxford University Press, 2000), 653. The instruments he discusses are flute, organ, Latin percussion, violin, banjo, tuba, euphonium, cello, French horn, oboe, English horn, bassoon, accordion, harmonica, kazoo, bagpipes, harp, and jazz whistling.

45. Black Music Poll, *Ebony,* October 1975, 64–65.

46. David Ake, *Jazz Cultures* (Berkeley: University of California Press, 2002), 42.

47. Dorn, "Makin' the Connection," 11.

48. Gillett, *Making Tracks,* 137.

49. It's an interesting coincidence that this quotation was published in 1974, the year Dorn left Atlantic Jazz. Even more interesting is that Mann was actually hired as head of Atlantic's jazz A&R in 1976, taking over the job that had

been vacated by Dorn; by this time the label's lineup included Jean-Luc Ponty, LesMcCann, Ray Barretto, and Billy Cobham, as well as others on distributed labels. Eliot Tiegel, "Jazz Gets Atlantic Jolt," *Billboard*, October 16, 1976, 1, 14.

50. Mike Gross, "Jazz Skipping New Beat as 'Poppouri,'" *Billboard*, May 11, 1968, 1, 66.

51. Joe Blum, "Straight Talk from Atlantic's Nesuhi Ertegun," *Jazz Times*, August 1987, 23.

CHAPTER 8

The Praxis of Composition-Improvisation and the Poetics of Creative Kinship

TAMAR BARZEL

It wasn't rock, it wasn't jazz, it wasn't "contemporary
music." . . . It was improvising but it was not jazz, it had
a lot of electronics but it wasn't rock, [and] it wasn't
really contemporary [concert] music because of the nature
of the performance style. . . . *What was it?*

—Anthony Coleman, describing his impression of the
rehearsals held in John Zorn's basement in the 1980s

A particular music can be part of more than one history.
And I think that there is a certain trend in jazz . . . a trend
that I notice starting with Thelonious Monk, and Ornette
Coleman's Prime Time Band, and Albert Ayler. These [artists]
can also be written into a history of rock. I have tried to
imagine a history of rock that includes these musicians.

—Marc Ribot, *Marc Ribot: La Corde Perdue*

With the recent publication of George E. Lewis's history of the Association for the Advancement of Creative Musicians (AACM) in New York
City and John Brackett's monograph on composer-improviser John Zorn—
as well as several shorter studies and a number of recent dissertations—
scholars of American music are beginning to give sustained attention to
the experimental music scene that developed on and around Manhattan's Lower East Side in the 1980s and 1990s.[1] The so-called "downtown

scene"—a phrase coined by critics to describe a collaborative network of composer-improvisers who lived and worked in the area—presents us with a body of innovative musical works, accompanied by a quandary. The quandary results both from the creative diversity of the scene and from the nature of its music.

First, there is the question of how to grapple with the nature of the Lower East Side's music world, a larger and more heterogeneous network of artists and ensembles than the one typically delineated by the phrase "downtown scene." It is impossible to generalize about the wider scene without flattening the very differences that animated it. No single rubric can do justice to a creative community that included Zorn's Naked City and Cobra ensembles, John Lurie's Lounge Lizards, Roy Nathanson and Curtis Fowlkes's Jazz Passengers, William Parker's Little Huey Creative Orchestra, Ikue Mori's drum machine and laptop improvisations, Elliott Sharp's Carbon compositions, Butch Morris's conduction orchestras, Shelley Hirsch's vocal performances and electronically manipulated sound canvases, and Marc Ribot's solo guitar work.[2]

Indeed, the wider scene was made up of individuals who took part in a dizzying variety of projects while carving out sui generis creative paths. Most have since built substantial oeuvres of recordings (as leaders and side musicians) and original compositions. Addressing individual works might thus seem more fruitful than attempting to delineate the scene as a unified community. On the other hand, because artists downtown shared myriad creative and professional connections, it is often impossible to abstract one part from the whole. Close readings are necessary but not sufficient: the "scene" resulted from real-time collaborations among composer-improvisers, and as such the scene had a collectively shaped character distinct from the sum of its parts.

The downtown scene presents scholars with two more key challenges. First, it puts into sharp relief the need for new language to address the developing discourse of composition-improvisation in the twentieth century—a discourse that both encompasses and is encompassed by jazz and yet is not fully coterminus with it. Second, the scene challenges us to develop new hermeneutic frames for music whose emblematic qualities include collage, genre blurring, syntactic rupture, and intertextuality.[3] At first reading, such qualities beg to be construed as postmodern. John Zorn's Cobra concept, his "file card" compositions, his epic piece *Locus Solus,* and the "jump cuts" typical of his speed-metal band Naked City are exemplary in this regard. As Brackett asserts, "In the relatively few academic essays that consider Zorn and his music, some link to post-modernity is generally nearby where the term is invoked to help explain the stark juxtapositions and stylistic incongruities that characterize Zorn's musical surfaces."[4]

Much downtown music is also prototypically postmodernist in its ubiquitous referentiality. John Lurie and the Lounge Lizards, for example, developed an aesthetic that audibly but seamlessly incorporates a wealth of timbral, rhythmic, formal, and syntactic influences—or inferences— into elaborate textures of interlocking riffs, precomposed instrumental parts, and improvised solo playing. Vocalist Shelley Hirsch, on the other hand, formulated a theatrical and multiply refracted referential aesthetic—for example, populating a four-part suite, *States,* with a se- quence of fragmented vocal personae set against a kaleidoscopically shifting stylistic texture, whose ostensible "references," as performed by Hirsch in character, function as multilayered simulacra of themselves.[5]

Some downtown music can be productively framed as postmodernist in that it rejects stylistic coherence while exploding both high and low cultural boundaries. Overdetermined webs of ever-refracting musical and textual references may be reasonably interpreted as ahistorical—or as skeptical of historical master narratives. However, while some down- town music may be designed to spurn close historical readings, much of it should be understood as participating in history rather than disengag- ing from it. Downtown's montage-oriented works were prefigured by the music of Frank Zappa and the Art Ensemble of Chicago, while par- alleling the sample-based aesthetic of hip-hop. As a conceptualist in the realm of concert music, John Cage, who engaged the notion of collage as a formal organizing principle in such pieces as *Imaginary Landscape No. 5* and *Williams Mix* (both 1952), was likewise a major influence on downtown composer-improvisers.[6] Indeed, the composer-improvisers discussed earlier may be written into a lineage of artists with like cre- ative concerns—a lineage of which, in interviews and writings and through their musical choices, downtown artists show themselves to be well aware.

Jazz's practices of signification also exerted a strong shaping force throughout the downtown scene. Such practices offer jazz musicians a means of manifesting historical awareness, even as they develop origi- nal ideas and assert a unique creative voice. Thus, saxophonist Charlie Parker's penchant for quoting works from outside the jazz canon is no- table not only as evidence of the artist's talent and wit, nor simply as an example of collage technique. Such quotations were also embedded in a discursive context that was itself intertextual. Working out new ideas amid jazz's intertextual field, composer-improvisers have long served as interlocutors between jazz's past and present. Jazz's near-ubiquitous influence and presence on the scene suggests that downtown's referential language, which may seem to imply a postmodernist ahistoricism, functions on similarly historicist grounds.

Ideally, as more studies are completed, they will interact to form a simulacrum of the whole, whose shape will shift depending on one's vantage point. Indeed, downtown artists were not beholden solely to jazz in developing new language in an improvisational context. In championing nonreferential language, European "free improvisers"—including guitarist Derek Bailey and saxophonist Evan Parker—also exerted a strong influence. However, as the scene's historiography unfolds, I suggest that its main hermeneutic frame should be downtown's function as a key site for developing the discourse of composition-improvisation, an art that in the United States has long been (apart from non-Western idioms) nearly coterminus with jazz. It will be crucial to stay cognizant of the connection of this discourse to, or its distance from, jazz as "Afrological" practice.[7]

As attested by the focus of the present volume, jazz's imperatives toward originality, individual creativity, and change have exerted an entropic force on the genre's core of common-practice language. Downtown artists often cite boundary-pushing composer-improvisers as major influences. A partial list would include Henry Threadgill and James "Blood" Ulmer (both active on the 1980s scene), as well as Duke Ellington, Thelonious Monk, Charles Mingus, Eric Dolphy, Ornette Coleman, Julius Hemphill, and Oliver Lake. Monk, for example, serves as a model both for his grammar of imperfection and for developing a sui generis compositional language with its own internal logic. The downtown scene represented a staging ground for forays into a realm of composition-improvisation that might be termed "postjazz," being unthinkable in the absence of jazz's performance practices and conceptual field but engaging only loosely (or sporadically) with jazz's received syntax. Most artists on the scene created a diverse body of composed-improvised work that varied in how audibly it was linked to jazz through style or repertoire, and that sometimes offered a metacommentary on its relationship to jazz—as in, for example, the music and moniker of the Lounge Lizards; Matt Darriau's avant-swing band Ballin' the Jack; and Elliott Sharp's electric blues band, Terraplane (a reference to Robert Johnson's "Terraplane Blues" from 1936).

In the 1980s the music scene on Manhattan's Lower East Side served as a kind of open-air lab whose artists hailed from widely varying musical backgrounds. Some had formal schooling in jazz or European concert music, while others came downtown after leading or working as side musicians in rock or soul bands. Some had experience in avant-garde theater, in the jazz avant-garde, or in experimental rock. Others were part of the No Wave scene. Some had played jazz professionally. Together these artists formed such a heterogeneous group, and followed such idiosyncratic creative paths, that it is fruitless (and misleading) to try to identify a common style or aesthetic.

But they did share some key concerns. First, they were creative misfits who had come of age during an era of radical changes in the musical landscape. As a result, those who undertook formal training in the 1970s and 1980s tended to be stymied by the creative constraints they encountered in their studies, while those who performed professionally recall searching for a forum that would allow them to synthesize their diverse interests and experiences. Anthony Coleman recalled the resistance he encountered, while studying for his master's degree in music composition at Yale, to the idea of engaging contemporary musical culture outside the concert sphere: "I came back to New York in '79, right after I graduated—after all that *shit* I really was fucked up. I was like *[takes deep breath, then lets it out],* oof! I felt like I'd been in the dryer, you know? Nyaaaaaaaaaaa! *[makes spinning motion accompanied by vibrating dryer whine].* I thought, 'Well, maybe I'm not cut out for this,' you know? And [then I found] Zorn . . . working with these people, in his basement, working on this music that sounded *completely* insane." As noted in the opening epigraph, the music Coleman encountered in Zorn's basement brought together his interests in rock, jazz, electronic music, composition, and improvisation in an exciting way:

> Zorn was doing what I was thinking about, except he had really made this other thing! It didn't sound like anything [else]! . . . I was really fascinated by it, 'cos I was thinking about integrating the stuff I was doing in high school, as a jazz player. At New England [Conservatory, where Coleman studied in the Third Stream department and received his bachelor's degree in music] there was always this feeling of three [separate] things [e.g., classical music, jazz, and popular music]. . . . So all my experimentation was sort of within the context of [challenging this way of thinking and hearing].[8]

Coleman's formal music education was not shared by many of his peers, but the creative frustration he describes was ubiquitous among downtown's newest cohort, most of whose members had witnessed—or, as young performers, had participated in—not only the creative upheavals of 1960s rock, soul, and funk but also the rise of rock counterculture, the New Thing in jazz, European free improvisation, and post-Cage developments in American composition. By the 1970s, however, as most were beginning their performing careers, it was evident that these waves had crested and that for the first time in several decades a generation was coming of age in the absence of a revolution in musical language uniquely suited to its moment. Those who moved downtown in the late 1970s caught the tail end of the revolution wrought by punk rock at the club CBGB, and the postpunk genre dubbed "No Wave" that followed captured the attention of many newcomers. As Don Byron recalled, after arriving downtown "the first cat I played with, that I put immediately on my résumé, was [No Wave punk-funk vocalist/saxophonist] James Chance. I was as proud of that as anything. [Chance] was one of my heroes in music. And I know that he can't play [Coltrane's] 'Giant Steps,' that's not what it was about . . . or [No Wave vocalist] Lydia Lunch. It was just some bad shit, that shit was bad!"[9] The avant-garde jazz and post-Cage compositional cohorts likewise served as beacons to a new generation of musical freethinkers seeking mentors and collaborators and hoping to forge original creative paradigms suited to their moment.

Second, most artists downtown shared an interest in noise, especially as this notion encompasses not only high volumes, dissonance, distortion, and "unmusical" sounds but also conceptual noise, that is, in a loosely Attalian sense, the breach of convention. In disrupting common practice, outré musical language amounted to a kind of defamiliarizing syntactical noise. Artists downtown tended to manifest this interest by juxtaposing idioms that ostensibly did not belong together, tweaking the hierarchies of taste and disrupting the semiotics of style that often underlay judgments of artistic quality. In Coleman's words, "what I'm looking for is to . . . let the references in language flow more freely and anarchically and make sense out of *that*. I'm interested in people who risk incoherence."[10]

Third, far from being militantly beholden to such avant-garde purposes, artists were resolutely pluralistic in their tastes. In addition to such concert music mavericks as Arnold Schoenberg, Karlheinz Stockhausen, and Anton Webern, they engaged the ideas of composer-improvisers from across the jazz pantheon. Their work often shows the influence of both blues-based idioms and pop-oriented, blues-free cartoon and film scores. The fidelity to syntactical noise did not imply a one-note attitude of ironic distance. The scene did not privilege abstract noise canvases over rock-fueled atavism or funk-inspired intensity. Rather, artists were intent on creating original work that stood alone, aspiring to explore new ideas in the absence of the epistemological constraints and possibilities delineated by style.

Finally, downtown artists shared the goal of developing a praxis of composition-improvisation with which to engage the music, and the ideas about music, they found most vital—whatever the era or idiom. Artists, including those not fluent in jazz, sought to develop modes of real-time interaction that would endow them with creative control while giving them a way to forge new musical syntax in collaboration with their colleagues. Individually and in ensembles, they worked out their own methods of composition-improvisation, adopting different creative foci and applying different ideas about which parameters of a work should be left up to the performing artists and which aspects precomposed or dictated by a leader. For creative models artists looked to jazz, to instrumental solos in blues and rock, to the nascent genre of free improvisation, to sound and noise experiments, or to non-Western genres.

Among all these models, an earlier generation of artists played a key role. Musicians affiliated with the jazz avant-garde—including those from Chicago's AACM and St. Louis's BAG (Black Artist Group)—had established themselves in the downtown music world by the 1970s. Their catholic approach to genre, their attention to African American music writ large, and their unorthodox fusions of composition with improvisation strongly influenced the aesthetics, performance practices, and creative aspirations of the 1980s downtown music scene.[11] As Zorn recalled, "I was attracted to the AACM because it seemed they were really involved with taking the emotionally charged blowing sessions that Coltrane and Albert Ayler had put together, and putting them in a new kind of context that created more of a compositional atmosphere instead of a strictly improvisational one."[12] By moving to the Lower East Side, both the AACM generation and their younger colleagues signaled an ambition to enter the ranks of restless thinkers who had been making the trip from hometown to downtown for several generations.

BEFORE AND AFTER THE "DOWNTOWN SCENE"

The Lower East Side's music scene had been reconstituting itself in different guises decades before one part of the scene was noted and dubbed "downtown" in the press.[13] Indeed, the area had long offered support to America's musical iconoclasts and transgressive creative thinkers. Described by artist Brandon LaBelle as an "interdisciplinary hive," the neighborhood saw numerous Cage-inspired happenings in the 1950s and 1960s—including those staged by Yoko Ono and the Fluxus group—and the subsequent influx of a new generation of "minimalist" composers. Living amid clusters of visual artists, filmmakers, and dancers allowed composer-performers such as Meredith Monk to develop interdisciplinary work, while others took advantage of downtown's collaborative ethos to develop new compositions in dedicated performing ensembles.

Giants of the midcentury jazz avant-garde held residencies at local clubs, lasting from one week to several months—Ornette Coleman, Thelonious Monk, and Cecil Taylor at the Five Spot; John Coltrane, Charles Mingus, the Modern Jazz Quartet, and Lennie Tristano at the Half Note; Albert Ayler at the Village Theater; and Sun Ra at Slug's. Such residencies served not only as paying gigs but also as incubators for new ideas, a function that helped forge downtown's reputation as a site of artistic daring. Musicians who lived in the neighborhood fueled this creative energy by using their converted loft-apartments to cultivate an after-hours scene. Musician-run organizations, notably the Jazz Composer's Guild of the mid-1960s, also offered support to local artists who were developing the experimentalist "New Thing" in jazz, thus serving as a key progenitor of the 1980s scene.[14]

Rock counterculture was another important precursor. In the late 1960s the neighborhood had hosted residencies by the Fugs at the Astor Place Playhouse and Frank Zappa and the Mothers of Invention at the Garrick Theater. A decade later, denizens of the club CBGB spurred the emergence of punk rock, an antivirtuosic rearguard aimed at recapturing rock's transgressive edge, a move presaged by such underground bands of the 1960s as the Stooges and the Velvet Underground. In the 1980s downtown venues were crucibles for No Wave, whose artists—including DNA, Mars, the Contortions, and the Theoretical Girls—created a genre of semiotically biting, socially transgressive antipop, partly in revolt against the commercial burnishing of punk rock into "New Wave" music and mod-punk style.

By the early 1970s the Lower East Side hosted a community whose creative multiplicity was unprecedented, but whose different scenes tended to overlap more conceptually than in practice. Gendron chronicles four venues that served the three primary "streams" of the 1970s scene: Studio RivBea (loft jazz); the Mercer Arts Center and CBGB (punk rock); and the Kitchen. By the mid-1970s the Kitchen, which originally focused on post-Cage experimental composers, had begun (under the leadership of trombonist George Lewis) programming avant-garde jazz.[15] As a new cohort of artists began convening downtown in the 1970s and 1980s, their work developed into a fourth stream. This work was shaped by each artist's intention to develop a creative paradigm delineated by a diverse array of musical interests and experiences. For example, vocalist Shelley Hirsch recounted her artistic projects of the late 1970s:

> I did a lot of different kinds of music. Like I was singing for a Korean dancer, I was working with a downtown minimalist composer . . . singing with [pianist] Kirk Nurock. . . . I'd hang out with . . . [Jeffrey Lohn's No Wave band] Theoretical Girls. . . . And then I met [pianist] Joel Forrester and started singing bebop songs with him. And then I joined a rock group. So I was always in different worlds! Always.[16]

Such accounts are typical of musicians in that time and place. For some artists, the search for new paradigms carried a social and political inflection. As clarinetist Marty Ehrlich explained,

> Anthony Braxton put out his solo saxophone record (*For Alto,* 1969)— and inside [in the liner notes] he said, "I listen to James Brown, Karlheinz Stockhausen, Charlie Parker, Mozart, and the [Baka] Pygmies, and Marvin Gaye," or something. . . . That blew my mind, as a young kid! . . . My generation's defined by that. Both a desire, and the fact that everything became available. . . . And I think that's a radical thing. I think we're breaking down the [walls]. And that's been one of my passions.[17]

For reasons pragmatic and creative, artists with the skills to do so also worked in a variety of professional contexts, both downtown and not. As Don Byron, whose primary instrument is clarinet, recalled,

> I was a working saxophone player. Playing a lot of baritone. And then I played a lot of gigs that were kinda in between the cracks of, kind of jazz and classical stuff. . . . I started playing with [guitarist Marc] Ribot [in Rootless Cosmopolitans], and I used to play with [vocalist/guitarist] Kazu [Makino]. . . . And me and [drummer] Ralph Peterson had our thing going [e.g., collaborating in the Ralph Peterson Fo'tet] I was playing with [tenor saxophonist] David Murray, with [trombonist] Craig Harris—and then I was subbing on Broadway. I was playing with [trumpeter/leader] Mario Bauzá, [and] I was doing the Ellington Band [Mercer Ellington Orchestra].[18]

Living and working in proximity was a necessity for composer-improvisers if they were to collectively forge new syntax that would be coherent enough to lead to fruitful interactions but flexible enough that each artist could develop it in unique directions. Both the imperative to play together and the economic scuffle faced by gigging musicians were evident in the challenge of finding spaces in which to congregate, rehearse, and work out new ideas. New arrivals looked to the strategies of colleagues, especially black experimentalists, who had been active in the "loft scene" of the 1960s and 1970s, when the closing of a number of supportive clubs left so few commercial venues for experimental jazz that artists began hosting jam sessions and concerts in their apartments. Composer-improvisers had developed this practice partly through necessity and partly through choice, "to develop alternative spaces that avoided the codes . . . of conventional jazz and classical performance."[19] In the 1980s a cohort of musicians began meeting to jam, rehearse, and perform in a small West Village basement space they called Studio Henry—the same space in which Anthony Coleman, in the opening epigraph, recalled first having participated in one of John Zorn's conducted improvisations.

In the 1980s Zorn's music, the "overproductive signifying community" that formed around it, and the critical attention paid to it, helped to codify the notion of the "downtown scene."[20] Zorn was undoubtedly a dynamic force whose ensembles, compositions, and conducted improvisations drew together a network of like-minded artists. However, the phrase "downtown scene" thus conceived was a misnomer. The music scene downtown was not singular but multiplex—a shifting formation of leaders, side musicians, and groups, with no clear boundaries and many internal differences. The 1980s scene was not a static object with Zorn fixed at its center but rather a shifting fabric of overlapping networks, Zorn's prominent among them, through which artists with different personal and professional backgrounds circulated freely.

In 1987 a club called the Knitting Factory opened on Houston Street on Manhattan's Lower East Side.[21] Following the Kitchen's example but with a focus on new developments in composition-improvisation, the "Knit" began to program work by artists hailing from downtown's many subscenes. Over the next decade, partly as a result of the audience and artist response to the Knitting Factory's programming, the scene's multiplicity became both more tangible to artists and more evident to observers. Although it opened in a scruffy, below-ground space with no air-conditioning, the Knit became a significant social and creative force, serving as a unique meeting point by booking performers from across downtown's creative spectrum.[22]

Rather than residing in any of its individual networks, the downtown scene was constituted by the concrete manifestation—at the Knit and elsewhere—of a unique creative formation. During the club's heyday in the late 1980s and early 1990s, downtown's imagined music community—the larger community implied by the presence of its various smaller ones—manifested itself as real, or at least as possible. This is not to say that downtown's freethinkers were immune to historical contingency or to the exigencies of privilege, access, and difference. The neighborhood's numerous creative scenes were delineated largely by race and to some extent class, and their makeup was determined by networks of professional, educational, and social opportunity as much as by musical focus.[23] The Lower East Side, moreover, was not the city's sole bastion of new developments in composition-improvisation. In parallel with the downtown scene of the 1980s, the M-Base collective, founded by saxophonist Steve Coleman and trumpeter Graham Haynes, was operating in Brooklyn, while free jazz had outposts not only downtown but also in Brooklyn and Harlem.[24] Salsa was still flourishing, not only in Loisada (i.e., the Lower East Side) and Spanish Harlem, but also in the South Bronx—a neighborhood where young MCs and DJs were developing the genre of hip-hop, engaging to new ends both composition-improvisation and collage technique.

The Knit was hardly a utopian space, and unlike such activist spaces as ABC No Rio, it was a commercial venue with no overt political mission.[25] The club also played a more important role as a gathering space for new arrivals in search of a community than it did for those working in free jazz circles established in the 1960s and 1970s. Indeed, the Knitting Factory scene was not a microcosm of the Lower East Side's music world. By and large the club did not program salsa or hip-hop, both of which were presented at other downtown venues. The Knit thus reified certain class- and race-based boundaries rather than redressing them.

Despite its limitations, the Knit of the late 1980s offered a moment of recognition for a culturally diverse community of like-minded artists, reflecting back to them, albeit imperfectly, both an image of the larger scene and the role played by their work and ideas in relation to the whole. As Byron recalled,

Everybody lived within walking distance from the old Knit [i.e., the club's original location]. . . . There was a lot of intermingling, and people heard and got to respect [one another]. . . . There's no place like that any more, where the scene is so alive that I just want to be there *tonight*, to see what's gonna come down. . . . Being able to hear that kind of a range of music, at one place I frequented. . . . I felt completely comfortable at the Knitting Factory. . . . Anything could happen on a given night. [That was] the way I thought about music. *I* could be playing anything on a given night. So, I liked going there more than I liked going to Bradley's [a jazz club in the West Village]. Bradley's didn't express all of me. Nor did going to the New York Philharmonic, or going to the Met. Those things only expressed a part of me. The Knitting Factory expressed quite a bit of me.[26]

Byron's warmth toward the sense of community engendered by the Knitting Factory was shared among many of my interviewees. Although the scene has since dissipated, artists continue to pride themselves on aesthetic choices now associated with the club: devoting themselves to uncompromising music; mastering and then rejecting stylistic norms; creating sonic and symbolic cross talk among distinct discursive modes (formal abstraction, unabashed noise, danceable grooves); and embracing pluralism while insisting on the primacy of the individual voice.

HISTORY, RESPONSIBILITY, TRADITION?

With this sketch of the 1980s scene in place, we can return to the question of how to approach its music analytically—and, accordingly, how to situate it culturally while developing a hermeneutic that takes into account its constituent ontologies. Although there are many possible points of entry, I find the question of jazz's role in regard to downtown music most salient. Jazz served as the main vehicle of and expression for the twentieth century's developing discourse of composition-improvisation. I would argue that one key aspect of jazz's self-fashioned identity should serve as "always-already" for nearly any analysis of contemporary composition-improvisation: its artists' evident sense of responsibility toward their idiom's history.

As asserted by both artists and jazz scholars, jazz's depth of expression results in part from its dialogic relationship to its own history and, consequently, from the particular cultural valences of that history in relation to each musician. Moreover, one of jazz's main tenets is the responsibility it confers on each performer to develop a personal sound— a timbre, instrumental (or vocal) character, and compositional syntax— to contribute uniquely to a dialogic whole. Jazz has thus long functioned as an intratextual discourse that signifies on its own history even as its artists develop the music in new directions. However, jazz artists have always been selective about the aspects of the idiom they choose to engage, and over time they have developed a disparate body of works and practices that, far from conforming to a single style, are linked by family resemblances into an irregular concatenation. As such, composer-improvisers developed a discourse that unfolded self-reflexively through a dialectic of continuity and rupture with jazz's own received tropes and practices. The downtown scene included many artists who chose to engage this dialectic, developing a practice of composition-improvisation that was fundamentally interpellated by jazz in method and philosophy but that also engaged wide interests beyond jazz per se.[27]

Jazz thus proffered to composer-improvisers not only a set of performance practices but also a sense of intimate contact with their predecessors' creative work, a relation artists often describe in terms of respect, appreciation, and responsibility. The substance of such responsibility is open to interpretation, and differences over this interpretation fueled the bitter conflicts of the 1980s between uptown (Lincoln Center) "traditionalists" and downtown "experimentalists."[28] Although musicians differ with respect to their engagement with jazz history and tradition, the nature of jazz discourse entails that such an engagement always be present. As such differences indicate, however, jazz musicians are not simply responsible for engaging "jazz history" per se, but they are also obligated to participate in constructing it.

To become a jazz musician is to take on a measure of responsibility toward both a musical idiom and a central aspect of African American cultural and intellectual history. However, composers or improvisers are not simply "tradition bearers" but also the architects of a sounded lineage of personal influence.[29] Over the course of an improvisation or a career, they sonically materialize their own unique, imagined creative tradition. What of jazz's dialogic system of meaning-making and its relationship to history on the downtown scene? Gauging some of their main interests, it might be assumed that many in the 1980s cohort would be hostile toward a notion of artistic responsibility in regard to history and tradition: free improvisation champions "a meticulous avoidance of any reference to pre-existing musical language," while No Wave casts a jaundiced eye toward convention, inserting itself into history mainly through constructing an aesthetic that savages all available musical precedents.[30] Downtown artists' purportedly postmodern panreferentiality can be taken similarly—as indicating a refusal to engage history or tradition beyond artistic traditions of transgression.[31]

Writing of the late 1970s, historian Luc Sante indicates that a disinterest in the history of the neighborhood was widely shared among the many aspiring culture makers who settled on the Lower East Side: "All of us were in that stage of youth when your star may not yet have risen, but your moment is the only one on the clock. . . . In our arrogance we were barely conscious of the much deeper past that lay all around." Referring to the remnants of turn-of-the-century immigrant culture in the now decaying neighborhood, Sante continues, "Our neighborhood was so chockablock with ruins we didn't question the existence of vast bulks of shuttered theaters, or wonder when they had been new. Our apartments were furnished exclusively through scavenging, but we didn't find it notable that nearly all our living rooms featured sewing-machine tables with cast-iron bases."[32]

In some senses, Sante's observation holds true for musicians downtown, most of whom were busy inventing themselves in a way that did not reflect directly on the historical import of their immediate surroundings. However, such ahistoricism belies my interactions with downtown-based artists and my understanding of their work. Although panhistorical referentiality can be construed as simply ahistorical, the artists I have encountered have been nothing if not attentive to the play of historical and cultural nuance between their own music and that which precedes and prefigures it. Recall Marc Ribot's suggestion in the opening epigraph that through his work he has tried to "write" certain composer-improvisers into a creative legacy—rock—from which they have been conventionally excluded. Ribot's free improvisation/noise band Spiritual Unity, whose musical conception is grounded in the work of saxophonist Albert Ayler (and whose name is taken from the title of a 1964 Ayler album), is one among many manifestations of this intention in his oeuvre.

Indeed, I read nearly all the music of the scene as deeply implicating itself in its historical legacy, rather than asserting an ahistorical stance. Although some downtown music may strive to float free of any cultural or historical context, much other work, through allusion and reference, implies a past-present dialogue that is jazz-based and, as such, Afrological in nature. As trumpeter Frank London recalled, artists from the AACM influenced his creative cohort "in absolutely every way. In their embracing the totality of their culture, in their demand to represent what they were doing and not be represented by others. . . . In their [embrace of] history in the biggest sense. In their absolute drive to creativity at every moment. In the goal of finding your personal essence beyond genre, beyond style. In walking and subverting the lines between insiders, outsider. . . . God, I can't think of a way that they didn't influence what we were doing."[33]

London's reference to history is one key to assessing downtown's aesthetic economy.

Even Zorn, whose statements and music often suggest an antipathy toward framing artists as tradition bearers, can surprise in this regard. As Brackett asserts, Zorn's compositional practice in his dedicated works functions as a form of "gift-giving," an artistic homage, rendered in sound, to one artist in his pantheon of influences. For example, the formal construction of Zorn's *Untitled* (Joseph Cornell) "invites a close, analytical reading where we might expect to uncover some sort of hidden logic or patterning," yet there is none discernible. Instead, Zorn uses "various combinations of recognizable gestures, harmonies, textures, and timbres . . . to create an emergent work" whose structure and affect mimic the varied repetition, and the implied but ambiguous relation among objects, typical of Cornell's work. Zorn thus makes manifest his creative debt to Cornell, while reciprocating through a musical gift.[34]

Zorn is not alone in such practices. Downtown artists have frequently paid tribute to creative progenitors, both through names and repertoire: hence, the band Jazz Passengers, whose name is derived from Art Blakey's Jazz Messengers; Anthony Coleman's *Freakish,* a solo piano recording interpreting the work of Jelly Roll Morton; and Shelley Hirsch's radical reimagining of the Rodgers and Hart song, "Blue Moon."[35] Most of their colleagues—whether more or less oriented toward jazz—have likewise shown themselves to be deeply invested in the question of what their music says, or should say, about their place in history and about their relationship to artists and thinkers who have preceded them. Each has taken on a dual task: not only developing original work through an idiosyncratic practice of composition-improvisation but also constructing an imagined tradition to which that work is literally and conceptually beholden. Each has thus created an oeuvre that manifests not only a creative vision but also an investment in an idea of historical relationality and responsibility. Although individual pieces function differently in this regard, over the course of a career an artist's work can be heard as enacting a historical dialogue that infers but does not flatten relationships among artists across time, space, and idiom. It is this dynamic that leads me to suggest that our understanding of composition-improvisation should hinge on a notion of praxis.

Thus, one artist's quick barrage of allusions to Stravinsky, Hendrix, Mingus, Wanda Jackson, and the Velvet Underground manifests not (or not only) a postmodern sensibility but rather the grounds for imagining a pantheon of predecessors to whom her work enacts a poetics of creative kinship. Brackett's illuminating analysis of Zorn's musical homages offers a finely tuned musicological model for analyzing the nature of such poetics. In assessing the music of the downtown scene, then, I suggest that we consider it as being embedded both in its wider creative community and in a larger cultural and historical discourse of composition-improvisation. In that this discourse is closely connected to jazz, it charges each artist with the responsibility of enacting a dialogic exchange between jazz's past and its present. In this sense, the discourse is Afrological. One key question to be asked of each work, then, is whether the tradition it conceptualizes is Afrological in substance as well as praxis. The possibility should of course remain open that some artists, and some musical works, are not especially invested in historical contingency or are, in fact, pursuing means to abstract themselves from such contingency, whether Afrological or otherwise. However, we should also keep in mind that a piece of the most wildly multifarious downtown music might effect the converse of what an ahistoricist analysis would suggest: not—or not only—enacting synaptic overload and syntactic rupture but also offering a concise and carefully coded reading of the particular artistic legacy in which it construes itself to be embedded.

NOTES

I would like extend my thanks to the editors of this volume, as well as to Gurminder Bhogal and Benjamin Piekut, for their close reading and comments.

1. The history of the scene can be roughly bracketed between the early 1980s and the early 2000s. Although many artists and organizations are still part of the downtown's cultural fabric, as a community the "scene" is now once again more imagined than concrete. Recent scholarly treatments include Bernard Gendron, "The Downtown Music Scene," in *The Downtown Book: The New York Art Scene 1974–1984*, ed. Marvin J. Taylor (Princeton, NJ: Princeton University Press, 2005), 41–65; George E. Lewis, *A Power Stronger Than Itself: The AACM and American Experimental Music* (Chicago: University of Chicago Press: 2008); Caroline O'Meara, "The Bush Tetras, 'Too Many Creeps,' and New York City," *American Music* 25, no. 2 (Summer 2007): 193–215; Scott A. Currie, "Sound Visions: An Ethnographic Study of Avant-Garde Jazz in New York City," PhD diss. (New York University, 2009); John Brackett, *John Zorn: Tradition and Transgression* (Bloomington: Indiana University Press, 2008); and Benjamin Piekut, *Experimentalism Otherwise: The New York Avant-Garde and Its Limits* (Berkeley: University of California Press, 2011). For writings by musicians, see the *Arcana* series of collected essays; the most recent volume is John Zorn, ed., *Arcana V: Music, Magic and Mysticism* (New York: Hips Road, 2010).

2. Downtown's earlier scenes were likewise resistant to easy summation. As Gendron observes in his discussion of CBGB's heyday in the 1970s, neither "punk" nor "New Wave" captured the diversity of a scene that included "the Ramones' 'dumbed-down' lyrics and speeded-up garage band riffs, Patti Smith's snarling poetry, the Talking Heads' spastic sounds . . . Television's meandering improvisations, the Voidoids' anthemic nihilism, and Blondie's retro girl-group posturings." "Downtown Music Scene," 53.

3. For a discussion of collage in electroacoustic music, including that of downtown vocalist Shelley Hirsch, see Ann LeBaron, "Reflections of Surrealism in Postmodern Musics," in *Postmodern Music/Postmodern Thought,* ed. Judy Lochhead and Joseph Auner (New York: Routledge, 2002), 49–61.

4. Brackett, *John Zorn,* xiii. For citations to literature that addresses Zorn's music vis-à-vis postmodernism, see note 2 on page 171. For a critical assessment of the relation between music and postmodernism, see David Brackett, "Where's It At? Postmodern Theory and the Contemporary Musical Field," in Lochhead and Auner, *Postmodern Music,* 207–34, esp. 213–15; and Vincent Cotro, "La résurgence du passé dans le jazz contemporain: Une problématique post-moderne?" [The resurgence of the past in contemporary jazz: A postmodern problematic?] *Revue de Musicologie* 91, no. 2 (2005): 425–54. For a productive reframing of musical traits typically discussed under the sign of postmodernism, see David Ake, "Sound and Time: Sex Mob and the Carnivalesque in Postwar Jazz," in *Jazz Matters: Sound, Place, and Time since Bebop* (Berkeley: University of California Press, 2010), 54–74.

5. John Zorn, *Locus Solus,* Rift 7, 1983, LP; Shelley Hirsch, "States," on *States,* Tellus TE-C003, 1997, compact disc; John Zorn, *Naked City,* Elektra Nonesuch 9 79238-2, 1990, LP; John Lurie/Lounge Lizards, *Voice of Chunk,* Strange and Beautiful Music SB 0012, 1988, LP.

6. Among the many other composers who have used collage, a few who have drawn the interest of musicians downtown include Mauricio Kagel, Gustav Mahler, Carl Stalling, and Karlheinz Stockhausen.

7. George E. Lewis, "Improvised Music after 1950: Afrological and Eurological Perspectives," *Black Music Research Journal* 16, no. 1 (Spring 1996): 110–11.

8. Anthony Coleman, interview with the author, August 13, 2001, New York.

9. Don Byron, interview with the author, February 12, 2004, New York.

10. Coleman, interview.

11. Although the scene was driven by artists' creative and professional interests, it was not wholly apolitical. Benefit concerts were common, including those held at the Knitting Factory, and many artists were involved with political causes, both individually and in ad hoc formations. Some artists also followed the AACM in chartering (and sustaining) not-for-profit organizations—including Roulette, ABC No Rio, and the Art for Arts/Vision Festival—devoted to fostering progressive politics, experimental arts, and community uplift.

12. Zorn, in William Duckworth, *Conversations with John Cage, Phillip Glass, Laurie Anderson, and Five Generations of American Experimental Composers* (New York: Da Capo, 1999), 457–58. Zorn's reproduction here of the familiar dichotomy between "emotional" improvisation (blowing) versus rational

composition illustrates how powerful this trope can be, even among artists who normally reject it.

13. Brandon LaBelle, *Background Noise: Perspectives on Sound Art* (New York: Continuum International), 58. Cf. "A Lower East Side Retrospective," ed. Lorenzo Thomas, special issue, *African American Review* 27, no. 4 (Winter, 1993): 569–98.

14. See Michael Dessen, "Decolonizing Art Music: Scenes from the Late Twentieth-Century United States" (PhD diss., University of California, San Diego, 2003), for a discussion of the racial politics involved in critics' creation of the "loft-jazz" moniker. By the 1980s, writes Lewis, the loft scene "was all but dead in New York, the victim of competition . . . from better-funded, higher-infrastructure New York spaces. . . . Moreover, the more established artists [from the loft scene] could obtain work at traditional club spaces . . . to say nothing of the expanded opportunities then becoming available in Europe." "Experimental Music," 123. For a discussion of the Jazz Composer's Guild, see Piekut, *Experimentalism Otherwise,* 102–39.

15. Gendron, "Downtown Music Scene," 44.

16. Shelley Hirsch, interview with the author, February 24, 2003, New York.

17. Marty Ehrlich, interview with the author, February 1, 2004, New York.

18. Byron, interview. This iteration of the Fo'tet also included Bryan Carrott (vibraphone) and Melissa Slocum (bass).

19. Lewis, "Experimental Music," 121.

20. Barry Shank, *Dissonant Identities: The Rock 'n' Roll Scene in Austin, Texas* (Hanover, CT: Wesleyan University Press, 1994), 120.

21. For a discussion of the Knit's early history by the club's cofounder, see Michael Ethan Dorf, *Knitting Music: A Five-Year History of the Knitting Factory* (New York: Knitting Factory Works, 1992).

22. In 1998 the club Tonic opened on the Lower East Side, supplanting the Knitting Factory as downtown's major commercial venue and gathering place. Tonic closed in 2007, even as artists who had once lived downtown moved away and a new generation of experimentalists settled in Brooklyn, which is now home to Roulette and Issue Project Room, two major nonprofit experimental music venues. Several commercial clubs in Manhattan and Brooklyn, including Le Poisson Rouge and Barbès, now program downtownish music, but the community is less cohesive without sharing a neighborhood, a de facto artists' space, or a community center. In 2009 the Knitting Factory (which had formerly relocated to TriBeCa) moved to Williamsburg, Brooklyn.

23. For an original and illuminating investigation into the theory of musical networks and the roles of race, class, and gender in shaping received notions of musical "experimentalism," see Piekut, *Experimentalism Otherwise,* 5–19.

24. For a brief discussion of M-Base, see Maureen Mahon, *Right To Rock: The Black Rock Coalition and the Cultural Politics of Race* (Durham, NC: Duke University Press, 2004).

25. ABC No Rio, which was founded in 1980, is a left-wing activist, artist, and performance collective that aims to "facilitate cross-pollination between artists and activists." "Overview," ABC No Rio, accessed February 1, 2011, www.abcnorio.org/about/overview.html.

26. Byron, interview. For a review of the club in its early years, see Jon Pareles, "Recordings: Fresh Shipments from the Knitting Factory," *New York Times*, April 30, 1989.

27. As asserted by Salim Washington, "The entire history of jazz, with its rapid advancement of styles and genres, could be understood as an avant-garde movement. . . . In many dominant narratives, however, certain black social and aesthetic practices have been routinely marginalized, if not rendered invisible. One way that these important emphases tend to be lost or misrepresented is by severing the avant-garde character from the mainstream of the music. Rather than explain avant-garde aesthetics as a primary *principle* of the music, jazz critics and writers have often chosen to isolate the avant-garde as a *style* practiced by a fringe element of the jazz community." "All the Things You Could Be by Now": Charles Mingus Presents Charles Mingus and the Limits of Avant-Garde Jazz," in *Uptown Conversation: The New Jazz Studies*, ed. Robert G. O'Meally, Brent Hayes Edwards, and Farah Jasmine Griffin (New York: Columbia University Press, 2004), 27.

28. For a useful framing of this conflict, see Jerome Harris, "Jazz on the Global Stage," in *The African Diaspora: A Musical Perspective*, ed. Ingrid Tolia Monson (New York: Garland, 2000), 103–36, esp. 120–22.

29. The phrase "tradition bearer" refers to Mellonee Burnim, "Culture Bearer and Tradition Bearer: An Ethnomusicologist's Research on Gospel Music," *Ethnomusicology* 29, no. 3 (1985): 432–447. Cf. John P. Murphy, "Jazz Improvisation: The Joy of Influence," *Black Perspective in Music* 18, no. 1–2 (1990): 7–19.

30. Marc Ribot, "The Representation of Jewish Identity in Downtown Music," unpublished essay, in the author's possession, ca. 1996.

31. Brackett, *John Zorn*, 167.

32. Luc Sante, "My Lost City," *New York Times Book Review* 50, no. 17 (November 6, 2003): www.nybooks.com/articles/16737. Cf. Holland Cotter, "Remembrance of Downtown Past," *New York Times*, September 1, 2006, and "A Return Trip to a Faraway Place Called Underground," *New York Times*, January 26, 2007.

33. Frank London, interview by Marcus Gammel, April 15, 1999, in Marcus Gammel, "Migration and Identity Politics in New York's Jewish Downtown Scene," Humboldt-Universität zu Berlin, Lerhstuhl fúr Theorie und Geschichte der populären Musik, www2.hu-berlin.de/fpm/wip/gammel_01.htm.

34. Brackett, *John Zorn*, 104, 108.

35. See Anthony Coleman, *Freakish: Anthony Coleman Plays Jelly Roll Morton*, Tzadik TZ 7631, 2009, compact disc; and Shelley Hirsch, "Blue Moon," on *The Far In, Far Out Worlds of Shelley Hirsch*, 1996–97, Tzadik TZ 7705, 2002, compact disc.

CHAPTER 9

The Sound of Struggle

Black Revolutionary Nationalism and
Asian American Jazz

LOREN KAJIKAWA

> Are you Chinese or Charlie Chan? Charlie was a white man.
> With his two buckteeth and his eyes pulled back,
> Vincent Chin lies dead from his racist attack.
> Are you Chinese or Charlie Chan? Charlie was a white man.

These lyrics form part of the chorus to "Are You Chinese or Charlie Chan?," the title track from pianist Jon Jang's independently produced 1983 album. Recorded at the height of the Asian American consciousness movement, the song's chorus refers repeatedly to the fictional Chinese American detective Charlie Chan, the lead character in more than forty films between 1931 and 1949. Much to the chagrin of Asian American activists who interpreted these films through the lens of post-1960s racial politics, Chan was played by a series of white actors, including Warner Oland, Sidney Toler, and Roland Winters.

The graphic design for Jang's album cover features two photographs: one taken from a Charlie Chan film and the other a satirical parody featuring Jang himself (fig. 9.1). Framed by a detective's magnifying glass held by a yellow hand, the costumed image of Jang, hand over mouth in a look of surprise, appears embarrassed to be unmasked as an imposter. The obvious point here is that one should strive to be authentically Chinese and not "Charlie Chan." Turning the album over, we read that *real* Chinese are those to whom the album is dedicated, "those Asian brothers and sisters who are struggling to create a better world."[1]

FIGURE 9.1. Jon Jang, *Are You Chinese or Charlie Chan?* RPM 5, 1983, cover. Courtesy of Jon Jang.

The chorus of "Are You Chinese or Charlie Chan?" also mentions Vincent Chin, a young Chinese American engineer from Detroit who was beaten to death in June 1982 after a barroom confrontation in which two laid-off auto workers, Ronald Ebens and Michael Nitz, blamed Chin for the loss of their jobs, assuming incorrectly that he was Japanese. Ebens and Nitz pursued Chin through the streets of Detroit, striking him repeatedly with a baseball bat. The two men were convicted of manslaughter after a plea bargain brought the charges down from second-degree murder. They served no jail time, only three years of probation. The judge presiding over the case defended the reduced sentence by explaining, "These weren't the kind of men you send to jail. . . . You don't make the punishment fit the crime; you make the punishment fit the criminal."[2] The lenient sentencing sparked a movement to bring Vincent Chin's case to nationwide attention, helping motivate and inspire a generation of Asian American activists.

Jang takes a unique approach to confronting these serious racial issues. Setting satirical lyrics to a bouncing boogie-woogie piano accompaniment,

Jang's performance provides some intriguing juxtapositions. By critiquing Asian minstrelsy, otherwise known as "yellowface," and suggesting that racial stereotypes perpetuate anti-Asian violence, the lyrics encourage listeners to be authentically Chinese—but the form of the song is a straight twelve-bar blues.[3] Similarly, in a spoken interlude, which is listed in the liner notes as the "no-fortune-cookie-jive-rap," Japanese Americans Woody Ichiyasu and Bob Matsueda critique anti-Asian racism using their own version of black vernacular speech (e.g., "Yo Brian! What's happenin' man?" and "Sheeeeyit. How many Asian brothers you know actually talk like that?"). Finally, "Are You Chinese or Charlie Chan?" takes some surprising musical turns, slipping between a conventional blues performance and a dissonant, freely improvised bridge.[4]

A song that refutes demeaning stereotypes and sets out a politicized Asian American identity by harnessing the power of black music and speech, "Are You Chinese or Charlie Chan?" encapsulates the main theme of this essay: the influence of African American culture on the formation of Asian American identity. The black liberation movement and the sounds of avant-garde jazz deeply affected the lives and musical activities of a group of mainly Chinese American and Japanese American musicians who came of age in the late 1960s and early 1970s and then gathered and supported one another in the 1980s under the rubric of "Asian American jazz."[5] African American music and politics provided a filter through which musicians like Jang understood their own musical efforts.[6] Jang himself employed the rhetoric of "self-determination" familiar to students of 1960s political culture in the liner notes to the album, remarking that "what is significant about this recording is that it is music about Asian Americans, by Asian Americans, for Asian Americans and created from the Asian American community."[7]

The work of these musicians underscores the fact that in the United States, black music is not simply a voice from the margins but rather a set of deeply embedded cultural forms that pervade a variety of racialized contexts. Asian American jazz musicians were highly aware that they were working a cultural field sown by African American artists, and their cultivation of an Asian voice within this tradition reflects the complicated cultural history of jazz. Rather than create a separate music that was uniquely Asian, the activities of these musicians speak to what scholar Lisa Lowe has termed the "hybridity" of Asian American culture. By "hybridity," Lowe refers to the "growing together" of cultural practices that results from the intersection of Asian American art with other communities and traditions. Rather than representing a "failed assimilation" to dominant forms (in this case, jazz) Lowe argues that Asian American art celebrates survival, refuses assimilation, and brings submerged histories to light.[8]

This essay explores the musical activities of Jon Jang and others to understand their attempts at creating Asian American hybrid art and addresses the following questions: Why was the music of the African American avant-garde so crucial and so relevant to Asian American musicians in the 1980s? What were Asian American musicians trying to accomplish with their music? What kind of framework did the black experimental music tradition provide for them? Finally, what challenges do the lives and work of Asian American musicians present to jazz historiography and hermeneutics?

ASIAN AMERICANS AND THE BLACK AVANT-GARDE

The diversity of Asian peoples in the United States makes the term "Asian American" problematic. I will not claim that there is an Asian American essence that can be expressed in music. Rather, the term is necessary for this examination because it is how the musicians in this study describe who they are and what they do; an *idea of Asian American music* has played an important role in shaping their endeavors.[9] By listening, performing, recording, publishing, and distributing their music, they and their supporters came together as "Asian Americans," proving sociologist Yen Le Espiritu's observation that "ethnicization—the process of boundary construction—is not only reactive, a response to pressures from the external environment, but also creative, a product of internally generated dynamics." Oliver Wang has argued, building on Espiritu's study of Asian American "panethnicity," that musical activity is a key *creative* force driving the construction of Asian American identity.[10] The shape that this identity took for Asian American jazz musicians depended heavily on the politics and art of the Black Power era.

In their work on "racial formation"—a theory that seeks to understand how racial meanings, far from being stable entities, are created, inhabited, and transformed by political struggle—Michael Omi and Howard Winant outline the growth of black nationalist projects in the 1960s. A key characteristic of nationalist politics, they argue, is an attempt to counter the racist logic of cultural domination by fostering "cultures of resistance."[11] In the 1960s nothing seemed to capture the restless energy and radical politics of black nationalism better than the growth of the experimental music that followed in the wake of

Ornette Coleman's historic Atlantic recording *Free Jazz* (1961). Referred to variously as "avant-garde," "the New Thing," "free jazz," and "creative music," the eclectic sounds of African American artists such as John Coltrane, Sun Ra, Archie Shepp, Cecil Taylor, members of the Art Ensemble of Chicago, and others contributed (sometimes willfully, sometimes not) to nationalist politics.[12]

Black activists, including many musicians, believed that the most experimental and cutting-edge sectors of the jazz world could contribute to political change. Saxophonist Archie Shepp offers a particularly vivid example of this perspective: "The Negro musician is a reflection of the Negro people as a social phenomenon. His purpose ought to be to liberate America aesthetically and socially from its inhumanity. The inhumanity of the white American to the black American, as well as the inhumanity of the white American to the white American, is not basic to America and can be exorcised. I think the Negro people through the force of their struggles are the only hope of saving America, the political or cultural America."[13]

Shepp's statement is emblematic of the nationalist impulse to promote culture as a means to achieve political and social progress. Omi and Winant explain that this idea was the result of a racial shift in the 1960s, a "great transformation" from the "ethnicity paradigm" of race to "new social movements," predicated on the rejection of cultural assimilation.[14] Rather than seeing the path to freedom paved by discarded ethnic characteristics (black speech, black music, etc.), many activists and artists in the late 1960s viewed the cultivation of certain racial traits as the best way to ensure that communities of color would not replicate what they believed to be the oppressive nature of white-dominated society. In avant-garde jazz circles, this nationalist impulse was often augmented by a modernist "Adornian" Marxism that equated aesthetic disruption with revolutionary politics.[15]

In many ways, Asian American musicians agreed with Shepp's ideas about the revolutionary potential of African American culture. Feeling that they too had experienced the degrading inhumanity of racism, black art and black politics gave them a way to begin coming to grips with their own marginality. Musician and writer Paul Yamazaki evocatively described this attraction as follows: "In the African American musical tradition, the musician is much more than an interpreter of formally organized sounds. He is a musical alchemist, fusing desire, spirit and intellect into a creation of the most subversive beauty. At his best, he is an insurrectionary who plays in a tradition that has its inspiration in a people's dream of freedom; and he creates in an aesthetic that challenges him to improvise, to seize, in performance, the moment of his own liberation. Among Asian Americans, it is this freedom, implicit in African-American music, which has inspired several generations to play jazz."[16]

Due to the influence of neoconservatism in politics and a neotraditionalist movement in jazz spearheaded by Wynton Marsalis, it may be tempting to regard the 1980s as a conservative period dominated by backlash against the perceived excesses of the 1960s. For Asian Americans, however, the Reagan-Bush years offered opportunities to put revolutionary nationalist ideas about race and music into practice. The Asian American movement was just reaching its peak. A key driving force was the growth of a nationwide movement to gain redress and reparations—an official apology and financial compensation—for the Japanese Americans who suffered preemptive incarceration during World War II. The issue of redress as well as cases of anti-Asian violence like the Vincent Chin incident energized Asian American activists and encouraged them to form coalitions. These activities fostered a sense of political empowerment and ethnic awareness that spilled over into other political and cultural activities. As Susan M. Asai argues, an understanding of Asian American jazz "requires an understanding of the motivations and aspirations involved in the larger context of the Asian American movement."[17]

Asian American jazz musicians saw their work as a part of this growing movement, and many were so committed to political activism that, risking family opprobrium and financial instability, they dropped out of prestigious university programs or turned their backs on white-collar jobs to devote their energies full-time to music and political organizing. Pianist Glenn Horiuchi dropped out of UC San Diego's graduate program in mathematics to work a series of blue-collar jobs, including a stint on a repair crew for the Los Angeles Department of Water and Power. Similarly, saxophonist Fred Ho graduated from Harvard in 1979 with a bachelor's degree in sociology but promptly took up work in construction. Most dramatically, pianist and future koto player Miya Masaoka shocked her parents by dropping out of high school to pursue revolutionary activism and union organizing. By expressing solidarity with the working class, these young activist musicians sought to unite their politics with their art, pledging their allegiance to a version of jazz authenticity derived from Charlie Parker's famous dictum that "if you don't live it, it won't come out of your horn."[18]

On a more practical level, refusing professional careers allowed these musicians to devote themselves full-time to political and cultural work.

As tenor saxophonist Francis Wong later recalled, the years from 1984 to 1988 were "high-water marks for the Asian American consciousness movement. We were trying to be active with our music and trying to identify with the movement. It was a very positive period. If it wasn't for that time we would not have been moved to create a lot of the work in the context that we did, with the content and substance that it had."[19] To understand this content, we must look more closely at the formative influence of avant-garde jazz on Asian American musicians' ideas about identity, race, and music.

While Asian American women were active in Japanese *taiko* drumming groups and in the world of jazz fusion, where June Kuramoto's improvised koto playing helped the group Hiroshima gain an international following, Asian American jazz was a masculine modernist space. Much like the black avant-gardists who inspired them, Asian American jazz artists—mainly second- and third-generation Chinese American and Japanese American males born between 1954 and 1957—set their bold musical experiments in opposition to the "feminized" world of popular music. Too young to participate in political struggle with the generation of 1968—most of them were still in grade school the year Malcolm X was assassinated—these young musicians' first encounter with radical black politics and culture was mediated by sound recordings, photographic images, and published writing. Listening to what they felt was the most exciting music to emerge from the 1960s, these musicians were awed by the moral and artistic power of black music and found it relevant to their own lives. Asian Americans' engagement with jazz—the politics, culture, and history behind it—enabled them to identify with the black musical experience as a form of resistance and encouraged them to develop their own identities.[20] And more than any other single inspiration, these musicians repeatedly testify to the transformative power of the late recordings of John Coltrane.

In the last years of his life, Coltrane, who had already become known for his musical restlessness and penchant for experimentation, broke radically with his past career as a giant of modal jazz. Entirely abandoning fixed key centers, chord progressions, and time signatures, Coltrane played whatever he wanted whenever he wished, moving from one key area to another at will.[21] The operative word here is indeed "will." As Scott Saul documents, the circuitous, aggressively pursued solo lines of Coltrane's late music, which often culminated in piercing screams, seemed to many listeners the result of some self-contained, personal logic.[22]

This effect resulted from a number of musical practices, including intense motivic work, extreme shifts in register, and free tempo. Coltrane continued to organize his long solos around short combinations of notes or motivic cells, such as the F–A♭–B♭ on which he bases his improvisation in the first movement of *A Love Supreme*. Driven, it seems, to explore all possible permutations, Coltrane subjected his melodic material to relentless recombination—turning it upside down, reversing it, and sequencing it—until it grew into an epic torrent of sound. Such dogged perseverance gave listeners the impression of someone chasing after a goal with the utmost commitment and resolve. In addition, Coltrane's use of extreme shifts in register, including his screams, modeled moments of transcendence. Coltrane developed the altissimo range of his saxophone up through a full octave above f'. Crafting solo lines that emphasized abrupt shifts in register—as if he were trying to play one melody in counterpoint with an accompanying part below—Coltrane created the impression that he could transcend the monophonic nature of his chosen instrument.[23] Indeed, the sound of Coltrane breaking into a soaring screech, of pushing beyond what his instrument was supposed to do, gave voice to the raw emotional quality of the era's quest for freedom. As observers noted, the result was a challenging, turbulent sound, only for the most committed and adventurous fans. For listeners searching for a form of expression suited to black nationalist politics, Coltrane's late music seemed to provide a musical analogue to political self-determination.

Like the militant rhetoric of Black Power, Coltrane's new sound had a polarizing effect on listeners, and his avant-garde experiments caused controversy among fans. Some felt puzzled, or worse, betrayed; others embraced the new sound, hearing in it seeds of resistance that could help ignite a global movement for black liberation. As Jamaican-born journalist, novelist, and playwright Lindsay Barrett exclaimed, "If a black man could grasp a Coltrane [saxophone] solo in its entirety as a club, and wield it with the force that first created it centuries before the white man moved Coltrane and his ancestors from the cave of history out into the bright flats of their enslavement, the battle would be near ending and in his favour." In another passage Barrett went on to make the connection between radical black art and Africa more explicit, arguing that Coltrane's piercing saxophone represented "the screams of a thousand lost and living voices whose existence has begun to demand the release of the soul's existence."[24] Scott Saul documents the gravitational pull of such nationalist rhetoric in the wake of Coltrane's death. Despite the fact that Coltrane himself adhered adamantly to a spiritual, universalist philosophy, Saul explores the ways in which he nonetheless became "a posthumous icon for a uniquely black epistemology."[25]

It is clear from my interviews that Coltrane also became an important touchstone for an emergent sense of Asian American identity. Japanese American bassist Mark Izu remembers how it was Coltrane in the late 1960s "who really turned me on to jazz. I had no idea what he was playing because it was more like his later years, *Ascension* and stuff like that. But there was something about it that really got me." Likewise, Francis Wong continues, "[African American] people are struggling for freedom in the music, and that's what [jazz] expresses. Well then that would be the next issue: As Asian Americans, what are we trying to get out of the music by playing [jazz]? And is it possible to create an Asian American version that's influenced by that? So we would listen to Trane." Finally, pianist Glenn Horiuchi recalls the potent combination of John Coltrane's music and Amiri Baraka's poetry: "That's when I really got into the later Coltrane [because of] my political studies, which revolved around the black liberation movement. And then you read Baraka's poem about Trane. You can't help but read that stuff and then turn on *A Love Supreme* or *Ascension* and be transformed."

These recollections support Deborah Wong's assertion that when Asian American music listeners choose one kind of music over another, their "act of choice and perception is no solipsistic mirror but rather a critical moment of representation."[26] In other words, listening to music is one way in which Asian Americans, and all people, assert identity and positionality. Emulating the political stances and performance styles of African American players, Asian American musicians used the cultural space opened up by revolutionary black nationalism and the jazz avant-garde to begin investigating their own identities.

DEFINING ASIAN AMERICAN IDENTITY THROUGH MUSIC

Jon Jang's first recording, the self-titled *Jang* (1982), does not feature any Asian-themed selections or overt markers. Instead, Jang positions himself alongside African American musicians as part of the jazz tradition while simultaneously critiquing the Eurocentrism of American cultural institutions. Jang attended Oberlin conservatory from 1974 to 1978, studying piano performance and composition with Wendell Logan, an African American professor. At Oberlin, Jang became disillusioned with what he characterized as the indifference of the classical music establishment toward African American jazz musicians and composers. The front of the album makes this point forcefully: it features an illustration of Jang's hands at the keyboard, shackled by handcuffs that read "U.S. Music Institutions." On the backside of the album, Jang stands with a defiant expression in front of a handwritten protest sign exclaiming, "[Thelonious] Monk Yes, Mozart No" (fig. 9.2).

These musicians studied texts such as *The Autobiography of Malcolm X* and the poetry and essays of Amiri Baraka; they listened closely to "freedom jazz" albums such as Max Roach and Abbey Lincoln's *We Insist! Freedom Now Suite.* In a conversation with Amy Ling, New York–based baritone saxophonist Fred Ho reported, "The Black revolution of the late 1960s and early 1970s, when I was a teenager, inspired my own awakening in terms of cultural identity, political and cultural consciousness. . . . The Black liberation struggle gave a framework and reference to understanding my own oppression and struggles."[27] As Asian American musicians were swept up by the political energy of the Asian American movement, however, their emphasis shifted toward defining forms of self-expression that would speak directly to their concerns and experiences. After jamming in a jazz fusion band with other Japanese American musicians in Los Angeles's Little Tokyo, pianist Glenn Horiuchi describes how he began to seek something more than imitating preexisting styles of jazz: "I started realizing that I wasn't satisfied musically; just playing jazz wasn't enough. I felt I had to find my own way. I thought there had to be *the* way that really captured for me the Japanese thing in the context of all the black music that I was really influenced by, like Coltrane and stuff."

It was the striking music and visual imagery of McCoy Tyner's album *Sahara* (1972) that caught Francis Wong's attention. The album cover shows Tyner playing a Japanese koto while seated on a wooden box amid urban decay, prompting reflection on the harsh environments, whether African desert or American postindustrial city, in which black people live (fig. 9.3). Wong remembers, "McCoy came out with this album that was the *Down Beat* album of the year. It was called *Sahara,* but on the cover of the album, he's holding a koto. The whole idea for Asian American jazz was born at that time for me." He continues, explaining that "it was the first time I thought that Asian music would contribute to jazz in a way that was respectful to both traditions. This served as a metaphor for the possibility that I could express my connection to

FIGURE 9.2. Jon Jang, *Jang*, RPM 4, 1982, cover and back. Courtesy of Jon Jang.

FIGURE 9.3. McCoy Tyner, *Sahara*, Milestone 311, 1972, cover. Courtesy of Concord Music Group.

my cultural heritage and be involved in jazz music." Much like Horiuchi in the previous quote, Wong finds himself looking to Asia through the eyes of a black artist.

Sahara is just one of many cases—ranging from Duke Ellington's two Asian-themed jazz albums *The Afro-Eurasian Eclipse* and *The Far East Suite* to Thelonious Monk's "Japanese Folk Song" to John Coltrane's "India"—in which African American jazz musicians looked East for inspiration.[28] These moments of musical cosmopolitanism, part of a general trend in the 1960s in which artists and intellectuals of color turned away from European influences and embraced other cultures in an era of heightened global consciousness and anticolonial struggles, were not lost on young Asian American musicians. Just as African American musicians like Tyner appropriated foreign instruments to further the construction of black culture, so too Asian American musicians realized that they could "appropriate" free jazz, among other resources, as they explored their own identities.

Asian American musicians experimented with the cultivation of an original Asian American "new" sound. Recalling his participation in the New York loft jazz scene in the late 1970s, violinist and bandleader Jason Kao Hwang explains, "I think the aesthetic was to explore the violin in an uncolonized way. The fundamentals of jazz harmony are a European concept. So to get away from fundamental harmony and the rules of music, not just as a formal reaction, but as an issue of cultural integrity and identity, I needed it to find out who I was."[29] Many musicians turned to traditional Asian musical forms. San Francisco–based bassist Mark Izu began studying with Togi Suenobu Sensei, an imperial court musician visiting from Japan whose gagaku workshops provided an opportunity for American musicians to learn about Japanese classical music. For jazz musicians interested in pursuing non-Western approaches to music, gagaku's approach to *ma* (organizing time) and coordinating an ensemble offered alternative paths for improvisation. Izu began performing on the *shô* (mouth organ), and, explaining that he was tired of hearing Asian American musicians complain about having nowhere to perform, he, along with George Leong and Paul Yamazaki, co-organized the first San Francisco Asian American Jazz festival, which took place on September 12 and 13, 1981.

In Los Angeles pianist Glenn Horiuchi began experimenting with Japanese folk tunes and taiko rhythms, explaining that he rejected conventional bebop harmony because he believed it was "fundamentally incompatible" with Japanese music. Significantly, although Horiuchi refused to "play a Japanese melody over chord changes," the performance styles of more experimental African American musicians were not off-limits. This hybrid approach takes shape on his 1988 recording "Issei Spirit," in which Horiuchi improvises on a Japanese transverse flute but also takes an extended piano solo, evoking the styles of McCoy Tyner and Cecil Taylor. In our interview, Horiuchi explained that in the 1980s he was trying to create a form of music that would help awaken other sansei to the legacy of discrimination and hardship faced by Japanese Americans: "I was very inspired when I read about what the issei did. I found that very moving. I was trying to tap where I felt there was this revolutionary potential too. I was trying to find, this kind of essence the issei had."[30] For Horiuchi, this Japanese American essence—or "truth" as he sometimes referred to it—was one of struggle, and he hoped to inspire other Japanese Americans to become more politically engaged.

Beginning with an improvisation on the *komabue* (Japanese flute), "Issei Spirit" clearly gestures toward the memory of the first generation of Japanese immigrants to the United States. The spirit of struggle seems to come later in the climactic moments of the piece, as Horiuchi pounds away at the keyboard and lets out a series of anguished screams, his piano playing reminiscent of Cecil Taylor's percussive, rapid-fire clusters. The connection to Taylor was conscious, as Horiuchi took to performing and being photographed for his album covers wearing a knit wool cap reminiscent of Taylor. In his liner notes for Horiuchi's album *Next Step,* Jon Jang played on this relationship, casting Horiuchi's piano style as "88 tuned taiko drums," a reference to Valerie Wilmer's description of Cecil Taylor's playing as "88 tuned drums."[31] In many ways, "Issei Spirit" seems to be Glenn Horiuchi's attempt at enacting Lindsay Barrett's conception of avant-garde musical practices that trigger "the screams of a thousand lost and living voices."[32]

AFRO-ASIAN ACTIVISM AND COALITION BUILDING

I am wary of oversimplifying the goals that Asian American musicians pursued in the 1980s, but it is helpful to note a few consistent themes. First, these musicians have been outspoken about their aims, and a number of them were politically active. Francis Wong, Glenn Horiuchi, Jon Jang, and Fred Ho all belonged to the most radical of these organizations, the Marxist-Leninist League of Revolutionary Struggle, which also counted Amiri Baraka among its most prominent members. The league gave Asian American musicians a direct link to the black liberation movement of the 1960s. By creating new forms of expression, Asian American musicians hoped to open a new front for the movement and help their brothers and sisters move beyond demeaning stereotypes at the margins of U.S. society.

Second, Asian American jazz musicians expressed solidarity with political struggles through recordings inspired by and dedicated to these movements as well as by playing benefit concerts and political demonstrations. In Los Angeles, Glenn Horiuchi received encouraging feedback at performances he gave at Japanese American redress movement events. In San Francisco Jang and Wong played at a number of political events seeking justice for Vincent Chin's death. Their music was most popular among young idealistic Asian American college students. Jang recalls how he received an especially friendly reception in 1983 at the Asian Pacific Student Union at Stanford University: "*Are You Chinese or Charlie Chan?* was released in March on the very day of a large APSU conference. The ensemble that performed on the recording performed at APSU.

We sold about 60 records at the conference. Students were asking me to autograph the record. There was a tremendous response."[33]

Are You Chinese or Charlie Chan? was issued on RPM records, a now defunct label cofounded by the group United Front, itself a collaboration between Japanese American musicians Mark Izu, African American musicians George Sams and Lewis Jordan, and Japanese-African American musician Anthony Brown. George Sams was a member of St. Louis's Black Arts Group and Lewis Jordan was a member of Chicago's Association for the Advancement of Creative Musicians (AACM). Sams and Jordan thus brought the "do-it-yourself" attitude toward independent production to the Asian American jazz movement. By 1987 RPM was no longer functioning, and Jang and Wong cofounded Asian Improv Records, primarily as a vehicle to produce recordings by Jang and Horiuchi.[34] With no established record companies showing interest in their work, Jang and Wong decided, "It's either [self-production] or self-censorship." Wong explains, "We didn't really have a choice because we were excluded and disenfranchised. We needed to have something. It's not like Jon could make a recording and then automatically have an outlet for his work." Reflecting on the historical importance of the record label, Wong continues, "So there wouldn't be an understanding that Asian Americans have a major voice in jazz if it wasn't for Asian Improv. There would still be Asian Americans playing the music, but there wouldn't be the recognition that it's some kind of collective expression by some people." He adds, "Asian Improv was politically in tune and trying to express what was happening [in the Asian American consciousness movement]."

Much of their music took its inspiration from the redress movement. With song titles such as Horiuchi's "Manzanar Voices," or Jang's "Never Give Up!" and "Reparations Now!," Jang and Horiuchi's musical efforts spoke to a relatively small but committed group of Asian American activists. Horiuchi remembers more than a few people from the community approaching him to say that his music had affected them deeply. Writing in the liner notes for Horiuchi's album *Manzanar Voices* (1989), redress activist and San Jose Taiko member Susan Hayase confessed that "[Horiuchi's] music is actually, kind of about my life."[35]

Third, in collaboration with African American musicians, Asian Americans also demonstrated a model of what cross-racial political coalition building could look and sound like. Fred Ho founded the interracial Afro Asian Music Ensemble in 1982. Likewise, Jon Jang's Pan-Asian Arkestra was a multiracial affair, inspired by Los Angeles–based African

American musician and community organizer Horace Tapscott's Pan Afrikan People's Arkestra. Indeed, Asian American jazz performances and recordings were rarely Asian-only affairs. In San Diego and Los Angeles, Glenn Horiuchi worked with bassist M'Chaka Uba, a Chicago transplant and member of the AACM. Uba educated him about the structure and activities of the AACM, and Horiuchi passed this information on to his Bay Area friends Jang and Wong, aiding them in the development of Asian Improv Records.[36] These musicians' collaborative efforts illustrate the creative possibilities of Afro-Asian cultural production.

As Deborah Wong notes in her essay "The Asian American Body in Performance," coalition building and cultural hybridity were much more celebrated and emphasized in Asian American jazz than they were in the black nationalist projects of the 1960s, both because Asian American jazz occurred in the "multicultural" 1980s and because the musicians were so clearly influenced by African American musicians. Writing about the collaborative efforts between Asian American and African American performers, Wong argues for a view of music as politics, claiming that minority coalition building always emerges from "specific need."[37]

I have observed that the specific need in the case of Asian American and African American experimental music revolves around the dialectical but equally problematic way African American and Asian American musicians are positioned in dominant discourses of race and music. With few points of "their own" to reference in U.S. popular culture, Asian American musicians had to counter their relative invisibility by improvising new identities. Thus, the experimentalism and freedom implicit in avant-garde jazz provided them with an ideal outlet for forging musical identities.

In contrast, many African Americans such as Cecil Taylor or the members of the Art Ensemble of Chicago suffered from a case of *hypervisibility*, in which their skin color predetermined what most listeners imagined they should sound like as jazz musicians. Thus, African American players have used the space created by the avant-garde to improvise their way out of mainstream expectations. As George Lewis argues in his history of the AACM, the term "jazz" has often been used to circumscribe and downplay the contributions that African American experimentalists have made to music. Groups such as the Art Ensemble went as far as to disassociate themselves from the label "jazz," preferring the term "creative music."

Despite facing very different obstacles, African American and Asian American musicians have found it useful and rewarding to support one another's efforts. By recognizing that their common problems stem from a creativity-stifling matrix of race and music, they have drawn on experimental musical practices to carve out pockets of freedom and resist dominant norms. In so doing, they have provided a particularly productive model for interracial coalition building.

ASIAN AMERICAN JAZZ AS PROCESS: GLENN HORIUCHI'S "TERMINAL ISLAND SWEEP"

For Asian American and African American avant-garde musicians, the line between music and politics has been fruitfully blurry. As they have sought to reconceptualize the artist/business and artist/community relationships, these groups have engaged in new forms of cooperative organization and political action. But social and political realities change with the times. For Asian American jazz musicians, the end of the 1980s ushered in a new set of challenging circumstances. Setting out in the mid-1980s to make music that would aid the Asian American movement, many of these musicians were unprepared for events lurking just over the political horizon. Toward the end of the decade, shifts in the political situation of Asian Americans created a crisis of meaning for musicians and cast doubt over the direction of their work. The experiences of pianist/composer Glenn Horiuchi illustrate how avant-garde jazz continued to provide a framework for Asian American musicians to negotiate the shifting terrain of race, politics, and cultural production.

In the 1980s Horiuchi was extremely active in the redress and reparations movement. The three recordings he released on Asian Improv Records at the end of the decade—*Next Step* (1988), *Issei Spirit* (1989), and *Manzanar Voices* (1989)—were inspired directly by these political activities. Horiuchi reports being particularly moved by the 1982 Commission on the Wartime Relocation and Internment of Civilians hearings, where former internees testified to Congress under oath about what they experienced during World War II: "The experience of seeing that was so profound. Just seeing the community actually one by one, all these people going up and testifying, that was a breakthrough for me. And then I started writing music a lot." Horiuchi came to regard his music as another way of contributing to the movement and potentially radicalizing fellow Japanese Americans, and we have already witnessed how an appreciation for the struggles of the issei inspired his approach to avant-garde jazz. His composition "Terminal Island Sweep," commissioned by the California Arts Council in 1991 and recorded in 1992 at

California Plaza in downtown Los Angeles, represents one of Horiuchi's last conscious attempts to distill the Japanese American spirit of struggle into music.

"Terminal Island Sweep" is part of a larger work titled *Little Tokyo Suite,* inspired by the history of Los Angeles's Japanese American community. It narrates the moment in which Japanese Americans living on San Pedro's Terminal Island at the start of World War II were literally swept from their homes and began the long journey to internment camps. Horiuchi uses *shamisen* (a three-stringed Japanese banjo), bass, piano, percussion, and woodwinds to tell the story of the forced evacuation. The programmatic piece opens with an "urgent" theme (so named in the score) performed by the woodwinds at a moderate march tempo. Played over a simple, one-note bass groove, the rapid-fire sixteenth-note groupings, doubled by a snare drum, evoke the menacing insistence of the military orders to evacuate. The urgent theme stomps through the first half minute of the performance and then fades out as a new sonic image fades in.

A repeated descending eighth-note motive in the woodwinds establishes a slow triple meter, and the "lyrical" theme (marked in the score) played by the shamisen sways gently above. Gone is the insistent bass groove. Instead, long tones from the winds blow a gentle breeze across the soundscape. The jagged chromaticism of the urgent theme gives way to the shamisen's flowing melody, introducing us to the unwitting Japanese American community of Terminal Island just before the evacuation. Having established his characters, Horiuchi wastes no time bringing them into conflict: the violence of the evacuation, represented by a loud drum solo, silences the lyrical melody of the shamisen. But the shamisen returns to embark on a series of eight-bar solos in a style derived from the Japanese *nagauta* repertoire. At the end of this solo section, motives built from fragments of the urgent theme spiral into oblivion and are abruptly quashed by the shamisen's closing gesture. Prompted by a final combined blast from the entire ensemble, we are encouraged to hear the spirit of the community triumphing over the forces that had sought to destroy it.

Despite the encouragement Horiuchi received from fellow musicians and activists, his reception in the broader Japanese American community was lukewarm. Although he hoped that his music would capture a "Japanese American essence" that would speak to and help transform the community, his penchant for artistic experimentation seemed to work against him achieving widespread popularity. One of the ironies of his artistic and political stance was that in resisting European American hegemony, Horiuchi and other Asian American musicians embraced an artistic ideology derived from Western modernism. Much like the black avant-garde musicians on whom they modeled themselves, Asian American jazz musicians found themselves engaged in a delicate balance between post-1960s identity politics and modernist values such as autonomy and individuality.[38] Put another way, to be truly "Asian American," to find the Japanese American "essence" he sought to convey, Horiuchi felt compelled to break free from existing musical conventions. In this 1991 performance of "Terminal Island Sweep," that meant composing an idiosyncratic piece of program music with unusual orchestration. Although this strategy voiced his political convictions, it also put him at odds with the very community he was trying so keenly to reach. As Horiuchi admits, "Okay, I'm trying to do this Japanese American thing and Japanese Americans don't like it."

By 1995 Horiuchi explains that he had "faced up" to the fact that the Japanese American community was not responding to his music the way he had hoped, and he also was confronting a dramatically different political landscape. Paradoxically, the success of the redress movement had taken away an important source of his inspiration. The radical trajectory of the Asian American movement, it seemed, was either dissipating or being redirected into mainstream academic institutions and nonprofit organizations. Horiuchi, and others like him who had been active in Marxist political organizations, were also deflated by the Tiananmen massacre. As Asian American movement scholar William Wei explains, "For Maoist groups like the league [of revolutionary struggle], the 3–4 June 1989 Tiananmen massacre of pro-democracy students was particularly disheartening. They, along with the rest of the world, watched in horror as their heroes, the Chinese Communists, murdered their young and lied about it afterwards."[39]

The year 1989 also saw the USSR disavow socialism and East Germany tear down the Berlin Wall. Rocked by these global events, as well as a scandal at Stanford University where the Marxist-Leninist League's clandestine practices were exposed and publicly criticized, the league voted to repudiate Marxist-Leninism and disband on September 8, 1990.[40] All these factors encouraged Horiuchi to reevaluate his past efforts. During one of our meetings, Horiuchi asked me to listen to another version of "Terminal Island Sweep" that was recorded years later, explaining that it might explain something about the changes he was experiencing in his life and music.

In 1995, Horiuchi rearranged "Terminal Island Sweep" for a recording session that featured tuba player William Roper, *erhu*/saxophonist Francis Wong, percussionist Jeanette Wrate, and Horiuchi himself on shamisen. In this version, he melted the original programmatic materials down into a framework for collective improvisation, abandoning the didactic narrative style of the original. Although the contrast between the "urgent" and "lyrical" themes serves as a reminder of the historical drama of internment, the performance does not seem intent on elaborating specific actions. Instead, through free improvisation, the performers disperse the thematic material, giving the piece a searching quality. In this recording, Horiuchi takes over for his aunt Lillian Nakano on the shamisen, performing with his own improvised autodidactic technique. San Francisco–based Chinese American musician Francis Wong adds his own radical reinterpretation of the erhu; in the process both musicians flout traditional Asian performance practice.

The syncopated groove created by "misplayed" Asian instruments foregrounds the hybridity of the players' own identities. No longer attempting to depict a Japanese American "essence," the shamisen becomes just one hybridized voice among others. The extended group improvisation revels in the present rather than a teleological chain of events. The sounds of seagulls simulated on the erhu, as well as the sounds of foghorns and tugboats imitated by the tuba, suggest the life of Japanese American fishermen at Terminal Island, but these objects, still charged with meaning, do not enact any kind of straightforward story. Horiuchi, it seems, traded in his dialectical dreams of political action for the more immediate and sensuous gratification of rehearsing utopian social interactions with his fellow musicians. As he put it, "I was a little more carefree. Because up until then I had always been concerned with audience. Politically being a Marxist, you're always concerned about the audience. But by [this recording] I didn't care anymore."

Hoping to overcome the contradictions of a modernist artistic position inspired by revolutionary nationalism, Horiuchi dramatically reconceptualized his aesthetic. Loosening his grip on the didactic, even stereotypical portrayal of Japanese American identity created by personifying the shamisen in the 1991 version of "Terminal Island Sweep," he fostered a more open and fluid approach to improvisation. Strikingly, Horiuchi's new version of "Terminal Island Sweep" was released on an album entitled *Kenzo's Vision* (1995), the name inspired by his then infant son. At times, in fact, the album's free improvisatory spirit seems intent on equating musical freedom with the subjective experience of an infant, from whose presymbolic position racial difference is quite literally a meaningless concept.

No longer driven to produce explicitly political music targeting the Japanese American community, Horiuchi did not relinquish his desire to create experimental jazz music. Instead, experimentalism continued to help him negotiate what it meant to be an Asian American musician playing jazz. Though the way in which race matters changes, Asian American identity remains an important interpretive framework for understanding both versions of "Terminal Island Sweep." As performer, composer, and scholar Michael Dessen has argued, despite the nationalist rhetoric surrounding the music in the 1960s and 1970s, avant-garde jazz practices have always been about much more than promoting a single political attitude or allegiance. Instead, the experimental nature of the music provided a space where successive generations of musicians from a variety of backgrounds could work out and renegotiate issues of identity and aesthetics. In Dessen's terms, they continued to see "artistic experimentation as a way to interrogate changing social realities in their full complexity," and, in the long run, a musician like Horiuchi gained much more than political slogans or musical gestures from his engagement with the experimental tradition.[41] Dessen's observations are also borne out by the increased diversity of the musicians who have recorded for Asian Improv Records in subsequent decades. Although they differ from the original core group in many ways, "Asian American jazz" continued to be a useful organizational concept in the 1990s and 2000s.

ASIAN AMERICAN MUSICIANS AND JAZZ HISTORIOGRAPHY

Horiuchi's story epitomizes a process of negotiation and growth experienced by many Asian American musicians of his generation. Yet what is the historiographic import of Asian American jazz in the 1980s? What can we learn by listening to these voices from (the margins of) the margins? How do the experiences of Jang, Horiuchi, and others help us reevaluate the recent musical past? By mapping Asian American jazz musicians onto the contentious field of jazz historiography, I seek to explain how taking the margins seriously can change the way we view dominant jazz narratives, leading us to richer and more nuanced understandings of the music's history.

Although veterans of the African American avant-garde face challenges in the current jazz world, few would deny their place in a musical history of the 1960s. In contrast, due to a racialized discourse of American culture that tends to view the world in black and white, Asian American musicians have been left outside not only discussions of jazz but American musical histories altogether. Drawing on Lisa Lowe's pioneering work on Asian American art and culture, Kevin Fellezs posits why such discourses exclude Asian American musicians as foreigners to the jazz tradition. Fellezs claims that the racialization of the jazz tradition and the racialization of Asian Americans "have worked in tandem to reduce Asian American jazz musicians' visibility as both 'real Americans' and 'real jazz musicians.' "[42] In other words, because most people regard jazz as distinctly "American" music, and because many people also presume Asian Americans to originate from "somewhere else," Asian American jazz musicians are cast as foreigners to the tradition in ways that are specific to their race. Through their musical endeavors, Asian American musicians have challenged these assumptions, helping to raise awareness about Asian American participation in jazz.[43] Their music says much about jazz's complicated cultural history and highlights the centrality of black cultural forms in the formation of diverse American identities. If nothing else, Asian American jazz should force us to reconsider the conventional view of jazz as a "black and white" affair.

In addition to expanding our knowledge of the music's past, the history of Asian American jazz can also help us to understand present and future developments. Despite the many changes in political and musical outlooks that have occurred since the 1980s, "Asian American" has continued to serve as an important rubric and rallying point for many musicians in the 1990s and 2000s. For musicians such as Anthony Brown, Fred Ho, Mark Izu, Jon Jang, Miya Masaoka, and Francis Wong, formative experiences in the Asian American movement of the 1980s have continued to inform their politics and art. Many of them have delved deeper into traditional Asian culture and history while continuing to use their music as a means to confront issues of social justice. Their efforts have helped to create space for Asian American musicians in the world of jazz and creative music and have established institutional networks that have benefited younger musicians.

Although the nonprofit Asian Improv Records was formed in the 1980s mainly to support Jang and Horiuchi's political music, the organization has since broadened its horizons. Under the leadership of Francis Wong, Asian Improv has provided assistance to new artists who do not necessarily use their music to confront racial issues or embrace nationalist politics. Yet these musicians, most of whom did not participate in the movement of the 1980s, have also found it advantageous to "come together" as Asian Americans. What they share is the awareness that as racially marked outsiders to the jazz tradition, they confront similar challenges. In the 1990s and 2000s a diverse crop of musicians, including Tatsu Aoki, Jeff Chan, Vijay Iyer, Kuni Mikami, Hafez Modirzadeh, and Jeff Song, have self-produced recordings on Asian Improv.

Although the rubric "Asian American" continues to be important, I want to avoid reducing the Asian American jazz movement of the 1980s and 1990s to an "Asian American problem" in jazz. Doing so would mask a very real hegemonic challenge that Asian American, African American, and other musicians must fight together. Ironically, the decade in which Asian American jazz flourished also witnessed the birth of a neotraditionalist wing of jazz criticism led by Wynton Marsalis. Drawing on ideas of Albert Murray and Ralph Ellison, combative critic Stanley Crouch—once a proponent of "freedom" jazz himself—cast Marsalis's rise to prominence as a salutary reaction against the excesses of the 1960s avant-garde, a development that in his eyes had taken jazz away from its roots. Marsalis and Crouch were concerned that by adopting a nationalist stance that equated jazz authenticity with the direct expression of struggle and protest, the avant-garde had unwittingly bought into a "noble savage" stereotype that cast jazz as an untutored expression of black emotion requiring little work or artistic ingenuity.[44] The conflation of jazz with complete musical freedom, they claim, threatens to undermine understandings of jazz rooted in black traditions that require sustained hard work to master. Interesting to note, however, is how closely Marsalis's counterargument—that jazz is "America's classical music"—parallels the rhetoric of color blindness espoused by certain politicians and their allies in the 1980s.

Countering the identity politics of new social movements of which black nationalism was perhaps the paradigm, neoliberal attitudes about race and politics encouraged Reagan's America to accept the construction of a "color-blind" society where race no longer matters. Supporters of color blindness in public policy have sought to erase the programmatic gains of the racial struggles of the 1960s, most notably affirmative action. In the 1980s this trend was mirrored in jazz by the neotraditionalist assault on the 1960s jazz avant-garde. In theory, Marsalis and his supporters put forward their own color-blind vision of jazz as a space potentially shared by musicians of all colors who prove their worth by playing bebop-derived styles. (Practically, however, Marsalis has been criticized for not hiring white musicians for his Lincoln Center performances.) Jazz may have started out as an "ethnic" music (or so the argument goes), but thanks to hard work and continual artistic development, it is now a timeless, universal musical language embodying American ideals like individualism, freedom, and democracy. As proponents of neoconservative and neoliberal ideologies posit a world where individual subjects are equally free to act according to their own interests and urge people to stop worrying about racial inequality, neotraditionalist jazz puts forward a model of artistic excellence that devalues music and musicians who appeal to the politics of race. These developments confirm Jocelyn Guilbault's position that musical discourses do not merely reflect hegemonic racial meanings; rather, musical discourses are actively engaged in the production of new understandings of race.[45]

I do not mean to suggest that Wynton Marsalis and Stanley Crouch are to blame for the decline of freedom jazz in the 1980s and 1990s. Many other forces both internal and external have compelled African American and Asian American musicians to recognize the limitations of such perspectives. Certainly the growth of interracial collaboration in traditions derived from avant-garde and the increasing presence of female experimentalists among the ranks count as positive developments that suggest new political possibilities. In fact, one of the most important legacies of avant-garde jazz and creative music movements might be their ability to articulate and symbolize epistemologies of freedom.

In the 1960s black musicians' thirst for intellectual and spiritual freedom led them to the avant-garde, which in turn fostered approaches seeking to liberate them from the essentialized stereotypes preventing them from realizing their full potential. What Asian American musicians of the 1980s found in avant-garde jazz was a cultural space that, despite its militant racial divisiveness, allowed them to exercise their creativity and collaborate meaningfully with their African American counterparts. The interracial encounter between African American and Asian American musicians thus exemplifies the "broader resonances" of the creative music movement, which at its best continues to feed a spirit of freedom and experimentation, a spirit that Paul Gilroy has described as our collective "hunger for a world that is undivided by the petty differences we retain and inflate by calling them racial."[46]

All musicians playing in styles derived from the 1960s avant-garde face continued marginalization both in the marketplace and in jazz historiography, and for those interested in countering such conservative strains, reclaiming the history of the intersection of Asian American jazz with black revolutionary nationalism offers a promising place to start.

If, however, we choose to ignore these musical threads in favor of a story of jazz that emphasizes unity over conflict, linear development from one dominant style to the next over the sometimes messy and unpredictable world of reality, such stories are in danger of being lost. I hope instead that we will not turn a deaf ear to musicians out of step with jazz's more familiar narratives and that we pursue a jazz history that continues to listen for the sound of struggle.

NOTES

1. Jon Jang, "Are You Chinese or Charlie Chan?" *Are You Chinese or Charlie Chan?* RPM 5, 1983, LP.

2. Helen Zia, *Asian American Dreams: The Emergence of an American People* (New York: Farrar, Straus and Giroux, 2000), 60.

3. See Krystyn R. Moon, *Yellowface: Creating the Chinese in American Popular Music and Performance, 1850s–1920s* (New Brunswick, NJ: Rutgers University Press, 2005); and Charles Hiroshi Garrett, "Chinatown, Whose Chinatown: Defining Americas Borders with Musical Orientalism," *Journal of the American Musicological Society* 57, no. 1 (2004): 119–74.

4. Jang explained to me that the dissonant free improvisation was meant to evoke the violence of the Vincent Chin murder; the four percussion punctuations represent the four times Chin was struck with a baseball bat.

5. Except where noted, the comments of these musicians have been excerpted from our personal conversations: Anthony Brown, Berkeley, CA, March 18, 1998 and May 17, 1998; Glenn Horiuchi, Los Angeles, CA, August 19, 1998 and October 31, 1998; Jason Kao Hwang, New York, June 16, 1999; Mark Izu, San Francisco, CA, June 6, 1999; Jon Jang, San Francisco, CA, June 5, 1999; Miya Masaoka, San Francisco, CA, September 16, 1999; and Francis Wong, San Francisco, CA, June 4, 1999.

6. Susan M. Asai, "Cultural Politics: The African American Connection in Asian American Jazz-Based Music," *Asian Music* 36, no. 1 (Winter/Spring 2005): 87–108.

7. Jang, *Are You Chinese?* Despite these assertions, this recording features African American musicians Cash Killion (cello) and George Sams (trumpet). The implications of cooperative efforts between African American and Asian American musicians are explored later.

8. Lisa Lowe, *Immigrant Acts: On Asian American Cultural Politics* (Durham, NC: Duke University Press, 1996), 67, 6.

9. The deliberate claiming of an Asian American identity and the self-conscious attempt to make Asian American music separates these musicians from people like Toshiko Akiyoshi and Akira Sakata who have also played in African American styles while inserting Asian elements.

10. Yen Le Espiritu, *Asian American Panethnicity: Bridging Institutions and Identities* (Philadelphia: Temple University Press, 1992), 176; Oliver Wang,

"Between the Notes: Finding Asian America in Popular Music," *American Music* 19, no. 4 (Winter 2001): 441.

11. Michael Omi and Howard Winant, *Racial Formation in the U.S.: 1960s to the 1990s* (New York: Routledge, 1994), 42.

12. These terms have been embraced or rejected at different times for different reasons by different people, making a single catchall term for experimental black music in the 1960s problematic. For more on this issue, see Ingrid Monson, *Freedom Sounds: Civil Rights Call Out to Jazz and Africa* (Oxford: Oxford University Press, 2007), 259–66.

13. Archie Shepp, quoted in Frank Kofsky, *Black Nationalism and the Revolution in Music* (New York: Pathfinder, 1970), 9.

14. Omi and Winant, *Racial Formation*, 95–104.

15. Monson, *Freedom Sounds*, 260.

16. Paul Yamazaki, "Oni-Gaku: Unholy Ghosts and Insurrectionary Spirits" in *Free Spirits: Annals of the Insurgent Imagination*, ed. Paul Buhle, et al. (San Francisco: City Lights Books, 1982), 100.

17. Susan M. Asai, "Transformations of Tradition: Three Generations of Japanese American Music Making," *Musical Quarterly*, 79, no. 3 (Autumn 1995): 438.

18. Michael Levin and John S. Wilson, "No Bop Roots in Jazz: Parker," *Down Beat*, February 1994, 24–26 (originally published in *Down Beat*, September 9, 1949).

19. Nic Paget-Clarke, "A Conversation with Jon Jang and Francis Wong," *Motion Magazine*, February 25, 1998, www.inmotionmagazine.com/jjfw1.html.

20. Asai, "Cultural Politics." See also Jere Takahashi, *Nisei/Sansei: Shifting Japanese American Identities and Politics* (Philadelphia: Temple University Press, 1997), 203.

21. Lewis Porter, *John Coltrane: His Life and Music* (Ann Arbor: University of Michigan Press, 1999), 277.

22. Scott Saul, *Freedom Is, Freedom Ain't: Jazz and the Making of the 1960s* (Cambridge, MA: Harvard University Press, 2003), 264.

23. Porter, *John Coltrane*, 279, 278.

24. Lindsay Barrett, "The Tide Inside, It Rages!" in *Black Fire: An Anthology of Afro-American Writing*, ed. Leroi Jones [Amiri Baraka] and Larry Neal (New York: William and Morrow, 1968), 149, 150.

25. Saul, *Freedom Is, Freedom Ain't*, 248.

26. Deborah Wong, *Speak It Louder: Asian Americans Making Music* (New York: Routledge, 2004), 259.

27. Fred Ho, "Response," in *Yellow Light: The Flowering of Asian American Arts*, ed. Amy Ling (Philadelphia: Temple University Press, 2000), 348.

28. In 1999 Anthony Brown's Asian American Jazz Orchestra earned a Grammy nomination for its new recording of the *Far East Suite*, which included the addition of traditional Middle Eastern and East Asian instruments.

29. Hwang's group, Commitment, boasted an Afro-Asian lineup that included William Parker, Takeshi Zen Matsuura, and Will Connell Jr. Before moving to New York, Connell had been a key member of Horace Tapscott's Pan Afrikan People's Arkestra in Los Angeles.

30. Issei, nisei, and sansei are the Japanese terms designating first, second, and third generations of Japanese immigrants and their offspring. Glenn Horiuchi's grandparents, who came from Japan, are issei; his parents, the first generation born in the United States, are nisei; and Horiuchi himself is sansei.

31. Valerie Wilmer, *As Serious as Your Life: The Story of the New Jazz* (London: Allison and Busby, 1977), 45.

32. Barrett, "Tide Inside," 150.

33. Paget-Clarke, "Conversation."

34. Asian Improv Records has also released recordings as AsianImprov Records. Both spellings refer to the same company.

35. Susan Hayase, liner notes to *Manzanar Voices*, AIR 6, 1989, LP.

36. Michael Dessen, "Asian Americans and Creative Music Legacies," *Critical Studies in Improvisation/Études critiques en improvisation* 1, no. 3 (2006): www.criticalimprov.com/article/view/56/89.

37. Wong, *Speak It Louder*, 177, 296.

38. Ibid., 177.

39. William Wei, *The Asian American Movement* (Philadelphia: Temple University Press, 1998), 237.

40. Ibid., 236–37.

41. Dessen, "Asian Americans."

42. Kevin Fellezs, "Silenced but Not Silent: Asian American and Jazz," in *Alien Encounters: Popular Culture in Asian America,* ed. Mimi Thi Nguyen and Thuy Linh Nguyen Tu (Durham, NC: Duke University Press, 2007), 73.

43. For example, the Asian American Jazz Orchestra's *Big Bands behind Barbed Wire* (AIR 45, 1998, compact disc) dramatizes the plight of Japanese Americans who found themselves in the ironic position of playing "all American" swing music while incarcerated in the United States' World War II internment camps.

44. Wynton Marsalis, "What Jazz Is—and Isn't" (excerpt), in *Keeping Time: Readings in Jazz History,* ed. Robert Walser (Oxford: Oxford University Press, 1999), 327–51.

45. Jocelyne Guilbault, "Racial Projects and Musical Discourses in Trinidad, West Indies," in *Music and the Racial Imagination,* ed. Ronald Radano and Philip Bohlman (Chicago: University of Chicago Press, 2000), 436.

46. Paul Gilroy, *Against Race: Imagining Political Culture beyond the Color Line* (Cambridge, MA: Harvard University Press, 2000), 356.

PART THREE

Education

CHAPTER 10

Voices from the Jazz Wilderness

Locating Pacific Northwest Vocal Ensembles within Jazz Education

JESSICA BISSETT PEREA

In 1944 a small shoeshine parlor adjacent to Seattle's Pike Place Market became a personal hangout for local high school student Fredrick Halsted "Hal" Malcolm, who often stopped by the parlor to listen to the music playing on its jukebox and frequented the area's numerous record shops in search of the latest releases. American popular music of the time was largely dominated by swing bands that featured both vocal soloists and vocal groups: the Tommy Dorsey Orchestra with Jo Stafford and the Pied Pipers, the Glenn Miller Orchestra with Tex Beneke and the Modernaires, and the Artie Shaw Orchestra with Mel Tormé and the Meltones. Malcolm recalled how he and his friends "emulated these professional groups by playing and singing in our high school dance band and vocal ensembles at school dances, military installations, U.S.O. shows, dance halls, and jam sessions throughout the Seattle-Tacoma area."[1]

After graduating from high school in 1947, Malcolm headed one hundred miles east to Ellensburg, enrolling as a music major at the Central Washington College of Education (CWCE). That fall, Malcolm, saxophonist Waldo King, and other music students approached the newly hired director of bands Albin Bert Christianson to see if he would sponsor an after-hours swing band. Christianson agreed, and the CWCEans (or Sweecians) dance band was born. In addition to playing at campus events, these student-musicians also secured outside work, including a steady gig at Yakima's Playland Ballroom, where they performed regularly to large crowds and attended shows by the touring orchestras of Gene Krupa, Charlie Barnet, Woody Herman, and others.

Listening to the local Ellensburg radio station (KXLE), Malcolm was particularly struck by the recording of Dave Lambert and His Bop Vocal Chorus performing their up-tempo rendition of Irving Berlin's "Always." Both King and Malcolm marveled at the "great sound" of Lambert's bebop-inflected arrangements, especially those written for Stan Kenton's vocal group, the Pastels.[2] In 1950 Hal Malcolm set out to replicate the Pastels' sound by transcribing its arrangements of "After You" and "There Is No Greater Love." He then selected a small group of men and women from the college's choral program and asked them to learn the transcribed parts. While the group read the notes flawlessly, Malcolm felt that the resulting sound resembled a "Wagnerian opera ensemble" that bordered on anarchy. As Malcolm recalled, "although I could hear the problems, I was simply too immature to understand and correct the perplexities involving timbre, harmonic extensions, placement, vibrato, etc. . . . That failure was a very important part of future success."[3]

In 1967 Malcolm accepted an offer to teach at Mount Hood Community College in Gresham, Oregon, where he was given license to establish the first ever institutionally supported vocal jazz ensemble. In the interest of building a strong pilot program, Malcolm recruited instrumentalists from the school's band and created a sixteen-voice ensemble known as the Mount Hood Swing Choir (forming a jazz ensemble remained largely prohibited in many music departments at the time). That same year CWCE alumni Waldo King and John "Coach" Moawad also initiated jazz-oriented "swing choirs" alongside their swing bands in the Seattle area public schools. Thanks to the pioneering efforts of Malcolm, King, and Moawad—the founding triumvirate of Pacific Northwest vocal-instrumental jazz education—vocal jazz ensembles consequently flourished in the Pacific Northwest, creating a regional focal point for innovative performance and pedagogical practices at both the secondary and collegiate levels.

Contemporary vocal jazz groups range in size and can be loosely designated as "combo" (roughly four to nine singers), "ensemble" (ten to twenty-four singers), and "choir" (twenty-five or more singers).[4] Instrumental accompaniment spans a wide continuum, from a large choir with a full jazz band and auxiliary percussionists, to a vocal ensemble with a rhythm section and instrumental soloists, to an a cappella vocal combo. The strength and quality of the Pacific Northwest vocal jazz community is now widely recognized nationwide, evidenced by an impressive number of *Down Beat* Student Music Awards and frequent invitations to perform at jazz and music education conferences nationwide.

Despite the popularity and successes of these groups, however, attempts to find a comfortable home for them within most college music programs, and also in the broader jazz discourse, have proven elusive. While vocal jazz ensembles draw from two well-established streams of influence—bop- and swing-based instrumental jazz and Western choral traditions—neither of these musical and cultural parents wants much to do with their offspring, as each tends to view vocal jazz as a transgression against their own aesthetic and cultural values. Choral traditionalists view vocal jazz as fun at best, potentially damaging at worst, while critics on the jazz side deride the vocal jazz subgenre as inauthentic, disingenuous, or just plain cheesy.

This chapter explores the aesthetic and ideological dissonances that underpin vocal jazz's orphan status. Drawing from my own experiences as a performer, director, and researcher within what we might call "jazz choir culture," I consider what has been gained and what has been lost in the shifts brought about by the institutionalization of jazz education. Aside from a few chronologically driven accounts of either instrumental or choral parent programs, this jazz phenomenon has yet to be analyzed in terms of either its integrated vocal-instrumental origins or its gendered implications.[5]

I begin by tracing briefly the original environment that led to a distinct Pacific Northwest jazz choir culture in the years following World War II, including how the vocal jazz community attempted to create, negotiate, and define its own jazz practices, and how this movement ultimately brought a greater number of women and vocalists into jazz education circuits. Next, I argue that both dominant jazz discourse and institutionalized music programs are equally complicit for the fragmentation of jazz education into separate spheres—instrumental versus vocal—and the resulting virtual exclusion of women and vocalists from what counts as jazz. I conclude by extending insights from jazz scholarship on gender, sexuality, and singing to the undertheorized realm of jazz education to explain how the marginalization of certain jazz ensembles relates to the masculine ethos that developed in modern jazz at midcentury. Since singing is one of the few sites where women have readily entered into jazz performance, I believe that the absence of vocal jazz groups in jazz lore and publications reveals a great deal about how we have studied, taught, performed, and understood jazz over the past half century.

The Pacific Northwest vocal jazz education movement blossomed on the campus of the Central Washington College of Education, located in the small farming town of Ellensburg, Washington. Although this may seem an unlikely site for the cultivation of innovative jazz pedagogy—located nearly three thousand miles west of the jazz epicenter in New York City—its rise to prominence can be attributed to three factors: the college's status as the state's premier institution for teacher preparation (est. 1892); an influx of military musicians brought to campus by the 1944 Servicemen's Readjustment Act (the GI Bill); and a literal and figurative distance from the comparatively more instrument-centric, competitive, and specialized East Coast jazz scene, allowing for new ways of thinking about performing jazz. Like their contemporaries across the nation, the first generation of Northwest jazz educators all came of age during the height of swing music's popularity. In addition, several of them served in the armed forces and took advantage of the GI Bill to complete degrees in music education. CWCE became the landmark degree-granting institution responsible for a healthy portion of the region's music educators who founded jazz programs within area high schools and community colleges.

Generally speaking, music education majors specialize in one of three degree tracks—choral, instrumental, or both ("broad area specialization"). Many influential jazz educators from this region—including Malcolm, King, and Moawad—chose broad area specialization and so were versed in both classical music (through their institutional education) and jazz (through their extracurricular and professional activities).[6] Likewise, these three educators all cited both choral and instrumental groups as primary inspirations for their unique approach to jazz ensemble singing. And over the course of the 1960s they experimented with vocal-instrumental jazz formats based on their own experiences performing in and directing jazz bands and vocal groups.

Like most musics that fall under the jazz umbrella, ensembles operating under the rubric of vocal jazz encompass a wide range of aesthetic allegiances and performance practices. Even so, Pacific Northwest vocal jazz ensembles typically feature arrangements of standards (as opposed to original compositions) performed by singers, vocal groups, or swing bands. Moreover, canonic jazz vocalists have been very influential. According to the jazz pianist and arranger Dave Barduhn, copying solo vocalists is "kind of how we've done it all along . . . trying to do an ensemble approach to Sarah Vaughan, an ensemble approach to Carmen [McRae], an ensemble approach to Mel Tormé."[7] To those not familiar with jazz choir culture, the thought of sixteen singers trying simultaneously to sound like Billie Holiday may seem incongruous, even comical. But just as in jazz-band section playing, Northwest directors attend to concerns of balance, blend, and timbre when creating a unified group sound while preserving the stylistic interpretations established by canonical performers and recordings.

From the outset, Northwest educators also sought to advance the aesthetic differences and alliances that mirrored their training and experiences in several key ways. To begin, there were two primary models that guided early experiments. First was the "big band for vocalists" model that included ample opportunity for vocal improvisation, like those featured on recordings by Dave Lambert's Bop Vocal Chorus. Lambert's groups epitomized an instrumental and improvisational approach to singing. Lambert's group was not the first large vocal ensemble to work with a rhythm section or jazz band, but they were one of the first groups to emphasize scat singing (i.e., improvisation using vocables). In the early 1950s Lambert also began to explore and popularize "vocalese"—a practice that Barry Keith Grant describes as the "setting/singing of lyrics (almost always composed rather than improvised) to jazz instrumentals, both melody and solo parts, arrangements and solos, note for note."[8]

When Lambert teamed up with singers Jon Hendricks and Annie Ross, their resulting collaborations (e.g., *Sing a Song of Basie,* 1958) demonstrated how an instrumental big band sound could be translated into a vocal ensemble format. In point of fact, the band Lambert, Hendricks & Ross met the same challenges with professional singers as Malcolm did with collegiate choral singers: neither the seasoned studio singers nor the newcomers to jazz singing could attain the balance, blend, timbre, and groove required to create a unified group sound. After failing to put together a successful full ensemble of singers, the trio turned to overdubbing technology: Ross sang the trumpet parts, Lambert sang the trombones, and Hendricks the saxes. It was this fleshed-out studio sound that Pacific Northwest jazz educators hoped to recreate live.[9] For instrumental-trained educators such as Malcolm, the trio's sound provided a professional model that embodied "a counterpart to the many things that have been done instrumentally for years and years."[10] To this day, Lambert, Hendricks & Ross hold an iconic status throughout the Northwest jazz education scene, as their bop-vocal aesthetics continue to inform the direction of vocal jazz ensemble performance practices.

The second aesthetic model that influenced Pacific Northwest jazz educators involved emulating the professional vocal groups that sang close-voiced harmonies, often in a cappella settings. Ensembles such as the Boswell Sisters, Mills Brothers, Four Freshman, Hi-Los, and Singers Unlimited helped popularize the practice of incorporating close jazz harmonies within the already well-established vocal group and a cappella singing traditions. They also honed closer to the vocal-instrumental or voices-as-horns approach of Lambert's groups and served as a bridge of sorts between the instrumental- and choral-trained educators of the Northwest.

In addition to forming these two alliances, early educators in the region also made clear how their ensembles differed from other vocal groups that sang popular musics, particularly the show choir phenomenon popularized by groups such as Fred Waring's Young Pennsylvanians. Waring's massive productions held wide-reaching appeal, due in no small part to the featured polished performances of pop songs complete with choreography, as well as the fact that Waring's orchestra and large chorus received ample nationwide exposure through their radio and television programs from the 1920s into the 1950s. Although show choirs do not have as strong a presence in the Pacific Northwest (the Midwest is known as the heart of show choir territory), their existence remains critical to various internal debates on whether vocal jazz ensembles do or do not count as jazz.

The development of Pacific Northwest jazz choir culture was also fostered by the establishment of major jazz publishing houses. As noted, the first jazz vocal educators both transcribed arrangements from recordings and created vocal adaptations of band charts. Renowned band director Hal Sherman explained, "publishers back then didn't release these charts they do now. . . . We did 'Little Pixie,' the Thad Jones thing and some of the hardest stuff from the Kenton book. . . . I'd play records of the tune and tell the kids, 'This is what we're going to do.' You couldn't help but get excited."[11] Moawad arranged the majority of the charts for his sixteen-piece swing choir to replicate jazz-band section writing and emphasize an instrumental approach to articulation, interpretation, and improvisation. This do-it-yourself approach ultimately produced the region's unique sound, in which "the primary concept [for vocalists] is to interpret the notation vocally in the same manner that an instrumental jazz ensemble would interpret the notation instrumentally."[12]

As their sound became more widely known during the 1970s, Northwest vocal jazz ensembles received more invitations to perform at local and national venues, and the demand for pedagogical materials and workshops grew. This rise in interest prompted Northwest educators to begin sorting out issues of repertoire and publishing rights, which primarily revolved around avoiding the "watered down" charts available through major commercial publishing houses. Malcolm recalled that "to satisfy publishers, we often bought 20 charts of *so and so,* filed them obviously, and then adapted or arranged our own version. It's what is known as 'dues payin' while avoiding canned soup, for a much preferred homemade variety."[13]

In the beginning, directors shared and circulated their adaptations and arrangements among themselves. However, with the advent of festivals and competitions, the difference between commercially available charts and the more hip arrangements being performed by Northwest groups became clear to educators nationwide. The demand for charts containing a blueprint for the desirable Pacific Northwest sound soon bumped into the realities of copyright law. As recently as 2006 Frank Eychaner noted that "many of the arrangements produced and performed in educational institutions throughout the country are written by individuals who have not secured permission from the copyright owners. Also, more institutions have begun recording and distributing recordings of their groups. Too often, these recordings feature illegally produced arrangements. Further, many recordings are unlicensed and the proper fees have not been paid to the copyright holders."[14] Thus, the boom in popularity of this region's sound ultimately led to the cessation of "under the table" practices, which were replaced by two legitimate publishing firms: the UNC Jazz Press (overseen by Gene Aitken) and Sound Music Publications (SMP, founded by Frank DeMiero and Ken Kraintz). In this fashion, Pacific Northwest vocal jazz ensembles have tried to define their own jazz space—musically, pedagogically, practically, and legally.

Jazz festivals too play an integral role in all forms of jazz education—setting standards of excellence, awarding appropriate aesthetics, gaining credibility for programs, recruitment of promising students, generating public support—and they have played a particularly important role in sustaining and defining the musical practices of vocal jazz ensembles.

By initiating the Northwest Swing Choir Festival (now the Northwest Vocal Jazz Festival) in 1968, Hal Malcolm not only provided a place for groups to perform but also began to formalize the parameters and performance practices of jazz choir culture through regulations and adjudication.[15]

Yet festivals have also led to telling clashes of musical cultures. In 1971, at a time when most jazz and choral festivals were not accustomed to hosting jazz choirs, Malcolm's group was invited to the Reno Jazz Festival. According to Malcolm, "Groups that added a visual element were a hit with audiences. . . . The first year in Reno, vocal jazz groups and Show-Pop groups performed on the same stage back-to-back. . . . Audiences went wild when the Show-pop groups performed. . . . Talented vocal jazz groups would come out and sing six-part arrangements and get just a polite applause."[16] It became clear that these two choral genres contrasted not only in style and performance but also in audience appeal. As a result, show choirs and vocal jazz ensembles were subsequently given separate performance stages and different adjudication sheets. In time the American Choral Directors Association also began drafting separate adjudication forms for jazz choirs and show choirs. In fact, the categories are virtually the same for jazz and show choirs; the fundamental difference hinges on the use (or not) of choreography. For Pacific Northwest vocal jazz educators, this critical distinction points to their efforts to have the vocal jazz movement distinguished as a movement *away* from show choirs.[17]

From this Reno Jazz Festival experience, Northwest vocal jazz educators continued their efforts to define for themselves and their colleagues the parameters of the vocal jazz movement. In 1980 Gene Aitken addressed the readership of *Jazz Educators Journal* on this very question by outlining three primary criteria in an article titled "What Is Vocal Jazz?" For Aitken, the first criterion for a vocal jazz ensemble is the absence of stage choreography, because "time spent on choreography takes away from the time an ensemble needs to spend time on the music . . . and in vocal jazz, emphasis must really be on the musical aspect." The second criterion hinges on the nature of repertoire. Although practices vary in jazz choir culture, Aitken posed three genres and styles widely accepted by instrumental and vocal jazz educators: nonmetric a cappella ballads that employ harmonic extensions common to jazz; straight-ahead swing charts, accompanied by a rhythm section, that highlight jazz techniques; and contemporary jazz styles, such as Latin jazz numbers, jazz waltzes, funk, and fusion charts. His final point emphasized the inclusion of improvisation, "for improvisation is the essence of jazz."[18] Although contemporary directors of jazz vocal ensembles would not all subscribe to the same aesthetic formula, it is clear that over the years this community of educators and practitioners has been just as active as the mainstream jazz community in attempting to define the nature, boundaries, and definitions of what is and is not (vocal) jazz.

Just as stage bands provided a point of entry for jazz instrumentalists into academia, vocal jazz ensembles continue to offer many opportunities for today's jazz singers and conductors. But despite the growing number of and interest in them, music educators and administrators frequently disagree about whether and where these groups should fit within music departments.[19] Vocal jazz still faces a number of significant roadblocks to full institutional acceptance and integration.

First, many classically trained choral directors have little experience with or no interest in forming or leading these groups. Indeed, some classically trained choral directors and voice instructors still view jazz singing as detrimental to vocal health. Of the relatively few directors who do want to (or have to) run a vocal jazz group, fewer still possess the background required to run a successful one. Hence, these educators often lead their vocal jazz ensembles in the same ways and with the same aesthetics as their other choral groups.

By contrast, Hal Malcolm's background in instrumental and vocal practices and pedagogies led him to develop his own idiosyncratic approach to jazz choir performance practices. Malcolm noted, "I don't even think in terms of gals' parts or guys' parts."[20] Instead, he organized his singers according to high, medium, and low vocal ranges, regardless of gender. He also freely experimented with placing female voices below male voices or writing unison lines in which male and female voices become indistinguishable—all to avoid his earlier "Wagnerian failure" brought about by applying operatic vocal techniques onto jazz charts. The use of heavy vibrato by classically trained singers could only obscure the close voicings and harmonic precision required by Lambert's arrangement, especially considering that his twelve vocalists were spread across six parts.[21] Likewise, timbre, attack, phrasing, and rhythmic sensibility differ greatly between choral singers and jazz singers. Ultimately, Malcolm discovered that concepts crucial to jazz are rendered ineffective when using a conventional choral approach.

Second, while Malcolm's unorthodox techniques became widely adopted among the early instrumentally trained vocal jazz educators, they represented a methodological departure from their more choral-oriented counterparts. As a result, various internal debates within the vocal jazz community have made it more difficult to deliver a consistent message about what and how to sing. Commenting on the divide, Gene Aitken explained that although many of the instrumentally trained vocal jazz directors "dealt effectively with style, they did not know how to work with the voice itself."[22] In response, Doug Anderson published his first *Jazz and Show Choir Handbook* (1978), and Aitken promoted vocal techniques for jazz choirs in his articles for the *Jazz Educators Journal* throughout the 1980s. Both sought to establish a middle ground between methods derived from Western choral and instrumental jazz amid the growing number of instrumental and improvisational pedagogical materials that emerged over the next decade.[23] Yet subsequent publications by vocal jazz educators served only to expand the methodological rift.

For example, in *Vocal Jazz Style* author Kirby Shaw contends that "it cannot be too strongly emphasized that the jazz choir bases its standards of tone production, blend, and balance upon the same Western European–derived choral practices found in the vast majority of American public school choral programs." Almost two decades later, Stephen Zegree's book *The Complete Guide to Teaching Vocal Jazz* only slightly qualifies Shaw's pronouncements, stating that "*in most cases,* the vocal jazz ensemble is a truly choral ensemble grounded in the classical concert choir tradition" and that "the ensemble should sing fundamentally well, emphasizing healthy vocal technique, blend, balance, diction, intonation, and tone." Zegree relies on the same choral vein as Shaw but permits more room for interpretation, acknowledging that "we must consider that some elements of jazz style (with West African derivations) and some elements of the Western European classical choral tradition are quite different. Therefore, opinions vary as to which stylistic elements are most important to a vocal jazz ensemble."[24]

Both publications openly support Western choral traditions and pedagogy and justify this position on the basis that the voice acts as the primary instrument. While this may alleviate the anxieties of choral directors inexperienced in jazz, it confuses the issue of locating institutional space for vocal jazz ensembles. On the one hand, Zegree's acknowledgment of flexibility in terms of style opens up jazz choir culture to include a variety of ensembles, even mixed repertoire groups, which becomes immediately problematic to jazz or choral educators concerned with notions of purity. On the other hand, Zegree admits the existence of regional differences, broadly understood, which recognizes the origins of the Pacific Northwest's idiosyncratic jazz choir culture and performance practices that emphasize vocal-instrumental concepts over choral traditions. Nonetheless, this methodological departure instigated further fragmentations within music education institutions.

In 2003 the debate over the official division of jazz and show choirs resurfaced once more. Vijay Singh, who took over vocal jazz instruction at Central Washington University after Moawad retired in 1998, led an official call for separation. From his position as the Repertoire and Standards chair for the American Choral Directors Association, Singh appealed to the membership by characterizing the main differences as follows: "Jazz music often employs dense harmonies, dissonances, complex rhythms, improvisation, a sense of 'swing,' and a strong instrumental-based history. The music is reflective of myriad human emotions and seeks to be provocative, individualistic, and make a statement. Dance or choreography are [sic] rarely the focus. 'Show/pop' music tends to be more harmonically and rhythmically simple, melodic, and seeks the entertainment value of popular styles, including dance, choreography, and scripts."[25] Although it took the association thirty years to recognize officially what Hal Malcolm had encountered in Reno in the early 1970s—that show choirs and vocal jazz ensembles have developed as fundamentally different idioms that require their own set of standards and resource distribution—this separation pitted choral-oriented against instrumental-oriented vocal jazz educators.

Such a division of camps has only further confused the placement of vocal jazz ensembles. An inflexible stance held by choral-minded educators serves to negate jazz choir's inclusion within jazz departments, and thus jazz culture at large. For instance, insisting that aspiring jazz singers take classical lessons (as many schools do) raises issues for purists on both sides who view "cross-over" musicians as problematic, diluted, or inauthentic. At the same time, an inflexible stance held by instrumentally minded educators carries a danger of claiming a certain status or legitimacy in the face of outright dismissal, a move, according to critic Lara Pellegrinelli, that simultaneously provides resistance to and proof of the marginalization of vocalists.[26]

This double bind points to a third challenge faced by vocal jazz ensembles: the prevalent hierarchy that privileges instruments over voices in jazz lore, as well as the gendered assumptions that help to fuel such perceptions. Historian Iain Anderson has traced how jazz studies initially entered academia in the 1960s through black studies departments by discursively aligning free jazz aesthetics with both the black arts movement and Western classical avant-garde musics. Since colleges and universities offered (and continue to offer) a comparably stable income and benefits for struggling musicians, such alliances with modernist classical music aesthetics could be read as a protective measure.[27] By the 1980s jazz studies departments became firmly entrenched within music departments, notably aided by the genre's designation as "America's Classical Music."[28]

An instrumental bias in jazz originated in the 1940s with the development of modernist aesthetics that invested deeply in notions of virtuosity, complexity, exclusivity, and anticommercialism. By contrast, conventional histories of the modern jazz era have deemed vocalists as inherently commercial or popular, and therefore not "real jazz," which is evidenced through the calculated inclusion of vocalists in the swing era (alternatively described as the "mainstream" or "entertainment" era) followed by the overt exclusion of vocalists beyond the 1940s.[29]

Yet a closer examination of the very jazz canons exalted within these same narratives reveals that previous instrumental-vocal relations were not as separate as modernist ideology would have one believe. Jazz vocalists (and vocal groups) developed alongside big bands of the swing era, bebop players of the postwar years, and so forth. Even just a cursory look at the lives and careers of the few singers accorded space throughout jazz historiography—Louis Armstrong, Billie Holiday, Ella Fitzgerald, and Sarah Vaughan—illustrates the point that vocalists thrived and survived within the major jazz scenes.[30] Despite this fact, most textbooks used for undergraduate jazz survey courses, most notably Mark Gridley's *Jazz Styles: History and Analysis,* mirror the near exclusion of vocalists and women, further realizing Burton Peretti's characterization of singing and piano playing as "virtual ghettos for jazzwomen."[31]

Gender inequities in jazz historiography have only recently begun to be addressed.[32] Moreover, the tendencies of conventional jazz narratives to marginalize or exclude dance bands, vocalists, and women as "mere" entertainment have fueled the gendering of jazz instrumentation. Lara Pellegrinelli, whose scholarship has explicitly addressed jazz singing as a gendered domain, traces the feminization of singing back to jazz's earliest days. She argues that vocal and instrumental jazz practices were "separated at birth" to legitimize jazz as an art tradition. Jazz historians have employed several strategies in congress: "'great man' histories that render the artist as hero, the divorce between jazz and its entertainment contexts, and the removal of its associations with vernacular culture, and, hence lyrics." In discussing the blues women that preceded jazz, Pellegrinelli further argues that "singing disappears from progress-oriented narratives after jazz's birth, its feminized role limited to the music's parentage. . . . The parentage of jazz, therefore, can be read as symbolically gendered: the blues is feminine, a natural product of the untrained voice associated with the body and the sexuality of its performers, whereas ragtime is masculine, associated with instruments as tools and technical skills."[33]

Such notions about masculinity and femininity are at stake as well when it comes to vocalists performing in jazz choir culture. If it is true that education is a form of social reproduction, what can be said about the systemic maintenance of "ideal communities" along gendered lines within institutionalized jazz education? Sherrie Tucker has argued, "The continued erasure of women from dominant jazz discourse, *despite* a dignified body of published knowledge on women in jazz, points to ideological morass impervious to pleas for the dignity and heroism of the women who played jazz and swing."[34] In other words, the issue is not that women were not actively performing, patronizing, or listening to jazz; it is that women have been written out of the narrative in favor of presenting jazz as a sphere of male accomplishment.

Recognizing a need to increase mentoring for young women in jazz education circuits, the International Association for Jazz Education instituted a Sisters in Jazz program in 1998, which featured a collegiate competition that rewarded its winning ensemble with professional mentoring and performance opportunities. The program's founders, a trio of women musician-educators from Michigan, explain, "Take a look at flourishing grade school and middle school music programs. Young women are not only playing in great numbers, they are sitting first chair and clearly interested in music. What happens in a young woman's life to discourage her from continuing?"[35] In 2000 Katherine Cartwright responded to this predicament by conducting a survey, titled "Sex/Instrument Survey," of college jazz programs with a view to investigate possible reasons for the shortage of women. Cartwright identified the following intertwined reasons: "early assignment of instruments by gender (girls on flute and voice, boys on trumpet and saxophone); institutionalized educational inequities based on instrument (division of programs into 'vocal jazz' and 'instrumental jazz' areas, with generally less-rigorous improvisational training in the former); a dearth of women as role models among senior jazz faculty (heads of jazz departments); and various other processes that are so common as to have become routine."[36]

Unsurprisingly, Cartwright's findings follow the familiar contours of a gendered instrumental-vocal divide: "Among our more stark findings was that among jazz programs that were sufficiently integrated with respect to voice and instruments to be headed by a single individual, 83% of these were headed by an instrumentalist. And to stress the over-arching issue of (a lack of) women in the jazz academy, we found no less than 98% of these department heads to be men—practically no women." In 1982 and 1985 Aitken compiled a "Directory of Collegiate Vocal Jazz Ensembles." The first year only thirty colleges and universities responded, and only one ensemble was directed by a woman. In 1985 seventy-four responded, and only eight ensembles were directed by women—a ratio of fewer than one woman for every nine men.[37]

As several scholars have argued, issues of gender and sexuality play a significant role in jazz culture's assessment of competency and authenticity (and therefore inclusion and exclusion). Pacific Northwest musician-educators were well positioned to develop a scene that subsequently diversified jazz education: women were accorded entry and men were presented with an alternate space to what Tucker describes as a "hyper-hetero-masculine" ethos of instrumental jazz. Tucker explains, "One of the most insidious performances of straightness in jazz continues to circulate in the normative division of labor by which men play instruments and women sing—the roles paired in such a way as to suggest complementary romantic or sexual union."[38]

Like Tucker, I am interested in the inevitable frisson when such constructed couplings become compromised. Such is the case with the irony underlying an ostensibly feminized jazz choir tradition that was developed by male instrumentalists who themselves were trained predominantly by male music educators. Yet, at the same time, most vocal jazz ensembles offer gender balance because of the practices fashioned by these educators. Because of early recruitment of male jazz instrumentalists to sing, combined with the reinforcement of choral part divisions—soprano, alto, tenor, and baritone—the male to female ratio is almost always equal.

Ultimately, there exists no easy resolution for the problematic and ambiguous placement of vocal jazz ensembles in higher education, for how a group is located within music institutions depends greatly on the ideological and pedagogical tactics at play.[39] Although vocal jazz ensembles and jazz choir culture have made enormous strides over the past four decades, their accomplishments continue to be marginalized in favor of conforming to the aims of dominant jazz narratives and discourse: "real jazz" is the sole province of (male) instrumentalists, and as a mixed gender enterprise, "vocal jazz" remains marginal to jazz history.

Although jazz choir culture has flourished in spite of numerous external struggles for recognition and authenticity, aforementioned instances of segregation between jazz and show choir practices raises critical internal contradictions. From an institutionalized jazz perspective, vocal jazz ensembles fall victim to negative stereotyping that usually associates them with a certain degree of "unhipness"—therefore undermining a jazz choir culture's aspiration to be taken seriously in jazz, a genre that tends to pride itself as being the most hip. Moreover, singers are often judged according to negative expectations—poor musical proficiency, low level of technical expertise—and are validated "in terms relative to the instrumental tradition."[40] The reality that leading vocal jazz educators have adopted many of the same dismissive and "hip" attitudes of an instrument-centric jazz discourse is indeed paradoxical and further complicates the location of jazz choir culture within music education institutions.

Even the stories told about jazz education in the Pacific Northwest have become notably instrument-centric. For example, Paul de Barros, the jazz critic for the *Seattle Times,* devoted a 2006 series to the development of jazz education in the Pacific Northwest. Hal Sherman was featured in an article titled "The Dean of High-School Jazz," which cited him as a nationwide legend and one of three "founding fathers" (alongside Moawad and King) of the Northwest region's impressive jazz tradition.[41] In 2008 de Barros described the region's forty-year "jazz education legacy" as a "dizzying genealogy of relationships and influences . . . handed down by four great teachers: Waldo King, Hal Sherman, John Moawad and Dave Barduhn."[42] An accompanying chart, titled "Jazz in Seattle-area schools: How it grew," illustrates the legacy's trajectory from the origins in the 1940s, to Barduhn's intermediary position in the 1970s, to present day high school ensembles chosen to participate in the prestigious Essentially Ellington Competition. While Sherman, Moawad, King, and Barduhn are indeed crucial to the story of Pacific Northwest jazz education, their vital roles in vocal jazz education have been obfuscated. That a history of jazz education would gloss over the simultaneous achievements of vocal jazz ensembles illustrates the high degree to which instrumental gains continue to be implied when talking about jazz.

It is clear that the institutionalization of jazz education in accordance with dominant jazz discourse has overwhelmingly edged out the contributions and activities of vocalists. That early jazz vocal ensembles offered one of the few opportunities for women to participate equally with men in jazz stands as a major accomplishment (the ratio of males to females is almost always equal in vocal jazz ensembles). The lack of a major gender gap in the Pacific Northwest jazz community is anomalous compared to other regions in the United States. Women who came up through these pioneering ensembles also now make up a healthy portion of today's vocal jazz educators and so serve as role models for future generations of jazz performers, teachers, and historians. But the jazz education community cannot become complacent. With the demise of the Sisters in Jazz program, it is of paramount importance that female students be encouraged to pursue jazz studies, because things are not equal until they truly are.

NOTES

This chapter is dedicated to the memory of two pioneers of Pacific Northwest jazz education, Frederick Halsted "Hal" Malcolm and John "Coach" Moawad.

1. Hal Malcolm, liner notes to *Genesis in Jazz Vocal Education,* Studios of Haystack Broadcasting, 1998, compact disc, 2.

2. Waldo King, quoted in Doug Anderson, *The Jazz and Show Choir Handbook II,* 2nd ed. (Chapel Hill, NC: Hinshaw Music Inc., 1993), 5.

3. Malcolm, *Genesis,* 3–4.

4. For clarity, I use "vocal jazz ensembles" interchangeably when referring to combos, ensembles, and choirs, unless otherwise specified.

5. Histories of jazz choirs in United States include Anderson, *Jazz and Show Choir,* and Eva Mae Pisciotta, "The History of Jazz Choir in the United States" (DMA diss., University of Missouri, 1992).

6. A more complete history of jazz choir culture would document how other influential jazz educators originally trained in a solely instrumental or choral path, and that CWCE was not the only center for Pacific Northwest jazz education. For instance, Ralph Manzo, who graduated from CWCE in 1948, ran a choral jazz program at Eastern Washington University that adopted a choral aesthetic. His Collegians, a mixed-repertoire chamber ensemble, performed a wider range of repertoire, from symphonic to swing music, that became an important model for music educators. Gene Aitken, another influential educator of the region, underscores the influence of an unofficial vocal jazz ensemble formed at the University of Washington in the late 1950s.

7. Dave Barduhn, interview with the author, September 12, 2002, Gresham, Oregon.

8. Although techniques approximated vocalese can be traced back the 1930s, it was popularized by King Pleasure's 1952 recording of "Moody's Mood," *King Pleasure—Original Moody's Mood,* Prestige PR 7586, LP. See Barry Keith Grant, "Purple Passages or Fiestas in Blue? Notes toward an Aesthetic of Voca-

lese," in *Representing Jazz,* ed. Krin Gabbard (Durham, NC: Duke University Press, 1995), 285–303.

9. It is certainly ironic that the live-performance choirs inspired by Lambert, Hendricks & Ross do not, or cannot, take advantage of the same studio techniques that helped enable that group's success.

10. Malcolm, quoted in Fred Crafts, "He's Got a Jazzy Cure for the Vocal Blahs," *Eugene Register-Guard,* March 2, 1978.

11. Hal Sherman, quoted in Paul de Barros, "The Dean of High-School Jazz," *Seattle Times,* February 6, 2006.

12. Anderson, *Jazz and Show Choir,* 92.

13. Malcolm, *Genesis,* 17.

14. Frank Eychaner, "Repertoire Standards: Vocal Jazz—the Jazz Choir Goes Legit: Copyright Law for the Vocal Music Educator," *Choral Journal* 46, no. 8 (2006): 41.

15. Vocal jazz ensemble adjudication forms illustrate the Pacific Northwest's aesthetic inclination toward instrumental jazz concepts, as opposed to choral ones, and provide insights into what types of performances are rewarded. See Anderson's handbook for samples of festival rules and regulations (from the Northwest Vocal Jazz Festival) as well as sample adjudication forms from both jazz and show choir competitions (Anderson, *Jazz and Show Choir*).

16. Malcolm, interview by Mike Weaver, February 2, 2001, in *Show Pop: The History of Show Choir,* www.angelfire.com/or3/tcsingers/SChistory.htm.

17. Anderson, *Jazz and Show Choir.* Several educators, critics, and audiences have described the scene as a "vocal jazz movement," and the term "movement," as used by educators in this context, does not necessarily imply political connotations.

18. Gene Aitken, "What Is Vocal Jazz?," *Jazz Educators Journal* 12, no. 1 (October/November 1980): 9, 10.

19. See Russ Baird, "Vocal Jazz: A Place in Choral Education," *Jazz Educators Journal* 25 (Winter 1993): 60–61; and Diana Spradling, "Vocal Jazz and Its Credibility in the University Curriculum," *Jazz Educators Journal* 32 (March 2000): 59–60, 62–64.

20. Crafts, "Jazzy Cure," 3D.

21. Jazz vocalists do employ vibrato but sparingly so in jazz choir settings.

22. Gene Aitken, "Vocal Jazz Vibrato," *Jazz Educators Journal* (October/November 1984), 16.

23. A few examples include Patty Coker and David Baker, *Vocal Improvisation: An Instrumental Approach* (Lebanon, IN: Studio P/R, 1981); Dennis DiBlasio, "Scat Singing: Imitating Instruments," *Jazz Educators Journal* 28, no. 5 (1996): 21, 33; Bob Stoloff, *Scat! Vocal Improvisation Techniques* (Brooklyn, NY: Gerard and Sarzin, 1999).

24. Kirby Shaw, *Vocal Jazz Style* (Milwaukee, WI: Leonard, 1987), 3; Stephen Zegree, *The Complete Guide to Teaching Vocal Jazz: Including Pop and Other Show Styles* (Dayton, OH: Heritage Music Press, 2002), 2; italics added.

25. Vijay Singh, "A Milestone in ACDA History," *Choral Journal* 44, no. 4 (2003): 65.

26. Lara V. Pellegrinelli, "The Song Is Who? Locating Singers on the Jazz Scene" (PhD diss., Harvard University, 2005), 8.

27. Iain Anderson, "Jazz outside the Marketplace," in *This Is Our Music: Free Jazz, the Sixties, and American Culture* (Philadelphia: University of Pennsylvania Press, 2007).

28. See Billy Taylor, "Jazz: America's Classical Music," *Black Perspectives in Music* 14, no. 1 (Winter 1986): 21–25.

29. To illustrate the point of vocalists' exclusion, Gridley's popular and authoritative jazz history text *Jazz Styles* dedicates 12 out of 442 pages (an approximate ratio of one to thirty-six) to discussing the important contributions jazz vocalists have made throughout this genre's inception. See Mark C. Gridley, *Jazz Styles: History and Analysis,* with contributions by David Cutler, 8th ed. (Upper Saddle River, NJ: Prentice Hall, 2003).

30. Scott DeVeaux, "Constructing the Jazz Tradition," *Black American Literature Forum* 25, no. 3 (Autumn 1991): 525–60.

31. Gridley, *Jazz Styles,* 2003; Burton W. Peretti, *The Creation of Jazz: Music, Race, and Culture in Urban America* (Urbana: University of Illinois Press, 1992), 122.

32. For instance, see Sherrie Tucker, *Swing Shift: "All-Girl" Bands of the 1940s* (Durham, NC: Duke University Press, 2000).

33. Lara V. Pellegrinelli, "Separated at 'Birth': Singing and the History of Jazz " in *Big Ears: Listening for Gender in Jazz Studies,* ed. Nichole T. Rustin and Sherrie Tucker (Durham, NC: Duke University Press, 2008), 42–44.

34. Tucker, *Swing Shift,* 21.

35. Marion Hayden, Diana Spradling, and Sunny Wilkinson, "Sisters in Jazz: Michigan Mentoring Pilot Program," *Jazz Educators Journal* 30, no. 1 (July 1997): 42.

36. The "Sex/Instrument Survey" findings were published in Katherine Cartwright, "Sisters in Jazz and Beyond: Through Mentorship, Musicianship, and Mobility," *Jazz Educators Journal* 33, no. 6 (May 2001): 70.

37. Gene Aitken, "Directory of Collegiate Vocal Jazz Ensembles," in *Jazz Educators Journal* 14 (October/November 1982): 72–73, and in *Jazz Educators Journal* 17 (October/November 1985): 19–21.

38. Sherrie Tucker, "When Did Jazz Go Straight? A Queer Question for Jazz Studies," *Critical Studies in Improvisation/Études Critiques en Improvisation* 4, no. 2 (2008): www.criticalimprov.com/article/viewArticle/850/1411.

39. This problem is further illustrated by my efforts to present a paper discussing the predicament facing vocal jazz ensembles at the 2005 Society for American Music Annual Meeting. Although there were two sessions dedicated to jazz, and even West Coast jazzes, I was placed in a session titled "Other Voices."

40. Pellegrinelli, "Song Is Who?," 3.

41. Barros, "High-School Jazz."

42. Paul de Barros, "Region's Jazz Legacy in Spotlight Again at Essentially Ellington," *Seattle Times,* May 28, 2008.

CHAPTER 11

Crossing the Street

Rethinking Jazz Education

DAVID AKE

In a scene from the 2004 Hollywood thriller *Collateral,* Vincent, a self-assured professional assassin (played by Tom Cruise), enters a Los Angeles jazz club with Max, a smart but timorous cab driver (Jamie Foxx), whom Vincent has forcibly enlisted to shuttle him from one hit job to another. The two men sit down at a table, ostensibly to listen to the band, led by a trumpeter named Daniel (Barry Shakaba Henley). It turns out that Vincent is not only a murderer but also a jazz aficionado. He lectures Max—no fan of the music—on the finer points of improvisation and, once the band finishes for the night, invites Daniel to their table. Daniel and Vincent commiserate on the current state of live jazz. Recalling a better era, Daniel described one life-changing evening—July 22, 1964—when his hero, Miles Davis, sat in with him at that very club. Only after Daniel finishes his reminiscence, and the wait staff, customers, and other musicians have left, does Vincent reveal to the two men that he has been hired to kill Daniel, who has run afoul of an international drug cartel. Daniel pleads to Vincent to let him go (as does Max). Apparently softened by Daniel's skillful musicianship, Vincent offers the trumpeter a way out. He just needs to provide the correct answer to one question:

VINCENT: Where did Miles learn music?

DANIEL *(defiantly):* I know everything there is to know about Miles.

MAX *(trying to help):* Music school! He got it in music school, right?

DANIEL: His father was a dentist. East Saint Louis. Invested in agriculture. Made plenty of money. Sent Miles to Juilliard School of Music. New York City. 1945.

MAX (relieved and impressed by Daniel's knowledge): Damn!

Vincent swiftly pulls out his handgun and fires three bullets between Daniel's eyes. Revealing a degree of sorrowfulness, Vincent swoops in before Daniel's head crashes down and gently rests the dead trumpeter on the table. Meanwhile, the action has visibly traumatized Max. Hadn't Daniel replied correctly to Vincent's question? Miles Davis *did* attend Juilliard, right? Yes, but Vincent had another answer in mind.

VINCENT (sotto voce): He dropped out of Juilliard after less than a year. Tracked down Charlie Parker on Fifty-Second Street, who mentored him for the next three years.

Vincent has taught Max an important lesson: real music—like real life— occurs on the streets, not in a school.

A pair of my earlier publications explores the ways in which the educational backgrounds of college-based jazz instructors influence what and how they teach, and thus what their students will hear as "good jazz."[1] Although there's a great deal more scholarship to be done on the aesthetics and pedagogical techniques emphasized within institutionalized jazz programs, this essay looks at a different side of music education. Namely, it shows how conservatory-style training for jazz musicians is generally understood by and represented in the broader jazz world, especially among the music's historians and journalists.

Why return to the topic of jazz education when most of the individuals involved in that field remain little known beyond their immediate regions? I do so because, by nearly any measure, college-based programs have replaced not only the proverbial street as the primary training grounds for young jazz musicians but also urban nightclubs as the main professional homes for hundreds of jazz performers and composers. Even so, this far-reaching and seemingly inexorable move from clubs to schools remains ignored, marginalized, or denigrated throughout a wide range of jazz discourse. And by examining some deeply held conceptions of both jazz history and music education, I hope to encourage jazz people to reconsider the roles schools now play in the development and dissemination of their favorite music.

DISCOURSE AND ANTIDISCOURSE

In January 2007 the *New York Times* featured an article on the front page of its Sunday Arts and Leisure section titled "Jazz Is Alive and Well, in the Classroom, Anyway." Timed to correspond with the thirty-fourth annual conference of the International Association of Jazz Education (IAJE) scheduled to meet in New York the following week, the piece tells of a jazz boom within America's high school and college music programs.[2] The article's author, Nate Chinen, relates some remarkable statistics: the 2007 conference was expected to draw more than eight thousand attendees from forty-five countries, and IAJE membership had quadrupled over the past two decades.[3] While Chinen closes his piece on an optimistic note, suggesting that the rise of college programs may help to sustain local jazz scenes throughout the United States, he also evinces wariness about the merits of this trend. Chinen writes that the profusion of information available to jazz students today "might be a mixed blessing" and cites Berklee College of Music faculty member Bill Pierce's concern: "You can learn every Coltrane solo there is without ever listening to a record. I'm not saying that's a good thing. But it's there."[4]

Pierce's comment alludes to the increase of commercially published notated transcriptions of solos by John Coltrane and other canonical jazz figures. No doubt, Pierce worries that young musicians who base their learning on written representations of improvisations forgo an important musical experience. In this case they couldn't hear the beauty of John Coltrane's recorded saxophone timbre or how Coltrane played within the context of the other performers in his band. Pierce is correct, of course, but he also seems to overlook how his attitudes and values regarding this matter have been shaped by his own historical situation. That is, Bill Pierce was nineteen years old when John Coltrane died, and he never attended a Coltrane performance himself.[5] Someone who *had* seen Coltrane play in person might argue that recordings offer just a limited glimpse into the power of Coltrane's music. Charles Mingus once commented along these lines when he said, "It's a funny society that's raised mainly on hearing records, they very seldom get the chance to know what the difference is, hearing live music."[6] Pierce's valorization of recordings over published transcriptions reveals how easily we can forget that one's historical, cultural, and geographic location influences how we study, hear, teach, and create music (and everything else).

My point is not that transcriptions make better learning tools than records, but rather that each generation of musicians uses the information available to it in the way it sees fit, and apprehensions over a specific pedagogical method should be understood in that light.[7] More important, I use this example to show that even parties who would seem to be sympathetic to jazz education—Pierce earns much of his livelihood from teaching at Berklee—tend to downplay its materials, techniques, and effectiveness.

A great number of other musicians, critics, and scholars also seem suspicious of college-based jazz education, favoring instead those customs, modes of learning, and venues prevalent during earlier eras or in other places. Christopher Small's position on this couldn't have been clearer: "Formal courses of training for jazz musicians may signal the end of jazz as a living force; an art that is truly living resists the codification, the establishment of canons of taste and of practice, that schools by nature impose."[8] The outstanding pianist (and longtime freelance educator) Hal Galper voiced a similar lament: "Used to be, back when there was less music theory available, the players developed more individual playing styles because of the lack of information, through the painful process of trial and error. I'm not promoting musical ignorance as a viable process for developing individuality but the delicate balance of how much to and not to teach a student should be a constant challenge for a teacher. An effective teacher should know how to get out of the way of a student's development. This is impossible in a classroom."[9]

Others are more circumspect in revealing their positions. In *Jazz Styles: History and Analysis,* author Mark Gridley points to the roles America's colleges and universities play in teaching and supporting jazz at a time when much of the country appears ambivalent about the music. His comments are worth quoting at length, as they both summarize widely held perceptions of the recent state of jazz in the United States and reveal a characteristic reluctance among writers to delve further into the music's changing practices and locations:

> With the exception of a few standouts, jazz had less exposure and fewer performance outlets during the 1990s and the beginning of the twenty-first century than at any other time in its history. The number of nightclubs featuring jazz on a regular basis was smaller than ever before, and the fees paid to the musicians in them were lower. . . . A number of eminent jazz musicians acquired full-time positions as college instructors and would not have been able to remain in the field of music without such jobs. Hundreds of excellent jazz players, including more than a handful of world-class musicians, served as adjunct instructors in colleges and universities. *In fact, most of the jazz improvising going on in America during this period occurred in high school and college bands. . . . And the level of musicianship among*

many young players was so high that a number of high school and college bands were better than some professional bands.[10]

Few would argue with Gridley's assessments. It's worth asking, though, why he would wait until literally the very last sentences of his 349-page textbook to point all this out to us. If colleges (and even high schools) have served as the most vibrant centers of jazz over the past generation or longer, why not note this trend earlier in his book and why devote only one paragraph to this circumstance while spending seven pages on a section called "Strategies for Album Buying"?[11] Certainly a shift of this magnitude would seem to bear more extensive comment in a history text.

Other examples reveal similar attitudes. In *Jazz: The First 100 Years,* authors Henry Martin and Keith Waters note, "The growth of jazz pedagogy . . . over the past three decades has been astonishing." Even so, these writers give roughly the same attention to this "astonishing" development as they give to discussing the styles of Big Bad Voodoo Daddy and the Brian Setzer Orchestra. Ted Gioia's *The History of Jazz* makes virtually no mention of music schools, nor does Ken Burns's ten-part PBS documentary. Gary Giddins's 2004 essay collection *Weather Bird* consists of 146 short essays covering a wide range of topics, including the programming policies at the annual JVC Jazz Festivals and the fluctuating reception of jazz within the hermetic world of the Pulitzer Prize's selection committees. Yet in a tome that runs to 632 pages and that bears the subtitle *Jazz at the Dawn of Its Second Century,* Giddins never broaches the topic of jazz education.[12] Lest one imagines that conservatory-style jazz programs emerged too recently for historians to concern themselves with the matter, we should bear in mind that the Berklee School (now College) of Music opened its doors in 1946, roughly the same moment when Charlie Parker, Dizzy Gillespie, and others were introducing bebop to the world, and that the National Association of Jazz Educators (precursor to the IAJE) was established in 1968, more than forty years ago, or half of the entire history of recorded jazz.

Not all writers have avoided or mistrusted jazz education. Charles Beale's essay for *The Oxford Companion to Jazz* provides an even-handed take on the history of and issues surrounding jazz pedagogy.[13] And one group of scholars has even commented, "One of the wondrous oddities of our current moment is that the best advice to a serious jazz player in training is not to drop out and study in New York's nightclubs but to attend one of the several conservatories where excellent jazz instruction, by accomplished jazz artists, is richly available."[14]

Yet most authors who have addressed this topic at any length seem skeptical, at best, of the relevance of America's college-level programs. In his 2005 book, *Is Jazz Dead?*, Stuart Nicholson opens the chapter called "Teachers Teaching Teachers: Jazz Education" by observing, "The institutionalization of jazz education in the final decades of the twentieth century has meant it is now playing an increasingly important role in shaping jazz in a way it did not in the past." He cites saxophonist and educator Bill Kirchner's remarks: "Jazz education—with all its imperfections and limitations—is the best way we now have of sustaining the mentoring process and enabling students to interact with their peers." After this seemingly dispassionate introduction, however, Nicholson abruptly trashes the whole of jazz pedagogy in the United States for what he sees as a fatal overemphasis on bebop- and modal-based forms and styles. He writes, "By copying the work of past masters, many students can acquire a superficial understanding of the art of improvisation, but they lack the deeper understanding of the processes involved that ultimately leads to originality of concept and execution." To counteract these supposed faults, the London-based Nicholson proposes that American jazz education be reoriented to function more like the jazz programs in Europe. In particular, he asserts that America's jazz students should incorporate a greater study of European classical styles. To support his position, he points out that Charlie Parker enjoyed listening to classical music and had expressed an interest in studying composition with Nadia Boulanger and Edgard Varèse.[15]

To be sure, Parker, and also Fats Waller, Billy Strayhorn, Charles Mingus, and many other important jazz musicians from previous generations, have studied and drawn inspiration from European art music, just as scores of jazz performers and composers continue to do today. And it's true that, as Nicholson notes, "Classical music provides a huge reservoir of musical knowledge to build upon."[16] But it's equally true that jazz artists have learned and borrowed from the music cultures of South America, the Caribbean, Japan, India, and Africa, as well as other sounds from across the United States, including rock, gospel, the blues, and country music—a much broader palate of potential influences that Nicholson chooses not to document. Nicholson's Europhilia, evident not just in his chapter on jazz education but throughout his book and beyond, suggests that he's less interested in encouraging young American musicians to develop their own jazz styles than in simply having them replace a bop-centric approach with a Eurocentric one.[17] (Moreover, we might consider why Nicholson thinks that it's a bad idea for jazz musicians to emulate "past masters" of jazz, but a good idea for them to emulate "past masters" of classical music.)

Gary Kennedy's "Jazz Education" entry in the second edition of the *New Grove Dictionary of Jazz,* published in 2002, takes an equally dim view of America's current education programs. Unlike Stuart Nicholson's preference for European-based models, though, Kennedy favors the practices of African American teachers and institutions of the late nineteenth and early twentieth centuries. His essay begins with an admiring historical overview of instruction and skill acquisition among important black musicians from the 1890s through the 1960s, followed by a section on the growth of jazz summer camps and the earliest college programs in the 1940s, '50s, and '60s. When his chronological account of the subject approaches the present day, Kennedy's tone turns decidedly less sanguine. "Even fifty years after the movement began, 'jazz education' has yet to reach any of the serious artistic goals that the term would imply. Much of the reason for this *failure,* at least in the USA, is that most undergraduate-level jazz programs are concerned more with creating generic professional musicians and educators than jazz musicians."[18]

Kennedy is right to credit the largely overlooked teachers who nurtured the first generations of jazz performers and composers.[19] Still, his *Grove* entry warrants comment for the assumptions buried just beneath the rhetoric. Most obviously, his position presumes that there exists, or existed in the past, a "real jazz" separate from the evidently pseudoversion taught and performed in schools today, though he never specifies the qualities that differentiate authentic from inauthentic styles. Nor does he describe the performance practices, sounds, tunes, or venues that supposedly separate "generic professional musicians" from "jazz musicians." Kennedy's disparagements seem particularly puzzling when one considers that they appear in the three-volume *New Grove Dictionary of Jazz.*

I have compiled a sample of American musicians, born since 1950, who studied jazz for at least some time at one of this country's colleges or universities (table 11.1).[20] The information comes directly from *Grove* itself, so the *Dictionary's* editorial staff, of which Kennedy was a member, evidently considered these individuals sufficiently authentic and accomplished to merit inclusion in their compendium. This list plainly illustrates the impact of school-trained performers and composers on all aspects of jazz over the past four decades or more and makes it difficult to justify Kennedy's portrayal of jazz education in the United States as a "failure."

TABLE 11.1 Sample of American jazz musicians born since 1950 who studied jazz at the college level

Musician (birth year)	School(s) attended	Musician (birth year)	School(s) attended
Carl Allen (1961)	William Paterson College	Joey Calderazzo (1965)	Berklee College of Music; Manhattan School of Music
Geri Allen (1957)	Howard University; University of Pittsburgh	Terri Lyne Carrington (1965)	Berklee College of Music
Ben Allison (1966)	New York University	Ndugu Leon Chancellor (1952)	California State University, Dominguez Hills
Jay Anderson (1955)	California State University, Long Beach	Cyrus Chestnut (1963)	Berklee College of Music
Joey Baron (1955)	Berklee College of Music	Billy Childs (1957)	University of Southern California
Bruce Barth (1958)	New England Conservatory	John Clayton (1952)	Indiana University
Bob Belden (1956)	North Texas State University	Scott Colley (1963)	California Institute of the Arts
Bob Berg (1951)	Juilliard School of Music	Ravi Coltrane (1965)	California Institute of the Arts
Jeff Berlin (1953)	Berklee College of Music	Harry Connick Jr. (1967)	Loyola University; Manhattan School of Music
Tim Berne (1954)	Lewis and Clark College		
Peter Bernstein (1967)	William Paterson College; New School for Social Research	Adam Cruz (1970)	New School for Social Research
		Bill Cunliffe (1956)	Duke University; Eastman School of Music
Jim Black (1967)	Berklee College of Music	Jesse Davis (1965)	William Paterson College
Cindy Blackman (1959)	Berklee College of Music	Al DiMeola (1954)	Berklee College of Music
Brian Blade (1970)	Loyola University; University of New Orleans	Dave Douglas (1963)	Berklee College of Music; New England Conservatory
Terence Blanchard (1962)	Rutgers University		
Luis Bonilla (1966)	California State University, Los Angeles	Mark Dresser (1952)	Indiana University; University of California, San Diego
Don Byron (1958)	New England Conservatory	Marty Ehrlich (1955)	New England Conservatory
Michael Cain (1966)	California Institute of the Arts	Peter Epstein (1967)	California Institute of the Arts; University of Nevada, Reno

Peter Erskine (1954)	Indiana University
Ellery Eskelin (1959)	Towson State University
Kevin Eubanks (1957)	Berklee College of Music
Robin Eubanks (1955)	Philadelphia College of Performing Arts
Jon Faddis (1953)	Manhattan School of Music
John Fedchock (1957)	Ohio State University; Eastman School of Music
Russell Ferrante (1952)	California State University, San Jose
Brandon Fields (1957)	California State University, Fullerton
David Fiucynski (1964)	New England Conservatory
Ricky Ford (1954)	New England Conservatory
Michael Formanek (1958)	California State University, Hayward
Curtis Fowlkes (1950)	Manhattan Community College
Rebecca Coupe Franks (1961)	Cabrillo Junior College; New School for Social Research
Bill Frisell (1951)	Berklee College of Music
Matthew Garrision (1970)	Berklee College of Music
George Garzone (1950)	Berklee College of Music
James Genus (1966)	Virginia Commonwealth University
Greg Gisbert (1966)	Berklee College of Music
Larry Goldings (1968)	New School for Social Research
Wycliffe Gordon (1967)	Florida A&M
Danny Gottlieb (1953)	University of Miami
Larry Grenadier (1966)	San Jose State; Stanford University
Drew Gress (1959)	Towson State; Manhattan School of Music
Russell Gunn (1971)	Jackson State University
Jamey Haddad (1952)	Berklee College of Music
Craig Handy (1962)	North Texas State University
Roy Hargrove (1969)	Berklee College of Music; New School for Social Research
Winard Harper (1962)	Cincinnati Conservatory of Music; Howard University; Hartt School of Music
Stefon Harris (1973)	Manhattan School of Music
Donald Harrison (1960)	Southern University; Berklee College of Music
Antonio Hart (1968)	Berklee College of Music
Graham Haynes (1960)	Queens College
Fred Hersch (1955)	New England Conservatory
Susie Ibarra (1970)	Mannes College of Music; Goddard College
Dennis Irwin (1951)	North Texas State University
Javon Jackson (1965)	Berklee College of Music
Mark Johnson (1953)	North Texas State University
Willie Jones III (1968)	California Institute of the Arts
Geoff Keezer (1970)	Berklee College of Music
Dave Kikoski (1961)	Berklee College of Music
Frank Kimbrough (1956)	Appalachian State University; Arizona State University
Kenny Kirkland (1955)	Manhattan School of Music
Larry Koonse (1961)	University of Southern California
Gene Lake (1966)	Berklee College of Music

(continued)

TABLE 11.1 (continued)

Musician (birth year)	School(s) attended
Will Lee (1952)	University of Miami
Joe Locke (1959)	Eastman School of Music
Joe Lovano (1952)	Berklee College of Music
Carmen Lundy (1954)	University of Miami
Brian Lynch (1956)	Wisconsin Conservatory of Music; New York University
Tony Malaby (1964)	Arizona State; William Paterson College
Rick Margitza (1961)	Wayne State; Berklee College of Music; University of Miami; Loyola University
Sherrie Maricle (1963)	State University of New York, Binghamton; New York University
Branford Marsalis (1960)	Southern University; Berklee College of Music
Delfeayo Marsalis (1965)	Berklee College of Music
Virginia Mayhew (1959)	New School for Social Research
John Medeski (1965)	New England Conservatory
Myra Melford (1957)	Evergreen State College; Cornish Institute
Pat Metheny (1954)	University of Miami
Ron Miles (1963)	University of Denver; Manhattan School of Music; University of Colorado
Ben Monder (1962)	University of Miami; Queens College
Jason Moran (1975)	Manhattan School of Music
David Murray (1955)	Pomona College
Lewis Nash (1958)	Arizona State
Steve Nelson (1954)	Rutgers University
James Newton (1953)	California State University, Los Angeles
Judy Niemack (1954)	Pasadena City College
Adam Nussbaum (1955)	City College of New York
Greg Osby (1960)	Howard University; Berklee College of Music
Jaco Pastorius (1951)	University of Miami
John Patitucci (1959)	San Francisco State; Long Beach State
Nicholas Payton (1973)	University of New Orleans
Ben Perowsky (1966)	Berklee College of Music; Manhattan School of Music
Chris Potter (1971)	Manhattan School of Music
Marcus Printup (1967)	University of North Florida
Tom Rainey (1957)	Berklee College of Music
Dianne Reeves (1956)	University of Denver
Lee Ritenour (1952)	University of Southern California
Herb Robertson (1951)	Berklee College of Music
Steve Rodby (1954)	Northwestern University

Marcus Rojas (1962)	New England Conservatory
Wallace Roney (1960)	Howard University; Berklee College of Music
Michelle Rosewoman (1953)	Laney Junior College
Jim Rotondi (1962)	North Texas State University
Patrice Rushen (1954)	University of Southern California
Michael Sarin (1965)	University of Washington; Cornish Institute
Maria Schneider (1960)	University of Minnesota; University of Miami; Eastman School of Music
Loren Schoenberg (1958)	Manhattan School of Music
John Scofield (1951)	Berklee College of Music
Brad Shepik (1966)	Cornish Institute
Bob Sheppard (1952)	Glassboro State; Eastman School of Music
Matthew Shipp (1960)	University of Delaware; New England Conservatory
Marvin "Smitty" Smith (1961)	Berklee College of Music
Jim Snidero (1958)	North Texas State University
Chris Speed (1967)	New England Conservatory
Mike Stern (1953)	Berklee College of Music
Bill Stewart (1966)	William Paterson College
Craig Taborn (1970)	University of Michigan
Akira Tana (1952)	New England Conservatory
Mark Turner (1965)	California State University, Long Beach; Berklee College of Music
Reginald Veal (1964)	Southern University
Chad Wackerman (1960)	California State University, Long Beach
Nasheet Waits (1971)	Morehouse College; Long Island University
Bobby Watson (1953)	University of Miami
Jeff "Tain" Watts (1960)	Berklee College of Music
Dave Weckl (1960)	University of Bridgeport
Kenny Werner (1951)	Berklee College of Music
James Williams (1951)	Memphis State
Matt Wilson (1964)	Wichita State
Kenny Wolleson (1966)	Cabrillo Junior College
Francis Wong (1957)	San Jose State
Rachel Z (1962)	New England Conservatory
John Zorn (1953)	Webster College

SOURCE: Barry Kernfeld, ed., *The New Grove Dictionary of Jazz*, vol. 2, 2nd ed. (New York: Macmillan, 2002).

We should be clear, too, that there are a great many other very fine musicians whose names do not appear in *Grove* but who studied jazz in school and who set up shop in towns large and small throughout this country and abroad. While many of these individuals may not have earned worldwide acclaim (though some have) or even make a full-time living in music (though some do), they continue to play, write, teach, learn, listen to, and, in all manner of ways, participate in jazz.[21] Granted, standard pedagogical methods are far from perfect; I have expressed my own reservations about some of these. But evading, deriding, or ignoring jazz programs tout court hardly constitutes healthy dialogue or an honest assessment of the music's current places and practices. And if we are to effect meaningful improvements in *how* jazz is taught, we must first accept this fundamental shift in *where* it is taught, played, and heard.

JAZZ MYTHOLOGIES

Having established a general reluctance among historians and others to credit America's music programs with playing a more positive role in recent jazz, I want to explore some of the reasons behind this reticence. Toward that end, I identify four predominant myths guiding negative perceptions of jazz education. I am not using the word *myth* here in the sense of an outright misconception or falsehood. Instead it should be understood as the stories that people tell themselves about themselves. Most important, people *believe* these stories; indeed, they live them, though usually without being aware they're doing so. As one writer described it, "Within myth, I do not see the myth itself, just as I do not see the lenses in my glasses; on the contrary, I see through the invisible or transparent myth in apprehending the world as—from my perspective—it simply is."[22] And if myths cause us to focus on events or activities from one view, they necessarily cause us to repudiate, ignore, or overlook other perspectives.

Myth #1: City Living

To start, there is the long-standing myth of jazz as a strictly urban genre. There are countless examples of a city-centric jazz narrative, so I will simply state here that as recently as 2002 the *New Grove Dictionary* stated categorically, "The history of jazz in terms of the venues that have fostered it is the history of nightlife in different cities."[23] Periodicals such as *Down Beat* and *Jazz Times* still dedicate the overwhelming majority of their print space to the activities of a relatively small circle of urban musicians, especially those who live and work in and around Manhattan. This New York nightclub mythology remains so deeply entrenched that the jazz studies program at New York University uses it as a marketing tool. The program's web page boasts about its location "in the heart of Greenwich Village, the world's Mecca for jazz music," where "students perform weekly at landmark venues including the Village Vanguard, Birdland, the Jazz Standard and the Knitting Factory."[24]

Without question, the clubs of New York, as well as of New Orleans, Chicago, Kansas City, Detroit, Philadelphia, Los Angeles, Paris, Copenhagen, Tokyo, and other large cities, have served as important centers for jazz from the music's inception. Those settings have provided not only places for performers to play in front of audiences but also crucial locations in which musicians could establish and build professional connections. Yet while jazz performers and their fans still convene in nightclubs and concert halls throughout the world, the diminishing number of such settings has forced jazz people to find other ways and places to interact.

Even New York University recognizes this trend. In the same paragraph as the one cited earlier, the school's promo reads, "With guidance from an up-to-date and nurturing faculty, NYU Jazz students learn to develop new venues, realize new concepts for distributing their music and create alternatives for successful careers in the modern jazz industry."[25] America's nonurban colleges and universities have long provided such "alternatives." Names such as Denton, Texas; Valencia, California; Bloomington, Indiana; Oberlin, Ohio; DeKalb, Illinois; Coral Gables, Florida; and Greeley, Colorado, may not stir the jazz imagination in the way that New York City and other major metropolitan areas do. Nevertheless, campuses in these and other towns now support and also utilize jazz in ways that many larger cities don't.

In some regions, on-campus concerts by visiting artists, student ensembles, and faculty groups represent some of the only live music available and so provide a service to the community while strengthening relations between "town and gown." Reaching these constituencies goes beyond simple goodwill for many schools. In an era of declining financial support from state coffers, it is no secret that colleges and universities must now raise a significant percentage of their budgets from private sources. Local audiences are increasingly seen as potential sources of that funding. And when institutions on campuses actively integrate their jazz education programs into their efforts to cultivate donor relationships, jazz's commentators should take note. Such situations illustrate as clearly as any Lincoln Center event ever could just how deeply the music has rooted itself at the nexus of politics, education, and business in the United States.[26]

Myth #2: What Is Hip (and Unhip and Nonhip)?

A second myth affecting perceptions of jazz education involves the aesthetic of hipness. The editorial preferences of the major jazz textbooks and fan publications serve more than simply to focus readers' attentions on jazz life in particular geographic areas. They also reinforce and shape understandings of how jazz is supposed to look and who is supposed to play it, which is to say that these publications promote an *image* of jazz as much as they report on the genre's sounds. And they have tended to portray jazz musicians as not just city based but also self-possessed, sophisticated, and utterly disdainful of the commonplace. In a word, hip.

The hip-jazz image is usually exemplified in one of two ways. First, there's the "venerable" icon from the 1950s or '60s. In 2006 *Down Beat* ran a cover story on the seventy-one-year-old Ramsey Lewis and another on Sun Ra, who died in 1993. Not to be outdone, *Jazz Times'* cover stories that same year featured Sonny Rollins, then seventy-six years old, and Ornette Coleman, also seventy-six, while another pictured Miles Davis, who passed away in 1991. Second, there's the "hot new thing," epitomized by the June 2007 cover in *Down Beat* with the breathless headline, "Who's Got Next? Jeremy Pelt Leads a Pack of Young Trumpeters Who Demand Attention. We've Got 25 You Need to Hear."[27] Note that these constituencies do not include figures from the 1930s or early '40s, when jazz reigned as the favorite genre in America, nor from practitioners of the immensely popular smooth-jazz subgenre of recent decades. Hip can be young or old (or even dead), but it must always distance itself from appearing too eager to please its audiences. That most readers who purchase these magazines will never possess the hip attributes of their jazz heroes does not detract from the allure of the published image, just as it does not hurt sales of *Vogue* or *Cosmopolitan* that very few readers of those magazines will ever look like cover models.

Yet while many musicians, journalists, scholars, and fans favor this urban-hip identity, it is not the only embodiment of jazz today. An ideal way to observe a clash of disparate jazz cultures is to attend one of America's many competitive jazz festivals. These events often force a panel of judges, typically consisting of representatives from both urban jazz centers and jazz education programs, and as many as twenty different bands, to face one another for eight hours a day, two or three days in a row. To sit among the adjudicators (and to watch the hip faction squirm, sneer, or wince) provides an eye-opening lesson in the breadth of practices and identities understood as jazz and reveals some of the activities and aesthetics that induce writers to disavow school programs. At least two of these traits have come to be stereotypically equated with America's college-level jazz education in general.

On one extreme of perceived unhipness lies the ensemble conductor who appears to wield a high degree of control over students (a.k.a. the infamous "band dictator"). It should come as no surprise that jazz's modernist and postmodernist contingents would look unfavorably on musical disciplinarians. As early as the 1940s tales of Lester Young, the prototypical hip musician, enduring a disastrous stint in the U.S. Army, circulated among jazz communities and engendered mistrust of authoritarians. Around that same time, Howard Becker reported on an attitude among white, bop-oriented performers who resisted any authority figure, musical or otherwise.[28] Even well-known bandleaders are not immune from jazz's contempt for hard-liners: Benny Goodman, Sun Ra, and Buddy Rich have all been mocked or disparaged for their strict policies.

On the other side of that same coin are those instructors who choose to present jazz as "fun." These teacher-directors select an upbeat repertoire while projecting an amiable stage presence. Again, it makes sense that an affable deportment and genial sound would draw the ire of hip-jazz devotees. Ever since the rise of bebop, a cadre of musicians, aficionados, and critics has worked to paint jazz as a serious art form. Such efforts have been guided in large measure by the desire to counteract racist notions that reduced creative African American musicians to charismatic but unthinking entertainers in the service of a predominantly white clientele. The "happy" band director undermines this serious-jazz front.

While the stereotypes of college jazz-band directors as either militaristic autocrats or incurably cheerful naifs represent diametrically opposed models of stage demeanor, they do share at least one flaw from the hipsters' point of view. Both typically favor big bands, whereas today's hip-jazz aesthetics prefer small ensembles, with their tendency toward looser, less scripted moments.[29] Another related factor here involves sartorial display. Today's urban-jazz proponents tend to perform in either well-tailored suits (see the much-photographed look sported by the neoclassicists) or in the decidedly casual, even sloppy, wardrobe favored by postmodernist groups like Medeski, Martin, and Wood. By comparison, many school jazz ensembles appear in matching uniforms, much like those worn during the institution's orchestra or wind ensemble performances. If the directors of these groups do make a concession to a "jazzy" style, it is often by substituting a red or green wrap-around bowtie for the traditional black one or going with an open-collared shirt, though some band members also compliment the style by donning berets and dark sunglasses. This uniform is especially common among vocal jazz ensembles, which, as Jessica Bissett Perea's essay in this collection shows, are widely dismissed—even within college jazz programs—as the cheesiest of all groups.

There is no question that race plays a fundamental role in all these presentations and perceptions. Ingrid Monson has written on how the hip aesthetic draws on, amplifies, reimagines, or otherwise involves notions of a streetwise black America.[30] Yet the vast majority of teachers and students in college-level jazz education programs are not African Americans. Thus, even while a handful of self-consciously nerdy white postmodern musicians—The Bad Plus and Bill Frisell come to mind—may participate in, if only by subverting, the same hip aesthetic as the sharp-dressed "cats," many other nonblack participants embody neither the modernist nor postmodernist stance and so do not accrue the honors associated with hipness. In other words, it can be hip to be square—but not to be cheesy. Simply being associated with schooling can mark students and teachers as eggheads, sheltered from the supposedly real life of the jazz streets. Beyond just *being* white (or Asian or Latino) many jazz program participants are dismissed as *sounding* white, perhaps the most cutting insult of all among proponents of a hip-jazz aesthetic. In this regard, Monson's essay is helpful in pointing to the lamentable legacy of attitudes that would equate hipness solely with notions of "badness." She exhorts us to realize that "discipline, dignity, and social consciousness are as important to defining hipness as transgression or social marginality."[31] This caveat serves as an important reminder to guard against simplistic generalizations linking jazz, or hip, or (more consequentially) African American authenticity with willful ignorance.

Consider, too, the gender aspect of the hipness myth. Historian Ann Douglas has chronicled how "over the course of the nineteenth century, women gradually came to constitute the overwhelming majority of grade-school teachers in America's public and private schools, a feat accomplished in no other country, and one which was to cause immense uneasiness in the men involved in American education by the turn of the twentieth century."[32] Teaching remains "women's work" even to this day. Men make up less than a quarter of this country's three million instructors at the kindergarten through twelfth grade levels; the number shrinks to a mere 9 percent when considering only kindergarten through eighth.[33] And while the occupation of university professor has traditionally been understood as somewhat more "manly" than grade school teacher, the college instructor hardly conjures images of an unambiguously hearty male heterosexuality in the manner of, say, construction worker, NASCAR driver, or Wall Street trader. Add all of this to the fact that male musicians (and not just jazz musicians) have long struggled against perceptions of their profession as a feminized activity, and it may be that for those invested in a hypermasculine image of jazz, combining a teacher with a musician is simply too much. In such ways, one might argue, the term "jazz education" doomed attitudes toward college programs from the start.[34]

We can see, then, why educators and education are largely left out of the jazz press. A magazine editor's primary responsibility is to raise the value of a publication. For the major jazz periodicals to draw the highest numbers of readers and advertisers, editors present what they deem to be the most attractive image of the genre. The harsh or happy jazz educator just does not fit this vision.[35] But even allowing for the hip-jazz bias, jazz people may need to reassess their perceptions of college instructors. Given the ever-increasing professionalization and specialization in jazz education over the past decade, more and more jazz programs are being led by musicians who uphold the hip-jazz aesthetics, making it difficult to argue, as even I have in the past, that those nonhip stereotypes and practices remain the rule.[36] Besides, if we may forgive magazine editors for ignoring some of the jazz identities displayed in institutional education (their professional situations are affected by such decisions, after all), musicologists do not have such an excuse. The scholar's job is to note significant developments in musical practices and meanings and to situate those developments within broader musical, social, cultural, and historical contexts.[37]

Myth #3: "You Either Got It or You Don't"

A third myth of jazz education states that school training stifles innovation (Gary Kennedy, Stuart Nicholson, Christopher Small, and Hal Galper all allude to this in their criticisms). With "the new" still valued within many, if not all, jazz circles, this criticism warrants consideration.[38] It is true that college programs have yet to show an ability to turn every promising talent into an influential artist. Yet just because jazz programs cannot systematically produce musical geniuses, it does not follow that students in those programs fail to learn, improve, and otherwise benefit from their studies. In jazz, as in every other discipline offered in higher education, good teachers provide students with a foundation in what has come before, offer suggestions to shore up perceived weaknesses, and foster a challenging, creative, and supportive environment in which students can focus on their work.

Values and practices differ from school to school, but in general the progress young performers make over the course of a few years, in terms of both technical facility on an instrument and the ability to "say something" with that instrument, is substantial and undeniable (recall that list of school-trained players). Some students become excellent, even important, musicians; some don't climb that high . . . just like those performers trained in the informal "schools" of New Orleans, Kansas City, or Fifty-Second Street in the past century. The resistance by jazz education's critics to acknowledge these improvements may have to do with their desire to mystify improvisational skill. For if anyone and everyone can learn to create music on the fly, perhaps jazz's "magic" is somehow diminished. Certainly, the Romantic conception of the Great Artist receiving inspiration directly from the musical gods accounts for much of the mystical aura hovering over a number of improvisers, most famously Keith Jarrett.

What is more, teaching private lessons, improvisation classes, ensembles, history, and the like represent only some aspects of what jazz educators do. Faculty members also mentor young players on the ways and means of the music profession, and many performers land their first significant gigs as a direct result of their teachers' intercessions. During the 1970s and '80s, the bands of Woody Herman, Maynard Ferguson, Buddy Rich, and Stan Kenton were regularly stocked with alumni of North Texas State University (now the University of North Texas) who were recommended for those jobs by their teachers. The vibraphonist and longtime Berklee College of Music faculty member Gary Burton showed a knack for recognizing and developing future standouts; his side musicians have included former Berklee students Mick Goodrick, John Scofield, Abe Laboriel, and Makoto Ozone. Saxophonist Steve Coleman met his frequent collaborators Ralph Alessi and Andy Milne when the latter two were studying under Coleman at the Banff International Workshop in Jazz and Creative Music in the 1980s. These same relationships can develop even during brief visiting artist workshops, such as when guitarist Ben Monder "discovered" drummer Ted Poor, now a highly sought-after performer himself, while Monder was giving a master class at the Eastman School of Music, where Poor was studying. One could find dozens, perhaps hundreds, of similar occurrences.

The benefits of these interactions run in many directions. Younger players gain experience, exposure, and financial rewards by playing alongside seasoned pros, while veterans may find that the fresh energy and ideas that youthful singers and instrumentalists bring to the stage can respark their own enthusiasm. The host institutions of these musicians can also profit, as the successes of teachers and their protégés in the professional field enhance their programs' reputations and so too their abilities to recruit still more talented students. In turn, schools contribute by providing a physical space in which musicians can congregate and play, as well as the equipment—pianos, drum sets, amplifiers, rehearsal rooms, recording studios—that facilitates the forging of social and professional connections. In short, while colleges may never unlock the alchemical secrets of creating musical geniuses, they do offer all of the benefits of the early twentieth-century nightclub-based mentoring system that Kennedy extolled in his *Grove* essay, albeit in an admittedly less colorful (but also less toxic) environment than the popular after-hours-session-in-a-smoky-gin-joint image.

Myth #4: Jazz and the "Free Market"

A fourth myth driving negative perceptions of jazz education involves market forces, specifically, that any style of jazz receiving support from an academic (or government) institution is inherently less authentic or artistically viable than that which seems to survive solely within the domain of commerce. Faculty positions have long been mocked as the refuge of individuals unfit for the so-called real world ("those who can't do, teach"). In jazz, the thinking goes that college instructors may possess theoretical knowledge *about* the music, but that their playing lacks either the requisite degree of technical skill or, worse, the elusive quality known as soul. This attitude is revealed even in a well-meaning *Down Beat* reviewer's praise: "There are academians and there are academians. The Brooklyn Conservatory Faculty Jazz Ensemble are academians in name only. . . . The B.C.F.J.E. confirm that, in jazz, technique and theory don't mean a thing without the aesthetic of swing."[39] The writer's point here being that this faculty group merits acclaim precisely because its members do not "sound like teachers."

At the same time, proponents of earlier ways and places of learning do want their favorite performers to be understood as smart, skilled, and serious. One way to encourage those perceptions is to designate the street as another—parallel, hipper—version of "higher education," hence the many references to "the Art Blakey School of Hard Bop," "the University of Miles Davis," "the Jazz College of Hard Knocks," and so on.[40] In this respect, critics of college programs want to have it both ways. On one hand, they would have us believe that jazz is like European classical music in that it merits study in conservatories. On the other hand, they also insist that "real jazz" survives and develops solely on the efforts of its musicians, nightclubs, and record companies, independent of any assistance from those same conservatories, or what one jazz writer described in another context as "the crutch of subsidy."[41] Of course, this free-market stance flies directly in the face of the deeply entrenched, anticommercial modernist position held by many of these same pundits, resulting in a situation where musicians are expected to make a living exclusively through gigs and recordings, while not seeming to be playing for money.[42]

Tied to such attitudes is the perception that jazz education is little more than a racket organized to sustain nothing but itself. This view underlies Stuart Nicholson's aforementioned "Teachers Teaching Teachers" chapter title and has even worked its way into jazz-education circles. In a letter to the editor responding to Nate Chinen's *New York Times* piece on the IAJE conference, an instructor wrote, "One of the positive consequences of—and perhaps a contributing factor toward—the significant expansion of the jazz education industry in the past 20 years is that it has allowed musicians to maintain a career in jazz. . . . As a 50-year-old jazz musician and educator, I have benefited from this expansion, but I do wonder if at some point the jazz education industry will exist more to perpetuate the industry than the music."[43]

As well intentioned as this soul-searching musician-educator seems to be, he need not wring his hands over the matter, for he's missing a fundamental point: the line scholars, journalists, and musicians maintain to separate "jazz" from "jazz education" is blurry, even illusory. Yes, students go to class, study, practice, and rehearse in classrooms, but they also play gigs, sometimes with faculty members, sometimes with other students, sometimes with performers unaffiliated with a formal music program.[44] When students (and also teachers) are not in school, they can often be found listening to recordings and attending gigs by other musicians. In other words, those studying jazz at Berklee, or the University of Kentucky, or the University of Oregon, or any of the dozens of other degree-granting programs in the United States are not just waiting until they graduate to become part of a jazz scene. They *are* the jazz scene, or a large portion of it, at any rate.[45]

A case in point is the quintet KneeBody. Four of the group's members, trumpeter Shane Endsley, bassist Kaveh Rastegar, keyboardist Adam Benjamin, and saxophonist Ben Wendel, graduated from the Eastman School of Music. Drummer Nate Wood earned his degree from the California Institute of the Arts (Cal Arts). Adam Benjamin returned to school in 2005, receiving a master's of fine arts degree from Cal Arts in spring of 2007. When the group performed at the University of Nevada (UNR) in 2006—that is, while Benjamin was still in grad school—it wasn't billed as "four professionals and a student," but simply as KneeBody. Those of us who attended their performance and clinic were astonished by the musicians' virtuosity, creativity, and, above all, the intricate musical cueing system they had devised.[46] KneeBody also profited from its appearances: UNR paid the group handsomely for its services and a number of students bought CDs after the show.

Now, KneeBody probably would not have even been aware to contact UNR about playing there were it not for the connections made and developed over the past two decades through the jazz programs at Eastman, New York's School for Improvisational Music, and especially Cal Arts, where not only Adam Benjamin and Nate Wood but also Peter Epstein (who directs UNR's Program in Jazz and Improvisational Music) and I both went to school. The lines of connection are too many and too interwoven to untangle here. Suffice it to say that the roles of teacher, student, professional performer, booking agent, colleague, festival adjudicator, friend, concert promoter, and audience member shift constantly. All this adds up to a much more complex interrelationship of music, schooling, aesthetics, and economics than the critics of the so-called jazz-education industry have recognized. And the University of Nevada is only one of many institutions that KneeBody has visited. The group's schedule for 2007 included appearances at Camden County

College, the University of Sioux Falls, the University of Colorado, and the Stanford Jazz Workshops, as well as Iridium in New York and Munich's Pinakothek der Moderne. Likewise, KneeBody is just one of the more than two dozen individuals and ensembles to have presented jazz concerts, workshops, and master classes at UNR over the past few years.[47]

CONCLUSIONS: PAST VERSUS PRESENT, IMAGE VERSUS REALITY

The image of the great jazz improviser mentored by streetwise hipsters is a powerful one; it's what drives the scene from *Collateral* I described at the outset of this chapter. But it is time we reassess this image in the face of twenty-first-century realities. If "the most important task of the contemporary historian is to write the history of the present," as Richard Taruskin has argued, then those writing on jazz must honestly begin to address the ascent, even the centrality, of today's college-level jazz programs.[48]

I am not suggesting that cities are finished as incubators of jazz talent; musicians and audiences continue to gather in New York and elsewhere and surely will for some time to come. Nor do I mean to say that school programs unerringly inspire jazz creativity: indiscriminately praising institutionalized jazz education would be just as misplaced as our current tendency to ridicule or overlook it. Students, teachers, administrators, and accreditation bodies must scrutinize and assess pedagogical practices, as well as such thorny issues as the disproportionately high number of white males enrolled (and also teaching) in these programs and the astronomical tuition costs charged by some conservatories.[49]

But the music's historians and other chroniclers must also take a more active and informed role in this conversation, not just because music schools will produce the next generation of jazz stars—though that is almost certain to happen, too—but more important, because this is where jazz musicians, good and not so good, now gather to learn from and play with one another, where audiences listen, and where individual and communal identities are formed, tested, challenged, and re-formed. Which is to say, this is one of the places where jazz matters most today, at least in this country. We need not fear that formal education somehow undermines or embarrasses "real jazz" or, as Christopher Small suggests, marks the end of jazz as a "living force." The saxophonist and longtime educator David Liebman and his fellow board members of the recently founded International Association of Schools of Jazz are right on the money with their motto, "The future of jazz is connected with the future of jazz education."[50] Ultimately, the fact that so many institutions now provide a home for widely differing understandings of and approaches to teaching, playing, and learning jazz is a cause for celebration, not despair.

NOTES

This piece originally appeared as chapter 5 in David Ake, *Jazz Matters: Sound, Place, and Time since Bebop* (Berkeley: University of California Press, 2010), 102–20.

1. David Ake, "Jazz 'Traning: John Coltrane and the Conservatory," in *Jazz Cultures* (Berkeley: University of California Press, 2002), 112–45; David Ake, "Learning Jazz/Teaching Jazz," in *The Cambridge Companion to Jazz*, ed. Mervyn Cooke and David Horn (Cambridge: Cambridge University Press, 2002), 255–69. Other recent scholarship on jazz pedagogy includes David Borgo, "Free Jazz in the Classroom: An Ecological Approach to Music Education," *Jazz Perspectives* 1, no. 1 (May 2007): 61–88; John P. Murphy, "Beyond the Improvisation Class: Learning to Improvise in a University Jazz Studies Program," in *Musical Improvisation: Sound, Education, Society*, ed. Gabriel Solis and Bruno Nettle (Urbana: University of Illinois Press, 2009); Kenneth Prouty, "Orality, Literacy, and Mediating Musical Experience: Rethinking Oral Tradition in the Learning of Jazz Improvisation," *Popular Music and Society* 29, no. 3 (July 2006): 317–34; and Ken Prouty, "The 'Finite' Art of Improvisation: Pedagogy and Power in Jazz Education," *Critical Studies in Improvisation* 4, no. 1 (2008): www.criticalimprov.com/index.php/csieci/article/view/346/966.

2. Nate Chinen, "Jazz Is Alive and Well, in the Classroom, Anyway," *New York Times*, January 7, 2007, sec. 2, p. 1. This would turn out to be the IAJE's final conference. The association declared bankruptcy in April 2008. By all accounts, that organization folded due to administrative incompetence, not from a decline in membership. In fact, it continued to grow at an impressive rate even as it lost large sums of money. See "IAJE R.I.P," *Jazz Times* 38 (July/August 2008): 82–86, 130–31.

3. To give music scholars a sense of the IAJE conference's scope, the 2000 Musical Intersections convention in Toronto, which brought together the meetings of fifteen professional organizations, including the American Musicological Society, the Society for Ethnomusicology, the Society for American Music, the Society for Music Theory and the International Association for the Study of Popular Music, drew "only" four thousand attendees. Ann Besser Scott, "Toronto, 2000," *AMS Newsletter* 31, no. 1 (February 2001): 1.

4. Chinen, "Jazz Is Alive," 1, 19.

5. Bill Pierce, e-mail message to author, March 27, 2007.

6. Charles Mingus, quoted in Brian Priestly, *Mingus: A Critical Biography* (New York: Da Capo, 1982), 174. Original interview by Nat Hentoff, November 2, 1964, BBC Radio.

7. John Coltrane, for instance, based much of his practice regimen and even part of his composition "Giant Steps" on Nicolas Slonimsky's *Thesaurus of Scales and Patterns* (1945; repr., New York: Amsco, 1975). And yet I have heard (though can find no hard evidence to substantiate) that word of Coltrane's famous *Thesaurus* studies amused Slonimsky, who reputedly dashed off his compendium merely as a kind of nerdy musical joke. For descriptions of Coltrane's use of Slonimsky's book, see Lewis Porter, *John Coltrane: His Life and Music* (Ann Arbor: University of Michigan Press, 1998), 149–50; Carl Woideck, *The John Coltrane Companion: Five Decades of Commentary* (New York: Schirmer, 1998), 172; and Ashley Kahn's interview with Joe Zawinul, in Ashley Kahn, *A Love Supreme* (New York: Viking, 2002), 28–29.

8. Christopher Small, *Music, Society, Education* (Hanover, NH: Wesleyan University Press, 1996), 198.

9. Hal Galper, "Rants and Raves: Jazz Pedagogy," accessed January 16, 2009, http://halgalper.com. See also Galper's "Articles: Jazz in Academia" at that same website.

10. Mark Gridley, *Jazz Styles: History and Analysis,* 9th ed. (Upper Saddle River, NJ: Pearson Prentice Hall, 2006), 349 (italics added).

11. Ibid., 380–86.

12. Henry Martin and Keith Waters, *Jazz: The First 100 Years,* 2nd ed. (Belmont, CA: Schirmer, 2006), 360, 376–77; Ted Gioia, *The History of Jazz* (New York: Oxford University Press, 1997); *Jazz,* directed by Ken Burns (Arlington, VA: PBS, 2001), DVD; Gary Giddins, *Weather Bird: Jazz at the Dawn of Its Second Century* (New York: Oxford University Press, 2004).

13. Charles Beale, "Jazz Education," in *The Oxford Companion to Jazz,* ed. Bill Kirchner (New York: Oxford University Press, 2000), 745–55.

14. Robert G. O'Meally, Brent Hayes Edwards, and Farah Jasmine Griffin, "Introductory Notes," in *Uptown Conversations: The New Jazz Studies,* ed. Robert G. O'Meally, Brent Hayes Edwards, and Farah Jasmine Griffin (New York: Columbia University Press, 2004), 1.

15. Stuart Nicholson, *Is Jazz Dead? (Or Has It Moved to a New Address)* (New York: Routledge, 2005), 99–100, 110, 120.

16. Ibid., 120.

17. See also Nicholson's three articles: "The Way It Is," *Jazzwise,* February 2007, 15; "Europeans Cut in with a New Sound and Beat," *New York Times,* June 3, 2001, Ar1; and "Crossing the Atlantic: Overseas Jazz Education," in "Jazz Education Guide," special annual issue, *Jazz Times* (2003–4): 46–50.

18. Gary Kennedy, "Jazz Education," in *The New Grove Dictionary of Jazz,* ed. Barry Kernfeld, 2nd ed., 3 vols. (New York: Macmillan, 2002), 2:396–98 (italics added).

19. For more on these important figures, see Andrew Goodrich, "Jazz in Historically Black Colleges," *Jazz Educators Journal* 34, no. 3 (November 2001): 54–58; and Al Kennedy, *Chord Changes on the Chalkboard: How Public*

School Teachers Shaped Jazz and the Music of New Orleans (Lanham, MD: Scarecrow, 2002).

20. I chose 1950 as a cut-off date for this list because those born in that year would have been eighteen years old (i.e., college age) in 1968, the year the National Association of Jazz Education was founded.

21. Now-prominent school-trained figures not mentioned in the *Grove Dictionary* include Ralph Alessi (California Institute of the Arts), Shane Endsley (Eastman), Briggan Krauss (Cornish College of the Arts), Donny McCaslin (Berklee), Cuong Vu (New England Conservatory), and Miguel Zénon (Berklee).

22. Dennis Ford, *The Search for Meaning: A Short History* (Berkeley: University of California Press, 2007), 43.

23. Bruce Johnson et al., "Nightclubs and Other Venues," in Kernfeld, *New Grove Dictionary*, 2:1.

24. See the New York University Jazz Studies website, accessed February 2, 2010, http://steinhardt.nyu.edu/music/jazz/.

25. Ibid.

26. "Development" efforts at the University of Nevada, Reno, include hosting meet-and-greet functions between donors and visiting jazz artists; freely distributing CD recordings by the Collective (the university's resident faculty jazz group) to donors and potential donors; and even using recordings by the Collective as "on-hold" music for the university's phone system.

27. J.K., "'Legends,' Season One," *Down Beat* 73, no. 4 (April 2006): 40; Jason Koransky, "Ra Uncovered," *Down Beat* 73, no. 12 (December 2006): 8; Ashley Kahn and Gary Giddins, "Tales of Two Sonnys: Gary Giddins Remembers Clashes of the Titans," *Jazz Times* 36, no. 2 (March 2006): 22–23; Marc Hopkins, "Selling the Dark Prince," *Jazz Times* 36, no. 8 (October 2006): 36–42; Nate Chinen, "In His Own Language, *Jazz Times* 36, no. 9 (November 2006): 46–51, 130; "Who's Got Next? Jeremy Pelt Leads a Pack of Young Trumpeters Who Demand Attention. We've Got 25 You Need to Hear," *Down Beat* 74, no. 6 (June 2007): cover.

28. Howard S. Becker, "The Professional Dance Musician and His Audience," *American Journal of Sociology* 57 (1951–52): 136–44; reprinted in *Keeping Time: Readings in Jazz History*, ed. Robert Walser (New York: Oxford University Press, 1999), 179–91.

29. For more on the preference for big bands in colleges, see Bruno Nettl, *Heartland Excursions: Ethnomusicological Reflections on Schools of Music* (Urbana: University of Illinois Press, 1995), 107; and Ake, "Jazz 'Traning," 113–14. Exceptions to the small-group bias among today's hip contingent include the Mingus Big Band and the larger groups led by Carla Bley, Charlie Haden, Dave Holland, and Maria Schneider. For an informed and insightful overview of practices and aesthetics in big bands today (including a critique of my work), see Alex Stewart, *Making the Scene: Contemporary New York City Big Band Jazz* (Berkeley: University of California Press, 2007).

30. Ingrid Monson, "The Problem with White Hipness: Race, Gender, and Cultural Conceptions in Jazz Historical Discourse," *Journal of the American*

Musicological Society 48 (Fall 1995): 396–422. See also Phil Ford, "Somewhere/ Nowhere: Hipness as an Aesthetic," *Musical Quarterly* 86, no. 1 (Spring 2002): 49–81; and Phil Ford, "Hip Sensibility in an Age of Mass Counterculture," *Jazz Perspectives* 2, no. 2 (November 2008): 121–63.

31. Monson, "White Hipness," 422.

32. Ann Douglas, *The Feminization of American Culture* (1977; repr., New York: Noonday, 1998), 76.

33. James White, "Male Teacher Shortage Hits Home," Men Teach, January 8, 2008, www.menteach.org/news/male_teacher_shortage_hits_home.

34. All of this also helps to explain the lingering homophobia in jazz, which as Monique Guillory noted, has remained "a hermetically sealed boys' club for nearly a century." "Black Bodies Swingin': Race, Gender, and Jazz," in *Soul: Black Power, Politics, and Pleasure,* ed. Monique Guillory and Richard C. Green (New York: New York University Press, 1998), 193. Taking on the mantle of what he jokingly described as the self-professed "poster boy for gay jazz musicians," Fred Hersch told me, "a lot of this masculinity stuff, if you let it get to you, it can" (telephone interview with the author, July 15, 2005). And while Hersch also noted that the situation for homosexual musicians had "changed a lot for the better over the twenty or thirty years," strong biases remain. See Giovanni Petranicht, "Gays in Jazz," *Jazz Times,* May 2002, 28; and Ajay Heble's discussion of Charles Gayle, "Up for Grabs: The Ethicopolitical Authority of Jazz," in *Landing on the Wrong Note: Jazz, Dissonance, and Cultural Practice* (New York: Routledge, 2000), 199–228.

35. To be fair to the larger magazines, they do sometimes feature "borderline" jazz acts, such as Yellowjackets and Chuck Mangione. Plus, *Down Beat* has long sponsored awards for student groups while providing advice columns from educators, and *Jazz Times* publishes its annual "Jazz Education Guide." Still, these publications overwhelmingly focus on the people and places I noted. One recent exception to this rule is *Jazz Ed.* First published in 2006, that periodical explicitly seeks to highlight both jazz stars and jazz educators. The September 2008 issue even featured a cover story on Kenny G.

36. See my "Jazz 'Traning" chapter.

37. One small step toward that end: Because the stereotypical jazz-education identities just outlined blithely forgo those qualities that have come to be understood as hip (or, in the case of the berets and sunglasses, work from an anachronistic approach to hipness), I offer that scholars and others might begin hearing, seeing, and describing such groups as "nonhip," rather than "unhip," a distinction that marks these musical presentations as alternatives to, rather than absences of, certain understandings of jazz identity and behavior.

38. James Lincoln Collier explored and explained this "problem" in jazz education as early as 1993. See his *Jazz: the American Theme Song* (New York: Oxford University Press, 1993), 153–54. Stanley Crouch expressed his very different take on the innovation aesthetic very clearly. See his article "Jazz Tradition Is Not Innovation," *Jazz Times,* January/February 2002, 26.

39. Bill Shoemaker, "Waxing On: Self-Produced Artists," *Down Beat,* August 1984, 42.

40. Thanks to Ken Prouty for reminding me of this tendency.

41. John McDonough, "Pro and Con: Failed Experiment" *Down Beat,* January 1992, 31. McDonough was writing on what he saw as evidence of the "failure" of free jazz as a viable subgenre because of the support its proponents have received from arts organizations.

42. The notion that jazz musicians should play solely "for the love of the music" without any thought to financial considerations has deep roots. See Scott DeVeaux, "The Emergence of the Jazz Concert, 1935–1945," special jazz issue, *American Music* 7, no.1 (Spring 1989), 11–12.

43. Mark Kross, "Letters: Jazz Education, in Service of the Music," *New York Times,* January 21, 2007, sec. 2, p. 6.

44. The director of the jazz studies program at the Manhattan School of Music approximated that between 60 and 70 percent of the jazz students at that school play professional gigs in New York. See Ben Ratliff, "A New Generation Knocks at the Gates of Jazz," *New York Times,* March 18, 1997, sec. C, p. 14.

45. Bill Milkowski, "Evolution of Jazz Education," in "Jazz Education Guide," special annual issue, *Jazz Times* (2001–2), 40.

46. KneeBody surely ranks among the most impressive examples of on-the-fly group decision making ever developed by a jazz ensemble. For any who may have the opportunity to see this group, it is well worth the time to talk to the musicians about how they devise arrangements and structure sets during *and through* their performances.

47. Or consider the "backwards" career path of keyboardist (and Eastman grad) Gary Versace. While many jazz musicians opt to leave the road for the more stable college environment, Versace went the opposite direction, relinquishing a tenured jazz studies position at the University of Oregon in 2002 to focus on playing. He now works alongside major artists, including Lee Konitz, John Scofield, and Maria Schneider . . . and gives numerous concerts and master classes at schools across the country.

48. Richard Taruskin, *Text and Act: Essays on Music and Performance* (New York: Oxford University Press, 1995), 18.

49. The 2002 figures from the International Association of Jazz Educators show that men outnumbered women in the association by a four-to-one ratio (4,800/1,200).

50. It remains to be seen whether that organization is as accurate with the second half of their tag line: ". . . and the IASJ is the chain." International Association of Schools of Jazz home page, accessed January 17, 2009, www.iasj.com/.

CHAPTER 12

Deconstructing the Jazz Tradition

The "Subjectless Subject" of New Jazz Studies

SHERRIE TUCKER

From its first publication in *Black Literature Forum* in 1991, through and beyond its reprinting in Robert O'Meally's edited volume *The Jazz Cadence of American Culture* in 1998, Scott DeVeaux's "Constructing the Jazz Tradition" remains one of the most influential essays in academic jazz studies.[1] So frequently do jazz studies scholars jumpstart their journal articles, book introductions, and dissertations with gestures toward DeVeaux's analysis of the jazz tradition as an interested narrative—rather than an objective account of a linear jazz past—that one could characterize much current work in new jazz studies under the rubric "Deconstructing the Jazz Tradition."

The key insight that scholars took from this essay was that the familiar account of jazz history as a logical march from one style to the next, forged by a procession of great men (and I do mean men), is of fairly recent vintage and achieved its hegemony at a particular moment and for specific reasons. This article challenged many of us to rethink the jazz history we thought we knew, one we prided ourselves in being able to recount in detail. For some of us already grappling with marginalized jazz topics, this essay suggested scholarly alternatives to the frustrating exercise of what I call "historical overdub"—or trying to pound our devalued jazz topics into the principal narrative that constructs itself, after all, by excluding them.

For my own work on all-woman bands, DeVeaux's essay bridged jazz studies and feminist historiography. I became convinced that it was not enough to prove that women's bands deserved a place in the canon. Rather, my study could contribute to a broader deconstruction of a monolithic narrative that elbowed out other understandings of what jazz had meant to people, who played it, who listened to it, who struggled and survived to it.

Although these may have been startling insights in jazz studies at the time, by 1991 many fields had been questioning canon formation as historiographical method—precisely because of its utility in consolidating power for dominant groups. Black studies, ethnic studies, and women's studies, for instance, had entered the U.S. academy in the 1960s and 1970s as parts of broader social movements that critiqued canon formation as one register of injustice among many that excluded people of color, poor people, women, gays, and lesbians. Judith Tick has compared American music scholarship and feminist historiography during this period, pointing out that both fields: (1) began as "outsider" fields to "conventional" disciplines, (2) not only critiqued the exclusions in the canonical work in the insider fields but questioned the very concept of the canon, (3) saw a need for, and produced, "foundational" studies to counter the historical exclusions and to make possible new kinds of scholarship, (4) were "receptive to social history and sociological interpretation, and finally (5) were open to "vernacular forms of cultural expressiveness."[2]

In fact, by the dawn of new jazz studies in the late 1980s, four book-length works documenting women's participation in jazz history had been published that share these affinities. As early as 1975 a graduate student named Susan Cavin had written about the absence of attention to women's participation in Congo Square drumming in New Orleans despite their presence in the primary sources used by jazz historians. Her article not only conveyed this evidence of women drummers but also documented jazz historians' "benign neglect" of what she called "the sex variable" that had enabled this canonical prejazz moment to appear to have an all-male cast.[3] Though published in the *Journal of Jazz Studies,* this article did not make much of a dent in jazz studies at large, but did inspire Sally Placksin and Linda Dahl, authors of *American Women in Jazz* and *Stormy Weather,* respectively, and D. Antoinette Handy, whose *Black Women in American Bands and Orchestras* must be located in a context of knowledge production about African American women's history in black studies, as well as in women's studies.[4]

All of these women-in-jazz books challenged jazz canon formation, provided foundational research that enabled new kinds of jazz scholarship, and located their historical subjects in social and cultural contexts rather than in parades of isolated geniuses. They also held out a wider net for areas of "vernacular expressive culture" that had included women but that had been defined as "not jazz" by jazz historiography (areas that included family bands, circus bands, all-woman bands, vaudeville, etc.)

In other words, this literature *could have* identified and challenged the jazz tradition narrative if it hadn't managed to fly under the radar of jazz studies scholars who were not explicitly interested in women in jazz. Excluded from the narrative that DeVeaux would later identify as "something of an official history" and *excluded again* from works in new jazz studies that critiqued this official history, narratives about women as jazz instrumentalists appeared to be taking shape as "something of a special interest"—perceived as supplemental jazz histories primarily by, for, and about women.[5] Although I was taking jazz classes in the music department and women's history classes in the women's studies department at the same time at San Francisco State in the 1980s, I never encountered the women-in-jazz literature in courses like Survey of Jazz, but rather in History of African American Women, which is also where I first learned about all-woman big bands of the 1930s and 1940s and started research on my book *Swing Shift: "All-Girl" Bands of the 1940s*.[6]

In 1991 two articles appeared that helped me to navigate the dissonance between the hidden histories of women in jazz and the exciting new work in interdisciplinary jazz studies. One is, of course, DeVeaux's essay, which, though not explicitly concerned with women or gender, identified and historicized the specific canon formation that carried jazz into the discourses of "high art" and "American culture" at the same time that women's studies and black studies were emerging from social movements that critiqued canon formation as a technology of exclusion, hierarchy, and power.

The other article is Elsa Barkley Brown's "Polyrhythms and Improvisation: Lessons for Women's History," published in the *History Workshop Journal*. Barkley Brown used jazz as a metaphor for the kinds of historiography that she thought would be useful for writing histories that did not construct parades of "great men," but instead approached history as "everyone talking at once. Multiple rhythms played simultaneously. The events and people we write about did not occur in isolation but in dialogue with a myriad of other people and events."[7] It became clear to me that most jazz histories were not this kind of narrative—though the women-in-jazz histories, by necessity, often *were*—and that other jazz histories might better account for women musicians, and other forgotten historical actors, if they took Barkley Brown's cue to adopt jazz as a model as well as a topic.

Similarly, DeVeaux's "Constructing the Jazz Tradition" provided an important analytic of power that helped me, and other jazz scholars, to understand *why* certain artists, musics, and histories had been overshadowed, why the straight line of one genius/one style leading to another prevailed as a dominant narrative. It also helped us to see how knowledge of marginalized jazz topics could interrupt the familiar cadences of the jazz tradition and help us to hear other jazz histories, approaches, analyses, voices, perspectives, and questions.

So, what were the interests behind constructing the jazz tradition as a principal narrative? According to DeVeaux's essay, a primary motivation stemmed from those working to pave the way for the grand entrance of jazz into mainstream institutional respectability. Many of us have become rather adept at identifying these moves in the narratives and policies of powerful institutions and media such as the Lincoln Center Jazz Orchestra and Ken Burns's PBS documentary *Jazz*.[8] But we also need to be attentive to DeVeaux's foregrounding of colleges and universities in his analysis of the relationship between narrating jazz history as linear and institution building. "Constructing the Jazz Tradition," after all, was a process that academics did not just describe, but in which they participated, and that enabled some of them to find institutional homes—sometimes known as jobs—from which to study, teach, and write about jazz.

The turn to "Deconstructing the Jazz Tradition" also marks a significant moment in the institutionalization of jazz in academia. The process of "Constructing the Jazz Tradition" enabled the academic careers of those who helped build this successful thoroughfare from the margins of mainstream society to the margins of music departments—but it has also produced and enabled careers of those of us bent on digging it up. Just as the jazz tradition narrative coalesced in a particular moment of the institutionalization of jazz, so has the critical response to it that we sometimes call academic jazz studies, interdisciplinary jazz studies, or new jazz studies. As has been noted by Mark Tucker, Robert O'Meally, Brent Hayes Edwards, Farah Jasmine Griffin, and others, the past fifteen years has seen the spread of academic jazz studies beyond the band rooms, bebop combos, and jazz appreciation classes that are the legacy of the jazz tradition, to its current array of emanations from lecture halls and seminars from a variety of nonmusic departments, where participants theorize anticanonical figures such as Sun Ra and study topics like race, gender, nationalism, and politics.[9]

We might mark this shift in 1988, with the appearance of the first jazz panel at the Modern Language Association. Featuring Krin Gabbard, Mike Jarrett, William Kenney, and Kathy Ogren, this panel helped to launch a watershed moment of new jazz studies publishing, with the anthology *Jazz in Mind: Essays on the History and Meanings of Jazz* and the volumes edited by Krin Gabbard: *Jazz among the Discourses* and *Representing Jazz.* None of these volumes made use of the women-in-jazz literature, nor did they acknowledge women jazz instrumentalists; there was very little, though some, gender analysis within their covers, but they did develop critical approaches that would prove useful for such work.[10]

The mid-1990s also saw the founding of interdisciplinary jazz studies conferences, such as the Leeds International Jazz Conference and the Guelph Jazz Festival and Colloquium, both founded in 1994, and new interdisciplinary academic programs such as the Center for Jazz Studies at Columbia (which grew out of the Jazz Study Group founded in 1995 by Robert O'Meally). Incidentally, 1995 also marks the year that Cobi Narita, founder of Universal Jazz Coalition, saw the necessity of establishing an organization called International Women in Jazz, which would mitigate against continuing exclusions of women jazz musicians from jazz practice, opportunities, and discourse.

This period also marks a migration of jazz history publishing from trade to academic presses, and a shift in who writes these histories, from critics and journalists to professors. This new wave of jazz studies academics has taken up the call to critically interrogate the official narrative, to deconstruct the binaries on which it established itself as whole (art/commerce, pure/contaminated, etc.), to interrupt its confidence, expose its exclusions, and insist on its historical particularity.

Many of us who participated in this shift, myself included, conceived our work as politically engaged, analyzing jazz not for its autonomous greatness, but, as Ajay Heble put it, for its usefulness in finding ways to contest "the kinds of objectifications, misrepresentations, and institutional disparagements that impede struggles for human agency."[11] Yet as someone who received tenure, thanks largely to these shifts, I'm also thinking about how some of us have benefited, or may eventually benefit, professionally from these institutional changes. Like those who shaped the jazz tradition paradigm, those of us who critiqued it not only described something as it happened but helped to shape it, through our teaching, our writing, our publishing, our institution building. And we still do. It seems an excellent time to reflect on the possibilities of jazz studies after the jazz tradition, but layered inside are a number of intellectual, institutional, and ethical concerns. We had the jazz tradition as a canon; now we have it as an outmoded idea to repudiate. What shall we do for an encore?

In asking, what is "jazz" in the new jazz studies, I am not asking the old form of the question that would find eager definitions in the jazz tradition paradigm (jazz is improvisation; it must swing; it is noncommercial; it is played on these instruments and not these, and so on—all of which have been debunked at one time or another in both old and new jazz studies). New jazz studies has done very well in appreciating and highlighting the blurriness of jazz categories, so I'm not expecting coherent parameters. But, for that very reason, I am interested in exploring what kind of category new jazz studies constitutes as its object of study.

Is jazz a genre, a culture, a discourse? Without the jazz tradition as stable ground, what do we teach in jazz studies classes? If there is no stable subject or object of study, is jazz studies in crisis, or is it developing exciting, new directions—theories and methods—as is sometimes argued about other fields such as women's studies, black studies, and American studies? Does new jazz studies pursue a "subjectless subject," as Ann Cacoullos has observed of both women's studies and American studies? (By the way, she meant this as a good factor—"conceptual and linguistic discomfort" as "an emancipatory alternative.")[12] If jazz studies is shifting from the study of knowable objects to that of "subjectless subjects," or subjects in the process of becoming, what is its future, and, well, is there one?

To what extent *has* new jazz studies diverged from the jazz tradition narrative? To what extent does new jazz studies continue to reify the jazz tradition as an object of study, even as the new jazz studies vociferously rejects old constructs? Are we really deconstructing the binaries we say we are, for example, or do substantial numbers of us still prefer jazz to be more art than commerce, more pure than contaminated (whatever that means to us), more populist than popular?[13] As Catherine Parsonage put it so succinctly, the "popularity of jazz . . . is still an unpopular problem" in jazz studies, despite calls for incorporating commerce in our analysis. I am not aware of a Kenny G jazz studies dissertation yet; despite Robert Walser's infamous chiding that jazz studies should not simply denounce Kenny G as beyond the boundaries of jazz artistry, but study the meanings of his massive success.

I live with the embarrassment that the first three or four times I publicly raised this question I had not realized that Christopher Washburne had published an outstanding chapter on Kenny G that raised these exact questions. I think I missed it because the title of the collection that presented it didn't sound like jazz to me. *Bad Music: The Music We Love to Hate* was a collection that I knew about but hadn't bothered to pick up. Did my subconscious whisper, *"I'm in jazz studies, therefore I have no need for a book about 'bad music'? I mean, it's not like I'm in popular music studies."*[14] In other words, does new jazz studies have fewer police at the gates of what counts as jazz, or do we simply have a new generation of police with different taste?

If the construction of the jazz tradition in the postwar years was, as DeVeaux suggests, "both symptom and cause" of the acceptance of jazz in music appreciation courses in colleges and universities, does it follow that the turn toward deconstructing the jazz tradition bears a coconstitutive relationship with the creation of new institutional strongholds of academic jazz studies *outside* the music departments and throughout the humanities? In other words, what are the institutional politics of constructing jazz studies as new? For instance, while there are new musicologists in new jazz studies, I think it is fair to say that there still exist the great chasms between jazz studies in nonmusic departments and in music departments that Mark Tucker lamented in 1998.[15] What can we do to ensure that constructing new jazz studies means more than a trophy in an academic turf war between humanities and music?

I am also concerned with wanting to make sure that new jazz studies means more than claiming the powerbase of jazz interpretation away from journalists, musicians, collectors, and fans, who frequently, though not always, of course, have less institutional support for their love of this music than do many academics.[16] Institutionalizing jazz studies in ways that narrowly define what counts as knowledge and power seems antithetical to the intellectual projects many of us are working on.

Finally, what kinds of narratives do we want to tell in new jazz studies? As we skillfully unsettle earlier definitions of jazz as an object of study, what narrative strategies are available to us and what is it that we hope to accomplish through their telling? As any decent deconstructionist will quickly tell you (well, maybe not *quickly*), this is not a method that offers a way out. The useful insight of desconstructionists, according to Gayatri Chakravorty Spivak, is the understanding that, "when a narrative is constructed, something is left out. When an end is defined, other ends are rejected, and one might not know what those ends are." But, at the same time, "we cannot but narrate." In other words, exposing error in received narratives does not exempt us from making them, nor does it make it possible for us to make them error free. Yet to narrate with an awareness of its limits, or what Spivak describes as "a radical acceptance of vulnerability," does offer an alternative to insisting on a particular version as the objective truth.[17]

So what kinds of narratives are up to the task of incorporating the insights gleaned from critiquing the old ones, as DeVeaux himself asked at the end of his 1991 essay? This important question is far less often cited than the exposure of the jazz tradition as an official history (though Washburne productively engaged this part in his outstanding *Bad Music* article on Kenny G) and deserves revisiting: "The narratives we have inherited to describe the history of jazz retain the patterns of outmoded forms of thought, especially the assumption that the progress of jazz as art necessitates increased distance from the popular. If we, as historians, critics, and educators, are to adapt to these new realities, we must be willing to construct new narratives to explain them."[18]

I'd liken this project to trying to capture something that we value precisely because it can't be contained. As specialists, we may rejoice in our clever attempts to invent porous bottles—narrative strategies that are multivocal and "relentlessly critical" and that refuse to hold our "subjectless subjects."[19] But while these experiments in leaky vessels may stimulate us as scholars, to what do we serve our students who may never have tried jazz before taking our course?

GENDER, RACE, AND JAZZ

Well, here's what I've been doing. In the first week of my undergraduate American Studies course, Gender, Race, and Jazz, I assign a jazz history text that takes the jazz tradition for granted. In the second week, I walk students through DeVeaux's "Constructing the Jazz Tradition," which some of them get right away and others find difficult. I have to say that it doesn't take long for most to become adept at identifying the parade of geniuses and styles described in the essay as a recurring way of crafting a kind of story but that passes itself off as the objective Jazz Truth. Inevitably, someone points out other instances in popular culture, news reportage, or high school and college textbooks where a dominant narrative is presented that excludes other possibilities. Students do not have to have prior knowledge of jazz, deconstruction, historiography, or theories about narrative to appreciate this insight. Usually, we are able to come up with an example of canon formation about which students are already critical.

And then I tell them that the rest of the class is called "Deconstructing the Jazz Tradition" and that they will not only learn about jazz in this class but develop some tools for analyzing culture as a place where people struggle over what matters to them. We then spend the next thirteen weeks analyzing jazz narratives for struggles over gender, race, class, sexuality, and nation. We explore narratives about jazz for their boundaries and binaries and analyze how people seem to be using jazz to make a range of meanings, often meanings in conflict with other meanings. And, yes, I assign Christopher Washburne's "Does Kenny G Play Bad Jazz? A Case Study," which does a great job of plunging us into the questions.

Like Alan Stanbridge, I use Ken Burns's PBS documentary *Jazz* "not simply as an objective resource, but rather as a cultural text which is, *itself* part of the discursive construction of jazz history."[20] I also encourage students to notice where else in culture they encounter narratives about jazz. I bring in examples culled from casting a wide cultural net. One of my favorites is a *Sponge Bob Square Pants* cartoon episode titled "Grandma's Kisses," in which Patrick the starfish teaches Sponge Bob how to be a man: "Puff out your chest. Now say 'tax exemption.' Now develop a taste for free-form jazz."[21] I use these kinds of popular culture references to jazz not to teach students the elements of jazz or jazz history but to stimulate critical readings of how jazz signifies in specific times and places of cultural life, including their own. Sponge Bob may seem out of his element in a course on jazz and American culture, but "Grandma's Kisses" is one of the best openings for discussions of jazz as a gendered discourse that I've found.

Throughout the course, I teach a variety of theories of gender and race and ask students to analyze competing notions of these categories as they play out in representations of jazz. I use my knowledge of women in jazz not only to supplement their historical knowledge but to get them to think critically about canon formation, narrative construction, and the multiple levels at which meanings compete.

One strategy I like to use is to present a series of conflicting narratives about a single figure, such as Lil Hardin Armstrong. Her contributions to jazz history are narrated very differently by, say, Geoff Ward, for whom she is remarkable only as Louis Armstrong's ambitious wife:

"Armstrong had grown unhappy at home. He didn't much like being a sideman in his wife's band and was embarrassed when his fellow musicians called him 'Henny' (for henpecked)," and by Linda Dahl, for whom she is an important woman in jazz: "The best known of these early jazz-women, and one of the hardiest survivors, was Lil Hardin Armstrong, whose career began in and centered around Chicago, in company with famous expatriate New Orleans players."[22] Sometimes I have them divide into groups and produce different kinds of narratives from the same packets of evidence: Lil Hardin Armstrong's contributions to jazz history, for example, narrated by the "great man" history group, the "exceptional woman" group, the "women-in-jazz" group, and so on.

I have them go out and listen to music and analyze what kinds of stories are being told through the ways the music is presented. I assign them a wide variety of music to listen to, picked by me, that I describe as having been defined as jazz either in its day or in retrospect, and I also assign them each week to write about something they listened to on their own that is either marketed as jazz or that sounds like jazz to them. And if they ask me, "Is Radiohead jazz?" "Is Norah Jones jazz?" or "Is the music on the Food Network jazz?" I say, "This isn't about me, or Mark Gridley—this is about what you hear as jazz, what you think of as jazz. This is about analyzing where you think you learned to hear jazz in the things you hear as jazz. What are the elements that make something sound like jazz, and what kinds of stories do you think are being told about jazz, or through jazz, in these sounds and the ways they are presented? This is about documenting what gets called jazz in the cultural spheres you frequent."

This raises what I've come to refer to as the Jazzercise dilemma, and I am deeply grateful to feminist musicologists Suzanne Cusick and Annie Randall for the imaginary Jazzercise Panel they have been half seriously planning for the American Musicological Society. In retaliation for conservative policies at the society about what constitutes music topics worthy of study, epitomized, I am told, by a paper titled "What Is Isorhythm?," Cusick and Randall began imagining aloud a panel called "What Is Jazzercise?"[23] When I heard about it, I jumped on board with an imaginary paper of my own, called "Where Is the Jazz in Jazzercise?" But then, the question arises of why the Jazzercise panel is a joke. I can easily see Jazzercise as a topic in American studies, women's studies, popular music studies, but probably not in jazz studies, new or old.

The Jazzercise dilemma really brings me back to the question: to what extent is new jazz studies a continuation of the jazz tradition? To what extent do we continue to reify that which we critique? I mean, it might be really helpful to know more about "Where is the jazz in Jazzercise?" The moves come from, I imagine, jazz dance, named after, as Brenda Dixon Gottschild points out, white appropriations of black dance aesthetics, all but forgotten in modern dance history, which sees itself as color-blind.[24] So maybe Jazzercise is a jazz studies project. Maybe we need to know more about Jazzercise and other Jazzerthings that trade on the cultural capital of jazz, and the gamut of associations of jazz with the body, sex, Otherness, modernity, pleasure, primitivism, and race.

If you're reading this and asking, "Where is the jazz in this paper?" then you are proving my point that new jazz studies is not completely wrenched from the jazz tradition, nor from what I think Scott DeVeaux means by his sense of the "core," as opposed to the "Core and Boundaries," of jazz.[25] Is jazz studies completely open to everything jazz means to all people in all instances? I call this dilemma, "When Sponge Bob leaps in, does Lester Leap Out?," and it chills me to the bone. As a cultural studies person, I agree with Stuart Hall in the "deadly seriousness" of popular culture as one of the sites where "struggle for and against culture of the powerful is engaged."[26] But as someone with particular hopes for the potential of jazz as critical practice, as black music, as bearing better democratic models than, say, television, I am ambivalent about having my students leave my class more attuned to noticing the place of jazz in constructing the "lifestyle" sold by Starbucks and Pottery Barn than the lives of jazz musicians.

On the other hand, I am in agreement with the authors of the introduction to *Uptown Conversations* that we need to know not only about *lives of great musicians* but about what "their images, including mistaken conceptions of who they were, tell us about cultures that mythologized them."[27] It is not enough to insist on the inclusion of Lil Hardin Armstrong into the jazz canon. This is what George Lipsitz has dubbed the "Blue Öyster Cult" problem, wherein the critique of the canon digresses into the noisy longing for one's own favorites to appear on the chart, in the documentary, or in the textbooks, with the other Giants of Rock (but in this case, of course, jazz). Where is Blue Öyster Cult? Where is Lil Hardin Armstrong?[28] We need not only to study those who are missing from the canon but to understand the desires for particular narratives that exclude them.

Maybe looking at the associations of jazz with particular kinds of manliness in Sponge Bob, what Ingrid Monson might identify as a spoof of "The Problem with White Hipness" *does* tell us something about meanings associated with jazz that have affected the lives of working jazz musicians.[29] Also, we need to bear in mind how evacuating the "popular" in old jazz studies often served to discount black musical practices and large segments of women's participation as jazz musicians. In a recent essay, Salim Washington deconstructs the binary avant-garde/ mainstream and shows how it serves to "render invisible . . . certain black social and aesthetic practices" even in a discourse that acknowledges that "jazz is an African American creation" and "that most of its innovators have been black."[30] The "all-girl" bands I wrote about were considered not real bands but novelty bands, even though the musicians in them considered themselves real.

Distinguishing real jazz from the popular, in other words, makes it easy to ignore artists, audiences, performance contexts, and discursive formations that may tell us a great deal about jazz histories and cultures. Another danger of distinguishing jazz studies too completely from popular music studies is that we may find ourselves out of the loop of conversations attempting to develop tools up to this very task, including Lawrence Grossberg's now ancient (by pop standards) conception of the object of rock music scholarship as "rock formation" rather than rock itself.[31]

JAZZ AS AN UNSTABLE OBJECT

Jazz studies entered academia by insisting that jazz is an autonomous art form, and then produced scholars who asked, "What is this thing called jazz?" In this respect, we are in good company; following women's studies, black studies, and American studies, for example, which also built academic homes by insisting on particularity in the face of exclusion; then used those home bases to explore issues of difference.

In women's studies, for the past couple of decades, several questions have arisen: What *is* the category 'woman'? What kind of work does it do? What about differences among women? What about cross-cultural and historical studies that show "woman" to be constructed differently in various times and places and social groups? What about all the little babies who are born who do not clearly fit on either side of the male/ female binary? Some programs have been renamed—gender studies, gender and sexuality studies—and some have kept the name of women's studies while interrogating the category of women.[32]

Questions in black studies correspond to those found in women's studies: Who is black? What is black if racial categories are never pure, never authentic, always mixed, in flux, and contested? What about black histories and identities that don't correspond to particular notions of U.S. blackness that often function as hegemonic in global diasporic contexts? Blackness did not disappear as a significant analytic even as program names shifted to African and African American studies, Africana studies, and African diaspora studies. Lately, blackness has received renewed emphasis even as it is reconfigured in frameworks such as global blackness studies and transnational blackness in department names, conference programs, and organizing themes of anthologies. Studies of mixed-race identity are also sites of critical interrogations of blackness as an organizing principle. Yet despite these contestations, and *because* of the paradoxes of race that propel these inquiries, the concept of blackness has not diminished in importance.[33]

In American studies, where I teach currently, students no longer study the United States by describing life in America or even by identifying American exceptionalism—the so-called frontier spirit, for example— but are trained to critically theorize notions of America and their operations; to locate national memories in histories of conquest, imperialism, and colonialism; to view U.S. borders not as natural results of manifest destiny but as contested, interested, violent, and movable; and to consider the United States in a global context. We train students to consider how ideas about America make indigenous nations within and overlapping U.S. national borders invisible, for example, and to study how colonialist discourse operates within U.S. international relations and justifies past and present global actions. Transnational approaches to theorizing America have transformed, invigorated, and improved the ability of the field to respond to urgent questions but have not obliterated America as an object of study.[34]

In jazz studies, as one can see quickly by reading recent titles of books, articles, and conference papers, many of us are not content to shore up a cohesive singular narrative about jazz, but we have been asking about the musics that were called jazz then but are not called jazz now. What about the radically different meanings that specific jazz performances articulated for different audiences? What about the artists who refuse the label of jazz, but who are important to others as jazz artists? What about the musics that have been called jazz in the jazz tradition narrative despite having little in common musically? What about the flows among genres, including popular and money-making ones excised by the boundaries of the jazz tradition narrative? What about the transnational, transcultural musical mixing throughout the history of jazz, including what took place earlier than jazz is said to have originated and that influenced musical forms that were called jazz as well as forms that were not, such as *danzón?*[35]

As Robyn Wiegman brilliantly notes, when scholars critically analyze an object of study as unstable, they do not necessarily lose their desire for the significance of that object. Gender, as an object of study, for example, has undergone several complete overhauls in its relatively short lifespan as a conceptual tool in women's studies, sexuality studies, gay and lesbian studies, queer theory, and gender studies—yet, Wiegman argues, gender continues to compel those who repudiate its earlier definitions and usages. Gender was once was interchangeable with "women," then became the culturally constructed superstructure of the biologically stable category "sex," then became that which is constituted through repeated performance with no biologically stable ground to stand on, then became that by which queer theory established itself by replacing gender with sexuality as its object of study. Now gender continues to operate as the locus of meaning for scholars who rework it, even those who work against it. Queer theory, for example, observes Wiegman, did not lose its "desire for gender" but "resurrected—and reconfigured" gender as a privileged object, this time as "mobile, proliferate, transitive."[36]

Wiegman urges other ways of dealing with the object of study—which she sees as an object of desire—ways that shift the focus from constituting the perfect category that will do the work we want done, to learning more about "the political desires that propel its analytic pursuit altogether." Rather than operating from a mode of repudiation, where each new cohort repudiates the assumptions of the previous one, she advocates a "thinking together" model, where scholars who come to their desire for the object at different historical moments, and from different disciplinary and interdisciplinary training, may think critically and differently together.[37] This, in fact, is a process I hear in jazz music making that interests me the most. When I see other uses of jazz as a privileged object not consistent with my political desires, I can repudiate those other uses as bad jazz studies, or I can try to think critically together with these other approaches about our shared and different political desires for jazz.

Okay, jazz is a different kind of category than gender, race, or nation. In fact, jazz is permeated with discourses of gender, race, and nation, as many jazz studies scholars argue. But let's entertain, for a moment, the idea that Wiegman's insights about the "desire for gender" may be usefully applied to the construction of the object of jazz studies. What does jazz studies want? Even as the movers and shakers of new jazz studies repudiate the canonical and discographical and metanarrative approaches of those who forged the jazz tradition, the desire for jazz must be alive and well in new jazz studies, or we wouldn't be so driven to make it new.

Some scholars prefer to work on jazz topics from frameworks of improvised music studies, black music studies, African diasporic music studies, or vernacular music studies. Yet many of us continue to call what we do, and name the places we do it from, "jazz studies." We are more attentive than we used to be in considering what we mean by blackness, Americanness, and gender. Perhaps we should give some more thought to what we hope to do by constituting jazz as our object of study? "Why jazz?" asks Ajay Heble in *Landing on the Wrong Note*. As Wiegman suggests in "The Desire for Gender," "If we find ourselves repeatedly disappointed" with some of the uses of our object of study, when we see it failing to live up to our hopes, "perhaps we should stop blaming the category or its user and explore instead what it is we expect our relationship to our objects of study *to do*."[38] Perhaps, instead of repudiating old jazz studies, or asking what is jazz in the new jazz studies, we should be asking what is our/my desire for jazz in the new jazz studies. What work do we want to do by facing this object, by constituting it as significant (dare I say, libratory?), by encountering and grappling with the limitations of the beloved object as a category?

For Heble, the dissonance of certain kinds of jazz, the kinds he likes, offers a useful model for critical thinking. Working with Nathaniel Mackey's concept of the "rickety, imperfect fit between word and world," Heble writes, "Jazz has provided me with the opportunity to test and develop my own understanding of the rickety fit between theory and practice, between academic and public worlds." For Heble, this dissonance includes the "out of tune-ness" between what academics write about jazz and "the musics and lives [they] seek to describe and interpret."[39] I would also include the dissonance among our various scholarly desires for jazz; the desires for jazz held by the cohorts that proceeded us (those we carry dear to our hearts and those we vigorously try to shake off); the desires that brought us to jazz studies (and how these may have changed through practice); the desires stimulated by representations of jazz in advertising and films; and the desires our students bring when they sign up for our courses.

I will close with a list of my own scholarly desires for new jazz studies, which includes many of the new directions described and implemented

.by the editors of *Uptown Conversations*. I am excited by the continued movement away from the focus on individual geniuses and toward the "immeasurably complex worlds through which they moved, and which they helped to shape." I'm all for learning more about the desires mapped onto representations of and narratives about jazz and the connections and disconnections between them and jazz practice. I am excited by recent emphases on transnational travels, interdisciplinarity, and relationships between musical forms we are accustomed to thinking of as jazz and those that may not fit into the jazz tradition notions of what counts as jazz. I am hopeful for the insights to be gained from what O'Meally, Edwards, and Griffin have identified as "moments, meetings, gatherings, gestures, and scenes."[40]

I guess what I would like to add to that agenda is a call for thinking about how new jazz studies might transform itself *in practice* to keep up with these promising conceptual transformations. Much of what I'm wishing for is directly inspired by "moments, meetings, [and] gatherings." I have had the honor and pleasure of attending the Jazz Study Group at Columbia and participating in the Guelph Jazz Festival and Colloquium (and more recently the Improvisation, Community, and Social Practice research initiative at Guelph), as well as in the Interdisciplinary Jazz Studies Group I and seven colleagues from five departments formed at University of Kansas. The areas I would like to highlight are collaborating across disciplinary difference, reevaluating dissonance in critical practice over repudiation, and maintaining a relentless awareness of our work as occurring in time and space and institutions that are often powerful, yet may not contain everything we need to know. Just as jazz musicians listen beyond the boundaries that critics and historians and even the most well-meaning fans construct for them, so must we listen beyond our institutional walls. (What if, for instance, jazz studies had better listened to women's studies in the early 1980s?)

In 1998 Mark Tucker urged the formation of "coalition(s) of scholars, journalists, critics, and musicians united in their passion for jazz and driven to understand the worlds of meaning people have found in this music."[41] What might that look like? What if we actually held workshops where musicologists and nonmusicologists paired off and—if we didn't kill each other first—actually made papers together? What if, as George Lewis recently suggested, we had workshops where creative musicians, who don't have time or institutional support to write critically about musical practice, produced papers?[42] Or what if there was a jazz camp for nonplaying jazz studies scholars, where collective listening and sounding and creative dissonance were valued over technical virtuosity? Nonplayers could suspend their excuses for not practicing and experience firsthand the tyranny of "right notes"—which can be quite different from what it is like for nonplayers to imagine metaphorically—and perhaps begin to sound the far cries between hitting clams and "landing on the wrong note" in the critical way described by Ajay Heble.

Working with Ajay Heble's ideas about dissonance may help us to develop approaches to difference that do not always demand hierarchy and that may open our ears to multiple and unexpected sources. We need to better hear differences sounding at once and to listen for their connections and disconnections without rushing for resolution. And we must bear in mind that, like jazz musicians, some jazz studies scholars benefit professionally from pursuing their desires, some do not benefit from institutional support, and all pursue this work without knowing what lies ahead.

NOTES

This chapter is a revised version of the paper "Deconstructing the Jazz Tradition: The Subjectless Subject of New Jazz Studies" that I first presented at the Leeds International Jazz Conference in England on March 11, 2005. An earlier version was published in *The Source: Challenging Jazz Criticism* 2 (2005): 31–46, © Equinox 2005. I am grateful to Tony Whyton, Catherine Parsonage, and the participants at the Leeds conference, the Creative Music Think Tank (Vancouver Jazz Festival, June 27, 2005), and the Columbia Jazz Study Group meeting on Jazz and Desire (Center for Jazz Studies, Columbia University, October 15, 2005). I appreciate the dialogue with Robyn Wiegman, as I continued to think through this paper and my ongoing relationship with my object of study.

1. Scott DeVeaux, "Constructing the Jazz Tradition," *Black Literature Forum* 25, no 3 (Fall 1991): 525–60, reprinted in *The Jazz Cadence of American Culture,* ed. Robert O'Meally (New York: Columbia University Press, 1998): 483–512.

2. Judith Tick, "Modern Feminist Scholarship and American Music" (paper presented at the national meeting of the Society for American Music, Eugene, OR, February 18, 2005).

3. Susan Cavin, "Missing Women: On the Voodoo Trail to Jazz," *Journal of Jazz Studies* 3, no. 1 (Fall 1975): 4–27.

4. Sally Placksin, *American Women in Jazz* (New York: Seaview Books, 1981); Linda Dahl, *Stormy Weather: The Music and Lives of a Century of Jazzwomen* (New York: Limelight, 1989); D. Antoinette Handy, *Black Women in American Bands and Orchestras* (Lanham, MD: Scarecrow, 1982). Black music studies of this period is very much a part of the emergence of the field of black studies. Although he chronicles black music historiography from the

1860s, Guthrie Ramsey situates the appearance of Eileen Southern's *The Music of Black Americans* (1971) as "a symbol of the epoch in which it appeared," during the "wake of Black Power" and the "radicalization of the word 'black,'" a time when students were demanding black studies across the curriculum. Guthrie Ramsey, "Cosmopolitan or Provincial? Ideology in Early Black Music Historiography, 1867–1940," *Black Music Research Journal* 16, no. 1 (Spring 1996): 11.

5. DeVeaux, "Constructing the Jazz Tradition," in O'Meally, *Jazz Cadence*, 483.

6. Sherrie Tucker, *Swing Shift: "All-Girl" Bands of the 1940s* (Durham, NC: Duke University Press, 2000).

7. Elsa Barkley Brown, "Polyrhythms and Improvisation: Lessons for Women's History," *History Workshop Journal* 31 (Spring 1991): 85.

8. *Jazz*, directed by Ken Burns (Arlington, VA: PBS, 2001), DVD.

9. Mark Tucker, "Musicology and the New Jazz Studies," *Journal of the American Musicological Society* 51, no. 1 (Spring 1998): 132–33; Robert G. O'Meally, Brent Hayes Edwards, and Farah Jasmine Griffin, "Introductory Notes," in *Uptown Conversations: The New Jazz Studies*, ed. Robert G. O'Meally, Brent Hayes Edwards, and Farah Jasmine Griffin (New York: Columbia University Press, 2004), 3.

10. Reginald T. Buckner and Steven Weiland, eds., *Jazz in Mind: Essays on the History and Meanings of Jazz* (Detroit: Wayne State University Press, 1991); Krin Gabbard, ed., *Jazz among the Discourses* and *Representing Jazz* (Durham, NC: Duke University Press, 1995). Gender analyses of men and masculinity is included in some pieces in *Jazz among the Discourses* and *Representing Jazz*, notably those essays authored by Krin Gabbard and Steven Elsworth. A landmark leap in jazz and gender studies of the 1980s came on the scene with Kathy Ogren's *The Jazz Revolution: Twenties America and the Meaning of Jazz* (New York: Oxford University Press, 1989).

11. Ajay Heble, *Landing on the Wrong Note: Jazz, Dissonance and Critical Practice* (New York: Routledge, 2000), 5.

12. Ann Cacoullos, "Feminist Ruptures in Women's Studies and American Studies," *American Studies International* 38, no. 3 (October 2000): 97.

13. Interestingly, popular culture is one of the few places in U.S. definitions of race where black has been conceived as pure, and white as a contaminant, at least in the sense that a diluting agent contaminates.

14. Catherine Parsonage, "The Popularity of Jazz—An Unpopular Problem: The Significance of *Swing When You're Winning*," *The Source: Challenging Jazz Criticism* 1 (2004): 59–80; Robert Walser, review of *Bad Music: The Music We Love to Hate*, ed. Christopher J. Washburne and Maiken Derno," *Journal of the Society for American Music* 1, no 4 (November 2007): 511–16; Christopher Washburne, "Does Kenny G Play Bad Jazz? A Case Study," in *Bad Music: The Music We Love to Hate*, ed. Christopher J. Washburne and Maiken Derno (New York: Routledge, 2004), 123–47.

15. Mark Tucker, review of *Representing Jazz* and *Jazz among the Discourses*, ed. Krin Gabbard, *Journal of the American Musicological Society* 51, no. 1 (Spring 1998): 131–48.

16. Travis Jackson has spoken eloquently about the dual traditions of sharing and stockpiling that have taken place in both academic and nonacademic jazz knowledge production. I was particularly struck by his identification of the record collectors on both sides of this divide, and I am compelled to acknowledge the music-loving record collectors who have generously plied me with sounds and knowledge over the years. I owe much to several informal teacher and conveners of such communities of jazz affinity, but let me single out and thank David Heymann. Travis Jackson, "All the Things You Are: The Changing Face(s) of Jazz Studies" (key note address, Jazz Changes Colloquium, University of Kansas, Lawrence, March 4, 2004).

17. Gayatri Chakravorty Spivak, *The Postcolonial Critic: Interviews, Strategies, Dialogues,* ed. Sarah Harasym (New York: Routledge, 1990), 18–19.

18. DeVeaux, "Constructing the Jazz Tradition," 505.

19. Spivak, *Postcolonial Critic.*

20. Alan Stanbridge, "Burns, Baby, Burns," *The Source: Challenging Jazz Criticism* 1 (2004): 94.

21. Patrick, quoted in "Grandma's Kisses," *Sponge Bob Square Pants, Seascape Capers* (New York: Viacom International, 2004), DVD.

22. Geoff Ward, *Jazz: A History of America's Music* (New York: Knopf, 2000), 157–58; Dahl, *Stormy Weather,* 22.

23. Thanks to Suzanne Cusick for recapping the history of the imaginary Jazzercise panel for me by e-mail message, February 6, 2005. Thanks to Suzanne and Annie Randall for letting me in on the panel planning and for permission to discuss it in this article.

24. Brenda Dixon Gottschild, *The Black Dancing Body: A Geography from Coon to Cool* (New York: Palgrave MacMillan, 2003), 20–22.

25. Scott DeVeaux, "Core and Boundaries" (keynote address, Brilliant Corners: Leeds International Jazz Conference, Leeds, England, March 11, 2005).

26. Stuart Hall, "Notes on Deconstructing the Popular," *Cultural Theory and Popular Culture: A Reader,* ed. John Storey, 2nd ed. (Athens: University of Georgia Press, 1998), 453.

27. O'Meally, Edwards, and Griffin, "Introductory Notes," 2.

28. George Lipsitz, quoted in David Sanjek et al., "Historiography and Popular Music Studies: Transcript of the IASPM/US 1997 Plenary Session," *Journal of Popular Music Studies* 8 (1996): 65.

29. Ingrid Monson, "The Problem with White Hipness: Race, Gender, and Cultural Conceptions in Jazz Historical Discourse," *Journal of the American Musicological Society* 48, no. 3 (Fall 1995): 396–422.

30. Salim Washington, "All the Things You Could Be by Now": Charles Mingus Presents Charles Mingus and the Limits of Avant-Garde Jazz," in O'Meally, Edwards, and Griffin, *Uptown Conversations,* 27.

31. Lawrence Grossberg, *We Gotta Get Out of This Place: Popular Conservatism and Postmodern Culture* (New York: Routledge, 1992).

32. Simone de Beauvoir raised the question "What is a woman?" as a feminist issue prior to the emergence of women's studies courses, and Sojourner Truth asked it a century prior to that in the context of the U.S. woman suffrage and abolitionist movements! See de Beauvoir, *The Second Sex* (New York: Ban-

tam, 1952); and Truth, "Woman's Rights," 1851, *Words of Fire: An Anthology of African-American Feminist Thought,* ed. Beverly Guy-Sheftall (New York: New Press, 1995), 36. These lines of inquiry acquire new valences and emphases in women's studies syllabi in the 1980s and 1990s, with such titles as Gloria T. Hull, Patricia Bell Scott, and Barbara Smith, eds., *All the Women Are White, All the Blacks Are Men, but Some of Us Are Brave: Black Women's Studies* (Old Westbury, NY: Feminist Press, 1982); Elizabeth Spelman, *Inessential Woman: Problems of Exclusion in Feminist Thought* (Boston: Beacon, 1988); Judith Butler, *Gender Trouble: Feminism and the Subversion of Identity* (New York: Routledge, 1999), to name but a few.

33. Think, for example, of Stuart Hall's widely cited essay, "What Is This Black in Black Popular Culture?," in *Black Popular Culture,* ed. Gina Dent (Seattle: Bay Ness, 1992), 21–33; or Marlon Riggs's posthumously completed film, *Black Is . . . Black Ain't* (San Francisco: California Newsreel, 1995). Many of us first became aware of the possibilities of global blackness studies through Paul Gilroy's *The Black Atlantic: Modernity and Double-Consciousness* (Cambridge, MA: Harvard University Press, 1993). For more recent scholarship that takes up global blackness in complex ways that do not reify, essentialize, or give up blackness as an analytical category, see, for instance, the essays collected in Kamari Maxine Clarke and Deborah Thomas, eds. *Globalization and Race: Transformations in the Cultural Production of Blackness* (Durham, NC: Duke University Press), 2006; as well as those in Manning Marable and Vanessa Agard Jones, eds., *Transnational Blackness: Navigating the Global Color Line* (New York: Palgrave Macmillan, 2008). For an approach to mixed-race studies that calls for combining an analysis of blackness and mixedness rather than conceptualizing mixed (black/white) hybridity as a "third space between bifurcations," see Naomi Pabst, "Blackness/Mixedness: Contestations over Crossing Signs," *Cultural Critique* 54 (2003): 178–212. In addition, Pabst argues that "black/white interraciality and transculturalism could be fruitfully situated within a framework of black difference, a framework that is usually reserved for other mitigating factors of identity such as gender, sexuality, class, and (trans) nationality" (180).

34. See, for instance, George Lipsitz, *American Studies in a Moment of Danger* (Minneapolis: University of Minnesota Press, 2001); Amy Kaplan and Donald E. Pease, eds., *Cultures of United States Imperialism* (Durham, NC: Duke University Press, 1993); John Carlos Rowe, *Post Nationalist American Studies* (Berkeley: University of California Press, 2000); Lucy Maddox, ed., *Locating American Studies: The Evolution of a Discipline* (Baltimore, MD: Johns Hopkins University Press, 1999); and Donald E. Pease and Robyn Wiegman, *The Futures of American Studies* (Durham, NC: Duke University Press, 2002). An influential work in the development of transnational American studies is Inderpal Grewal's *Transnational America: Feminisms, Diasporas, Neoliberalisms* (Durham, NC: Duke University Press, 2005).

35. Bruce Boyd Rayburn made this point eloquently in his conference paper, "Submerging Ethnicity: Creole of Color Jazz Musicians of Italian Heritage," delivered at the Creole Studies Conference, New Orleans, Louisiana, October 25, 2003. Ragtime and *danzón* (from Cuba) emerged simultaneously in the late

1800s, and by the 1920s both forms could be heard in New Orleans and Havana. See Raul Fernandez, *Latin Jazz: The Perfect Combination/La Combinación Perfecta* (San Francisco: Chronicle Books, 2002), 14–24.

36. Robyn Wiegman, "The Desire for Gender," in *A Companion to Lesbian, Gay, Bisexual, Transgender, and Queer Studies,* ed. George E. Haggerty and Molly McGarry (Malden, MA: Blackwell, 2007), 219.

37. Robyn Wiegman, opening remarks in an earlier version of the paper "The Desire for Gender," presented at Yale University, New Haven, CT, February 17, 2005. See also her article, "On Being in Time with Feminism," *Modern Language Quarterly* 65, no. 1 (March 2004): 161–76.

38. Heble, *Wrong Note;* Wiegman, "Desire for Gender," in Haggerty and McGarry, *Companion,* 232.

39. Nathaniel Mackey, *Discrepant Engagement: Dissonance, Cross-Culturality, and Experimental Writing* (Cambridge: Cambridge University Press, 1993), 19, quoted in Heble, *Wrong Note,* 2; see also page x.

40. O'Meally, Edwards, and Griffin, "Introductory Notes," 2.

41. Tucker, "Musicology," 148.

42. Conversation with George Lewis, during a refreshment gathering at a meeting of the Jazz Study Group, March 6, 2005, Columbia University.

Contributors

DAVID AKE is the director of the School of the Arts at the University of Nevada, Reno. His publications include the books *Jazz Cultures* (2002) and *Jazz Matters* (2010) for the University of California Press. An active pianist and composer, he has recorded and performed alongside many of today's outstanding improvising musicians.

TAMAR BARZEL is an assistant professor of ethnomusicology at Wellesley College, where she teaches courses on jazz, American popular music, and the avant-garde. Her published work includes articles in the *Journal of the Society for American Music* and in *People Get Ready! The Future of Jazz Is Now*, forthcoming from Duke University Press. She is working on a book manuscript, titled *Downtown and Disorderly: "Radical Jewish Culture" and Its Discontents on New York's Experimental Music Scene*.

JESSICA BISSETT PEREA is a University of California President's Postdoctoral Fellow in the Department of Music at the University of California, Berkeley. She completed her PhD in musicology from the University of California, Los Angeles, in 2011 with a dissertation on the politics of contemporary Alaskan Inuit musical life from 1959 to the present. She has lectured at San Francisco State University's Department of American Indian Studies, College of Ethnic Studies, where she teaches courses on Native American women studies and Alaska Native cultural and music studies.

CHARLES HIROSHI GARRETT is an associate professor of musicology at the University of Michigan School of Music, Theatre & Dance. His graduate studies in musicology at the University of California, Los Angeles, led to his book *Struggling to Define a Nation: American Music and the Twentieth Century* (University of California Press, 2008), which received the Irving Lowens Memorial Book Award from the Society for American Music. He also served as editor in chief for *The Grove Dictionary of American Music*, second edition.

DANIEL GOLDMARK is an associate professor of music at Case Western Reserve University in Cleveland. He is the series editor of the Oxford Music/Media Series and is the author and/or editor of several books on animation, film, and music, including *Tunes for 'Toons: Music and the Hollywood Cartoon* (University of California Press, 2005).

JOHN HOWLAND is an associate professor of music history at Rutgers University–Newark and the author of *Ellington Uptown: Duke Ellington, James P. Johnson, and the Birth of Concert Jazz* (University of Michigan Press, 2009). He is a former editor in chief and cofounder of *Jazz Perspectives,* an interdisciplinary jazz studies journal (Routledge). He specializes in the study of arranging traditions across popular music, big band jazz, and jazz-related orchestral idioms in dance bands, musical theater, and the media of film and radio.

LOREN KAJIKAWA is an assistant professor of ethnomusicology and musicology at the University of Oregon, School of Music and Dance. He teaches courses on music of the Americas, music of the twentieth and twenty-first centuries, and U.S. popular music. He also serves as an affiliated faculty member in the Departments of Ethnic Studies and Folklore. His current research explores how conceptions of race become audible in hip-hop music.

ERIC PORTER is a professor of American studies at University of California–Santa Cruz. His research interests include black cultural and intellectual history, U.S. cultural history, comparative ethnic studies, and jazz studies. He is the author of *What Is This Thing Called Jazz? African American Musicians as Artists, Critics, and Activists* (University of California Press, 2002) and *The Problem of the Future World: W. E. B. Du Bois and the Race Concept at Midcentury* (Duke University Press, 2010).

KEN PROUTY is an assistant professor of musicology and jazz studies at Michigan State University. He holds a PhD in ethnomusicology from the University of Pittsburgh and completed a master's degree in jazz performance at the University of North Texas, where he played trombone with the acclaimed One O'clock Lab Band. His book *Knowing Jazz: Community, Pedagogy and Canon in the Information Age* is forthcoming from the University Press of Mississippi in early 2012. Ken is a regular presenter on jazz topics at conferences and symposia around the world.

SHERRIE TUCKER is an associate professor in American studies at the University of Kansas. She is the author of *Swing Shift: "All-Girl" Bands of the 1940s* (Duke University Press, 2000) and coeditor, with Nichole T. Rustin, of *Big Ears: Listening for Gender in Jazz Studies* (Duke University Press, 2008). She is currently completing a book on swing culture as war memory, *Dance Floor Democracy: the Social Geography of Memory at the Hollywood Canteen* (forthcoming, Duke University Press).

ELIJAH WALD is a musician and writer who has toured on five continents and published more than a thousand articles on music and other subjects. His books include *How the Beatles Destroyed Rock 'n' Roll: An Alternative History of American Popular Music* (Oxford University Press, 2009); *Escaping the Delta: Robert Johnson and the Invention of the Blues* (Amistad, 2004); and *Narco-*

corrido (Rayo, 2001), about the modern Mexican ballads of drug trafficking and political corruption. He has taught blues history at UCLA and won multiple awards, including a 2002 Grammy.

CHRISTOPHER WASHBURNE is an associate professor of ethnomusicology at Columbia University and the founding director of Columbia's Louis Armstrong Jazz Performance Program. His books include *Sounding Salsa: Performing Latin Music in New York* (Temple University Press, 2008) and *Bad Music* (Routledge, 2004). He is currently working on a book on Latin jazz, which will be published by Oxford University Press. As a performer he has been called "one of the best trombonists in New York" by the *New York Times* and was voted as a "Rising Star of the Trombone" in the 2008, 2009, and 2010 *Down Beat* Critic's Poll. He has recorded more than 150 albums and performed with numerous jazz, pop, and Latin figures and groups, including Tito Puente, Ray Barretto, Anthony Braxton, Duke Ellington Orchestra, Eddie Palmieri, Celia Cruz, Ruben Blades, Marc Anthony, and Justin Timberlake.

Index

TEXT
10/13 Sabon Open Type

DISPLAY
Sabon Open Type

COMPOSITOR
Westchester Book Group

PRINTER/BINDER
IBT Global